PROFESSIONAL RESPONSIBILITY AND REGULATION

SECOND EDITION

By

DEBORAH L. RHODE
Ernest W. McFarland Professor of Law
and
Director, Stanford Center on Ethics
Stanford University

GEOFFREY C. HAZARD, JR.
Distinguished Professor of Law
Hastings College of the Law
University of California
Trustee Professor, University of Pennsylvania

CONCEPTS AND INSIGHTS SERIES

FOUNDATION PRESS
2007

Cover Design: Keith Stout
Cover Art: Yale Law School (with thanks)

© 2002 FOUNDATION PRESS
© 2007 By FOUNDATION PRESS
        395 Hudson Street
        New York, NY 10014
        Phone Toll Free 1–877–888–1330
        Fax (212) 367–6799
        foundation–press.com

Printed in the United States of America

ISBN 978–1–59941–142–2

 TEXT IS PRINTED ON 10% POST CONSUMER RECYCLED PAPER

For
Mary Tye

*

ACKNOWLEDGMENTS

We are deeply grateful to Mary Tye, to whom the book is dedicated, for her invaluable contributions in preparing the manuscript for publication.

*

TABLE OF CONTENTS

TABLE OF CONTENTS

*

PROFESSIONAL RESPONSIBILITY AND REGULATION

*

Chapter I

THE PROFESSION AND ITS REGULATION

A. The Concept of a Profession

In a book about the legal profession, it is appropriate to begin with an understanding of what membership in a profession implies. Occupations that we now consider "professional" have been in existence for well over 2000 years, although the term itself and the distinctive features of these vocational groups did not begin to emerge until the sixteenth century. "Profession" comes from the Latin term, "professionem," meaning to make a public declaration. The term evolved to describe occupations that required new entrants to take an oath professing their dedication to the ideals and practices associated with a learned calling.

Contemporary definitions of professions generally emphasize their special expertise and ethical responsibilities, which give rise to other defining features, such as self-regulation, prescribed qualifications, codes of conduct, occupational associations, and monopolies over certain work. American lawyers have long prided themselves on being a profession. According to a prominent report by the American Bar Association (ABA), professionals are those who are "pursuing a learned art ... in the spirit of public service."[1] By the same token, lawyers also have long been concerned about a loss of professionalism and the "decline of law into a business." Over a century ago, one American commentator captured widespread views in observing that the bar had lost its "fine sense of dignity" and had become "contaminated with the spirit of commerce."[2]

During the past two decades, expression of these concerns has intensified, fueled by increasing competition and commercialism in the market for legal services, and by a sense of decreasing professional control over the regulation of lawyers and the scope of their monopoly. To a growing extent, the bar shares its authority over lawyers' conduct with courts, legislatures, employers, and administrative agencies. The profession's efforts to prevent the "unauthorized practice of law" by nonlawyer competitors has been eroded by

---

1. American Bar Association (ABA) Commission on Professionalism, "In the Spirit of a Public Service:" A Blueprint for the Rekindling of Lawyer Professionalism 3 (1986).

2. American Lawyer, quoted in Deborah L. Rhode, In the Interests of Justice: Reforming the Legal Profession 1 (2001). See also Geoffrey C. Hazard, Jr. & Angelo Dondi, Legal Ethics: A Comparative Study 45 (2004).

market pressures and technological advances. Increasing specialization within the profession has also raised questions about the usefulness of treating lawyers as a single unified group subject to the same education and regulatory standards.

The practice of law has traditionally been regulated at the state level rather than nationally or locally (as in Europe). In modern times, legal practice has increasingly crossed jurisdictional boundaries, both state and national. This growth of "multi-jurisdictional practice" has compounded other ambiguities in the boundaries of lawyers' work. In many nations, much of what lawyers do in this country is not reserved to members of the bar or is divided among subgroups of the legal profession. For example, in European and South American countries, some types of legal documents are exclusively prepared by *notaires,* who have legal training and significantly more status and official responsibility than their American counterparts. And in Japan, a large number of individuals in business and the professions have legal education and perform legal tasks, but only about two percent of these individuals pass the bar and are able to represent litigants in court.[3] Other nations generally permit non-lawyers to give legal advice and to join with lawyers in multidisciplinary partnerships. As a consequence, multinational accounting firms have eclipsed law firms as the world's largest providers of legal services.

How the American bar is responding to regulatory issues is the focus of Chapter IX. For present purposes, what bears emphasis is the challenge that they raise to traditional understandings of the profession. Those understandings have been subject to criticism on several levels. First, critics from both the right and left have questioned whether professions like law are qualitatively different in terms of expertise or public spiritedness from others that have not attained professional status. Not all legal practice requires greater skill and training than what is necessary in other occupations that lack professional status, such as investment banking or information technology. Nor is it apparent that lawyers have been less self-interested than other occupational groups in structuring their own regulation and in policing their own membership. Popular opinion polls demonstrate considerable public skepticism about the profession's claims to public spiritedness. Fewer than a fifth of Americans rate lawyers' ethical standards as "very high or high"; as "honest and ethical;" three-fifths view lawyers as "greedy," and four-fifths believe some of their work could be done as well with

---

3. See Rhode, supra note 2, at 119.

less expense by others.[4] To many observers, the bar's rhetoric about professionalism often serves as window dressing for economic protectionism and an inflated self-image.[5]

By contrast, bar leaders generally view recent market trends and opinion polls as a reason not to relinquish claims of special status, but rather to rekindle professional ideals. To that end, state and local bar associations have launched a broad range of professionalism initiatives, including conferences, commissions, centers, and civility codes. How much effect these efforts have on practice remains an open question. But the underlying aspiration is surely worth preserving. Whatever its other limitations, the bar's commitment to professionalism has made an enormous contribution to the rule of law and the pursuit of justice. Lawyers inspired by that commitment have been at the forefront of every major public interest cause in American history. Their efforts to provide pro bono assistance, to protect individual liberties, and to serve as an independent check on governmental overreaching have been models for other bars throughout the world. Many individuals choose law as a career at least in part out of a desire to advance social justice, and they seek a professional identity that will serve that end.

B. Professional Norms: Law, Morality, and Legal Ethics

A key concept in a book about the regulation of lawyers is "legal ethics." The term is often used interchangeably with "professional responsibility" to describe the bar's governing norms. A threshold question is what is the "ethics" in legal ethics, and how is it related to the law of lawyering.

As a definitional matter, most scholars trace *ethics* to the Greek words *ethikos*, which means pertaining to custom, and *ethos*, which refers to character. *Morality* comes from the Latin *mores*, which refers to character or custom and habit. In contemporary societies, both terms have become somewhat detached from their

---

4. Id., at 4; Roper Center for Public Opinion Research, Gallup Poll, Dec. 1, 2005; Gary A. Hengstler, "Vox Populi: The Public Perception of Lawyers: ABA Poll" A.B.A. J., Sept. 1993, at 60; Randall Samborn, "Anti–Lawyer Attitude Up," National L. J., Aug. 9, 1993, at 20; Stephen Budiansky, Ted Gest, & David Fisher, "How Lawyers Abuse the Law," U.S. News & World Report, Jan. 30, 1995, at 50; Gallup Poll Releases, Nov. 1999.

5. For the classic conservative position, see Milton Friedman, Capitalism and Freedom 144–149 (1962). See also Richard Posner, Overcoming Law 37–38, 91–93 (1995). For criticisms from the left, see Rhode, supra note 1, at 1–22, 135–41, 207–08. Russell G. Pearce, "Law Day 2050: Post–Professionalism, Moral Leadership, and the Law-as-Business Paradigm," 27 Fla. St. U. L. Rev. 9 (1999); Richard Abel, American Lawyers 12 (1989); Richard L. Abel, "The Contradictions of Professionalism," in Lawyers and Society: The Common Law World 186–243 (Richard L. Abel & Philip Lewis, eds. 1989).

original meaning. Philosophers generally consider "ethics" to be the study of morality, or to refer to the customary norms in a given society (i.e., its *ethos)*, and "morality" to involve universal principles of right and wrong.[6] However, because philosophical principles overlap with customary norms, many contemporary theorists doubt the usefulness of any general distinction between ethics and morality, and use the terms interchangeably.

In one sense, legal ethics is a branch of trans-legal norms that reflect and reinforce broader concepts of morality drawn from religious and philosophical traditions. In another, equally coherent sense, legal ethics is simply a form of regulation that incorporates mandatory rules of conduct adopted by courts, legislatures, and administrative agencies. On both these dimensions, legal ethics is central to the working lives of lawyers. The bar's code of conduct determines their continued eligibility to practice, and helps shape their moral identity as professionals.

The application of much contemporary moral philosophy to problems of legal practice is limited by two of its defining features: its commitment to universal principles and its assumption of knowledge about the facts on which normative judgments rest. Yet in the working lives of lawyers, knowledge is incomplete and context matters. Moreover, the very fact that legal ethics involves the practice of law is centrally important. "Lawyer" is not simply a job description but a legally defined occupation with legally prescribed powers and duties, such as the duty to keep a client's confidences. As a general matter, the dominant traditions of moral philosophy may help frame questions, but they do not supply determinate answers to the concrete dilemmas of practice.[7]

The two philosophical traditions generally viewed as most relevant for legal ethics are utilitarianism and deontology (or rights-based theory). In its classic form, utilitarianism holds that the morally right action is the one that produces the greatest good for the greatest number. Under this theory, each person's happiness is equally important. Deontology, a term derived from the Greek word "deon," or duty, holds that the morally right action is one that conforms to universal, generalizable principles of obligation. Immanuel Kant, a leading deontological theorist, believed that ethically justifiable conduct must satisfy one ultimate moral principle, the categorical imperative. Kant gave this principle two formulations. The first is that individuals are to "act only according

---

6. G.W.F. Hegel, Phenomenology of Spirit 266–94 (A.V. Miller trans., 1977); John Hartland–Swann, An Analysis of Morals (1960).

7. See Geoffrey C. Hazard, Jr., "Law Practice and the Limits of Moral Philosophy," in Ethics in Practice 75, 77 (Deborah L. Rhode, ed., 2000).

to that maxim ... [which] should become a universal law." A second is to "treat others only as an end, and never as a means only."[8] In applying deontological theory, philosophers have attempted to identify obligations that would satisfy the requirements of universalization, generalization, and respect for others. Such obligations typically include duties of fidelity (keeping promises, avoiding deception), duties of benevolence (helping others and avoiding harm), and duties of justice (treating similar cases similarly). Because these obligations imply corresponding rights, deontological frameworks are often referred to as rights-based theories.

Both utilitarian and right-based approaches have been applied to legal ethics issues, and each has been subject to criticisms that are relevant for such issues. One problem with utilitarianism involves the difficulty of objectively identifying, weighing, and comparing the consequences of a particular act against all the alternatives. A further problem is that the theory provides no way of protecting individual rights against majority preferences, or of distinguishing qualitatively between preferences, such as between those founded on irrationality, bigotry, or addiction, and those founded on socially beneficial values.[9] By the same token, deontological theories have also been criticized as indeterminate. Principles like the categorical imperative are of little assistance in resolving ethical dilemmas that implicate competing values such as protection of the rights of apparently guilty clients as against those of innocent third parties. A requirement that rules be generalized and that individual rights be respected is of little help when the issue is which rule we should generalize and whose individual rights should have priority.[10]

These limitations become even more apparent in the context of particular legal ethics issues. A representative example involves the classic dilemma, discussed more fully in Chapter VI, of whether lawyers should disclose a client's confidences in order to prevent serious harm to third parties. It is possible to justify broad protections for client confidences on both rights-based and utilitarian grounds; it is equally possible to critique such protections on similar grounds.

8. Immanuel Kant, Foundations of the Metaphysics of Morals 46 (Lewis White Beck, trans. 2d ed. 1990).

9. See Consequentialism and its Critics (Samuel Scheffler, ed. 1988); Utilitarianism and Beyond (Amartya Sen and Bernard Williams, eds. 1982); Amartya Sen, Collective Choice and Social Welfare 118–48 (1970); J.J.C. Smart & Bernard Williams, Utilitarianism: For and Against 33 (1973).

10. Consequentialism and its Critics (Samuel Scheffler, ed. 1988); Utilitarianism and Beyond (Amartya Sen and Bernard Williams, eds. 1982); Roberto Mangabeira Unger, Knowledge and Politics 54 (1975); Alasdair MacIntyre, A Short History of Ethics 197–98 (1966).

The basic rights-based argument for confidentiality obligations builds on several assumptions about societal values and client conduct. The first assumption is that an overarching objective of the legal system is to preserve individual rights. In an advanced industrial society, people have an array of legal rights (due process, privacy, the right to contract, for example) that are vulnerable to infringement, either by the government or by other private interests. Preventing or redressing infringement often requires the assistance of lawyers. Lawyers cannot provide adequate representation unless clients feel free to provide all relevant information. Many individuals will be unwilling to seek legal assistance or to disclose essential facts without assurances that their communications will remain confidential. Protection of such confidences serves not only to safeguard legal rights in general, but also to preserve certain specific entitlements such as constitutional guarantees for criminal defendants. If lawyers could disclose inculpating client communications, persons accused of a crime could not fully exercise both their Sixth Amendment right to counsel and their Fifth Amendment privilege against self-incrimination.

Critics of broad confidentiality protections make several responses. First, they note that concerns about criminal defendants' constitutional rights do not justify sweeping protections in civil contexts. Nor do concerns about individual liberty and privacy explain the extension of broad confidentiality safeguards to corporations. It is also not self-evident why the rights of clients, especially corporate clients, should always take priority over the rights of others, particularly where their health or safety concerns are at risk. Moreover, current confidentiality rules are subject to exceptions and indeterminacies; existing research leaves doubt whether some further limitations on the protection of confidentiality would significantly alter client behavior.[11]

An alternative utilitarian justification for broad confidentiality rules is that they promote the greatest good for the greatest number by facilitating compliance with legal norms. Lawyers who can acquire confidential information can counsel individuals about their legal obligations and encourage appropriate resolution of legal disputes. However, for all the reasons noted above, critics of broad confidentiality protections argue that allowing some disclosures in order to prevent injuries to third parties would not significantly intrude on the lawyer's beneficial counseling role. Exceptions to confidentiality safeguards already exist, most individuals are unaware of their scope, and many clients have sufficient reasons to

11. See the discussion in Chapter VI infra.

confide in their attorneys regardless of the precise scope of ethical obligations.

The merits of these arguments are explored more fully in Chapter VI. The point here is simply to underscore the contributions and limitations of ethical theory in addressing legal ethics issues. Abstract moral principles may help in framing the relevant inquiry. But the resolution will generally depend on concrete factual information about the effects of particular ethical decisions, and contextual judgments about how to reconcile competing moral claims. In the confidentiality case just noted, it is important to know how different disclosure rules affect clients' behavior and how to weigh their interests against those of third parties affected by the rules. However, that kind of information is virtually unattainable. Debates over the issue necessarily proceed on a level of unsupported assumptions on both sides.

It does not, however, follow that moral theory is useless and that an entirely relativist approach to ethics is appropriate. In its extreme form, relativism holds that there is no objective basis for justifying one set of ethical beliefs over another. Relativism is appealing because it combines a healthy skepticism towards universal truths and an equally healthy tolerance for cultural diversity. From a relativist standpoint, disagreements about facts look qualitatively different from disagreements about morality. On factual issues, consistent empirical information can produce consensus. On moral claims, such information is far less available. So, for example, in contexts of professional responsibility, we lack an objective basis for determining how different confidentiality rules would affect lawyer-client relationships, or how to weigh the needs of clients against other individuals affected by the rules. Ethical judgments are generally "subjective" to a degree that factual judgments are not. Moreover, ethical convictions vary widely across cultures. To take only the most obvious examples, practices that contemporary Americans would find abhorrent—torture, subjugation of women, or infanticide—have been widely accepted in other societies.

However, as critics of relativism note, factual claims may also be subject to dispute, but few of us conclude that convincing answers are impossible. Many societies long argued about whether the earth was flat; we do not therefore doubt the possibility of valid claims about geography. Moreover, few individuals are prepared to follow relativism to its logical conclusion, and view actions like genocide and terrorism as beyond judgment by universal moral principle.[12] Over time, substantial consensus has emerged on cer-

---

12. W. Bradley Wendel, "Teaching Ethics in an Atmosphere of Skepticism and Relativism," 36 U.S. F. Law Review 711 (2002); Morris Ginsburg, On the

tain basic moral premises. Given full information and an opportunity for dispassionate and disinterested judgment, most individuals will agree about core essential principles, such as honesty, benevolence, fairness, and so forth. Although disagreements will remain about the application of those principles in particular cases, including those in legal ethics, some positions will often seem more persuasive than others—more rational, informed, and internally consistent.

In any event, however lawyers resolve the philosophical debate over relativism, they must make considered ethical judgments of the kind that are the subject of this book. Their challenge is to avoid moral arrogance without abdicating moral convictions. On many issues of legal ethics, lawyers with high principles may disagree about what those principles require in hard cases. Particularly where competing values and factual uncertainties are involved, the most professionally responsible approach may require tolerance for differing views. How to arrive at well-considered judgments in the face of conflict and ambiguity is a key focus of the chapters that follow.

C. The Law of Lawyering

In the United States, law is a highly regulated profession. American lawyers are subject to a complex set of formal and informal norms that are largely under the influence of the profession but that are also affected by other forms of regulation. The most important sources of authority are as follows.

Courts

The judicial branch traditionally has asserted "inherent power" to regulate the practice of law, an authority rooted in the proposition that lawyers are officers of the court. In the American context, that judicial authority rests on constitutional provisions governing the separation of government power. Some exercises of the judiciary's oversight are simply instances of common law adjudication. For example, courts have applied contract, fiduciary, and related principles to govern lawyers in areas such as malpractice, fee disputes, and conflicts of interest.

In addition, the judiciary has asserted authority to adopt general procedural rules and ethical codes. Virtually every state supreme court has exercised control over bar admission, discipline, and unauthorized practice of law. Federal judges enjoy comparable

Diversity of Morals, in 1 Essays on Sociology and Social Philosophy 97–129   (1956); Michael Moore, "Moral Reality," 1982 Wis. L. Rev. 1061, 1088–1096.

inherent authority as well as statutory power to regulate admission, discipline, and trial conduct in their own court system. For substantive standards, federal courts generally rely on the ethical codes and common law of the jurisdictions in which they sit. To varying degrees, judges in both state and federal systems have enforced legislative regulation that they view as not inconsistent with their own oversight powers.

Bar Associations

In exercising their regulatory responsibilities, courts frequently have deferred or delegated authority to bar associations. About two-thirds of the states have "integrated" bars, which require lawyers to belong to state bar associations as a condition of practice. In some states, bar organizations largely administer admission and disciplinary structures, although the judiciary exercises nominal supervision. Other states have separate regulatory bodies that are subject to judicial review. In either case, although non-lawyers often have some representation on disciplinary committees, members of the profession exercise control. The organized bar generally has shaped the relevant ethical standards through committee recommendations and lobbying efforts.

In addition to state bar associations, many lawyers belong to national, local, or other bar organizations, including those structured around fields of practice, political and legal causes, or race, gender, and ethnicity. The largest of these organizations, representing about 40 percent of the nation's attorneys, is the American Bar Association (ABA).

Ethical Codes

One of bar associations' most significant activities has been formulating ethical codes that are adopted by courts. The ABA is responsible for the three model codes that have formed the basis for states' ethical rules. The Canons of Ethics (1908), the Code of Professional Responsibility (1970, amended 1981), and the Model Rules of Professional Conduct (1983, amended 2003). By 2005, the supreme courts in all but six states, including California, had adopted standards based on the Model Rules, generally after consultation with state bar organizations.[13] California has a unique system that grants its Board of Bar Governors statutory power to promulgate rules directly, subject to approval by the California Supreme Court. That court has adopted Rules of Professional Conduct that draw on the ABA Code but are in some respects

---

13. State Ethics Rules, ABA/BNA Lawyers' Manual on Professional Conduct, April 20, 2005, 273.

different. The California legislature has also adopted a broad Business and Professions Code that has provisions applicable to lawyers.

In almost all jurisdictions, bar ethical codes have the force of law as a result of their adoption by state supreme courts. In a minority of jurisdictions, courts have ratified these codes only as guidelines, which can then be given force in judicial and bar disciplinary proceedings. Ethical codes are designed to set standards only for lawyer discipline and expressly disclaim any intent to establish a basis for civil liability.[14] However, most courts have relied on codified rules in malpractice cases. During the late 1980s and 1990s, many state and local bars also adopted codes of civility. For the most part, these codes establish voluntary standards, but several of them have been approved or adopted by a court.

D. Sources of Regulatory Authority

Other primary sources of regulatory standards include bar ethics committees, legislatures, administrative agencies, specialized bar organizations, and legal employers. Rulings by state, local, and national bar committees have played a significant, although declining, role in defining lawyers' ethical responsibilities. Traditionally, these opinions have responded to inquiries by attorneys and have attempted to interpret or amplify codified standards. However, as courts have grown increasingly active in disciplinary, malpractice, and disqualification proceedings, and as voluntary bar organizations have grown increasingly concerned about avoiding antitrust violations, ethics committee opinions have become less influential.[15]

At the same time, the role of legislatures and administrative agencies has expanded. Courts generally have allowed these bodies to define standards for parties appearing in administrative tribunals and to establish other rules of conduct that are consistent with judicially approved rules. Some administrative agencies, such as workers' compensation boards and tax commissions, permit nonlawyers who meet specified qualifications to represent parties in their proceedings. Certain agencies, such as the Securities and Exchange Commission and the Internal Revenue Service, also have power to impose sanctions for unethical conduct by those appearing before them.

14. The introductory provision governing the "scope" of the Model Rules of Professional Conduct asserts that they are "not designed to be a basis for civil liability." The Preliminary Statement to the Code of Professional Responsibility included a similar disclaimer.

15. In the aftermath of the settlement of a government antitrust suit against the ABA, its ethics committee issued an opinion declaring that its rulings were not binding on lawyers. ABA Comm. on Ethics and Professional Responsibility, Informal Op. 1420 (1978).

The complexity of these overlapping regulatory structures is compounded in multi-jurisdictional practice. Much of lawyers' work cuts across state or national boundaries, and is therefore subject to more than one ethical code. Although the ABA's Model Rules establish principles for resolving conflicts between state codes, application of these principles can be problematic in practice.[16]

Other bar entities also play a significant regulatory role. State boards of bar examiners exercise authority over admission standards and procedures. These boards administer bar exams, moral character requirements, and procedures for admitting out-of-state attorneys. Other professional organizations have promulgated standards for lawyers that can be an important source of guidance for practitioners, courts, bar committees, and drafters of ethical codes. The American Law Institute's Restatement of the Law Governing Lawyers is the most comprehensive and influential of these works. Other examples include the ABA's Standards Relating to the Administration of Criminal Justice, and the Standards of Conduct of the American Academy of Matrimonial Lawyers.

A final source of influence involves the formal and informal norms of legal workplaces. Employers often have specific policies, procedures, committees and/or advisors concerning ethical issues. For example, many large firms, corporate in-house counsel offices, and government agencies have elaborate structures for dealing with ethical issues such as conflicts of interests. Employer policies typically supplement as well as incorporate governing ethical codes, and often reflect other sources of authority, such as conditions imposed by insurance companies in malpractice liability policies.

Of equal or greater importance are informal norms. A wide array of evidence documents the importance of peer influence on ethical behavior.[17] Lawyers' sense of appropriate conduct depends heavily on prevailing standards in their workplace, community, and field of practice. A desire to fit in, to be team players, and to protect their reputation, often plays a powerful, not always fully conscious role, in lawyers' ethical decisionmaking. Depending on the context,

16. ABA Model Rules of Professional Conduct, Rule 8.5. As Chapter X notes, the American Bar Association on recommendation of the Commission on Multi-jurisdictional Practice, adopted amendments to its Model Rule that facilitate practice across state boundaries under specified circumstances.

17. See sources cited in Deborah L. Rhode, Where Is the Leadership In Moral Leadership, in Moral Leadership: The Theory and Practice of Power, Judgment, and Policy 29, 32 (ed. Deborah L. Rhode, 2006); Linda Trevino and Gary R. Weaver, Managing Ethics in Business Organizations; Social Scientific Perspective (2003); Bradley Wendel, "Informal Methods of Enhancing the Accountability of Lawyers," 54 U. S. Car. L. Rev. 967 (2003); Fran Zemans & Victor Rosenblum, The Making of a Public Profession 172 (1984).

the result can be to reinforce, reshape, or repress moral commitments.

In this complicated regulatory environment with overlapping (sometimes competing) practice norms, "doing the right thing" both morally and legally can pose substantial challenges. Those challenges are the subject of this book.

Chapter II

THE AMERICAN LEGAL PROFESSION AND BAR REGULATORY STRUCTURES

A. The Origins of the Profession

The Anglo American Tradition

The practice of law dates back over two millenia. By the mid-fourth century B.C.E. in Greece, advocates argued for parties at trial and legal counselors handled commercial matters and drafted legislative proposals. However, these individuals did not constitute a "professional" community in the contemporary sense of the term. Formal ethical standards were reportedly nonexistent, and systematic education and discipline were lacking. Payment for these law-related services was prohibited, but gifts may often have been expected.[1] Later Roman practice gave rise to a somewhat more professionalized culture of advocates and advisors. Between the first and third centuries A.C.E., associations of advocates with formal training and disciplinary standards emerged around the courts of major cities. However, with the fall of the Holy Roman Empire, the professional tradition also declined.[2]

In England, prior to the Norman invasion, disputes ordinarily were settled through informal community pressure or, more formally, through ordeal or trial by "compurgation." Ordeals were a form of adjudication based on divine intervention; the accused was placed at risk (such as by drowning or burning) and the result was interpreted as a sign from God indicating guilt or innocence. Under an alternative trial procedure, a critical issue was the credibility of the accused, which was established through oaths by a specified number of compurgators. In order for their oaths to be valid, compurgators had to complete their recitation without any verbal slips. Tradition has it that the earliest Anglo–American legal practitioners were those who could be counted on to deliver their oaths without a sneeze or a stumble.[3]

---

1. See Thomas Holton, Preface to Law: The Professional Milieu 2–4 (1980); Douglas M. MacDowell, The Law in Classical Athens (1978); Robert J. Bonner, Lawyers and Litigants in Ancient Athens: The Genesis of the Legal Profession 200–13, 218–43 (1927).

2. J. A. Crook, Legal Advocacy in the Roman World 172–75 (1995); Wolfgang

Kunkel, An Introduction to Roman Legal and Constitutional History 105–16 (J. M. Kelly trans. 1973); Hans Julius Wolff, Roman Law: An Historical Introduction 95–117 (1951).

3. S. F. Milsom, Historical Foundations of the Common Law 28 (1969); Marion Neef & Stuart Nagel, "The Ad-

Over time, a more professional culture evolved. Church courts on the Continent and in England (which adjudicated various civil as well as religious matters) developed more rational procedures of factual and legal argument. The Normans who invaded England also brought with them traditions of trial by combat, use of "juries" for investigation and trial, and expansion of church court jurisdiction. As the forms of adjudication became more sophisticated, a greater role for advocates developed.[4] And as the economy became more complex, a greater need also emerged for advisors who could provide assistance with legal documents, transactions, and commercial disputes. Practitioners in these matters evolved into two groups. Barristers provided trial representation and prepared for this role by attending one of four Inns of Court and then by serving as apprentices to a practicing barrister. Solicitors provided other forms of legal assistance and were governed by professional associations and rules of court, supplemented by legislative enactments.

Efforts to establish law as a "gentlemen's" profession resulted in restrictive entry practices. For a substantial period, barristers excluded certain presumptively unfit groups including Catholics, tradesmen, journalists, and women. Class also served as a filtering device; the costs of obtaining an education and establishing a practice limited access to those with substantial means. Although solicitors were less exclusive in their entrance standards, lengthy apprenticeship requirements and selective referral networks discouraged female applicants and candidates from economically and racially subordinate groups until the later twentieth century.[5] In recent years, the British profession has become much more diverse, and the differences between barristers and solicitors have diminished.

The colonists who settled America were generally not eager to import English legal traditions. Some colonies attempted to exclude lawyers entirely, either by barring them from courts or by prohibit-

versary Nature of the American Legal System: A Historical Perspective," in Lawyers' Ethics: Contemporary Dilemmas, 73, 75–80 (Allan Gerson ed. 1980); Henry S. Drinker, Legal Ethics, 12–14 (1953).

4. Theodore F. T. Plucknett, A Concise History of the Common Law 216–17 (5th ed. 1956). See also Geoffrey Hazard and Angelo Dondi, Legal Ethics: A Comparative Study, Ch. 1 (2004); Herman Cohen, A History of the English Bar and Attornatus to 1450, 18–35 (1929); Roscoe Pound, The Lawyer from Antiquity to Modern Times (1953); J. H. Baker, "The English Legal Profession 1450–1550," in Lawyers in Early Modern Europe and America 16 (Wilfrid Prest ed. 1981).

5. Michael Birks, Gentlemen of the Law (1960); W. J. Reader, Professional Men: The Rise of the Professional Classes in Nineteenth–Century England (1966); Deborah L. Rhode, "Moral Character as a Professional Credential," 94 Yale L. J. 491, 494–95 (1981).

ing payment for legal services. This hostility had multiple sources. Many colonists had been victims of government persecution in England and retained a strong distrust of all officers of the court. Merchants and landowners often wanted to run their own affairs without interference by law and lawyers. Some religious and political leaders were equally wary of inviting legal limits on their authority or coping with the contentiousness that lawyers might encourage. The idea that "lawyers' law" conflicted with God's law was widely shared. Class prejudice was also at work. Lawyers were frequently disparaged by reason of their association with unpopular upper-income groups.

Qualifications for the Bar and Discriminatory Practices

Yet as historian Lawrence Friedman concludes, "lawyers were, in the end, a necessary evil."[6] In a developing economy, legal rules and institutions evolved and with them legal skills became increasingly useful. A growing class of practitioners accordingly emerged. Their training was uneven and often slipshod. With a few short-lived exceptions, law schools were not available until the late nineteenth century. The dominant method of preparation during the bar's formative era was apprenticeship, which often left much to be desired. Many aspiring lawyers trained as not very glorified clerks, with a heavy concentration of drudgery and little formal instruction.[7]

Admission standards were sporadically imposed, but until the twentieth century, they were seldom demanding. In 1800, most states required some brief preparatory period of study but even these minimal requirements largely vanished during the Jacksonian populist era. As Chapter XI indicates, bar exams were usually perfunctory. Many were oral, and involved only a few rudimentary questions and an exchange of pleasantries.[8]

Not all applicants benefited from this open admission system. Although formal entry requirements were fairly lax until the late nineteenth century, informal screening occurred through educational, apprenticeship, and hiring practices. Such practices were strongly colored by class, racial, ethnic, and religious prejudices. The first black student graduated from law school in 1869, and a number of predominantly black institutions formed graduate programs in law around this same period, but few of the programs

---

6. Lawrence M. Friedman, A History of American Law 83 (1973).

7. James Willard Hurst, The Growth of American Law: The Law Makers 285–94 (1950); Friedman, supra note 6 at 96.

8. Len Yang Smith, "Abraham Lincoln as a Bar Examiner," 51 Bar Examiner 35, 37 (1982). See also Hurst, supra note 7, at 282.

survived after the Reconstruction era. Estimates suggest that blacks constituted less than one percent of the profession at the turn of the century, and that they remained under two percent until the 1960s.[9] Other racial minorities were similarly underrepresented. In the 1930s, a series of legal actions began challenging segregation in legal education. This litigation initially forced establishment of "separate but equal" minority law schools, and eventually required integration of previously all-white institutions. However, even after changes in formal policies, the absence of financial aid, affirmative action, recruitment efforts, or supportive academic environments worked against minority admissions. Discrimination by employers, clients, and bar associations further deterred applicants of color.[10]

Bias against religious and ethnic minorities was also common. During the late nineteenth and early twentieth centuries, some universities maintained quotas on Jewish applicants. Many bar leaders also spearheaded campaigns to upgrade entry requirements in the hope of screening out those with immigrant and lower class backgrounds. Antisemitic and nativist attitudes were similarly apparent among some state bar moral character committees and prominent law firms during this period.[11]

Discrimination against women was also pervasive. In the Colonial period, a few women participated in legal transactions by acting as their husbands' representatives or by obtaining powers of attorney.[12] However, the gradual formalization of bar entrance criteria in the late eighteenth century made it increasingly difficult for women to act as agents in legal matters. After the Civil War, the rise in female education, political consciousness, and reform activity sparked increasing challenges to sex-based admission standards. In 1867, Iowa became the first state to license a woman attorney, and,

---

9. Geraldine Segal, Blacks in the Law (1983); Walter J. Leonard, "The Development of the Black Bar," 407 Annals of the Amer. Acad. of Pol. and Soc. Science 134, 136–43 (1973); Kellis E. Parker & Betty J. Stebman, "Legal Education for Blacks," 407 Annals of the Amer. Acad. of Pol. and Soc. Science 144 (1973).

10. See sources cited in note 9 and Jerold S. Auerbach, Unequal Justice: Lawyers and Social Change in Modern America 106–07 (1976).

11. Robert Stevens, Law School: Legal Education in America from the 1850s to the 1980s at 100–01 (1983); Rhode, supra note 5, at 500–02.

12. Karen Morello, The Invisible Bar: The Woman Lawyer in America 1638 to the Present (1986); Deborah L. Rhode, Justice and Gender: Sex Discrimination and the Law 20–24 (1989); Deborah L. Rhode, "Perspectives on Professional Women," 40 Stan. L. Rev. 1163 (1988). See generally, Barbara J. Harris, Beyond Her Sphere: Women and the Professions in American History (1978); Marylynn Salmon, "The Legal Status of Women in Early America: A Reappraisal," Law and Hist. Rev. 129 (1983).

in 1872, Howard University conferred the first law school degree on a female graduate.

The reception for these women in practice was generally less than welcoming. In a celebrated 1873 decision, the United States Supreme Court affirmed Myra Bradwell's exclusion from the Illinois bar. The concurring opinions by Justice Bradley summarized prevailing assumptions about the "separate spheres" of the sexes: "[T]he natural and proper timidity and delicacy which belongs to the female sex evidently unfits it for many of the occupations of civil life.... The paramount destiny and mission of woman are to fulfil the noble and benign offices of wife and mother. This is the law of the Creator."[13] To many courts, the "peculiar qualities of womanhood" seemed ill-suited for "forensic strife."[14]

By the turn of the century, sustained political and legal challenges had secured women's formal right to admission in most states, but significant informal barriers remained. Not until 1972 did all ABA-accredited law schools admit female applicants. Throughout the first half of the century, women constituted less than three percent of the profession, and women of color were even more underrepresented. Biases in salary, hiring, promotion, and placement were common.[15]

The Conditions of Practice

Until the beginning of the twentieth century, lawyers practiced largely in single-person offices or firms of two or three members. The nature of practice varied, and changed over time, partly because lawyers proved exceptionally "nimble in identifying new forms of work and new ways of doing it."[16] When edged out of one area by other service providers like realtors, accountants, or banks, attorneys generally found other areas. But obtaining paid work and restraining competition, both from within and outside the profession, were ongoing challenges. As one struggling mid-nineteenth century practitioner put it, "I wish the fees came in half as fast as the cases."[17]

Still, American lawyers were more successful in securing a strong market for their services than their counterparts in other nations. A primary reason was the centrality of the law in Ameri-

13. Bradwell v. State, 83 U.S. 130, 141 (1872) (Bradley, J. concurring).

14. In re Goodell, 39 Wis. 232, 245 (1875).

15. See Rhode, Justice and Gender, supra note 12, at 23; Cynthia Fuchs Epstein, Women in Law 79–95 (1981).

16. Friedman, supra note 6, at 634.

17. See Maxwell Bloomfield, "The Texas Bar in the Nineteenth Century," 32 Vand. L. Rev. 261, 270 (1979).

can society. A pivotal judicial decision was that of the Supreme Court in *Marbury v. Madison* in 1803. There Chief Justice Marshall proclaimed that "it is emphatically the province and duty of the judicial department to say what the law is."[18] Since the judiciary determines what the law is, and the role of lawyers derives from the role of the judiciary, the centrality of judicial review, including Constitutional review, helps define the function of lawyers in the American system. "Court challenges" are a normal part of our political decision-making.

The corresponding importance of the legal profession in public life prompted Alexis de Tocqueville's celebrated description of attorneys as the nation's "natural aristocracy." Compared with other countries, he noted, the United States had placed more power in the hands of lawyers and less in a hereditary class, or in the military, church, or civil service. That allocation of authority both reflected and reinforced the importance of law in American culture. As Tocqueville also famously noted, "[s]carcely any political question arises in the United States that is not resolved, sooner or later, into a judicial question.... As most public men are or have been legal practitioners, they introduce the customs and technicalities of their profession into the management of public affairs." Another reason for the centrality of lawyers, according to de Tocqueville, involved their ability to serve as a "connecting link" between classes. They belonged to the "people by birth and interest" and to the aristocracy by "habit and taste." Their "love of order and formalities" aligned them with the upper class; their middle and upper middle class backgrounds aligned them with ordinary citizens and inspired the trust necessary for social influence.[19] As Supreme Court Justice Louis Brandeis noted in an influential 1905 address at Harvard Law School, during the nation's formative years, nearly "every great lawyer was then a statesmen, and nearly every statesmen, great or small, was a lawyer."[20]

The extent to which lawyers actually fulfilled the exalted role portrayed by de Tocqueville and other bar leaders is uncertain. The extent to which they can do so today is equally open to question. As Chapter I noted, popular opinion surveys reflect little public confidence in attorneys' ethics and integrity. Lawyers still edge out used car salesmen, but not by much. Yet the negative public image of the

---

18. Marbury v. Madison, 5 U.S. (1 Cranch) 137, 177 (1803).

19. Alexis de Tocqueville, 1 Democracy in America 273–80 (H. Reeve trans., P. Bradley ed. F. Bowen rev. 1989) (1st ed. 1835). See also Geoffrey C.

Hazard Jr., "The Future of Legal Ethics," 100 Yale L. J. 1239 (1991).

20. Louis D. Brandeis, "The Opportunity in the Law," in Business—A Profession 329, 330 (1914).

bar has done little to deter law school applicants or to deny leadership opportunities. Attorneys are well represented in prominent roles in government, business, academic, and non-profit institutions. Given the continued centrality of law in American public life, it seems likely that members of the legal profession will retain considerable influence in both public and private sectors.

B. Bar Regulatory Structures and Professional Associations

As soon as lawyers formed a critical mass in any local practice setting, they also tended to form professional organizations. After the Revolutionary War, the largest cities generally had voluntary bar associations, which served primarily social functions but sometimes played a significant role in admissions and discipline. During the early nineteenth century, as entry standards became more lax, these regulatory functions largely ceased. They resurfaced at the end of the century in response to several concerns. Leading lawyers saw bar associations as a way not only to socialize with other elite members of the profession, but also to raise ethical standards, combat municipal corruption, curb unlicensed practice, and discourage competition.[21] One of the first undertakings of the American Bar Association, formed in 1878 at the Saratoga Springs summer resort, was to draft Canons of Ethics. The goal was both to promote integrity and to restrain overtly commercial activity. These Canons prohibited advertising, solicitation, and other related practices which, according to an accompanying report, had "debased [lawyers'] high calling in the eyes of the public." In the eyes of bar leaders, a growing number of new entrants, lacking "fixed ideals of ethical conduct," were threatening to reduce the profession "to the level of a trade." Sanctions were needed to stay their "itching fingers" in the "eager quest for lucre."[22]

However, as critics noted, the effect of these anticompetitive prohibitions was not so much to prevent the pursuit of profits as to restrict its methods and beneficiaries. Well-connected members of the bar could attract clients through business and social networks without resort to overtly commercial forms of self-promotion. The bans on advertising and solicitation hindered less established lawyers from targeting their services to unsophisticated and low-income clients, who lacked access to legal assistance and knowledge

---

21. Hurst, supra note 7, at 286–289; Auerbach, supra note 10, at 62–67.

22. American Bar Association, Report of the Committee on [the] Code of Professional Ethics, 1906 American Bar Association Reports 600, 604.

about how to obtain it.[23] Moreover, other early ethical rules, such as those requiring adherence to bar-established minimum fee schedules, were designed to reduce competition within the profession. The ABA's Practice Manual recommended presenting clients with lists of minimum charges in expensive leather folders suggesting a "degree of dignity and substance."[24]

Other bar activities were directed more toward the public interest. The profession promoted law reform and judicial independence; it sought to reduce corrupt or unduly partisan influences over governmental policy and judicial appointments; and by the late twentieth century it supported legal services for the poor and pro bono contributions by its members.[25] Lawyers were at the forefront of almost every major social reform movement of the last two centuries and many viewed public service as part of their professional responsibilities.

However, as the profession has grown larger, more specialized, more diverse, and more profit-oriented, it has faced greater challenges both in speaking with one voice and in playing a civic role. The assumption that inspired many early bar associations—that the profession was, and should remain "above trade"—is hard to sustain in today's legal market. Increasing competition and consumer activism have broken down many of the traditional restraints on commercialism and placed growing emphasis on earnings as a measure of professional achievement.

Yet lawyers also continue to be leaders in public interest movements. And on some issues, the increasing diversity within the profession has enabled bar associations to play a more informed role in public policy. On matters such as equal opportunity and the elimination of bias, the organized bar has been at the forefront of progressive social change.

C.   Diversity Within the Profession

Beginning in the late 1960s, the representation of women and racial and ethnic minorities in the legal profession began to increase substantially. Women's representation among new entrants to the bar grew from about three percent in the 1960s to fifty percent at the turn of the twenty-first century; minorities increased

23. Auerbach, supra note 10, at 64 ; Philip Shuchman, "Ethics and Legal Ethics: The Propriety of the Canons as a Group Moral Code," 37 Geo. Wash. L. Rev. 244 (1968).

24. Deborah L. Rhode, In the Interests of Justice: Reforming the Legal Profession 169 (2000).

25. Robert W. Gordon, "The Ideal and the Actual in the Law: Fantasies and Practices of New York City Lawyers, 1870–1970," in The New High Priests: Lawyers in Post–Civil War America 52–53, 56–59, 65–66 (G. Gawalt ed., 1984); Deborah L. Rhode, Access to Justice 59–66 (2004).

from one percent to twenty percent. Whether or not the proportion of gays and lesbians has changed remains unclear, given their traditionally closeted status, but the number who are able to be open about their sexual orientation has grown significantly.[26] Yet despite such progress, women and minorities remain overrepresented at the bottom and underrepresented at the top of professional status and reward structures. For example, women account for half of law school graduates, and about thirty percent of the profession, but less than a fifth of law firm partners, law school deans, and *Fortune* 500 general counsels.[27] Minorities account for about ten percent of the profession, but only four percent of law firm partners and general counsel at *Fortune* 1000 companies; forty percent of firms have no partners of color.[28] Salaries are substantially lower for women, minority men, and openly gay and lesbian attorneys than for other lawyers with comparable qualifications and positions.[29] Women are half as likely to achieve partnership as similarly situated men. And the limited data available on minority, gay, and lesbian lawyers document significant disparities in retention and promotion.[30]

Part of the discrepancy is related to historic patterns. Lawyers generally achieve higher positions in the profession as they advance

26. William N. Eskridge, Jr. and Nan P. Hunter, Sexuality, Gender, and the Law (2d ed. 2004); Deborah L. Rhode & David Luban, Legal Ethics 98–100 (4th ed., 2004); Leigh Jones, "Smaller Firms More Up Front About Their Gay Employees," Nat'l. L. J., Dec. 12, 2005, at 12.

27. Paula Patton, "Women Lawyers: Their Status, Influence, and Retention in the Legal Profession," 11 William & Mary J. Women & Law 173,174 (2004); American Bar Association Commission on Women in the Profession, Current Glance of Women and the Law 1(Chicago: ABA Commission on Women in the Profession, 2003); Association of American Law Schools, Statistical Report on Law School Faculty and Candidates for Law Faculty Positions (2004–2005).

28. Elizabeth Chambliss, Miles to Go, Progress of Minorities in the Legal Profession 5, 2 (American Bar Association Commission on Racial and Ethnic Diversity in the Profession, 2005); National Association of Law Placement, NALP, Women and Attorneys of Color at Law Firms (2004).

29. Chambliss, supra note 28, at 5; David B. Wilkins & G. Mitu Gulati,

"Why Are There So Few Black Lawyers in Corporate Law Firms? An Institutional Analysis," 84 Cal. L. Rev. 493, 503 (1996); Darryl Van Duch, "Minority GC's Are Few, Far Between," The National Law Journal, Oct. 18, 1999, at A1; Kathleen E. Hull & Robert Nelson, "Divergent Patterns: Gender Differences in the Careers of Urban Lawyers," 10 Researching Law 3, 51 (American Bar Foundation News, Summer 1999); The State Bar of California, Report and Recommendations Regarding Sexual Orientation Discrimination in the California Legal Profession 2 (1996).

30. See State Bar of California Report supra note 29; Rhode & Luban, supra note 26, at 98–110. See also Symposia: Homophobia in the Halls of Justice: Sexual Orientation Bias and Its Implications Within the Legal System, 11 Am. U. J. Gender, Social Pol'y & L. 1 (2002), particularly Amelia Craig Cramer, Discovering and Addressing Sexual Orientation Bias in Arizona's Legal System, 11 Am. U. J. Gender, Social Pol'y & L. 25, 31 (2002).

in practice, and women and minorities constitute a smaller percentage of the most experienced attorneys than of the bar generally. Another factor in the case of women is the difficulty that many face in accommodating work and family responsibilities. Almost a fifth of women with graduate and professional degrees are not in the paid labor force compared with five percent of similarly credentialed men.[31]

However, other factors are also at work. Part of the problem is the lack of recognition that there is a serious problem. Ironically enough, recent progress has created its own obstacles to further change. A widespread perception is that barriers are coming down, women and minorities are moving up, and discrimination has largely been eradicated; whatever racial or gender disparities remain are often attributed to different choices and capabilities.

Yet much depends on how discrimination is defined and whose definition matters. To many attorneys, discrimination implies overt intentional prejudice, and the professional workplaces that they inhabit produce few clear examples. By contrast, other attorneys see bias in more subtle forms, such as unconscious racial and gender stereotypes, exclusion from informal networks of support and professional development opportunities, and inadequate work/family policies. From this perspective, most legal workplaces have ample room for improvement. Over the last two decades, some sixty studies have surveyed bias in the profession, and they consistently find substantial race and gender gaps in perceptions of discrimination. Between two-thirds and three-quarters of women lawyers report experiencing gender bias, while only a quarter to a third of men report observing it.[32] About two-thirds of black attorneys, but only about ten percent of white attorneys, believe that minorities are treated less fairly in hiring and promotion processes.[33] Similar race and gender gaps emerge concerning selections for partnership.[34]

---

31. Claudia Wallis, The Case for Staying Home, Time, March 22, 2004, 51, 53; See also Sylvia Ann Hewlett and Carolyn Buck Luce, Off Ramps and On Ramps: Keeping Talented Women on the Road to Success, Harvard Business Review, March 2005, 43–45 (forty percent of surveyed women with professional, graduate, or undergraduate honors degrees had dropped out of labor force, primarily for family reasons, left the labor force compared with 10 percent of similarly credentialed men).

32. See sources cited in Rhode, supra note 24, at 39.

33. Arthur S. Hayes, "Color–Coded Hurdle," 85 ABA Journal, 56 (1999).

34. Abbie F. Willard, Perceptions of Partnership: The Allure and Accessibility of the Brass Ring 33 (Washington, D.C.: National Association for Law Placement, 1999).

Both psychological research and empirical surveys suggest that differential treatment remains common. Part of the reason involves the lingering, largely unconscious, influence of gender and racial stereotypes. Women and minorities often do not enjoy the same presumption of competence as their white male colleagues. Traditionally disfavored groups find that their mistakes are more readily noticed and their achievements more often attributed to luck or special treatment.[35] So too, the mismatch between characteristics traditionally associated with women and those typically associated with professional success leave female lawyers in a persistent double bind. They are faulted as too assertive or not assertive enough and what is viewed as assertive in a man often is perceived as abrasive in a woman.[36]

The force of traditional stereotypes is compounded by other cognitive biases. People are more likely to notice and recall information that confirms their prior assumptions than information that contradicts them.[37] Attorneys who assume that their minority colleagues are beneficiaries of affirmative action, not meritocratic selection, will recall their errors more readily than their insights. Attorneys who assume that working mothers are less committed to their careers will remember the times that they leave early, not the times they stay late. A related problem is that people share what psychologists label a "just world" bias.[38] They want to believe that individuals generally get what they deserve and deserve what they get. Perceptions of performance frequently are adjusted to match observed outcomes. If women and minorities are underrepresented in positions of greatest prominence, the most psychologically conve-

35. Deborah L. Rhode, The Unfinished Agenda: Women and the Legal Profession 15 (ABA Commission on Women and the Legal Profession, 2001); Martha Foschi, "Double Standards for Competence: Theory and Research," 26 Annual Rev. Soc. 21 (2000); Wilkins & Gulati, supra note 29, at 557, 571; Chambliss, supra note 28, at 85; David A. Thomas & Karen L. Proudford, "Making Sense of Race Relations in Organizations," in Addressing Cultural Diversity in Organizations: Beyond the Corporate Context 51 (Robert J. Carter, ed. 1999).

36. Deborah L. Rhode and Joan Williams, "Legal Perspectives on Employment Discrimination, in Sex Discrimination in Employment: An Interdisciplinary Approach" (Faye Crosby, Margaret Stockdale, and S. Ann Ropp,

eds., forthcoming); Rhode, Unfinished Agenda, supra note 35, at 15; Peter Glick and Susan T. Fiske, "Ambivalent Sexism," in 33 Advances in Experimental Social Psychology 115 (M. P. Zanna, ed. 2001).

37. Linda Hamilton Krieger, "The Content of our Categories: A Cognitive Bias Approach to Discrimination and Equal Employment Opportunity," 47 Stan. L. Rev. 1161 (1995); Deborah L. Rhode, "The Difference 'Difference' Makes," in The Difference Difference Makes: Women and Leadership 3, 30–32 (Deborah L. Rhode, ed., 2003); Willard, supra note 34, at 93.

38. Melvin J. Lerner, The Belief in a Just World: A Fundamental Delusion vii-viii (1980).

nient explanation is that they lack the necessary qualifications or commitment.

However, a more adequate explanation would acknowledge that careers can also be waylaid by adverse stereotypes, race-or sex-based harassment, inadequate access to mentoring and client networks, and inflexible workplace structures. A wide array of research finds that people feel more comfortable with those who are like them in important respects such as race or sex, and are more likely to assist those with similar backgrounds. Women, minority men, and gay and lesbian attorneys frequently report being left out of the loop of advice, collaboration, and business development.[39] A significant number also experience race or sex-based harassment.[40] So too, because women generally bear a disproportionate share of family obligations, they pay a similarly disproportionate price for inflexible workplace structures. Although most legal employers in theory permit part-time schedules, only about four percent of lawyers, few of them men, feel free to take advantage of that option.[41]

These problems are compounded by the disincentives to challenge them. Most targets of bias are reluctant to appear confrontational, and discrimination claims are generally far too expensive to litigate in both personal and financial terms. Plaintiffs risk having all their deficiencies publicly aired, and the rare individuals who win in court may lose in life by being labeled as troublemakers.[42]

39. ABA Commission on Women in the Profession, Visible Invisibility: Women of Color in Law Firms (2006); Ida O. Abbott, The Lawyers' Guide to Mentoring (2000); Rhode, Unfinished Agenda, supra note 35, at 16; Rhode & Williams, supra note 36; Chambliss, supra note 28, at 84; Catalyst, Women in Law (2001); Willard, supra note 34, at 54–58.

40. Deborah L. Rhode & Jennifer Drobac, Sex–Based Harassment: Workplace Policies for Lawyers (ABA Commission on Women in the Profession, 2002).

41. See sources cited in Patton, supra note 27, at 189; Deborah L. Rhode, Balanced Lives: Changing the Culture of Legal Practice (ABA Commission on Women in the Profession, 2001); Deborah L. Rhode, "Balanced Lives for Lawyers," 70 Fordham L. Rev. 2207 (2002).

42. Brenda Major & Cheryl Kaiser, "Perceiving and Claiming Discrimina-tion," in The Handbook on Employment Discrimination Research: Rights and Realities (Laura B. Nielsen & Robert Nelson, ed. 2006); Laura B. Nielsen & Robert Nelson, "Scaling the Pyramid: A Sociological Model of Employment Discrimination Litigation," in Handbook of Employment Discrimination Research: Rights and Realities 3 (Laura B. Nielsen & Robert Nelson, ed. 2005); The Special Committee on Lesbians and Gay Men in the Legal Profession, "Report of Findings from the Survey on Barriers and Opportunities Related to Sexual Orientation," 51 The Record 130 (Association of the Bar for the City of New York, 1996); Thomas & Proudford, supra note 35. For case histories of the costs of these suits, see Paul M. Barrett, The Good Black: A True Story of Race in America 59 (1998); Deborah L. Rhode, "What's Sex Got to Do With It?: Diversity in the Legal Profession," in Legal Ethics: Law Stories 233 (Deborah L. Rhode & David Luban, ed. 2006).

How best to respond to these problems is subject to dispute. One of the most controversial issues involves preferential treatment for attorneys of color in hiring and promotion. Opponents view such forms of affirmative action as perpetuating a color consciousness that society should be seeking to eradicate. They also worry that such treatment implies that lawyers of color require special advantages, which perpetuates the problem. By contrast, supporters of proactive policies emphasize the costs of inaction. In their view, only by insuring a critical mass of minorities in top positions can the legal profession secure a workplace that is fair in fact as well as form. In some contexts, "special" treatment may be essential to counteract the special obstacles facing underrepresented groups.

Other disputed issues involve the need for special gender-related initiatives to counteract unconscious bias and to accommodate family responsibilities. For example, lawyers differ over the value of diversity training, the appropriate terms of part-time policies, and the need for special women's networks.[43]

However these issues are resolved, the situation in the United States is much more favorable to minorities than that in other countries. In many contemporary legal systems, effective entry into the profession still depends primarily on family affiliation.[44] In this nation, most lawyers agree about the underlying goal of equal opportunity. A premise of the bar's self-concept is that an attorney becomes successful by merit and professional diligence. Difference in identity or background should not make a difference in professional opportunities.

American lawyers also generally agree, at least in principle, about the value of diversity and balanced lives. Full representation in the profession of those from varying backgrounds should be a high priority in order to reflect diverse perspectives on legal issues; to create the fact and appearance of fairness in legal decision-making, and to provide adequate legal services to all sectors of the American community. A balance between professional and personal commitments should be widely available. Policies that address work/family concerns generally prove cost-effective by improving recruitment and retention and reducing stress-related dysfunc-

---

43. For discussion of such strategies, see Rhode, Unfinished Agenda, supra note 35, at 34–35; Rhode, "Difference," supra note 37; Rhode & Drobac, supra note 38; Susan Bisom–Rapp, "Fixing Watches with Sledgehammers: The Questionable Embrace of Employee Sexual Harassment Training by the Legal Profession," 24 U. Ark. Little Rock L. Rev. (2001) 147; Kimberly D. Krawiec, Cosmetic Compliance and the Failure of Negotiated Governance, 81 Wash. U. L. Qu. 487 (2003).

44. Hazard and Dondi, supra note 4, ch. 1.

tions.[45] Equal opportunity and balanced lives are issues in which the entire profession has a stake.

45. Rhode supra note 24, at 41–44, 47; Deborah L. Rhode, Profits and Professionalism, 33 Ford. Urb. L. J.49, 66–68 (2005).

Chapter III

THE FORMS AND ECONOMICS
OF LEGAL PRACTICE

A. The Structure of Practice

The term "law practice" is an abstraction that covers a wide range of professional activities whose only common denominator is that lawyers engage in them. Indeed, the variety of what practicing attorneys do makes it difficult to identify shared experiences, beyond graduation from law school and membership in a bar. Similarity of educational background and equality in formal status make for certain common interests and commitments, but these can often be eclipsed by the diversity in daily experience. "Lawyers" include law school graduates who do not practice law, but who pursue other careers such as politics, journalism, management, the judiciary, legal education, government, and nonprofit organizations. Their legal background remains an important element of their outlook and role in society. In European and Asian countries an even higher proportion of university graduates who have majored in law proceed to such other vocations.

The work of practicing lawyers varies along several dimensions: core functions, substantive fields, and practice contexts. A lawyer's minimal function, viewed analytically, is providing advice and advocacy concerning legal rights. From these core functions derive further specializations, cutting across substantive areas. The portfolio of required skills includes the knowledge of substantive and procedural law, understanding of legal institutions such as courts and government agencies, and various interpersonal, analytic, writing, and verbal capabilities. It is conventional to classify lawyers according to which of these skills or substantive fields predominate in their professional repertoire. Thus, we speak of litigators and labor negotiators, or of tax and securities specialists.

Another variation involves "situation in practice." This concept can include locality (small town, metropolitan area, etc.), work context (solo practitioner, small firm lawyer, large firm lawyer, government lawyer, etc.) or professional experience and status (senior partner, junior associate, etc.). A different form of classification is premised on the attorney's primary clientele. Such distinctions depend on the proportion of professional assistance that involves indigents, individuals of modest means, small businesses, large corporations, governmental institutions, and so forth.

When considered along all these dimensions, the American legal profession is quite diverse, and it has changed significantly over the last half century. In 1950, the United States had about 200,000 lawyers, one for every 695 persons. By the beginning of the twenty-first century, the number had grown to over a million, roughly one for every 265 persons. About three-quarters of today's lawyers are in private practice, and are close to equally divided in solo practice (48 percent) and firms (52 percent). The percentage of lawyers in large and midsize firms has increased, as has the size of the firms. In the 1950s, only about forty firms had more than fifty lawyers. Now, of the lawyers in firms, slightly over a quarter are in offices of over 100 lawyers. Another 25 percent are in offices of two to four practitioners; about 30 percent are in offices of five to twenty, and 20 percent are in offices of twenty-one to a hundred.[1] About a third of the lawyers in firms are associates; the remainder are partners or lawyers in firms with no associates.[2] Of the lawyers not in private practice, about eight percent are in private industry, ten percent are in government, three percent are in the judiciary, one percent are in academia, and one percent are in legal aid, public defender, or public interest offices. Five percent are retired or inactive.[3]

The functions that lawyers perform are also quite diverse. They range from counseling ordinary citizens about ordinary legal problems to orchestrating "megalaw" mergers, litigating transnational disputes, and representing various client interests before and on behalf of governmental institutions. Over time, lawyers tend to specialize and, while they may move around in the system, most do not stray far from where they started.

The effect of such specialization is a pronounced stratification within the profession. In broad terms, that stratification corresponds to types of practice and, more particularly, to types of clientele. In a classic study, John Heinz and Edward Laumann found a profession divided into two hemispheres. Clients in one hemisphere included individuals and small businesses; in the other were large organizations such as corporations and governmental bodies. Few lawyers regularly crossed the equator, and those who served large organizations had greater status within the profession than those who served other clients. The demand for services remained strongest in the corporate sector. About 60 percent of private practitioners' work is now devoted to business clients.[4]

1. Clara Carson, The Lawyer Statistical Report 8 (American Bar Association, 2004).

2. Id., at 9.

3. Id. At 6–7.

4. John P. Heinz, Edward O. Laumann, Robert L. Nelson & Ethan Michelson, "The Changing Character of

B. The Conditions of Practice: Balanced Lives and Bottom Lines

Legal practice has changed in other important ways over the last half century. For most lawyers, the workplace has become more competitive, more commercial, and more time consuming. Billable hour requirements have substantially increased, and many attorneys work at least 55 to 60 hours per week.[5] Technological innovations have also increased the pace of legal practice and encouraged expectations of constant availability and instant responsiveness. Lawyers remain tethered to their worksites by cell phones, e-mails, faxes, and beepers. Unsurprisingly, most lawyers feel that they do not have enough time for themselves, and close to half feel that they lack sufficient time for their families.[6] To an important degree, this pattern mirrors similar change in other white-collar vocations.

Although the extent and causes of lengthening workweeks vary somewhat across practice contexts, some dysfunctional patterns are widely shared. One involves performance. Bleary, burnt-out lawyers seldom provide cost-effective services for clients, and overwork is a leading cause of lawyers' own disproportionate rates of stress, substance abuse, and other health-related disorders.[7] In addition, extended hours and inflexible schedules pose special problems for those with substantial family responsibilities. Because women assume a disproportionate share of those responsibilities, women lawyers pay a disproportionate price in professional opportunities. The lack of adequate alternative schedules and leave policies is part of the reason for persistent glass ceilings for women, and excessive attrition and recruitment costs for their employers.[8] Finally, as Chapter IX notes, increases in billable hours have curtailed the time available for pro bono work. The result is to deny lawyers valuable opportunities for training, trial experience, and community networks in the service of causes to which these individuals are committed.

Lawyers' Work: Chicago in 1975 and 1995," 32 Law & Soc. Rev. 751, 765 (1998).

5. Deborah L. Rhode, Profits and Professionalism, 33 Fordh. Urb. L. J 44, 64–66 (2006); Judith N. Collins, Nat'l Ass'n for Law Placement, Billable Hours: What Do Forms Really Require? (2005). See Deborah L. Rhode, In the Interests of Justice 35 (2001).

6. See studies cited in Patrick S. Schiltz, "On Being a Happy, Healthy, and Ethical Member of an Unhappy, Un-

healthy, and Unethical Profession," 52 Vand. L. Rev. 871, 888–95 (1999).

7. See Deborah L. Rhode, Balanced Lives: Changing the Culture of Legal Practice 21 (ABA Commission on Women in the Profession, 2002); Rhode, "Profits and Professionalism," supra note 5, at 66.

8. Rhode, supra note 7, at 21; Catalyst, Women in Law: Making the Case (2001); and discussion in Chapter II.

The increasingly demanding nature of professional work is part of a larger global trend. Growing competition within and across occupations and nations is intensifying workplace pressures, and shows no signs of diminishing. The problem is compounded by the priority on profits in advanced industrial societies that is eclipsing other values. Yet for well-paid professionals, this priority may often be self-defeating; it can squeeze out time for family, friends, public service, and personal interests that would ultimately prove more satisfying than the incremental income generated by excessive workloads.[9] In some practice contexts, growing numbers of practitioners wonder whether their well-paid work is worth the price.

Considerable evidence indicates that money plays a much smaller role in promoting personal satisfaction than is commonly assumed. Researchers consistently find that for individuals at lawyers' income levels, differences in compensation bear relatively little relationship to differences in satisfaction.[10] There is also no relationship between compensation and fulfillment across different fields of practice. Discontent is greatest among well-paid large firm associates and least pronounced among relatively low-earning academics, public interest, and public sector employees.[11] One reason for this disconnect between wealth and satisfaction is that most of what high incomes can buy does not yield enduring happiness. Desires, expectations, and standards of comparison tend to increase as rapidly as they are satisfied. As psychologists note, the transitory pleasure that comes through non-essential purchases is less critical in promoting well-being than other factors, such as individuals' relationship with families, friends, and communities, and their sense of contributing to larger societal ends.[12]

Yet several dynamics converge to produce choices that overvalue income. One dynamic involves the difficulty of downward

---

9. For further discussion of the self-defeating dynamics described in the text accompanying notes 10–17, see Rhode, "Profits and Professionalism," supra note 5, at 72–74, and Rhode, In the Interests of Justice, supra note 5, at 29–38.

10. David G. Myers & Ed Diener, Who is Happy?, 6 Psychol. Sci. 12, 13 (1995); Juliet B. Schor, The Overspent American 9 (1998); Robert H. Frank, Luxury Fever 72, 112–113 (1999); Matthew Herper, Money Won't Buy You Happiness, Forbes, Sept. 21, 2004, available at http://www.forbes.com/technology/sciences/2004/09/21/cx_mh_0921happiness.html (last visited Nov. 25, 2005).

11. NALP Found. & The American Bar Found., After the JD: First Result of a National Survey of Legal Careers, 8, 10 (2004); Boston Bar Ass'n Task Force on Prof. Fulfillment, Expectations, Reality, & Recommendations for Change, Aug. 15, 1997, available at http://www.bostonbar.org/prs/fulfillment.htm.

12. Martin E. P. Seligman, Authentic Happiness 9 (2002) (arguing that pleasure is less related to enduring happiness than engagement in relationships and a sense of meaning, which involves using personal capacities to make a broader societal contribution); Herper, supra note 10.

economic mobility. Attorneys who initially chose well-paying jobs in order to gain training and prestige, or to pay off student loans, often become habituated to the lifestyle that such positions make possible.[13] So too, the work required to generate high income creates a heightened sense of deprivation that fuels heightened demands. Attorneys working long hours feel entitled to goods and services that will make their lives easier and more pleasurable. This pattern of compensatory consumption can become self-perpetuating. Part of the reason many professionals accept grueling schedules is to afford "extras" for themselves or their families that they have little time to enjoy. But luxuries can come to seem like necessities and prevent attorneys from opting for a more satisfying balance of personal, professional, and public service pursuits.

A desire for relative status pushes in a similar and equally corrosive direction. For many individuals, including lawyers, money is a key measure of achievement and self-esteem, and spending money is a way to signal success and social status. The desire to impress and display is deeply rooted in human nature, and in America's increasingly materialist culture, self-worth is linked to net worth.[14] Income is, to large extent, a "positional good;" individuals' perceptions of their own pay depends on its position relative to others.[15] The frequently public nature of personal salaries has made the competition for relative status easier to play and harder to win.[16] As economists note, this kind of arms race has few winners and many losers. There is, in fact, no room at the top. Attorneys who look hard enough can always find someone getting something more.

These dynamics skew the priorities not only of individual lawyers but also of the firms that employ them. Because money is at the top of almost everyone's scale, it is easier to reach consensus on maximizing compensation than on other values such as reducing hours or subsidizing substantial pro bono commitments. Firms that sacrifice profits for other workplace satisfactions risk losing talented partners and recruits who prefer greater earnings. Once high pay scales are established, they are difficult to dislodge. Downward mobility is painful, and the working conditions necessary to sustain

13. John R. O'Neil, The Paradox of Success 132 (2006); William R. Keates, Proceed With Caution 126–27 (1997).

14. Richard Conniff, A Natural History of the Rich 145 (2002).

15. Robert H. Frank, How Not to Buy Happiness, Daedalus, Spr. 2004, at 69, 79.

16. As Steven Brill, the former editor of the American Lawyer, has noted, once legal periodicals began comparing law firm salaries, "suddenly all it took for a happy partner making $250,000 to become a malcontent was to read that at the firm on the next block a classmate was pulling down $300,000." Steven Brill, "Ruining" the Profession, Am. Law., July–Aug. 1996, at 5.

such incomes then encourage the sense of deprivation and entitle-
ment that fuel desires for further financial compensation. Even
attorneys who initially entered the profession with modest financial
aspirations and strong social justice commitments often become
trapped in these reward cycles. If these lawyers cannot afford to do
the kind of public-interest work that they would really like, they
want at least to be very well paid for what they are doing.

For other practitioners, however, high incomes are not a major
priority. What motivates their long hours are interesting and challenging issues. Many of these lawyers are addicted to their work
and they assume that those who work with them should feel the
same.

There are no simple solutions but there are real choices for
attorneys who want something different. Lawyers who are dissatisfied with current workplace structures can take collective action or
vote with their feet. Competitive pressures may be inevitable but
attorneys, both individually and institutionally, can redefine what
they are competing over. The desire for status is deeply rooted, but
professional cultures can change the way status is measured, and
practitioners can live by their own definitions of success and self-
worth.

C. Lawyers in the Private Sector: Solo, Small Firm and Large Firm Practice

Over the last two decades, the proportion of lawyers in private
practice has grown from about two-thirds to three-quarters of the
bar. As noted earlier, they practice in a range of different settings
that carry distinctive rewards and challenges.

The third of the profession who work on their own generally
are seeking advantages such as flexibility, independence, client
contact, and escape from office politics.[17] Solo practitioners often
can have more control over their caseloads and schedules than
other lawyers. Some solo practitioners work out of home offices,
which helps to reduce expenses and work/family conflicts. Yet the
price for such advantages is often paid in greater isolation and
economic instability, fewer intellectually challenging cases, and
lower income and status.[18] Additional stress can come from the
absence of mentoring and back-up support, and the complexities of
running a small business while also serving current clients and

---

17. Carroll Seron, The Business of
Practicing Law: The Work Lives of Solo
and Small–Firm Attorneys 12, 79–80
(1996).

18. Seron, supra note 13, at 80; Kim-
mel, supra note 13, at 12–13; Clyde Jay
Eisman, "The Ups and Downs of Practicing Alone," N.Y. L.J., Nov. 12, 1999,
at 24.

developing new ones. Cooperative office sharing arrangements and referral networks with other lawyers can help minimize some of these difficulties. An increasing number of bar associations have also established support groups and educational materials specifically designed for solo practitioners.[19]

At the other end of the spectrum is the third of the profession that is in firms of over fifty lawyers. As noted earlier, the number and size of these firms has increased dramatically over the last half century; the largest now has over two thousand attorneys spread across over thirty-five countries. Big firms typically have a pyramid structure with a built-in growth imperative. In this structure, partners at the top profit from their skills, experience, reputation, and relationships by supervising and marketing the work of associates. Junior lawyers accept salaries that give the firm a surcharge for their labor in exchange for training and for the chance to compete for partnership.[20] Growth is inevitable unless the firm hires or promotes only to fill the positions of departing partners, a limitation that may be unappealing to both partners and associates.

The trend to growth is further encouraged by the cultural tendency to view size as a measure of status and to assume that the largest firms are also the leading firms. Large firms also can achieve substantial competitive advantages and economies of scale by providing full service for clients' needs that cut across substantive fields and jurisdictional boundaries.

These firms are generally decentralized constellations of internal departments or teams that are typically headed by a senior partner and coordinated by a management committee. A few law firms also have nonlawyer managers serving under such a committee. Coordination is required to avoid conflicts of interest in the service of various clients. The rules governing conflict of interest, considered in Chapter VIII, require constant attention in large firms, and are a constraint on their growth and reach.

Lawyers choose such settings for a variety of reasons. In general, large firms offer high incomes and status, generous benefits and support services, rewarding pro bono opportunities and the possibility of working on intellectually challenging cases under the supervision of talented senior lawyers. Many new entrants to the profession accept such positions, despite the limited prospects for advancement, in order to pay off law school debts and to acquire

19. Jill Schachner Chanen, "Solace for Stressed Solos," ABA J., Aug. 1999, at 82.

20. Carson, supra note 1, at 8–9; Marc Galanter & Thomas Palay, Tournament of Lawyers: The Transformation of the Big Law Firm 94–100 (1991).

valuable training and credentials. However, the price for these advantages may sometimes be extended hours, inflexible or unpredictable schedules, lack of caseload control, and an excessive share of routine work. In some firms with high associate/partner ratios, inadequate supervision, limited mentoring and client contact, and restricted promotion opportunities can result in substantial rates of dissatisfaction and attrition, which are costly for all involved.[21]

Increases in size also can carry a cost in terms of bureaucratization, impersonality, and pressure to generate business for additional attorneys. Particularly in the largest firms, which have hundreds of lawyers spread across multiple offices with high turnover rates, a sense of collegiality and institutional loyalty becomes harder to sustain. However, many firms and bar associations are now making increased efforts to address such concerns and to improve lawyers' quality of life, particularly among junior associates. Many offices have added flexibility to the traditional two-tiered up-or-out system by creating multiple statuses, such as permanent associates, nonequity partners, "of counsel" positions, and temporary contract lawyers. In general, the demand for such positions and the profitability of large firms remain strong.

Another group of private practitioners are those in small firms (two to twelve lawyers) or in midsize firms (twelve to fifty lawyers). These vary enormously in scope and structure. The smallest generally resemble solo practice; a few lawyers join together to share space, staff, and support services, and to provide backup caseload coverage when necessary. Practitioners in many of these firms "have it all": an interesting and profitable practice carried out in small offices by specialists with substantial personal control over their work schedules. Other midsize firms resemble, and aspire to become, large firms. Some small offices are local affiliates of national firms, and specialize in providing low-cost routine services to individuals of modest means. However, the effort to grow "H & R Block" law practice has come to an unsuccessful end, evidently because managing such a practice requires skills that are better compensated in independent settings. Another group of small to midsize firms offer specialized "boutique" services in restricted fields, or provide general services but choose, or are unable to move beyond limited growth.

How the structure of private practice will evolve over this next century remains an open question. Most experts predict a period of

---

21. Rhode, supra note 7, at 35–37, 41–42; National Association of Law Placement, Keeping the Keepers: Strategies for Associate Retention in Times of Attrition (1998).

continued fluidity and experimentation, as firms adapt to an increasingly competitive and global market. As Chapter X notes, the demand for multidisciplinary and multijurisdictional practice are likely to encourage further growth and diversity of organizations providing legal services. However, constraints imposed by conflict of interest rules impose some ceilings on size. Concerns about balanced lives are also likely to affect the structure of workplaces, and to introduce greater flexibility in schedules and status.

D. Legal Counsel to Organizations

Although the percentage of lawyers working for private industry has remained fairly stable over the last half-century, the absolute number and status of those lawyers has grown substantially. Since the 1980s, in-house counsel have increasingly assumed responsibility for providing business and organizational clients with an array of basic legal services, as well as for selecting and monitoring outside attorneys, implementing legal compliance programs, and preventing legal problems from arising. Departments range in size from one to hundreds of attorneys and perform a wide variety of tasks that reflect their employers' nature and scope. The needs of small real estate companies may rarely extend beyond routine property, contracts, and taxation issues; a multinational corporation will encounter practically every kind of legal problem at one time or another.

A number of factors have accounted for the increased role of lawyers for organizations. From the standpoint of individual attorneys, positions in a client's law department hold several appeals. The time demands can be more manageable than in many private practice settings, and inside attorneys can avoid the pressures of juggling the needs of multiple clients while attempting to attract new ones. From the standpoint of organizations, it is often possible to achieve substantial savings by relying on in-house counsel who are familiar with their employers' structure, workforce, culture, and objectives; who do not need to divide their attention among other clients; and who do not have incentives created by hourly fee structures to bill for unnecessary work. During the 1980s and early 1990s, many companies began to reserve basic routine work for their own legal departments, and to rely on outside firms for more episodic or specialized needs. However, that trend has slowed somewhat in recent years, as outside firms have grown increasingly competitive in their fees, and as corporations have faced pressure to downsize staff and outsource non-core functions. One obvious disadvantage of corporate employment for individual lawyers is the dependence on a single client whose attitude toward legal services may shift with different management and economic conditions.

In-house counsel is the client's employee. In that sense, the attorney's role appears to lack the autonomy that is a defining feature of professionalism. But in practice, the degree of independence exercised by in-house counsel can vary widely. If the organization is itself complex—a multidivision multinational corporation, for example—its lawyer-client relationships can be as diverse as those of an outside law firm. Given the diffusion of power and competing interests within many organizational structures, one of the lawyer's most critical tasks may be determining who speaks for the client. This fragmentation of authority often gives in-house counsel considerable flexibility and bargaining leverage. Although they lack some of the autonomy of outside counsel, their greater familiarity with the client often expands opportunities for influence.

The role that in-house lawyers play in particular organizational settings reflects a complex mix of personal preferences and situational factors. In the most systematic study of contemporary corporate law departments, lawyers generally clustered into three basic roles. About a fifth described their function as largely gate keeping; their work was highly "rule-based" and focused on assessing legal risks, monitoring legal compliance, and approving legal transactions. A second group, about half the sample, described their role as predominantly counseling; their work involved not just keeping corporations within legal bounds, but also looking for ways to maximize business profits through creative legal strategies. A final group of lawyers, about a third of the sample, identified themselves as entrepreneurs; their emphasis was on assisting with business planning, particularly in areas with legal implications.[22]

Whatever role they choose, in-house counsel often face special challenges in protecting the organization's legal interests while also protecting their own relationships with management and other employees. These challenges play out in a number of settings involving confidentiality and conflicts of interest, discussed in Chapters VI and VIII below.

E. The Public Sector: Government Service, Legal Aid, and Public Interest Law

The roughly ten percent of lawyers in government provide a range of services as diverse as those in private practice, such as

---

22. Robert L. Nelson & Laura Beth Nielsen, "Cops, Counsel, and Entrepreneurs: Considering the Role of Inside Counsel in Large Corporations," 34 Law & Soc'y Rev. 457 (2000). See also Carl D. Liggio, "A Look at the Role of Corporate Counsel—Back to the Future—Or is it the Past?" 44 Ariz. L. Rev. 621 (2002).

counseling, litigating civil and criminal cases, and implementing legislative and administrative regulations. These tasks cut across a variety of substantive areas, encompassing most private law specialties.

All government lawyers have the same "situation in practice" in that they are all public employees. Behind this resemblance lie many significant variations. For example, district attorneys in sparsely populated rural jurisdictions may handle all the public legal work in the area, often on a part-time basis, including criminal prosecutions, indigent child support claims, and representation of county commissioners. On the other hand, the district attorney's office in a large metropolitan center may have hundreds of lawyers, diversified across many specialties. At both the state and local levels are myriad agencies, departments, and commissions, each having specialized legal problems and specialized legal counsel. Many government agencies engage private firms for some or most of their legal work and lawyers who specialize in this work could be plausibly classified as in private practice or in government service. In addition to such variations at the state and local level of government, some twenty-five thousand federal employees perform virtually all kinds of legal tasks.

Although the government lawyer's client is usually the agency for which he or she works, this is not always the case; public defenders and civil legal aid attorneys owe traditional duties of loyalty to the individuals they assist. However, when lawyers represent "the government," their relationship with the client ordinarily is not the same as in a private context. The legal agency itself will often have independent authority over matters within its jurisdiction. Thus, a district attorney has discretion over whom to prosecute without being answerable to any other public official. Prosecutors have no clients except in the metaphorical sense. Or, to put it differently, they have the authority of both client and lawyer in the representation. This independence is, of course, by no means complete. Government lawyers are responsible for implementing legislative and executive policy with which they may not agree. High-level officials are accountable to those who elect or appoint them. Junior lawyers are also subject to direction from supervisors, whose policy interpretations may appear problematic at best. Many government attorneys are employed in agencies with specialized subject matter, such as public hospitals or universities, where their relationship to higher authority in the organization is similar to that of in-house lawyers in the private sector.

Nonetheless, relative independence is one of the attractions of government service, along with its tendency to offer generous benefits, manageable schedules, and freedom from competitive and business development pressures. The price is paid in lower salaries and limited opportunities for advancement. As Chapter VIII notes, these countervailing costs and benefits have led to a revolving door between public and private sector employment. That structure has its advantages in keeping government accountable as well as attractive to talented attorneys, but it also poses special challenges concerning loyalty and conflicts of interest that will be explored in the chapters that follow.

As noted at the outset of this chapter, approximately one percent of the profession works in legal aid, public defender, and public interest organizations. The term "public interest" is relatively new, but the concept has its origins in earlier movements concerning civil rights, civil liberties, and legal services for the poor. The Council for Public Interest Law, now the Alliance for Justice, has defined the term to include "tax exempt non-profit groups devoting at least 30 percent of their resources to representing previously unrepresented interests on matters of public policy." By that standard, the Council has estimated that until the 1970s, there were only about 25 centers with a total of fewer than 50 full time attorneys. By the 1990s, the number had grown to about 200 organizations employing slightly over a thousand attorneys.[23] In addition, a substantial number of law school clinics and private firms that are not tax exempt provide representation on such matters. A growing number of conservative legal foundations consider themselves to be public interest organizations, although they may not always satisfy the Council's definition because they often take positions that are already well represented by their corporate funding sources.[24]

Public interest organizations generally receive their funding from a mix of government and foundation grants, membership fees, private contributions, and court-awarded attorneys fees. Their work spans a broad array of substantive fields, including environmental, consumer, poverty, immigration, civil rights, women's rights, gay rights, disability rights, and civil liberties issues. Despite their modest numbers, public interest lawyers have had a significant social impact, in part through careful targeting of resources, and in part by enlisting assistance from the private bar as well as from non-legal organizations and coalitions.

---

23. Nan Aron, Liberty and Justice for All: Public Interest Law in the 1980's and Beyond (1989). See Deborah L. Rhode, Access to Justice 66–68 (2004).

24. Aron, supra note 23, at 78.

Government-subsidized legal aid programs have a longer history, although their numbers and mission expanded dramatically during the 1960s and 1970s. Like public interest lawyers, civil legal aid attorneys confront a highly expandable universe of legal needs, and often exercise considerable discretion in allocating their assistance. As the materials in Chapter IX reflect, the appropriate exercise of that discretion remains a subject of continuing controversy. Ironically enough, the effectiveness of legal aid lawyers in court has led to negative responses in legislatures. During the Reagan administration, Congress imposed the first of a series of budgetary cutbacks and restrictions on the cases and clients eligible for federally-funded legal services, and a further wave of restrictions followed in the late 1990s.[25] The result has been to curtail salaries and support services, and to prevent much of the impact litigation that attracts attorneys to poverty law.

Public defender services have been subject to similar budgetary constraints. In many offices, lawyers' salaries are shamefully low and caseloads are unmanageably high. Some defenders handle as many as 500 felony matters per year, and few have adequate time or resources for factual investigation and trial preparation.[26] The problems are compounded in the growing number of jurisdictions that rely on competitive bids to award indigent defense. The underpricing of services that is often necessary in order to win contracts also undercuts effective representation.[27]

Despite these challenges, many public defenders and legal aid organizations, like their public interest counterparts, manage to sustain high levels of professionalism and commitment. Financial rewards may be low, but psychic income is high. Lawyers in these practice settings generally take considerable satisfaction in representing clients and causes that would otherwise lack representation in the justice system. These practitioners do, however, deserve increased financial resources, and the profession has a critical role to play in lobbying and public education to make that support possible.

25. See discussion in Rhode, supra note 23, at 58–64 and Chapter IX infra.

26. Rhode, supra note 25, at 11–12, 123–30; Bruce Green, "Criminal Neglect: Indigent Representation from a Legal Ethics Perspective," 52 Emory L. J. 1169, 1179–83 (2003).

27. See sources cited supra note 26.

Chapter IV

THE "CONSTITUTIONAL" FUNCTIONS
OF THE LEGAL PROFESSION

A. The Rule of Law and Individual Rights

As an historical fact, the legal profession has most fully evolved
in political regimes based on the "rule of law," including legal
guaranties of civil rights and rights of individuals and corporate
entities to own and manage property. The rule of law signifies legal
mandates that are prescribed in advance and applied impartially.
No legal system is perfect in fulfilling these requirements, but the
modern industrialized systems more or less approximate doing so.

The concept of individual rights generally is understood to
include freedom of speech and conscience, freedom from arbitrary
imprisonment, unreasonable searches and seizures, and procedural
unfairness; and, in more recent times, freedom from discrimination
based on race, gender, religious affiliation, or national origin.
Individual rights also encompass the right to ownership of property
and participation in contractual transactions for employment,
goods, and services. An extension of these individual rights is the
right to form organizations, such as religious congregations, private
nonprofit institutions, business partnerships, and political parties.

B. Lawyers and Individual Rights

Individual rights are merely formal guarantees unless there are
adequate procedures for recognition and enforcement. Although
there remain regimes in which judges are presumed to be a sufficient safeguard of individual rights, all regimes professing the rule
of law recognize the right to legal representation in court and the
right to consult a lawyer in out-of-court matters. Governments also
rely heavily on lawyers in law enforcement and administrative
agencies. As a practical matter, legal services are an essential
means of safeguarding the rule of law and protection of individual
rights.

This functional relationship between the rule of law and the
role of counsel poses constitutional questions of major and continuing importance: To what extent does intervention of lawyers introduce not only formal regularity but also excessive "technicality" in
court proceedings and other legal transactions? To what extent
should public subsidies be available to provide legal aid for people
who cannot afford a lawyer? Such issues involving the distribution

of legal services are the focus of Chapter IX. But another, perhaps less visible constitutional issue is involved in debates over the lawyer's role. What is the justification for legal representation of individuals and organizations that can afford assistance of counsel, particularly the high-priced legal talent engaged by business corporations and wealthy individuals?

C. Lawyers for Business Enterprise

It is accepted in modern political regimes that a business corporation can employ lawyers to further its operations. Virtually all corporations of any size regularly engage lawyers to assist in minimizing their tax obligations, monitoring their regulatory obligations, and protecting their interests in relationships with employees, customers, suppliers, creditors, stockholders, and the government. All large corporations have sizable staffs of in-house lawyers. Most large, independent law firms are primarily engaged in corporate law practice. A substantial part of the practice of most smaller law firms deals with matters of property and business.

Nevertheless, in the modern era, ethical discourse about the legal profession has involved criticism of lawyers' allegedly disproportionate assistance to business organizations and wealthy individuals. A main theme of the profession's own pronouncements has been the assertion of independence from client interests and a distinction between legal practice and commercial activity, as in the often-repeated assertion that "the practice of law is a profession, not a business."[1] Yet a large fraction of lawyer's work, especially in prestigious firms, has always been in the service of business. Eminent leaders of the profession, such as Alexander Hamilton, Daniel Webster, and Abraham Lincoln, all obtained most of their income from business clients.

D. The Critiques of Corporate Capitalism

Underlying much of the traditional criticism of corporate law practice are critiques of corporate capitalism and its constituent legal institutions, including private contracts (particularly the adhesion contracts that pervade modern commerce) and the aggregation of power in large business organizations. These critiques are symbolized in the demonstrations against global capitalism that have now become a common world event and in the denunciations that have accompanied recent corporate scandals. The foundations for

---

1. See American Bar Association Commission on Professionalism, In the Spirit of a Public Service: A Blueprint for the Rekindling of Lawyer Profession-alism (1986); see also sources cited in Deborah L. Rhode, In the Interests of Justice: Reforming the Legal Profession 1 (2000).

these critiques emerged in the nineteenth century in works by Marx and other prominent socialists.

The critiques are familiar. Corporate capitalism involves relentless competition, "commodification" of labor, preoccupation with "the bottom line" at the expense of broader values, domination by bureaucratic hierarchies, and manipulation of legal rules for the benefit of wealthy owners and overly powerful business interests. Much in these critiques still needs to be taken seriously by the legal profession. A wide range of critics from within and outside the American bar have raised such concerns about corporate legal practice.[2]

A comprehensive response to these critiques is beyond the scope of this volume (and our own expertise). However, the outline of such a defense on constitutional grounds is fairly straightforward: individuals have rights to own property, to enter contracts and to engage in economic production; individuals have a right to legal assistance in pursuing their objectives; the right to legal assistance includes the right to seek out the most competent available legal assistance; an effective means of implementing individual objectives is through cooperative activity in the form of organizations; the business corporation is a well-developed form of cooperative organization; as such, a corporation is entitled, on behalf of its owners and managers, to employ competent legal assistance.[3]

However, each step in this constitutional logic is open to debate. The right to own property does not entail the right to own or manage corporate entities in their current form; the right to enter contracts does not legitimate adhesion contracts dictated by the stronger party; the right to engage in cooperative activity does not justify all practices by multinational corporations, and so forth. The gaps in the logic can be illustrated by comparison. Compare, for example, the enforcement of a contract that is mutually agreed upon more or less by equal bargainers, with enforcement of a form contract prepared by lawyers for one party that is unread and unreadable by the other party. Such comparisons reflect deeper debates in contemporary politics over how modern society should be structured and how power should be exercised.

---

2. Among the most prominent critics have been Louis D. Brandeis, Business: A Profession 329–43 (1914); Harlan Fiske Stone, Law and Its Administration (1924); and Jimmy Carter, Speech to the Los Angeles Bar Association, May 4, 1978.

3. In Upjohn Co. v. United States, 449 U.S. 383 (1981), the leading American case recognizing the corporate attorney-client privilege, the majority opinion offers a summary form of this analysis.

These debates have grown increasingly important as multinational corporations have grown increasingly powerful. Capitalist enterprises exercise substantial influence over matters of enormous societal significance, including employment, the environment, the availability of goods and services, and health, safety, and financial security of stakeholders.[4] Multinational organizations have achieved their dominance because they have developed efficient ways of satisfying market demands, and effective ways of responding to attempted oversight. International experience suggests that the corporate form permits the most disciplined coordination of cooperative effort; such disciplined coordination permits the most cost-effective matching of labor, components, and intelligent direction; and maximum cost-effectiveness in production results in more abundant goods and services, whatever their eventual distribution. However, granting these advantages still leaves open the questions of how such activities should be regulated and how their profits should be distributed. On these questions, lawyers for both the private and public sector have always played a highly influential role.

E. The Plausibility of Alternatives

In considering the legitimacy of corporate practices, and the role of lawyers who assist them, the critical question is always: compared to what? Few believe that returning to small-scale enterprises is a plausible alternative. If it could be somehow achieved, the result would likely be massive inefficiencies and a reduction in the standard of living for most of the world's population. A second possibility—state ownership of major enterprises—generally has not proved compatible with a healthy economic and democratic structure. Under socialism, those in control have a monopoly of financial as well as political power and have typically stifled opposition and innovation. A chief virtue of capitalism is that economic power is more decentralized, and governmental power is more constrained.

To most contemporary commentators, the only viable response to capitalist critiques is more effective regulation. However, a major problem has always been the extent to which business has been able to capture its regulators. "Crony capitalism" is all too pervasive and corrosive. A crucial issue about capitalism—perhaps *the* fundamental issue—involves the capacity of governments to control corporate self-interest. Of particular concern are the state's ability

4. Milton C. Regan, "The Professional Responsibility of the Corporate Lawyer," 13 Georgetown J. Legal Ethics, 197, 206 (2000).

to protect individuals' rights from corporate overreaching, and to redistribute a fair share of profits from corporate activity.

In constitutional regimes, these issues are posed, debated, and resolved in terms of legal rules. Attorneys are involved in all aspects of the process. In the public sector, lawyers play a critical role in legislatures that are drafting statutes; in administrative agencies that are formulating and implementing regulations; and in courts that are enforcing these bodies of law. In the private sector, in-house and outside counsel assist clients in interpreting, implementing, and challenging relevant law. These professional roles involve complex interdependent relationships. Some lawyers over their careers serve in both sectors, and may pass through the "revolving door" on multiple occasions. However, whatever their position, attorneys generally share a commitment to the rule of law even while disagreeing about specific interpretations and applications. After all, a lawyer's vocation and livelihood depends on maintaining that commitment to legal principles and procedures.

Chapter V

BASIC PROFESSIONAL NORMS

The ethical rules governing American lawyers express several core values that guide legal practice. Those values and their corresponding obligations include independence, competence, loyalty, confidentiality, candor, and integrity in personal and professional conduct. These obligations extend to clients, courts, and the public. Similar responsibilities are required in other legal systems throughout the world, although their implementation takes somewhat different forms and reflects different priorities.

A. Responsibilities as a Profession: Independence in Professional Regulation and Professional Judgment

A primary norm of professional ethics is independence. It has two dimensions. The first involves ensuring the bar's freedom from government control. As the Preamble to the ABA's Model Rules of Professional Conduct notes, "An independent legal profession is an important force in preserving government under law, for abuse of legal authority is more readily challenged by a profession whose members are not dependent on government for the right to practice." Experience under totalitarian regimes makes clear that a bar that is overly subject to state regulation and control will be unable adequately to protect individual rights, check official misconduct, or insure due process. Lawyers defending unpopular clients and causes require some safeguards from political backlash.

The primary threat to professional independence comes from the political branch of government, as distinct from the judicial branch. The bar generally considers the courts to be a more appropriate regulatory authority than the legislature or executive. Indeed, judges have often invoked the concept of professional independence as a basis for their own oversight of the bar. Thus, American courts have asserted inherent authority to regulate legal practice, and have permitted further legislative or administrative regulation only to the extent that it is consistent with judicial supervision of the bar.[1] In the exercise of their inherent authority, courts have delegated much of the day-to-day control over admission and disciplinary systems to the organized bar, or to agencies

---

1. Charles W. Wolfram, Modern Legal Ethics 32–33 (1986). For a critical historical overview of the inherent power doctrine, see Charles W. Wolfram, "Toward A History Of The Legalization Of American Legal Ethics—II The Modern Era," 15 Geo. J. Legal Ethics 205, 210–18 (2002).

that are nominally independent but closely aligned with bar associations.

This structure of self regulation imposes corresponding obligations. As the Model Rules Preamble notes:

> The legal profession's relative autonomy carries with it special responsibilities of self-government. The profession has a responsibility to assure that its regulations are conceived in the public interest and not in furtherance of parochial or self-interested concerns of the bar. Every lawyer is responsible for observance of the Rules of Professional Conduct. A lawyer should also aid in securing their observance by other lawyers. Neglect of these responsibilities compromises the independence of the profession and the public interest which it serves.

How well the profession has discharged its regulatory responsibilities is subject to dispute, which subsequent chapters will explore in the context of specific rules and oversight structures. The overarching concern is whether the bar's lack of public accountability compromises the performance of its regulatory process. As one critic puts it:

> The problem is not that bar policies are baldly self-serving. Lawyers and judges who control regulatory decisions generally want to advance the public's interest as well as the profession's. Rather, the difficulty is one of tunnel vision, compounded by inadequate accountability. No matter how well intentioned, lawyers and former lawyers who regulate other lawyers cannot escape the economic, psychological, and political constraints of their position. Without external checks, these decision makers too often lose perspective about the points at which occupational and societal interests conflict.... Protecting the bar from state control clearly serves important values, and nations that lack an independent profession have had difficulty safeguarding individual rights and checking official misconduct. But professional autonomy and government domination are not the only alternatives. Many countries with an independent bar impose far more checks on its self-regulatory powers. Governmental efforts to increase lawyers' accountability do not necessarily pose significant risks of retaliation or threats to the proper administration of justice.[2]

Another consideration is the cost of regulation. Effective monitoring of the large and diffuse American legal profession would cost

---

2. Deborah L. Rhode, In the Interests of Justice: Reforming the Legal Profession 143–45 (2000). See Geoffrey Hazard and Angelo Dondi, Legal Ethics: A Comparative Study, ch. 4 (2004).

considerably more than the modest amounts now devoted to the effort. The bar has not wanted to pay for closer supervision. Nor have government agencies wanted to assume the cost, as they do in other contexts such as the regulation of banks or the securities market. Whether the American legal system should strengthen or supplement bar oversight processes will be a focus of the chapters that follow.

A second dimension of professional independence involves lawyers' individual capacity to exercise judgment on behalf of clients free from improper external influences. Such influences include: pressure from judicial or governmental officials; the interests of other clients or potential clients; the concerns of colleagues, legal employers, or third parties who are subsidizing representation; and the lawyer's own financial, ideological, or reputational interests. Attempts to prevent such interference have generated an extensive body of ethical requirements and legal doctrine. Rule 2.1 of the ABA's Model Rules of Professional Conduct sets forth the basic standard: "In representing a client, a lawyer shall exercise independent professional judgment and render candid advice." The Model Rules and Model Code also include more specific mandates governing conflicts of interest, discussed in Chapter VIII.

However, some influences do not readily lend themselves to specific regulations or external enforcement. Lawyers typically want to maintain good working relationships, both with clients and others whose concerns do not necessarily coincide with those of their clients. The biases that may arise from such relationships are often difficult to prevent or police. For example, lawyers' desire to maintain a good reputation with judges, other lawyers, and other potential sources of business may argue against pursuing certain causes or positions. In-house lawyers may face particular difficulties maintaining their independence, because their reputations and livelihoods are tied to a single client. For that reason, some countries, such as Germany, have rules on professional independence that deny lawyers working as employees the privilege of receiving confidences that will be legally protected from disclosure. Similarly, in many countries, such as Japan, lawyers admitted to practice before the courts are not permitted to serve as employees of private organizations.[3]

By contrast, American ethical rules have no such categorical prohibitions. Rather, the bar fosters professional independence by

3. German Code of Legal Ethics, "Protection of Professional Independence," Richtl § 40. Individuals with legal training who work in-house form a separate profession—Syndikusanwalte—and cannot join the bar. See David Luban, "Asking the Right Questions," 72 Temp. L. Rev. 839, 853 (1999).

more context-specific requirements designed to minimize inappropriate external influences.

B.   Responsibilities to Clients: Loyalty, Competence, and Confidentiality

The legal relationship between lawyers and clients is one of agency. An agency relationship entails several basic responsibilities: loyalty, competence, and confidentiality. As agents, attorneys often occupy positions of knowledge and influence that present opportunities for exploitation, coercion, and paternalism. Maintaining loyalty to the client's interests as the client defines them requires a measure of self-restraint that is central to the lawyer's role.

Of course, lawyers can play an important part in helping clients identify their interests. One of the most valuable functions of a loyal advocate is to provide advice on the full range of considerations, moral as well as legal, that should inform a client's decision making. That counseling process will often prompt clients to reassess their short term desires in light of their long term objectives and ethical commitments. But ultimately, as ABA Model Rule 1.2 makes clear, a lawyer generally "shall abide by a client's decisions concerning the objectives of representation . . . and shall consult with the client as to the means by which they are to be pursued." If the client "insists upon pursuing an objective that the lawyer considers repugnant or imprudent," then Model Rule 1.16, along with settled case law, permits the lawyer to withdraw. If the client is seeking assistance in a criminal or fraudulent act, or in other conduct that would violate rules of professional conduct, the lawyer must withdraw.

As a practical matter, withdrawal is an unattractive option. Terminating representation is likely to result in acrimony and loss of fees, and may have other costs in terms of reputation, contractual disputes, or malpractice claims. To avoid such difficulties, lawyers generally try to screen out clients, cases, and work assignments that may pose ethical difficulties. When such screening processes are successful, the obligation of loyalty to clients generally will be consistent with lawyers' own financial and reputational interests in providing effective assistance.

In representation of individuals, the client-lawyer relationship is usually face-to-face, and many ethical problems are more or less obvious. For example, a lawyer may have direct information about whether a document provided by the client is authentic or was contrived after the fact. Some individuals, of course, deceive their lawyers, but seldom easily. More complications arise, however, where the client is an organization or a group whose members have competing concerns and it is unclear who speaks for the client. In organizational settings, as Chapter VII notes, lawyers are normally accountable to management, but their ultimate obligation is to the entity. Under Model Rule 1.13, if the lawyer knows that the organization's employees are engaging in illegal conduct that may be attributable to the organization, then the lawyer has an obligation to act in the organization's best interest. That obligation may include attempts to force reconsideration of the conduct, reports to its highest authority, or withdrawal from representation. When the organization is a governmental entity, as the Comment to Model Rule 1.13 notes, lawyers may have even more extensive responsibilities to prevent or remedy wrongful conduct because their obligation runs to the government as a whole, rather than to specific officials or agencies. When the client is a group, as in a class action lawsuit, lawyers' responsibilities run to the entire membership. Significant conflicts of interest among individual class members ordinarily should be brought to the presiding court's attention; separate subclasses with separate representation may be necessary.

Loyalty to clients' interests also entails competence in representing them. Model Rule 1.1 of the ABA's Model Rules sets forth the basic mandate: "A lawyer shall provide competent representation to a client. Competent representation requires the legal knowledge, skill, thoroughness and preparation reasonably necessary for the representation." The Comment to the Rule adds that "[a] lawyer may accept representation where the requisite level of competence can be achieved by reasonable preparation." Chapter XII explores what this requirement demands in specific circumstances. As a general matter, the important point is that lawyers have an ethical obligation to undertake only those cases that they have sufficient expertise to handle effectively, unless they can acquire the necessary competence without undue expense to the client. This obligation assumes special force where the client is an individual with limited ability to evaluate the lawyer's qualifications for the services required. Three years of law school and passage of a bar exam does not endow a lawyer with the diversity of skills and substantive knowledge that is necessary in every context. In an era of increasing specialization, one important dimension of competence is lawyers' ability to recognize the limits of their own expertise.

A closely related professional norm is confidentiality. A commitment not to disclose information acquired during the course of representation is a central aspect of loyalty to the client and a prerequisite of competent assistance. A basic expectation of privacy is essential to ensuring trust and candor in the lawyer-client relationship. Model Rule 1.6 defines the core obligation: "A lawyer shall not reveal information relating to representation of a client unless the client consents after consultation, except for disclosures that are impliedly authorized in order to carry out the representation." The Rule also provides some important exceptions, discussed more fully in Chapter VI. Lawyers may reveal information to the extent that they believe necessary "to prevent the client from committing a criminal act that the lawyer believes is likely to result in imminent death or substantial bodily harm." Disclosure of confidences is also permitted to prevent fraud on a tribunal or a third party, or to establish a claim or defense in a dispute with the client.

As Chapter VI notes, the appropriate scope of confidentiality rules is one of the most controversial issues in American legal ethics. The ABA has had several divisive debates over whether disclosure should be permitted to prevent consummation of a client's fraud. State bar associations have had similar battles, and almost all states permit or require such disclosure.[4] In 2002, Congress passed federal legislation, the Sarbanes–Oxley Act, which requires lawyers for companies whose stock is publicly traded to take corrective measures upon learning of client fraud. These measures include internal reporting: lawyers must "go up the ladder" and notify corporate management and boards to obtain corrective measures.[5]

Issues concerning confidentiality have been more intensively debated in the United States than in other nations. One reason is simply that all issues concerning lawyers' professional responsibilities are addressed much more fully by the academic and legal community in this country than elsewhere. A further reason for the greater attention is the centrality of lawyers in American life, and the extent to which confidentiality obligations run counter to generally accepted values of openness in public affairs. In a society in which freedom of information is prized and official records are presumptively available for scrutiny, lawyers' broad claims of confidentiality are a jarring exception. Public support for "openness" has encouraged law enforcement agencies to constrain the attorney-client privilege, particularly in investigations of "white-collar"

---

4. See Deborah L. Rhode & David Luban, Legal Ethics, 265–75, 284–97 (4th ed. 2004).

5. See William Duffey, "Corporate Fraud and Accountability: A Primer on the Sarbanes–Oxley Act of 2002," 54 South Carolina L. Rev. 405 (2202); Susan Koniak, "When the Hurleyburly's Done: The Bar's Struggle With the SEC," 103 Columbia L. Rev. 1236 (2003).

crimes.[6] In other nations that lack such traditions of openness, confidentiality protections are less controversial. A second reason for the greater disclosure disputes in this society involves the greater frequency of malpractice claims against lawyers. The bar has often resisted even discretionary disclosure provisions for fear that attorneys would be subject to civil liability if they failed to take advantage of such rules by revealing client secrets.

Because the stakes in the confidentiality debate are substantial for both the profession and the public, the proper scope of confidentiality protections is likely to remain contested. But while the extent of those protections will be subject to dispute, the general responsibility to maintain client secrets will not. To provide effective representation, lawyers need access to potentially compromising information. And to gain access, they need to provide assurance that such information generally will not be disclosed without the client's consent.

C. Responsibilities to the System of Justice and the Rule of Law

The Preamble to the Model Rules of Professional Conduct defines lawyers' basic obligations as officers of the court:

> A lawyer's conduct should conform to the requirements of the law, both in professional service to clients and in the lawyer's business and personal affairs. . . .

> A lawyer should demonstrate respect for the legal system and for those who serve it, including judges, other lawyers and public officials. . . .

> As a public citizen, a lawyer should seek improvement of the law, the administration of justice and the quality of service rendered by the legal profession.

Model Rule 8.4 elaborates these obligations:

> It is professional misconduct for a lawyer to:

> (a) violate or attempt to violate the Rules of Professional Conduct . . . ;

> (b) commit a criminal act that reflects adversely on the lawyer's honesty, trustworthiness or fitness as a lawyer in other respects;

> (c) engage in conduct involving dishonesty, fraud, deceit or misrepresentation;

6. Lance Cole, "Revoking Our Privileges: Federal Law Enforcement's Multi-Front Assault on the Attorney–Client Privilege," 48 Vill. L. Rev. 469 (2003).

(d) engage in conduct that is prejudicial to the administration of justice;

(e) state or imply an ability to influence improperly a government agency or official; or

(f) knowingly assist a judge or judicial official in conduct that is a violation of applicable rules of judicial conduct or other law.

Model Rule 3.3 also impose specific obligations of candor to the tribunal:

A lawyer shall not knowingly:

(a) make a false statement of material fact or law to a tribunal;

(b) fail to disclose to the tribunal legal authority in the controlling jurisdiction known to the lawyer to be directly adverse to the position of the client and not disclosed by opposing counsel; or

(c) offer evidence that the lawyer knows to be false.

In addition, as Chapter VI notes, many jurisdictions have established voluntary civility codes specifying further responsibilities for lawyers as officers of the court. These codes range from matters of decorum (such as dress and punctuality) to trial tactics (such as bullying witnesses or opposing counsel). How much effect these aspirational standards have on behavior is an open question. But they clearly serve an important admonitory function in reaffirming the bar's commitment to basic professional norms of propriety and integrity.

Many experts on legal ethics also believe that lawyers have an obligation to preserve the rule of law on which a just society and efficient market depend. That obligation necessarily involves concern for third parties and commitment to core values of honesty and fair dealing that are necessary to effective legal and commercial processes.[7] What these values entail in specific practice, and how they can be balanced with client responsibilities, are a primary focus of the chapters to follow.

---

7. Deborah L. Rhode, "Moral Counseling," Fordham L. Rev. (2006); Geoffrey C. Hazard, Jr., "Lawyers for the Situation," 39 Val. U. L. Rev., 377, 388– 90 (2004); Robert Gordon, "A New Role for Lawyers?: The Corporate Counselor After Enron," 35 Conn. L. Rev. 1185 (2003).

Chapter VI

THE ADVERSARY SYSTEM, CONFIDENTIALITY, AND ALTERNATIVE DISPUTE RESOLUTION

A. The Premises of an Adversary System

The American system of justice is "adversarial." The term carries several connotations. In a narrow sense, it describes a litigation system that depends on opposing parties to investigate, organize, and present the evidence and legal arguments in disputes that go to court. This contrasts, to some extent, with the "inquisitorial" model of civil law systems in Europe, most notably in France, Germany, Italy, and Spain. In those systems, the judge has greater control over a case after the pleading stage, particularly in questioning witnesses and in defining and sequencing the issues that parties should address.

A broader connotation, or implication, of an "adversarial" system is the priority that it places on individual adversaries' legal rights. This priority is apparent not only in litigation (as in the right to take discovery, or to cross-examine opposing parties and witnesses) but also in legislative and administrative proceedings and in contractual negotiations. Thus, many hearings before legislative bodies resemble courtroom trials, and administrative agency procedures generally draw on models from civil litigation. In contractual negotiations, particularly major business transactions, lawyers in the United States generally play a far greater and more partisan role than lawyers in other countries.

A final connotation of "adversarial" involves the nature of interactions between opposing counsel. Compared with legal proceedings in other nations, the American system tends to be more contentious, but paradoxically, it also involves more cooperation between opposing counsel. Legal matters in Europe, Canada, Australia, and Asia, particularly in civil law systems, give rise to less incivility than in the United States, but also to less interaction of all kinds.[1]

As a general matter, the American public has deep faith in its system of justice; the vast majority believe that, despite its flaws, it

---

1. Geoffrey Hazard and Angelo Dondi, Legal Ethics: A Comparative Study 67–69 (2004).

is the best in the world.[2] That faith rests on two central premises. The first premise, drawing on utilitarian principles, is that an adversarial presentation is the best available way to discover the truth and thus achieve fair outcomes for the greatest number of parties. A second premise, drawing on deontological rights-based principles, is that an adversarial process provides the most effective protection for individual rights.

Justifications and Critiques

The argument that the adversary system is the best available means of discovering truth depends on several core assumptions. Their fullest elaboration appears in an influential report by Lon Fuller and John Randall for a joint conference by the American Bar Association and Association of American Law Schools. In essence, these assumptions are that:

- The prospect of victory will motivate adversaries to put maximum effort into developing their case, while in inquisitorial systems, adjudicators lack such competitive incentives;
- Proof requires hypotheses and, if adjudicators develop the proof, their preliminary hypotheses will too easily bias their final decision;
- Reliance on an independent legal profession for developing the record provides a check on official power; and
- The advantages of competitive, party-controlled processes outweigh their costs.[3]

This faith in partisan processes is part of a broader world view that underpins America's basic social and economic institutions. Robert Kutak, chair of the ABA commission that drafted the Model Rules of Professional Conduct, observed that our commitment to an adversarial framework reflects "the same deep-seated values we place on competition" in other contexts.[4]

This truth-based justification for adversarial processes has, however, attracted considerable criticism. First and most obviously, as Plato pointed out centuries ago, the advocate is not a seeker of truth but a producer of belief.[5] Presentations by opposing counsel

2. American Bar Association, Perceptions of the U.S. Justice System 59 (1999).

3. American Bar Association and Association of American Law Schools, "Report of the Joint Conference on Professional Responsibility," reprinted in 44 ABA Journal 1161(1958). See Geoffrey

C. Hazard, Jr., Ethics in the Practice of Law 120–35 (1978).

4. Robert J. Kutak, "The Adversary System and the Practice of Law," in The Good Lawyer: Lawyers' Roles and Lawyers' Ethics 172, 174 (David Luban, ed., 1983).

5. Plato, Gorgias (T. Irwin trans., 1979), discussed in Anthony T. Kron-

intent on victory rather than justice will not necessarily produce justice. Marvin Frankel, a former federal court judge and member of the ABA's Model Rules Commission, voiced a widely quoted and widely shared concern that American adversarial processes rank truth too low.

> Despite our untested statements of self-congratulation, we know that others searching after facts—in history, geography, medicine, whatever—do not emulate our adversary system. We know that most countries of the world seek justice by different routes. What is much more to the point, we know that many of the rules and devices of adversary litigation as we conduct it are not geared for, but are often aptly suited to defeat, the development of the truth.... Employed by interested parties, the process often achieves truth only as a convenience, a byproduct, or an accidental approximation. The business of the advocate, simply stated, is to win.... His is not the search for truth as such. To put that thought more exactly, the truth and victory are mutually incompatible for some considerable percentage of the attorneys trying cases at any given time.[6]

As the discussion below reflects, common techniques of discovery, witness preparation, and cross-examination often serve to obfuscate rather than reveal relevant information.

Moreover, in an adversarial model, the merits will be more or less likely to prevail only if the contest is a balanced one. As critics note:

> The conventional model presupposes adversaries with roughly equal incentives, resources, capabilities and access to relevant information. But those conditions are more the exception than the rule in a society that tolerates vast disparities in wealth, high litigation costs, and grossly inadequate access to legal assistance.... In law, as in life, the "haves" generally come out ahead.[7]

Marc Galanter's classic account of why the "haves" do better identifies certain systematic advantages enjoyed by "repeat players" [RPs] who frequently engage in similar litigation against "one shot" [OS] adversaries.[8] Although acknowledging that these charac-

---

man, "Forward: Legal Scholarship and Moral Education," 90 Yale L.J. 955, 959 (1981).

6. Marvin E. Frankel, "The Search for Truth: An Umpireal View," 123 U. Pa. L. Rev. 1031, 1036–37 (1975).

7. Deborah L. Rhode, In the Interests of Justice: Reforming the Legal Pro-

fession 55–56 (2000); Deborah L. Rhode, "Legal Ethics in an Adversary System: The Persistent Questions," 34 Hofstra L. Rev. 641 643–44 (2006).

8. Marc Galanter, "Why the 'Haves' Come Out Ahead: Speculations on the Limits of Legal Change," 9 Law & Soc'y. Rev. 95, 97 (1974).

terizations are somewhat oversimplified, Galanter finds them useful to illustrate the advantages available to frequent litigators such as prosecutors, creditors, or insurance companies:

> RPs, having done it before, have advance intelligence; they are able to structure the next transaction and build a record. It is the RP who writes the form contract, requires the security deposit, and the like.
>
> RPs develop expertise and have ready access to specialists. They enjoy economies of scale and have low start-up costs for any case.
>
> RPs have opportunities to develop [helpful] relations with institutional [players such as court clerks or police]. . . .
>
> RPs can play the odds . . . [and] adopt strategies calculated to maximize gain over a long series of cases, even where this involves the risk of maximum loss in some cases.
>
> RPs can play for rules as well as immediate gains. First, it pays an RP to expend resources in influencing the making of the relevant rules by such methods as lobbying. (And his accumulated expertise enables him to do this persuasively) . . .
>
> RPs, by virtue of experience and expertise, are more likely to be able to discern which rules are likely to [make a tangible difference] and which are likely to remain merely symbolic commitments.[9]

In short, one-shot players are unlikely to succeed unless they have access to resources from other sources. These resources may be available for certain claims such as personal injuries, civil rights, and corporate fraud. In these contexts, the availability of contingent or court-awarded fees has given rise to a highly competent and generally well organized plaintiff's bar. The individual claimants are One Shot litigants, but the lawyers on their behalf are distinctly Repeat Players. Their primary professional organizations, including the American Trial Lawyers Association, have become very influential not only in litigation as such, but also in legislative drafting, lobbying, and judicial elections.

Yet for too many cases, these equalizing resources are absent and the adversary system falls short in its capacity to promote "truth." Its defenders often concede as much, but rely on an alternative justification: the system's capacity to protect individual rights and the underlying values of autonomy and dignity that such

---

9. Id. at 98–103. See Marc Galanter, "Farther Along," 33 Law & Soc'y Rev. 1113 (1999).

rights preserve. Giving parties an opportunity to control the agenda of their "day in court" fosters self-esteem and builds confidence in the legitimacy of the process. A wide range of research indicates that, for most people, an opportunity to be heard under a procedurally fair system is more important than the outcome of that system in shaping their judgment about whether justice has been done.[10]

Criminal Versus Civil Cases

This rights-based rationale for an adversarial system assumes special force in criminal cases. Individuals whose lives, liberty, and reputation are at risk are especially deserving of an advocate without competing loyalties to the state. The consequences of an alternative model are readily apparent in many totalitarian countries that lack an adversarial process and an independent profession. Where defense lawyers' role is to "serve justice," rather than their clients, what passes for "justice" often is simply deference to prosecutorial authority.[11] In this country, experience also teaches that a vigorous defense is necessary to give law enforcement officials adequate incentives to respect constitutional rights and to investigate facts thoroughly. In the long run, providing adversarial protections for individuals who are guilty also protects those who are not.

Yet how well the current adversary system serves rights-based goals is open to question. As critics note, one threshold question is why the rights of a particular client should trump those of all other parties whose interests are inadequately represented. In a system in which not everyone can afford effective advocacy, adversarial models may leave many individual rights unprotected.

Critics also question whether the justifications for adversarial norms in criminal defense extend to civil contexts. Criminal proceedings account for a relatively small portion of lawyers' work and are distinctive in several respects: the role of state power, the potential for governmental oppression, and the impact on individual life, liberty, and reputation. For these reasons, American constitutional traditions impose special protections for criminal defendants, such as proof beyond a reasonable doubt and the privilege against self-incrimination. By the same token, the justifications for adversarial procedures are strongest in criminal cases.[12] Of course, some civil matters raise concerns about abusive power or funda-

10. E. Allan Lind & Tom R. Tyler, The Social Psychology of Procedural Justice, 64–67 (1988).

11. See the cases discussed in Deborah L. Rhode, supra note 7, at 54.

12. See id. at 54–55; Richard Wasserstrom, "Lawyers as Professionals: Some Moral Issues," 5 Human Rights 1 (1975).

mental rights that are analogous to those at issue in criminal proceedings. But such cases do not constitute the mainstay of legal work. And, as discussion below reflects, for many ordinary civil disputes, some qualification of adversarial norms or resort to alternative dispute resolution procedures might yield significant benefits.

Given all the limitations in conventional rationales for adversarial processes, some commentators argue that the current system is justifiable only on weak pragmatic grounds: it is not demonstrably worse than other systems, the costs of radical restructuring would be substantial, and the devil you know is better than the devil you don't.[13] Many experts also note the difficulties of moving toward a more "judge-centered" system. In civil law regimes, such systems often suffer from serious understaffing, and from indifference or resignation on the part of the judiciary.[14] In any case, it is clear that some imperfections in American adversarial processes are inevitable and that imposes certain responsibilities on lawyers to address, not exploit, the weaknesses in existing structures.

B. Litigation Tactics and Adversarial Abuses

The last quarter century has witnessed increased concerns about frivolous and abusive adversarial practices. A number of factors have contributed to these concerns:

- The growth in substantive rights that can give rise to legal claims;

- The growth in scale and complexity of some forms of litigation;

- The growth in size and competitiveness of the bar; and

- The related decline in informal community relationships of social control.

Frivolous Cases

Although perceptions of "the problem" have clearly heightened, the scope of that problem remains open to dispute. Whether "frivolous" cases have increased is particularly hard to measure, given inherent difficulties in defining frivolity. Available data indicate that the United States' current litigation rates are not exceptionally high, in comparison either with prior historical eras or with other western nations not known for undue contentiousness.[15]

---

13. David Luban, Lawyers and Justice: An Ethical Study 92–93 (1988).

14. Hazard and Dondi, Legal Ethics:, supra note 1.

15. Deborah L. Rhode, "Frivolous Cases and Civil Justice Reform: Miscasting the Problem, Recasting the Solution," 54 Duke L. J. 447, 456 (2004).

Many arguments about America's "legal hypochondria" or "hyper-lexis" rest on largely anecdotal evidence of trivial cases: football fans suing referees, suitors suing dates, and beauty contestants suing each other.[16] However, examples such as these do not of themselves establish that America has exceptional problems with frivolous suits or that they occupy an undue amount of judicial time. The issue is always: compared with what?

Historical and cross-cultural research reveals similar examples of trivial claims, and what qualifies as frivolous is often in the eye of the beholder. Consider, for instance, one example of an "inappro-priate" claim once cited by a prominent law school dean: sex discrimination suits against Little Leagues.[17] It is not self-evident that such claims are a "waste" of judicial resources, given the importance this nation attaches to sports, the longstanding inequal-ities in male and female athletic opportunities, and the gender stereotypes that such inequalities reinforce. Some substantial num-ber of complaints about litigiousness may, in reality, be complaints about the reach of the substantive law; the "line between vindic-tiveness and vindication is often difficult to draw."[18]

Litigation Abuse

Although the exact scope and nature of adversarial abuse is subject to dispute, there is little disagreement that some problems exist. Over four-fifths of the American public and about four-fifths of surveyed jurors agree that too many meritless cases are filed.[19] Over 90 percent of bar leaders view incivility as a serious concern.[20] More cases of intentional destruction of evidence have been report-ed in one recent decade than in the preceding two centuries.[21] In large, complex cases, researchers report chronic difficulties with discovery. Although most litigation involves relatively few pretrial problems, high-stakes lawsuits often result in excessive costs, eva-sion, and delay.[22] In some significant percentage of such suits,

16. Id., at 447–449. See James L. Percelay, Whiplash: America's Most Frivolous Lawsuits 54 (2000); Philip K. Howard, The Lost Art of Drawing the Line 14–15 (2001).

17. Bayless Manning, "Hyperlexis: Our National Disease," 71 Nw. U.L. Rev. 767 (1977).

18. Rhode, supra note 7, at 121.

19. Rhode, supra note 15, at 449–50.

20. N. Lee Cooper, "Courtesy Call," ABA Journal, March, 1997, at 8.

21. David K. Isom, "Electronic Dis-covery Primer for Judges," 2005 Fed. Cts. L. Rev. § II.L.1.

22. James S. Kakalik, et al., Discov-ery Management: Further Analysis of the Civil Justice Reform Act Evaluation Data xx, 55 (1998); Austin Sarat, "Eth-ics in Litigation," in Ethics in Practice, (Deborah L. Rhode, ed. 2000); John S. Beckerman, "Confronting Civil Discov-ery's Fatal Flaws," 84 Minn. L. Rev. 505, 506 (2000); Jeffrey W. Stempel, "Ulysses Tied to the Generic Whipping Post: The Continuing Odyssey of Discov-

material information is never discovered by opposing parties.[23]

Catalogues of discovery abuse abound. Common techniques for evading or exhausting an adversary include:

- Overuse of depositions and interrogatories;

- Abusive scheduling practices, such as arranging depositions in order to impose maximum inconvenience and expense, and refusing to acquiesce in reasonable requests for extensions of time;

- Objectionable questioning techniques, such as seeking embarrassing but unnecessary information, objecting to reasonable inquiries, or inappropriately coaching witnesses or instructing them not to answer;

- Evasive strategies, such as promising to answer at a later date; recycling vague allegations of a complaint or answer; reassigning potential witnesses to inaccessible locations; reshuffling documents so that an adversary has little sense of how files are kept and how relevant materials can be located; destroying or burying the "smoking pistol" where it is almost impossible to locate ("dump truck discovery").[24]

These practices arise from a complex set of economic, social, and psychological factors. By prolonging proceedings, some clients can continue to engage in legally dubious but financially profitable activity, avoid publicizing unfavorable facts, or buy time to prevent adverse events such as a corporate acquisition. By turning litigation into an expensive war of attrition, parties may also be able to force a favorable settlement, discourage other potential adversaries from filing suit, or retaliate for perceived abuses.

Lawyers' own incentives also contribute to procedural problems. Attorneys seeking to maximize billable hours have an obvious interest in meter-running, a practice that litigators frequently report having experienced, although they do not acknowledge having committed.[25] Many litigators are understandably risk-averse, and leaving no stone unturned has obvious advantages "if you can charge by the stone."[26] Some types of claims have "blackmail" value beyond their legal merits, which gives settlement leverage to the claimant. Prolonging pretrial maneuvers to force settlements can also avoid the risks of defeat and the loss of reputation that it

---

ery 'Reform'," 64 Law & Contemp. Problems 197, 219 (2001).

23. See sources cited in Rhode, supra note 7, at 88–89.

24. Beckerman, supra note 22, at 525; Rhode, supra note 7, at 83–85.

25. Rhode, supra note 7, at 84.

26. Id. at 61, 84.

might entail. Finally, lawyers as well as clients can easily become used to a combative approach, and retaliation has its own rewards.

There are, however, significant countervailing interests. In the short run, abusive behavior can be counterproductive if it provokes sanctions or a response in kind, and undercuts constructive settlement efforts. In the long term, such conduct can compromise a lawyer's reputation for integrity and reasonableness. The result is likely to be less credibility and fewer referrals, as well as more unpleasant working environments.[27] Relations with clients may also suffer. Many individuals recognize that when litigation becomes an arms race, the major beneficiaries are often the lawyers; the parties pay an undue price in aggravation, acrimony, and legal bills. Moreover, the costs of procedural abuse are not borne by the litigants alone. Legal costs are passed on to consumers in the form of higher prices, and subsidized by taxpayers through public funding for the courts and tax deductions for corporate legal expenses. How to modify the incentive structures that contribute to abusive tactics is a matter of public as well as professional interest.

Sanctions: FRCP Rule 11 and Bar Discipline

Bar disciplinary agencies rarely impose sanctions for litigation misconduct. Rather, the principle legal means of regulating such misconduct has been Rule 11 of the Federal Rules of Civil Procedure, and its state court analogues. The rule provides that the lawyer's signature on any filing signifies that: "to the best of the [signer's] knowledge, information, and belief, formed after an inquiry reasonable under the circumstances;" the filing has "evidentiary support" or is likely to have such support after a "reasonable opportunity for further investigation;" the filing is "warranted by existing law or a good faith argument for the extension, modification, or reversal of existing law or the establishment of new law;" and is "not being presented for any improper purpose, such as to harass or to cause unnecessary delay or needless increase in the cost of litigation." When parties move for sanctions for a violation of Rule 11, their opponents have a 21–day "safe harbor" interval, during which they can withdraw the offending papers without penalty. A court that finds a violation may impose an "appropriate sanction," which may include monetary or non-monetary remedies. Absent special circumstances, a law firm can be held jointly liable for violations committed by its partners, associates, or employees.

---

27. Rhode, supra note 7, at 85; Allen K. Harris, "Increasing Ethics, Professionalism and Civility: Key to Preserving the American Common Law and Adversarial System," Professional Lawyer 92 (2005).

The terms of this Rule and its state court analogues have been a matter of ongoing controversy. Until its amendment in 1983, Rule 11 sanctions were discretionary with the court rather than mandatory. The Rule imposed no requirement of reasonable inquiry by the lawyer. In effect, this earlier version was violated only on a finding of subjective bad faith, and that standard was almost never met. The 1983 amendments required a reasonable inquiry, made sanctions mandatory if a violation occurred, and permitted fines payable to the opposing party. As a result, Rule 11 enforcement escalated rapidly. Motions for sanctions became a standard part of the advocate's arsenal and generated some of the harassing litigation that it was meant to deter. The problem was exacerbated by the ambiguity of standards governing "reasonable inquiry," "good faith," and "well grounded in fact." According to some studies, courts also disproportionately exercised their discretion to penalize civil rights plaintiffs.[28]

These concerns have prompted amendments that made sanctions once again discretionary, imposed a safe harbor option, and made financial penalties normally payable to the court, unless payment to the adversary was warranted for purposes of deterrence. Modifications in the discovery provisions of Rule 26 also created an optional "core discovery" system that became mandatory for federal districts in 2000. Under this system, parties must automatically disclose certain categories of information. Amendments to Federal Rules of Civil Procedure 30 and 31 also limited the number of depositions and interrogatories available without explicit court approval.

This history is instructive in several respects. First, it helps to explain why bar ethical standards have been largely ineffectual in response to procedural abuse. Although the ABA Model Code and Model Rules both enjoin lawyers from asserting frivolous positions or taking positions merely to harass, these provisions have proven largely unenforceable in practice. Not only is the burden of proving a violation unrealistically high, but litigants have little if anything to gain from referring the case to bar disciplinary agencies. Those agencies generally will not act during the pendency of litigation, will not impose fines that compensate complainants, and, except in the most egregious cases, will not expend scarce resources on matters where an alternative judicial remedy is available.

28. Mark Spiegel, "The Rule 11 Studies and Civil Rights Cases: An Inquiry into the Neutrality of Procedural Rules," 32 Conn. L. Rev. 155 (1999); David B. Wilkins, "Who Should Regulate Lawyers?," 105 Harv. L. Rev. 799, 869, n. 308 (1992).

Moreover, courts are generally reluctant to impose sanctions except for the most serious instances of litigation misconduct. Sorting out who is at fault in pretrial disputes is a time-consuming and frequently thankless enterprise. It often requires more knowledge than overburdened judges would otherwise need to acquire, particularly on matters that are unlikely to require a trial or that do not involve clear villains and victims.[29] Most judges also dislike antagonizing lawyers by imposing sanctions, since that can interfere with facilitating settlement, risk reversal on appeal, or make the proceedings even more contentious. If counsel cannot manage to behave civilly toward one another, a traditional judicial response has been to let them pay the price.

Civility Codes

In response to the persistence of abusive behavior and the limitations of enforcement structures, over a hundred bar associations have adopted voluntary civility codes. Their content varies but many largely consist of general exhortations, such as avoid "excessive zeal," "cooperate in scheduling," and "value integrity above all."[30] These codes are meant to be aspirational, but a few courts have adopted them as enforceable procedural rules, or have invoked them to justify sanctions. The appeal of these codes is obvious; they are a concrete response at little cost. Lawyers who oppose such aspirational standards can simply ignore them. Yet without enforcement mechanisms, the effectiveness of civility codes is difficult to determine. The bar's current enthusiasm for such standards rests on no evidence that they significantly influence behavior. A few jurisdictions require lawyers to take a civility oath or certify that they have read the applicable code; none have attempted to assess compliance or even to measure awareness of its requirements. Yet it seems doubtful that voluntary standards will be sufficient to cope with lawyers most likely to violate them.

An effective response to adversarial abuses requires multiple strategies. One obvious priority is to increase penalties, an approach which a growing number of courts are pursuing in cases of serious misconduct. Other options include publicizing sanctions, improving disciplinary agencies' responses, and requiring employers of sanctioned attorneys to institute educational and monitoring programs in their organizations. More resources could also be available for oversight, not only by trial courts but also by magistrates, special masters, and volunteer referees from local bar associ-

---

29. Stempel, supra note 22, at 209–10; Arthur R. Miller, "The Adversary System: Dinosaur or Phoenix," 69 Minn. L. Rev. 1 (1984).

30. Rhode, supra note 7, at 91–92; Robert E. Huie, "Uneasy Bedfellows," National L. J., March 6, 2006, 23.

ations.[31] Other commonly proposed responses to procedural abuse include internal employer policies and training programs; more disciplinary measures directed against entire law firms; replacement of hourly billing structures with flat-fee rates that would reduce incentives for over-discovery; and orders that parties who make burdensome discovery requests subsidize their opponents' compliance.

For many attorneys, however, the most powerful influences will come through informal norms of reciprocity and retribution, rather than formal sanctioning structures.[32] Victims of procedural abuse can refuse to cooperate with ill-behaved adversaries, exploit their otherwise excusable mistakes, insist on formalities, and tarnish their reputations with influential third parties. Conversely, practitioners can reward civility and fair dealing by responding in kind. For obvious reasons, these informal norms work best among lawyers who have continuing interactions. Small communities, practice specialties, and bar associations can be powerful socializing forces. Other larger professional organizations can also attempt to institutionalize approval for appropriate conduct through awards and election or appointment to desirable bar positions. The respect of colleagues is, for most attorneys, the most powerful force in sustaining standards of conduct that serve broader societal interests.

C. Candor and Confidentiality

Rules governing candor and confidentiality in lawyer-client relationships must balance several, sometimes competing, concerns. One is to provide sufficient protection for confidential communications to ensure candor and trust in lawyer-client relationships. A second concern is to prevent lawyers from assisting criminal or fraudulent conduct or withholding information necessary to protect innocent third parties and promote legal compliance. A third concern is to preserve some incentives for parties to prepare their own cases adequately without freeloading on their opponents' efforts.

These concerns have shaped both bar ethical obligations and evidentiary rules governing the attorney client privilege. The privilege protects confidential client communications from disclosure in legal proceedings. The duty of confidentiality set forth in bar ethical codes is broader than the privilege in two primary respects. This duty encompasses information from any source, including, but

---

31. Rhode, supra note 7, at 95; Wilkins, supra note 28, at 835–39; Stempel, supra note 22, at 239–41.

32. Geoffrey C. Hazard, Jr., "The Lawyer for the Situation," 39 Val. L. Rev. 377, 382 (2004).

not limited to, clients. The ethical obligation also applies in all contexts, including office practice, not just legal proceedings. Unlike the privilege, which is a rule of evidence developed by courts and legislatures, the ethical duty is part of lawyers own self-regulatory structure, developed in the first instance by bar associations, and approved by courts.

The Attorney–Client Privilege

The attorney-client privilege arose in the seventeenth century as an outgrowth of the general principle that it is dishonorable to reveal another's confidence.[33] Originally, the privilege belonged to the lawyer. During the eighteenth and nineteenth centuries, the rationale gradually shifted to the needs of a proper functioning legal system, and authority to assert or waive the right shifted to the client. In its traditional formulation, the law of privilege holds that:

> (1) Where legal advice of any kind is sought (2) from a professional legal adviser in the lawyer's capacity as such, (3) the communications relating to that purpose, (4) made in confidence (5) by the client, (6) are ... permanently protected (7) from disclosure by [the client] himself or by the legal adviser, (8) except [if] the protection be waived.[34]

The attorney-client privilege as now understood also includes communications from the lawyer to the client if they refer, explicitly or implicitly, to communications originating from the client. An auxiliary rule extends protection against disclosure to the attorney's "work product," i.e., information assembled in anticipation of litigation and lawyers' analysis of that information.[35]

Application of the privilege has generated an extensive body of case law and several important exceptions. One exception involves waivers. The privilege is waived if the communication takes place in the presence of a third party, if the client discloses the communication to a third party, or if the client or his agent implicitly or explicitly consents to disclosure. The privilege also does not apply to disclosures by jointly represented clients in any subsequent dispute arising between those clients. The waivers in these cases are not

---

33. Geoffrey C. Hazard, Jr., "An Historical Perspective on the Attorney–Client Privilege," 66 Cal. L. Rev. 1061, 1069–73 (1978); John H. Wigmore, A Treatise on the Anglo–American System of Evidence in Trials at Common Law § 2290 (John T. McNaughton ed., rev. ed. 1961).

34. Wigmore, supra note 33, § 2292.

35. The original formulation of the privilege appears in Hickman v. Taylor, 329 U.S. 495 (1947). Exceptions to the privilege include statements given by a litigant or independent witness to an opponent's investigator, and experts who will be called as witnesses. See Fed. R.Civ.P. 26(b)(3).

always voluntary in the conventional sense of the term. Some occur inadvertently, such as through misdirected documents.[36] Others are required by government prosecutors as a condition of avoiding certain criminal charges, a practice that is highly controversial within the bar.[37]

Other significant exceptions to the privilege involve information regarding client identity, future crimes, and continuing frauds. The theory behind these exceptions is that the purpose behind the privilege is to encourage clients to seek advice that will assist their compliance with legal obligations or their vindication of legal rights. That purpose is not well served by enabling clients to shield their identity or violate legal mandates.

Ethical Duties of Confidentiality

Attorneys' confidentiality obligations are also defined by bar ethical codes. These obligations are more recent than the lawyer-client privilege. They are generally traced to David Dudley Field's 1849 Civil Procedure Code, which was later incorporated in bar ethical codes. Both the ABA Model Code and the Model Rules prohibit lawyers not only from offering evidence of privileged communications with clients but also from disclosing confidential information from any source in any setting in or outside the courtroom. Model Rule 1.6(a) states simply that "[a] lawyer shall not reveal information relating to representation of a client."[38]

This ethical responsibility is subject to exceptions. Lawyers may reveal confidences if the client consents or if they are "impliedly authorized in order to carry out the representation." Model Rule 1.6(a.). This is a principle of agency law and recognizes that most aspects of law practice involve communicating with others, including opposing counsel, about the matter being handled for a

---

36. Rule 4.4(b) of the ABA Model Rules requires lawyers who receive misdirected confidential documents to notify the sender but leave to lawyers' discretion whether to return the document unread. For conflicting state and national ethics opinions on the subject, see Deborah L. Rhode & David Luban, Legal Ethics 141–46 (4th ed., 2004).

37. For the government's increasingly common practice of requiring waivers, see Jonathan D. Glater, The Squeezing of the Lawyer–Client Privilege, N.Y. Times, Sept. 7, 2005, at C6; Association of Corporate Counsel, The Decline of the Attorney–Client Privilege in the Corporate Context (2006). For the bar's concern, see ABA Task Force on the Attor-

ney–Client Privilege, "Report of the American Bar Association Task Force on the Attorney–Client Privilege," 60 Bus. Law. 1029 (2005); Bruce Green & David C. Clifton, "Feeling a Chill," ABA J., Dec. 2005, at 61.

38. Disciplinary Rule 4–101 of the Code protects both "confidence(s)," which encompass any information protected by the attorney-client privilege, and "secret(s)," which encompass "other information gained in the professional relationship that the client has requested be held inviolate or the disclosure of which would be embarrassing or would be likely to be detrimental to the client."

client. Most authorities agree that disclosures required by law are also so authorized.[39] Lawyers may also divulge information to protect themselves or third party interests in certain circumstances. Model Rule 1.6(b) allows attorneys to reveal information necessary to establish their own claims or defenses in a controversy with the client or in proceedings concerning their representation of the client. The Rule permits but does not require a lawyer to disclose confidential information "to the extent the lawyer reasonably believes necessary . . . to prevent reasonably certain death or substantial bodily harm." Lawyers may also reveal confidences in order to prevent crimes or frauds reasonably certain to result in substantial injury in which the lawyer's services have been used and in order to prevent, mitigate, or rectify injuries from these unlawful acts.[40]

These exceptions in effect allow lawyers to "blow the whistle" on a client regarding certain unlawful transactions that they have assisted. Under Model Rule 1.2(d), a matter that plainly involves crime or fraud is not one in which a lawyer should be involved in the first place. However, determining whether a transaction is fraudulent can be difficult, because clients in such a situation will usually make every effort to conceal its character from counsel. Where lawyers manage to discover such misconduct, they should attempt to dissuade the client or halt the transaction before withdrawing from the matter or revealing confidential information. It should be expected that a confrontation with a client over such issues may be disagreeable, going on ugly. Lawyers don't like to talk about such a situation, and many of them don't even want to think about it. Professional discussions are larded with euphemisms. When lawyers fail to disclose, or remain willfully ignorant of illegal conduct, matters can grow worse. Counsel with deep pockets may often face civil liability claims if their role comes to light.[41]

In addition, the Model Rules, like its predecessor, the Model Code, impose obligations of candor toward tribunals. Model Rule 3.3 provides:

A lawyer shall not knowingly:

39. Disciplinary Rule 4–101 of the Code similarly allows lawyers to reveal confidences if required by law or court order.

40. Disciplinary Rule 4–101(C)(3) of the Code permits but does not require a lawyer to reveal "the intention of his client to commit a crime and the information necessary to prevent the crime."

One version of DR 7–102(B) obligates lawyers to rectify frauds perpetrated during the course of representation.

41. For examples, see Rhode & Luban, supra note 34, at 284–297. See also Emma Schwartz, "Sharp Rise in Big Suits Against Firms: Study Shows Increased Costs, Prompting Insurance Fears," Legal Times, May 9, 2005, at 1.

(1) make a false statement of material fact or law to a tribunal or fail to correct a false statement of material fact or law made to the tribunal by the lawyer;

(2) fail to disclose to the tribunal legal authority in the controlling jurisdiction known to the lawyer to be directly adverse to the position of the client and not disclosed by opposing counsel; or

(3) offer evidence that the lawyer knows to be false. If a lawyer has offered material evidence and comes to know of its falsity, the lawyer shall take reasonable remedial measures, including, if necessary, disclosure to the tribunal. A lawyer may refuse to offer evidence, other than the testimony of a defendant in a criminal matter, that the lawyer reasonably believes is false.

Model Rule 3.4 also prohibits lawyers from unlawfully obstructing access to evidence or unlawfully destroying or concealing material of evidentiary value.[42]

Many legal ethics experts have criticized the bar's confidentiality obligations as overly broad. As they note, Model Rule 1.6(b) does not require disclosure of confidential information in any circumstances except those involving fraud on a tribunal. Nor does the rule permit disclosures to prevent financial rather than physical injuries unless the lawyers' services have been used. In those cases, the lawyer's only recourse is to withdraw from representation. Rule 1.6, Comment.

Confidentiality in Representing Organizations

In representing organizations, a lawyer may, and in some contexts must, report legal violations within the organization. In the wake of massive corporate scandals, Congress in 2002 passed the Sarbanes–Oxley Act, which mandated reporting for lawyers representing organizations subject to federal securities law. In the wake of this Congressional action, the ABA then amended Model Rule 1.13 to strengthen lawyers' internal disclosure obligations in all organizational contexts. Rule 1.13(b) provides that lawyers who know of a legal violation that might be imputed to the organization should proceed in a manner "reasonably necessary in the best interest of the organization," including referral to the organiza-

---

42. For Model Code provisions on candor to the tribunal, see DR 7–102 and 7–106. For destruction of evidence, see Dr 7–109. The Restatement of the Law Governing Lawyers (Third), §§ 66 and 67, permits lawyers to disclose confidences to prevent reasonably certain death or serious bodily harm, or to rectify client crimes or frauds threatening substantial financial loss if the lawyers' services have been used in that matter.

tion's highest authority. If that authority fails to address the matter in a timely and appropriate manner, and lawyers reasonably believe that the legal violation is reasonably certain to result in substantial injury to the organization, they may disclose the information unless they have been retained to investigate or defend the organization with respect to a legal violation.

Regulations promulgated by the Securities and Exchange Commission (SEC) under the Sarbanes–Oxley Act require lawyers to report evidence of a material violation of securities law to an organization's chief legal officer or the officer and the CEO, or to a qualified legal compliance committee. If the officer does not make an appropriate response within a reasonable time, the attorney must report the matter to the highest authority. The regulations also permit lawyers representing securities issuers to reveal client confidences in order to prevent or rectify frauds in which the lawyers' services have been used. The SEC also considered, but did not approve, regulations opposed by the organized bar that would have required lawyers who did not get an appropriate response to their reports to withdraw and to notify the SEC and successor counsel of their withdrawal.[43]

The scope of lawyers' disclosure obligations has been a matter of intense controversy. State ethical rules vary. Some are broader than the Model Rules and a few require, not just permit, disclosure of certain illegal acts. Other state standards are narrower than the Model Rules and do not even permit disclosure to prevent financial injuries in contexts where the Model Rules and Sarbanes–Oxley regulations permit. The conflict between state and federal mandates, as well as the interpretation of lawyers' responsibilities and potential malpractice liability in particular contexts, are likely to remain matters of continuing debate and further reform.[44]

Justifications for Confidentiality Protections

The justifications for broad confidentiality protections closely parallel the justifications for the adversary system. One rationale rests on the value of individual legal rights and the importance of confidentiality in securing them. A second rationale focuses on the instrumental value of confidentiality in promoting just resolution of legal issues and in encouraging compliance with legal obligations.

---

43. See "Federal Lawmakers Get Earful on SEC's Proposed 'Noisy Withdrawal' Rule," BNA Litigation Feb. 11, 2004.

44. For an overview, see Roger C. Cramton, George M. Cohen, & Susan P. Koniak, "Legal and Ethical Duties of Lawyers After Sarbanes–Oxley," 49 Vi. L. Rev. 725, 783 (2004); Fred C. Zacharias, "Coercing Clients: Can Lawyer Gatekeeper Rules Work?," 47 Boston College L. Rev. 455 (2006).

The rights-based argument for confidentiality obligations builds on several assumptions about societal values and client conduct. First, an overarching objective of the legal system is to preserve individual rights, which often requires legal assistance. Lawyers cannot provide adequate assistance unless clients feel free to communicate relevant information. Many people will be unwilling to consult lawyers or to disclose essential facts without assurances that the information will not be used against them. Confidentiality obligations serve not only to safeguard legal rights in general, but also to preserve certain specific entitlements such as those of privacy, effective assistance of counsel, and the protection against self-incrimination. In the absence of confidentiality safeguards, clients who are unaware of legal defenses might withhold helpful information.

A second justification for broad confidentiality protections is that they promote just outcomes. By encouraging individuals to seek legal advice and to disclose all relevant information, the attorney-client privilege and related ethical rules facilitate compliance with legal norms. Well-informed lawyers can counsel individuals about their legal obligations and encourage appropriate resolution of legal disputes. To perform this function, attorneys need a level of trust that is incompatible with whistle-blowing obligations.[45]

Critiques of Current Confidentiality Rules

Whether these arguments justify the current scope of confidentiality protections is subject to dispute. Critics of broad confidentiality rules note that concerns about criminal defendants' constitutional rights do not justify sweeping protections in civil contexts. Nor is it self-evident why the rights of clients should always take priority over the rights of others, particularly where the client is an organization and other individuals' health and safety interests are implicated.[46] Similarly, critics also challenge the implicit hierarchy in current bar codes, which require disclosure to prevent fraud on a tribunal but only permit (not require) disclosure to save a life, and which permit disclosure to enable lawyers to collect their fees but not to protect others from financial injuries. On general principles, a preference for lawyers as compared with third party victims is difficult to justify, since the lawyer is likely to be in a better position than others to prevent the wrong or to mitigate its impact.

---

45. For an overview, see Rosemary Pattenden, The Law of Professional–Client Confidentiality: Regulating the Disclosure of Confidential Personal Information, §§ 1.17, 1.19 (2003).

46. See sources cited in Rhode, supra note 7, at 110–12.

Some commentators also challenge the effectiveness of broad confidentiality protections in safeguarding legal rights. As they note, many individuals are reluctant to confide in lawyers who might have competing loyalties, whatever the rules on confidentiality. Other individuals, particularly corporate officials, have little choice but to consult lawyers, whatever the rules, because failure to do so would deprive them of essential advice or the right to invoke the "advice of counsel" defense in a criminal case, or the "business judgment" defense in a civil case.[47] Moreover, current confidentiality rules are riddled with exceptions and indeterminacies that few clients now comprehend. In organizational contexts, those who give information to attorneys cannot assume that it will remain confidential because the privilege belongs to the organization and can be waived when that will serve organizational interests.

Available research also leaves doubt whether modest qualifications of existing rules would significantly alter client behavior. The most systematic studies reveal only a tenuous connection between confidentiality rules and the willingness of clients to reveal sensitive information to their lawyers.[48] For example, one study of New York lawyers and clients, produced findings that: lawyers almost never inform their clients about the duty of confidentiality; clients substantially misunderstand the scope of confidentiality; and only about a third of former clients said that they gave information to their lawyers that they would not have given without a guarantee of confidentiality.[49] So too, historical, cross-cultural, and cross-professional research makes clear that practitioners can provide effective assistance with more qualified confidentiality safeguards than those now prescribed in many state ethical codes.[50] Subsequent chapters will explore whether changing confidentiality rules would serve professional or public interests in specific contexts such as negotiation and counseling. For present purposes, several of the most contested issues regarding general confidentiality norms merit closer scrutiny: client perjury, client fraud, secrecy clauses, and whistle-blower protections.

Client Perjury

How lawyers should respond to client perjury has generated considerable controversy, particularly in the context of criminal defense. In his influential treatment of the subject, Monroe Freed-

---

47. William Simon, "The Confidentiality Fetish," Atlantic Monthly, Dec. 2004, at 1134.

48. Rhode & Luban, supra note 36, at 190–91; Fred C. Zacharias, "Rethink-ing Confidentiality," 74 Iowa L. Rev. 351, 382–83 (1989).

49. Zacharias, supra note 48, at 379–86.

50. Rhode, supra note 7, at 111.

man analyzes what he labels the "perjury trilemma," which arises from competing ethical obligations.[51] In order to provide effective advocacy, the criminal defense attorney must learn all the significant facts. At the same time, the attorney has obligations of confidentiality to the client and a duty of candor to the court. The trilemma arises if the client demonstrates an intent to give false testimony from the witness stand. Although attorneys often maintain that they can never know with certainty that the client's trial testimony is untrue, in some situations they certainly would have to "know" in the ordinary sense of the term.

According to Freedman, attorneys confronting client perjury can fulfill at most two of their three obligations. If they have acquired all relevant information, they will know that the testimony is perjurious, and then must breach either their duty of confidentiality or the duty of candor. Those duties can be reconciled only if lawyers remain selectively ignorant, which compromises their ability to provide effective advocacy. Freedman argues that in cases of conflict, the obligation of candor to the court must give way. In his view, the duties of confidentiality and zealous advocacy are of paramount constitutional and moral significance in criminal cases, for they are essential to the Fifth Amendment privilege against self-incrimination and the Sixth Amendment right to representation. A 1992 ethics opinion of the National Association of Criminal Defense Lawyers came to a similar conclusion on similar reasoning.[52]

By contrast, the initial formulation of the Comment to Model Rule 3.3 summarized the organized bar's traditional response to the problem of client perjury:

> While it is agreed that the lawyer should seek to persuade the client to refrain from perjurious testimony, there has been dispute concerning the lawyer's duty when that persuasion fails [and when withdrawal is not possible]. . . .
>
> Three resolutions of this dilemma have been proposed. One is to permit the accused to testify by a narrative without guidance through the lawyer's questioning. This compromises both contending principles; it exempts the lawyer from the duty to disclose false evidence but subjects the client to an implicit disclosure of information imparted to counsel. Another suggested resolution, of relatively recent origin, is that the advocate be entirely excused from the duty to reveal perjury if

51. Monroe H. Freedman, Lawyers' Ethics in an Adversary System 27–41 (1975). See also Monroe H. Freedman & Abbe Smith, Understanding Lawyers' Ethics (2d ed. 2002).

52. The Ethics Advisory Committee of NACDL, Formal Op. 92–2, reprinted in The Champion, March 1993, at 23.

the perjury is that of the client. This is a coherent solution but makes the advocate a knowing instrument of perjury.

The other resolution of the dilemma is that the lawyer must reveal the client's perjury if necessary to rectify the situation. A criminal accused has a right to the assistance of an advocate, a right to testify and a right of confidential communication with counsel. However, an accused should not have a right to assistance of counsel in committing perjury. Furthermore, an advocate has an obligation, not only in professional ethics but under the law as well, to avoid implication in the commission of perjury or other falsification of evidence. . . .

The Comment endorsed the last approach, which would leave to the court's discretion how to address the matter and whether to declare a mistrial. However, the Comment also noted that some jurisdictions had interpreted constitutional requirements of due process and the right to counsel as requiring that counsel permit the defendant's testimony or allow the defendant to provide an account in narrative form. In those jurisdictions, the lawyers' obligations would be "subordinate to such a constitutional requirement."

In its revision to the Model Rules in 2002, the ABA deleted its discussion of various responses to client perjury and noted simply that criminal defense lawyers were subject to Rule 3.3, but that constitutional requirements might supercede bar ethical obligations in some jurisdictions. The ABA also added new language to the Rule and Comment making clear that the lawyers' general discretion to refuse to offer evidence they "reasonably believed" was false did not extend to testimony by a criminal defendant; they must honor that defendant's right to testify unless they "knew" that the testimony was false.

In *Nix v. Whiteside*, 475 U.S. 157 (1986), the Supreme Court offered some guidance about responses to the client perjury problem. There, the Court held that a lawyer did not provide ineffective assistance of counsel by discouraging his client from giving what the lawyer concluded would be false testimony. However, the *Nix* decision did not directly overrule lower court holdings that disclosure of perjury violated a client's due process rights. Nor did *Nix* clarify what level of knowledge is necessary to trigger disclosure obligations. Under the Model Rules' somewhat circular standard, "knowingly" means "actual knowledge of the facts in question . . . [which] may be inferred from circumstances." The Commentary to former ABA Criminal Defense Standard 4–7.7 interpreted "knowledge" to require a defendant's admission of inculpating facts to his lawyer that are corroborated by the lawyer's own investigations.[53] Some jurisdictions have imposed similar standards concerning the lawyer's knowledge, while other courts have proceeded with less rigorous requirements.[54] At a minimum, it would seem appropriate for trial courts to make some factual inquiry into the basis of lawyers' judgments about the falsity of their clients' testimony.

In most cases, however, it is in the lawyer's own interest to resolve doubts in favor of their clients and avoid information that would unequivocally establish perjury. The main check against false testimony is not fear of disciplinary charges (which would generally be extraordinarily difficult if not impossible to prove) but concerns about effectiveness. That is, if a defense lawyer is convinced that testimony will be false, judges and jurors also are likely to be convinced, at least in contexts where they have access to the same information as the lawyer. Effective representation will include advising the client accordingly.

Client Fraud

A related set of issues involves client fraud. As noted earlier, most states permit disclosure of client frauds in at least some circumstances, and a small number require it. Both the ABA Model Rules, as amended in 2002, and Section 67 of the Restatement of Law Governing Lawyers permit disclosure to prevent or rectify client crime or fraud involving "substantial" financial loss in which the lawyers' services are used.

Opponents of stronger disclosure requirements worry that they will encourage litigation against lawyers for failure to prevent client misconduct. Underlying this opposition is the assumption that a categorical requirement of confidentiality will protect lawyers against such suits. However, as legal ethics experts have noted, this protection is often illusory: third parties can claim that lawyers aided and abetted the fraud, and jurors will often be sympathetic to such claims whether or not they are supported by direct evidence. Even if lawyers ultimately can establish their lack of complicity and persuade decision makers that ethics rules demanded confidentiality, the financial and reputational costs of litigation are likely to be substantial. And even in the absence of third party claims, lawyers whose services are implicated in fraud may suffer a loss of credibili-

---

53. That standard was withdrawn in 1979 on the understanding that it would be supplanted by the Model Rules ABA Standards Relating to the Administration of Criminal Justice 4.94–4.95 (2d ed. 1980) (Editorial Note to deleted Standard 4–7.7).

54. Compare cases discussed in Developments, "Client Perjury and the Duty of Candor," 6 Geo. J. Legal Ethics 1003, 1008–1009 (1993), and Rhode & Luban, supra note 36, at 330–32.

ty with judges, regulatory officials, colleagues, and the broader legal community. Prudent attorneys generally want the ability to prevent the fraud in the first instance, and rules allowing disclosure are necessary to that end. It bears note that loss prevention specialists in malpractice insurance companies typically support discretionary disclosure rules.[55]

From a societal standpoint, there is also a strong case for mandatory disclosure of frauds involving substantial financial loss, particularly those in which lawyers' services were used. Honest clients have little to fear from such requirements; dishonest clients have no right to secrecy, and innocent third parties could benefit from early warnings. Although systematic data are lacking, no evidence suggests that mandatory disclosure rules have proven unworkable in the jurisdictions that have adopted them.

Whatever the formal ethical rules concerning disclosure, lawyers have an interest in creating safeguards against involvement in client fraud. Workplace structures are often necessary to counteract financial temptations, peer pressure, diffusion of responsibility, and psychological predispositions that encourage see-no-evil, hear-no-evil attitudes toward client misconduct. Individuals generally tend toward reduction of "cognitive dissonance"; they are especially likely to register and retain information that is compatible with established beliefs or earlier decisions, and to suppress or reconstrue information that casts doubts on those decisions.[56] Once lawyers have determined to represent a particular client, they may become less sensitive to ethical problems arising from that choice. Crafting internal reporting structures and external regulatory systems that will address such biases is an ongoing challenge for the profession and the public.

Secrecy Clauses

Another issue concerning confidentiality obligations involves the lawyer's role in crafting litigation settlements that include secrecy clauses, which enjoin parties from discussing or releasing evidence concerning the litigation. Such clauses have obvious benefits to the litigants: they reduce defendants' legal exposure and adverse publicity, and increase plaintiffs' bargaining leverage. But these benefits carry a cost for other claimants and third parties. Many unsafe or unlawful practices would come to light sooner if

55. Geoffrey C. Hazard, Jr., "Lawyer as Whistleblower," National L. J. March 5, 2001, at A19.

56. Deborah L. Rhode, "Moral Counseling," Fordham L. Rev. (forthcoming);

Donald C. Langevoort, "Where Were the Lawyers? A Behavioral Inquiry Into Lawyers' Responsibility for Clients' Fraud," 46 Vand. L. Rev. 75 (1993).

there were more legislative or ethical prohibitions on such secrecy clauses. Highly publicized examples involve cases of defective tires, exploding gas tanks, and sexual abuse by Catholic priests.[57]

The Ethics 2000 Commission that considered amendments to the Model Rules debated a proposal supported by many legal ethics professors that would have prohibited lawyers from facilitating secrecy agreements. The recommended addition to Model Rule 3.2 provided:

> A lawyer shall not participate in offering or making an agreement, whether in connection with a lawsuit or otherwise, to prevent or restrict the availability to the public of information that the lawyer reasonably believes directly concerns a substantial danger to the public health or safety, or to the health or safety of any particular individual(s).[58]

The Ethics 2000 Commission rejected the proposal on the grounds that the appropriateness of such provisions was a policy decision that should not be resolved by ethical codes.[59]

Several states have addressed that policy issue with "sunshine in litigation" statutes, one federal district court has adopted a widely publicized prohibition on sealed agreements, and other legislatures, courts, and bar associations are considering such reforms. The statutes prohibit courts from granting secrecy orders in cases involving public hazards, such as product defects, medical malpractice, or environmental dangers. The District Court for the District of South Carolina adopted changes to its local rules banning any sealed settlements unless "good cause is shown."[60] A few judicial decisions have also restricted the use of confidentiality agreements in particular cases.[61]

By contrast, the ABA Section of Litigation has proposed Guidelines for Negotiation of Settlements in Litigation that expressly

---

57. See Elizabeth Spainhour, "Unsealing Settlements: Recent Efforts to Expose Settlement Agreements that Conceal Public Hazards," 82 N.C. L. Rev. 2155 (2004); Richard A. Zitrin, "The Fault Lies in the Ethics Rules," National L. J., July 8, 2001, at A25; Adam Liptak, "A Case that Grew in the Shadows," N.Y. Times, March 24, 2002, at D3.

58. Richard A. Zitrin, "The Case Against Secret Settlements (Or, What You Don't Know *Can* Hurt You)," 2 J. Inst. for the Study of Legal Ethics 115, 116 (1999).

59. Kevin Livingston, "Open Secrets," The San Francisco Recorder, May 8, 2001, at 1 (quoting Nancy Moore, reporter for the Commission).

60. Joseph Anderson, Jr. "Hidden From the Public by Order of the Court: The Case Against Government–Enforced Secrecy," 55 S. C. L. Rev. 711, 720 (2002).

61. See Martha Neil, "Confidential Settlements Scrutinized," ABA J. July 2002, at 20–21; Eric Frazier, "Judges Veto Sealed Deals," Natl L. J. Aug. 12, 2002 at A1; David Luban, "Settlements and the Public Realm," 83 Geo. L. J. 2619, 2651 n. 126–29, 2652–59 (1995).

recognize the legitimacy of secrecy provisions, including provisions for turning over discovery products such as inculpating documents.[62] Opponents generally claim that secrecy restrictions are unnecessary and unwise: public risks eventually come to light despite settlements incorporating secrecy provisions; such provisions are essential to protect trade secrets and other proprietary information; and preventing secrecy clauses will deter settlements, fuel lengthy discovery fights, and encourage frivolous copy cat claims.[63] Proponents respond that such adverse consequences have not been demonstrated in states with legislative prohibitions, that substantial harms often occur before certain risks become public, and that secrecy provisions burden the legal system by necessitating duplicate suits with duplicate discovery.[64] Whether the bar should take a stand on these provisions is likely to remain an issue of ongoing professional debate.

Whistle-blower Protections

A final area of controversy involves protection for in-house counsel who are fired for blowing the whistle on illegal conduct. Courts have divided over whether lawyers can sue for wrongful discharge and whether they can use confidential information to support their claims. About half of jurisdictions have established public policy exceptions to employers' rights to fire at will in response to ethical resistance. A dozen have extended protections to lawyers; a half dozen have barred wrongful discharge claims and the remainder have not addressed the issue. The scope of existing protections is also unsettled. They generally safeguard employees who are fired for refusing to do something illegal, but not necessarily those who have suffered retaliation for aggressively reporting illegalities.[65] Courts also have divided on whether to allow lawyers to reveal client confidences essential to prove their claims. The issue is complicated because lawyers' interests line up on both sides of the debate. Opponents of disclosure worry about the chilling effects on clients; the concern is that individuals will be less candid if they fear that confidences may later be revealed by disgruntled in-house counsel. By contrast, proponents of wrongful discharge protections stress the chilling effect on attorneys; the concern is that in-house counsel will be less likely to take an ethical stand if

62. See ABA/BNA Lawyers' Manual, June 5, 2001, at 346.

63. Frazier, supra note 61, at A11; David Hechler, "Secrecy in Settlements as a Public Safety Issue," Nat'l L. J., Jan. 12, 2004, at 1, 33.

64. Frazier, supra note 61, at A11; Diana Digges, Confidential Settlements Under Fire in 13 States, 2 Ann. 2001 ATLA–CLE 2769 (2001); Luban, supra note 61, at 2652–59.

65. Rhode & Luban, supra note 41, at 407. John Gibeaut, "Telling Secrets," ABA J. (Nov. 2004) at 39, 41.

they cannot expect safeguards against retaliation. How courts and bar associations should weigh these competing concerns is likely to remain another subject of continuing controversy.

D. Alternative Dispute Resolution

Lawyers have always been involved in alternative dispute resolution processes (ADR). The vast majority of legal controversies eventually settle rather than go to trial. Negotiating out-of-court settlements is therefore a major part of every litigator's role. What distinguishes contemporary practice is a formalization of "ADR" and an emergence of specialists in mediation and arbitration. Interest in these processes has grown rapidly over the last quarter century. A broad range of factors fuel that interest: dissatisfaction with the expense, delays, and contentious nature of adjudication; concerns about undue litigiousness and unequal access to justice; desires for increased client participation, community empowerment, and remedial flexibility; heightened interest in preserving relationships and exploring root causes as well as legal symptoms of problems; and perceived inadequacies in other family, religious, and community institutions for mediating grievances.[66]

Advocates of ADR typically advocate "fitting the forum to the fuss."[67] Their approach assumes that different types of disputes and dispute resolution procedures have distinctive characteristics and should be matched accordingly. Lon Fuller, one of the principal architects of this framework, argued that adjudication was appropriate for cases implicating fundamental rights or unsettled legal principles but that other procedures might be more suitable for routine matters, for parties with ongoing relationships, or for grievances that affect multiple individuals and that do not lend themselves to principled win-lose decisions.[68]

A range of processes has emerged. Some ADR procedures have evolved through private initiatives, while others have developed

---

66. See Carrie Menkel–Meadow, "From Legal Disputes to Conflict Resolution and Human Problem Solving: Legal Dispute Resolution in a Multidisciplinary Context," 54 J. Legal Education 7 (2004); Carrie Menkel–Meadow, "Many Doors? Closing Doors? Alternative Dispute Resolution and Adjudication," 10 Ohio St. J. on Dispute Resolution 211 (1995); David D. Hechler, "ADR Finds True Believers," Nat'l L. J. July 2, 2001, at A1. For a review of issues surrounding ADR, see Rhode & Luban supra note 36, at 871–82.

67. Frank E. A. Sander and Stephen B. Goldberg, "Fitting the Forum to the Fuss: A User–Friendly Guide to Selecting an ADR Procedure," 10 Negotiation J. 49, 67 (1994) (crediting the phrase to Maurice Rosenberg).

68. Lon L. Fuller, "The Forms and Limits of Adjudication," 92 Harv. L. Rev. 353 (1978); Lon L. Fuller, "Mediation—Its Forms and Functions," 44 S. Cal. L. Rev. 305 (1971).

under federal and state legislation or judicial decrees. For example, the Federal Judicial Improvements Act (Civil Justice Reform Act) of 1990 requires every federal district court to study its caseload and to develop a plan to "facilitate ... adjudication of civil cases on the merits ... and ensure just, speedy and inexpensive resolutions of civil disputes."[69] Among the strategies that courts are required to consider is referral of appropriate cases to alternative dispute resolution.

ADR procedures vary along several dimensions:

- *The role of the decision maker or facilitator.* Who selects that individual and by what criteria? What expertise is required?

- *The enforceability of the outcome.* Is the outcome advisory (mediation) or is it binding (arbitration) and, if the latter, is it subject to review?

- *Consent.* Is the procedure voluntary or mandatory?

- *Relationship to the adjudicative system.* Is the procedure connected to a state or federal court system, and if so, does it rely on in-house staff or outside experts who are trained and subsidized by the system?

- *Relationship to the community.* Is the procedure part of a religious or ethnic community's traditional method of dispute resolution?

- *Formality.* Is the procedure formally structured by fixed rules or by agreement of the parties, or is it relatively informal and flexible?

The most common forms of ADR are as follows.

Arbitration. In arbitration, parties submit their dispute to a neutral decision maker, often someone who has particular expertise in the matters at issue. Typically, the arbitrator is chosen by mutual agreement of the contending parties from a list of professionals. Some consumer agencies and industry groups such as the Better Business Bureau also have systems for arbitrating claims. Most states have statutes modeled on the Uniform Arbitration Act, 7 U.L.A. 5 (1985), which govern enforcement of arbitration agreements. Enforcement may also be available under the Federal Arbitration Act, and the Labor Management Relations Act of 1947. Arbiters' judgments are usually final; review is available only in limited scope, generally involving procedural violations. A number

---

69. 28 U.S.C. § 471. See Federal Judicial Center, Guide to Judicial Management of Cases in ADR (2001).

of federal and state courts require submission of certain cases to court-annexed arbitration, although parties typically have a right to trial de novo.

Private Adjudication. Some statutes and rules of court permit referral of cases to privately selected and compensated adjudicators, often retired judges. These referral programs, sometimes labeled "rent-a-judge," authorize the private adjudicator's decision to be entered as the judgment of the court. Unlike an arbitrator's award, such a judgment is normally subject to appellate review.

Summary Jury Trials. Under this procedure, lawyers give a summary of their trial presentation to a jury, usually without witnesses or exhibits. The jury then renders a verdict that is not binding, although the jurors are not informed of this fact before reaching their decision. This verdict can assist parties evaluate their claims and negotiate a reasonable settlement.

Mini-trials. Mini-trials, or "structured settlement" negotiations, offer opportunities for lawyers to present an abbreviated version of their case to a decision-making panel. In one common variation, the panel includes a neutral advisor and executives of the opposing parties. The aim is to enable the parties to hear a forceful presentation of their adversary's case. The advisor predicts what would happen if the case were litigated, and the principals then attempt to negotiate a settlement. In some mini-trials, the neutral advisor will render an advisory opinion only if the parties initially fail to reach an agreement.

Early Neutral Evaluation or Expert Evaluation. This technique, which is used both in private dispute resolution and in court-annexed programs, involves reliance on a third party neutral with relevant experience or expertise to evaluate a case. After summary presentations by counsel and the parties, the evaluator assesses the issues in dispute in an effort to facilitate settlement negotiations.

Mediation. Mediation is an informal process in which a neutral third party helps the parties resolve a dispute or structure a transaction. Ordinarily, this third party facilitates but does not impose a solution, and the parties voluntarily choose the mediator. However, some courts require mediation for certain types of cases, such as child custody disputes, and provide a panel of mediators for those cases.

Ombudsperson. Ombudspersons are officials appointed by organizations to prevent, investigate, and informally resolve disputes. In the private sector, ombudspersons function primarily in employer/employee relations, but in the public sector their role is often broader.

Neighborhood Justice Centers. Neighborhood justice centers, citizen complaint bureaus, and other community-based centers function as free-standing institutions or court-affiliated agencies. These organizations typically receive referrals from courts, prosecutors, police, or other community agencies, as well as walk-in clients. Professional mediators or community volunteers with mediation training handle a variety of disputes, including landlord-tenant, family, and neighbor relations.

On-line Dispute Resolution. A newly emerging option involves on-line processes for negotiation or mediation of disputes. Although these processes initially targeted disputes that had originated on-line, they now encompass a broad variety of other controversies. Among the options are direct negotiation technologies that help parties quickly identify settlement points; panels that referee small claims based on parties' on-line submissions of evidence and arguments; and on-line mediators that facilitate settlements.

At the most abstract level, supporters of such alternative dispute resolution share certain common objectives. They join in what then Chief Justice Burger summarized as the true goals of the legal profession: "to gain an acceptable result in the shortest possible time with the least amount of stress and at the lowest possible cost to the client."[70] At the concrete level, however, what constitutes "acceptable" results remains a matter of some disagreement, and ADR goals are not always consistent. Conflicts may arise between cost and quality; between enhancing access and reducing judicial overload and court delays; and between facilitating parties' objectives and serving societal interests.

These tradeoffs have sparked criticism along several lines. Alternative dispute resolution has been faulted for being both too available and not available enough. Some commentators complain that options such as rent-a-judge or mini-trials are accessible only to the wealthy. In their view, such a market-based structure institutionalizes "legal apartheid"—convenient, speedy justice for the haves and cumbersome, inefficient processes for the have-nots. The existence of a two-track system may reduce pressure to reform the judicial system that makes such alternatives necessary.

Conversely, another group of critics charges that ADR is too available: it is too often imposed on middle and low income clients with "simple" cases or contractual obligations to arbitrate disputes, and it too often offers second-class justice. From this perspective,

---

70. Commission on Professionalism, American Bar Association, In the Spirit of Public Service: A Blueprint for the Rekindling of Lawyer Professionalism 41 (1986) (quoting Chief Justice Warren Burger).

informal, streamlined structures appear to deprive weaker parties of crucial protections. For example, according to one study, the odds of employers winning in ADR proceedings with employees were five to one. Only employers who were repeat players had incentives to investigate the past records and predispositions of ostensibly neutral decision makers, and these decision makers often had incentives to please parties who would be sources of future business.[71] So too, mediation between parties with unequal power may reinforce their inequality and encourage negotiation of rights that should be non-negotiable. Cases involving domestic violence pose well-documented risks.[72]

Although some mediators attempt to mitigate disparities in parties' bargaining capacities, or refuse to ratify settlements that seem clearly unfair, such non-neutral conduct raises its own set of ethical difficulties. Active intervention by ostensibly neutral mediators can compromise their credibility and capacity to achieve solutions. And it can expose participants to manipulation under undisclosed standards and unstructured procedures lacking formal mechanisms of accountability.

A related concern is that informal processes oriented toward private settlements may undervalue society's interest in having publicly accountable judges interpret and implement publicly acceptable norms. A process geared toward compromise may also provide inadequate deterrence of unlawful conduct. Where ADR decision makers or facilitators need not adhere to formal rules or give reasons for their judgments, the process appears arbitrary in a sense that adjudication does not.[73]

Yet as ADR supporters note, these criticisms often proceed by comparing alternative processes to an idealized image of adjudication. Before denouncing such processes as second-class justice, it is important to inquire whether first class is actually available and for whom. The preferred trial procedure implicit in criticism of ADR is a well-functioning adversary system: each party is assumed to be represented by a competent advocate, making presentations before a competent and disinterested judge. That model is very expensive,

---

71. Richard C. Reuben, "Lawyer Turns Peacemaker," ABA J., Aug. 1996, at 61; Richard C. Reuben, "The Bias Factor," California Lawyer, Nov. 1999, at 25; See Jeffrey W. Stempel, "Reflections on Judicial ADR and the Multidoor Courthouse at Twenty: Fait Accompli, Failed Overture or Fledgling Adulthood," 11 Ohio State J. in Disp. Resol. 297, 319, 339, 351 (1996).

72. Leigh Goodmark, "Alternative Dispute Resolution and the Potential for Gender Bias," Judges Journal, Spring 2000, at 21.

73. Owen M. Fiss, "Against Settlement," 93 Yale L.J. 1073, 1085–87 (1984).

for it involves at least three professionals each with substantial income expectations. Also implicit in a "fair" adversarial procedure is discovery such as that afforded under the Federal Rules of Civil Procedure, which itself is a costly process compared to many ADR hearings. If a jury is also included, there are the additional expenses of assembling and providing for the jury panels. The process is too costly for all but a small percentage of disputes. And even for those disputes, it is not clear that society is well served by a system that enables wealthy parties to spend whatever they consider worthwhile on resolving their controversy.

It also bears note that the limited empirical evidence available suggests that in some contexts, parties prefer informal dispute resolution to current alternatives.[74] Although parties' satisfaction should not be the sole criteria for evaluation, it is surely relevant, particularly given the difficulties of determining which processes produce the "best" result in a given context. Not only do we lack empirical data, we have no commonly accepted measures of what would make an outcome "best" or "fairest."[75]

In evaluating these critiques and defenses of ADR, the safest generalization may be that no single process is necessarily preferable under all circumstances in accomplishing all dispute resolution objectives. Those objectives include: insuring full disclosure of relevant facts, offering widely accepted remedies, providing principled guidance for future cases, encouraging compliance, and fostering confidence and good relations between the parties and other stakeholders. Available research does not establish that either adjudication or ADR is always more effective in realizing any of these objectives.[76] Nor does that research suggest consistent differences between ADR and adjudication in cost, speed, and party satisfaction.[77]

Given that no process is clearly preferable for every context, many experts argue that parties should have a broad range of dispute resolution choices and the information necessary to make them. The public should also have ways to insure that the parties' procedural choices are subject to reasonable constraints based on the societal values at stake. So, for example, many commentators

74. Lisa Brenner, "What Lawyers Like: Mediation," National Law Journal, July 2, 2001; Robert J. MacCoun, E. Allan Lind, & Tom R. Tyler, "Alternative Dispute Resolution in Trial and Appellate Courts," in Handbook of Psychology and Law 95, 99–100 (D.K. Kagehiro & W. S. Laufer, eds. 1992).

75. Menkel–Meadow, "From Legal Disputes," supra note 66, at 23.

76. Marc Galanter & Mia Cahill, "Most Cases Settle: Judicial Promotion and Regulation of Settlements," 46 Stan. L. Rev. 1339, 1388 (1994).

77. Id.; Rhode, supra note 7, at 132–34.

support "multidoor courthouses" that have been established in a growing number of jurisdictions. These court systems allocate different types of cases to "appropriate dispute resolution" processes based on several key criteria: the nature of the controversy; the relationship between the parties; the priorities that the participants attach to various features of the dispute resolution process; and the public interests at issue. Cases involving relatively small monetary damages and the application of settled legal precedents may not justify the expense of full-scale adjudication. In other contexts, the relationship between the parties may argue for ADR procedures that are best to address power disparities or foster long-term working relationships, and engage in productive problem-solving for multiple stakeholders.[78] Some cases, like those involving domestic violence, may call for specialized "holistic" courts that can address all aspects of the dispute and connect parties with a broad range of services.[79]

More comprehensive ethical rules for ADR practitioners are also necessary. Not all of these individuals are lawyers and their practices vary considerably concerning issues such as fairness, confidentiality, and conflicts of interest. There are similar variations in the ethical codes drafted by different professional organizations, such as the American Arbitration Association, the Society of Professionals in Dispute Resolution, and the CPR–Georgetown Commission on Ethics and Standards in ADR.[80] Questions remain as to whether all ADR professionals should be held to some uniform standards and, if so, how they should be defined and enforced.

However, commentators generally agree that lawyers should discuss ADR options with their clients and that when lawyers act as third party neutrals, they should be subject to ethical rules analogous to those applicable in other contexts. So, for example, lawyers serving as third party neutrals should exercise independent judgment and disclose all circumstances that might reasonably be perceived to constitute conflicts of interest or to jeopardize their impartiality.[81] The American Bar Association's Model Rules of Professional Conduct include a provision governing neutrals. See Model Rule 2.4. Other proposed ethical rules direct lawyers to "discuss confidentiality rules and requirements at the beginning of the

---

78. Rhode, supra note 7, at 133–34.

79. See Deborah L. Rhode, Access to Justice 85–86 (2004).

80. See CPR–Georgetown Commission on Ethics and Standards in ADR, Proposed Model Rule of Professional Conduct for the Lawyer as Third Party Neutral (Discussion Draft, April 1999),

and sources cited. See also "Symposium on ADR and the Professional Responsibility of Lawyers," 28 Fordham Urban L.J. 991 (2001).

81. CPR–Georgetown Commission, supra note 80 (Proposed Model Rule 4.5.3).

proceeding and obtain party consent with respect to any ex parte communication or practice.''[82] Whether or not lawyers become subject to more formal ethical rules on such ADR issues, practitioners in this area have an obvious financial and reputational interest in upholding broadly shared norms of fairness and integrity. And the entire legal profession has a stake in addressing legitimate criticism of present dispute resolution procedures.

82. Id., Proposed Model Rule 4.5.2.

Chapter VII

TRANSACTIONAL PRACTICE

A. Introduction

Although the cultural image of the American lawyer is that of a courtroom advocate, in reality, most legal practice occurs in transactional settings. What attorneys do on a day-to-day basis typically involves document preparation, counseling, negotiation, and lobbying. Even litigation matters are seldom fully litigated; over 90 percent of all civil and criminal cases settle prior to trial.

The fact that most of lawyers' work occurs outside the structure of court procedure has obvious ethical significance. That point was underscored a half-century ago in a prominent Joint Conference Report on Professional Responsibility by the American Bar Association and the Association of American Law Schools. As the Report noted:

> The most effective realization of the law's aims often takes place in the attorney's office, where litigation is forestalled by anticipating its outcome, where the lawyer's quiet counsel takes place of public force. Contrary to popular belief, the compliance with the law thus brought about is not generally lip-serving and narrow, for by reminding him of its long-run costs the lawyer often deters his client from a course of conduct technically permissible under existing law, though inconsistent with its underlying spirit and purpose.
>
> Although the lawyer serves the administration of justice indispensably both as advocate and as office counselor, the demands imposed on him by these two roles must be sharply distinguished. The man who has been called into court to answer for his own actions is entitled to a fair hearing. Partisan advocacy plays its essential part in such a hearing, and the lawyer pleading his client's case may properly present it in the most favorable light. A similar resolution of doubts in one direction becomes inappropriate when the lawyer acts as counselor. The reasons that justify and even require partisan advocacy in the trial of a cause do not grant any license to the lawyer to participate as legal adviser in a line of conduct that is immoral, unfair, or of doubtful legality. In saving himself from this unworthy involvement, the lawyer cannot be guided solely by an unreflective inner sense of good faith; he must be at pains to preserve a sufficient detachment from his client's

interests so that he remains capable of a sound and objective appraisal of the propriety of what his client proposes to do.[1]

No systematic data is available, nor is it clear how such data could be compiled, on the extent to which lawyers have provided such "sound and objective appraisal." However, bar codes and commentary have long recognized that responsibility, and most members of the bar accept it in principle. The challenges of realizing it in practice are the focus of the discussion that follows.

B. Document Preparation, Retention, and Destruction

Two of lawyers' most critical transactional roles involve documents: creating documents to govern transactions, and crafting policies and practices concerning document retention. Documents are of critical importance in a legal relationship because they have the formality and particularity necessary to create, modify, or negate legal obligations. Once created, a document, unlike an oral communication, is permanent proof of its content—unless, of course, the document is destroyed. Hence the phrase "smoking gun." As Chapter VI notes, most ethical obligations governing lawyers in litigation draw on other law, especially rules of evidence and procedure. The same is true of ethical obligations governing lawyers' transactional work. Bar disciplinary rules governing such conduct largely track criminal and civil prohibitions.

With respect to preparing documents or providing document-related advice, a lawyer "shall not counsel a client to engage, or assist a client, in conduct that the lawyer knows is criminal or fraudulent." Model Rules of Professional Conduct, Rule 1.2(d). See also DR 7–102(A)(7). Nor may a lawyer knowingly "make a false statement of material fact or law to a third person," or "fail to disclose a material fact when disclosure is necessary to avoid assisting a criminal or fraudulent act by a client, unless disclosure is prohibited by [the rule governing client confidences]." Model Rule 4.1. See also DR 7–102. In essence, the rules governing documentation simply incorporate the background law of fraudulent misrepresentation. Lawyers may also be subject to ethics-related statutory obligations regarding the preparation of legal documents.[2]

1. Lon L. Fuller & John D. Randall, "Professional Responsibility: Report to the Joint Conference," 44 ABA J. 1159, 1161 (1958).

2. Prominent examples involve securities and tax filings. For securities, see the discussion of the Sarbanes–Oxley Act in Chapter VI. For tax shelters, see 31 C.F.R. § 10.35 (2005); and Tanina Rostain, "Sheltering Lawyers: The Organized Tax Bar and the Tax Shelter Industry," 23 Yale J. Reg. 77 (2006).

With respect to document production and retention, Rule 3.4 of the Model Rules provides that lawyers may not "unlawfully obstruct another party's access to evidence or unlawfully alter, destroy or conceal a document or other material having potential evidentiary value." See also DR 7–109. The Model Rules also prohibit conduct "prejudicial to the administration of justice," which would include unlawful document destruction. Model Rule 8.4. See also DR 1–102(A).

These rules, although clear in their intended purpose, can be difficult to interpret in practice. Part of the problem involves indeterminacies in the law of fraud as applied to particular transactions. Whether statements are materially misleading, or whether disclosures are necessary to prevent a third party's misapprehension of a material fact, often may be open to dispute. So too, although many state, local, and federal laws regarding document retention are unambiguous, others leave room for argument about their applicability in a particular setting. Typically, these provisions prohibit destruction or concealment only if the individual believes that an official proceeding is pending or about to be instituted. Some statutes also cover investigations.[3] A few states impose liability for actions intended to prevent production of evidence in a legal proceeding regardless of when the actions take place. Lawyers' ethical responsibilities thus depend on the relevant statutes, the timing of the contemplated actions, and the pendency or likelihood of proceedings. If an attorney discovers documents establishing that a client is liable to a third party, but does not know with certainty whether that party will file suit, then it will be arguable whether the documents must be retained. Similar ambiguities may arise concerning the level of factual certainty required before a lawyer "knows" that the client is engaging in fraud.

In resolving these ambiguities, prudent lawyers generally consider pragmatic as well as ethical considerations. In many transactional contexts, one of lawyers' primary functions is to provide assurances that the matter complies with all legal requirements. In some instances, those assurances must include a statement that the lawyer has conducted an appropriate inquiry or investigation, for example concerning whether specified contracts are presently still in force. Such inquiries are often referred to as "due diligence" investigations. Fulfillment of this function is often called "gate-

---

3. See the Sarbanes–Oxley Act, 18 U.S.C. § 1519, discussed infra, and Model Penal Code § 241.7 (1962). Other jurisdictions prohibit destruction or concealment if the material is relevant to pending criminal proceedings or to any ongoing investigation. Thousands of state, federal, and local laws require retention of certain records for specified periods. See Deborah L. Rhode & David Luban, Legal Ethics 342–43, 347 (4th ed. 2004).

keeping," meaning that the lawyer's approval is required for the transaction to go forward. In other circumstances, a third party's reasonable reliance will create similar obligations. Lawyers who do not responsibly perform this gatekeeping role risk being held accountable by government regulators or defrauded parties. Even if lawyers ultimately manage to escape legal liability, the financial, psychological, and reputational costs of their defense are likely to be substantial.

So too, the risks to clients of arguably illegal conduct may be greater than they anticipate, and lawyers play an important role in persuasively communicating those risks. If, for example, relevant documents are destroyed when a legal proceeding is clearly foreseeable, the judge and jury may be permitted to draw adverse inferences about their contents. In many cases, those inferences will be more damaging than the contents themselves. Compromising documents can sometimes be explained; the destruction of documents removes that possibility. Intentional failure to comply with discovery obligations can also help justify large punitive damage awards. Moreover, in an age of widespread photocopying and electronic transmission, it can be difficult to destroy all copies of inculpating material. Unsuccessful efforts to do so are likely to be extremely damaging for all concerned, including lawyers. One crucial counseling function is to help clients establish appropriate document retention policies that will ensure conformity with applicable laws while avoiding unnecessary storage.

The complexities of these issues are well illustrated by the prosecution of the Arthur Andersen accounting firm arising from document destruction during the Enron scandal. The conduct at issue involved an October 12, 2002 memo that in-house counsel Nancy Temple sent to a supervising partner suggesting that it might be "useful to consider reminding" Andersen employees working on Enron of the Andersen firm's document and retention policy. The files at issue related to the audit of questionable investment vehicles for Enron, and to the certification of the company's potentially misleading financial statements. Andersen had a standard document retention policy calling for the destruction of all nonessential draft documents or conflicting documentation relating to an audit.[4] Temple's conduct was the subject of a 2002 Congressional hearing in which she characterized her actions as customary house-

---

4. A complete copy of the Andersen policy, Client Engagement Information–Organization, Retention and Destruction, Feb. 1, 2000, is reprinted in Destruction of Enron–Related Documents by Andersen Personnel: Hearing Before the House of Representatives Committee on Energy, 107th Cong. 1 (Jan. 24, 2002), at 79–103. http://www.access.gpo.gov/congress/house.

keeping duties. In that hearing, she admitted awareness, prior to drafting her memo, of allegations of inappropriate accounting procedures, as well as an investigation of those allegations by outside counsel. In addition, Temple's notes from a conference call on October 8 noted: "Highly probable some SEC investigation."[5] On October 19, the SEC notified Enron, with a copy to Andersen, that it was under investigation. On October 23, Andersen's supervising partner on the Enron audit ordered his team to comply with Andersen's policy. The result was an extraordinary volume of document destruction over the next several weeks, which the firm stopped only on November 9, when the SEC served a subpoena on Andersen for Enron-related documents.

The Justice Department subsequently prosecuted Andersen under a federal statute imposing criminal liability on anyone who "corruptly persuades another person" to destroy documents so that they will be unavailable "in an official proceeding."[6] The jury convicted Andersen based on an instruction that defined "corruptly" to mean "having an improper purpose, . . . an intent to subvert, undermine or impede the fact-finding ability of an official proceeding." On appeal, the Supreme Court reversed, and agreed with firm that the statute required a finding that its employees knew that their actions were unlawful. The Court also maintained that it was not "wrongful" for a manager to instruct employees to comply with a lawful document retention policy "under ordinary circumstances" even if the policy was designed to keep certain materials from the Government.[7]

This holding, however, did not entirely restore the reputation of the Andersen firm, which dissolved during the Enron proceedings. Nor will it exonerate lawyers and clients in subsequent similar cases because Congress, in the Sarbanes–Oxley Act of 2002, amended the statute. As modified, the law eliminates the term "corruptly" and imposes criminal liability on those who "knowingly" destroys or falsify records "in relation to or contemplation of any [federal] matter or case." If other jurisdictions and bar disciplinary committees begin following this trend, then as one commentator notes, a prudent lawyer or manager would be well advised to avoid "even wistful glances at the delete key."[8]

---

5. April Witt & Peter Behr, "Losses, Conflicts Threaten Survival," *Washington Post*, July 31, 2002, at A1.

6. 18 U.S.C. § 1512.

7. Arthur Andersen v. United States, 544 U.S. 696 (2005).

8. 18 U.S.C. § 1519. David G. Savage, "Of Motives and Memos," ABA J. April 2005, 34 (quoting James Dabney Miller).

C. Counseling

Bar ethical rules on counseling again mirror broader civil and criminal prohibitions. A lawyer "shall not counsel a client to engage, or assist a client, in conduct that the lawyer knows is criminal or fraudulent, but a lawyer may discuss the legal consequences of any proposed course of conduct. . . ." Model Rules, Rule 1.2(d). See also DR 7–102(A)(7). If lawyers discover that a client is engaging in criminal or fraudulent conduct, they must avoid any assistance and withdraw from the representation. The Comment adds: "In some cases, withdrawal alone might be insufficient. It may be necessary for the lawyer to give notice of the fact of withdrawal and disaffirm any opinion, document, affirmation or the like." Model Rules, Rule 1.2 Comment. See also Rule 1.16(a) and Rule 4.1. In providing legal advice, "a lawyer may refer not only to law but to other considerations such as moral, economic, social, and political factors, that may be relevant to the client's situation." Model Rules, Rule 2.1.

Some evidence suggests that clients are more likely to welcome non-legal advice than lawyers often assume, and that such advice will be most effective when it is framed in pragmatic rather than explicitly moral terms.[9] Private practitioners rarely report giving advice that expressly invokes "the public interest."[10] Yet concerns about public welfare will often inform even the most pragmatic "bottom line" counseling. By exploring the full costs of ethically dubious conduct, such as adverse publicity, loss of reputation, and risks of litigation, lawyers frequently demonstrate that the "right" course of conduct is also the economically prudent one.[11]

The most difficult dilemmas in counseling arise when that form of persuasion falls short, or is expected by the lawyer to be ineffective. Such dilemmas require analysis on two levels. First, how should lawyers, like other decision makers, determine the

9. Milton C. Regan, Jr., "Professional Responsibility and the Corporate Lawyer," 13 Geo. J. Legal Ethics 197, 202 (2000) (noting the importance of non-legal advice by in-house counsel); Edward A. Dauer, "Attorneys Underestimate Clients' Desire for Business Involvement, Survey Shows," Preventive Law Reporter, Dec. 1988, at 19 (finding that clients were more likely than lawyers to believe that non-legal advice was generally appropriate); Robert Jackall, Moral Mazes: The World of Corporate Managers 108–24 (1988) (noting the reluctance of corporate decision makers to frame issues in moral terms); Rhode & Luban, Legal Ethics, supra note 3, at 434–35 (noting reasons for preference for pragmatic rather than explicitly ethical counseling).

10. Robert L. Nelson, "Ideology, Practice, and Professional Autonomy: Social Values and Client Relationships in the Large Law Firm," 37 Stan. L. Rev. 503, 533 (1985).

11. See e.g. Lynn Sharp Paine, "Moral Thinking in Management: An Essential Capability," in Ethics in Practice 59 (Deborah L. Rhode ed., 2000).

propriety of particular conduct when competing values are involved? Second, under what, if any, circumstances, should lawyers decline to assist lawful client conduct that they find morally objectionable? Little in abstract ethical philosophy provides concrete guidance concerning these issues. There is, of course, agreement on some general principles: that dishonesty and theft are wrong and that unnecessary harm to third parties should be avoided. But, to borrow the celebrated phrase from Justice Oliver Wendell Holmes, "general principles do not decide concrete cases." In this respect, ethics in professional practice is no different from ethics in ordinary life; in both contexts, the "right thing to do" usually depends on circumstances.

Hard Cases

Since counseling issues cannot be resolved in the abstract, it is helpful to consider some concrete factual contexts. For example, how should lawyers respond when they believe that a corporate client is selling products, permitting workplace conditions, or releasing industrial pollutants that are not clearly unlawful but that pose excessive safety risks?[12] What should lawyers do if management decides to permit regulatory violations that are unlikely to result in detection or serious sanctions?[13] Should lawyers assist transactions that are not clearly unlawful but which could well mislead investors about the financial health of the company?[14] These problems are most likely to arise in circumstances where legal standards are ambiguous or set too low due to lack of information or political leverage, or where enforcement is too infrequent due to inadequate regulatory resources or difficulties in policing compliance.

Such examples come from corporate practice, but similar problems arise in representing individuals and government entities. For example, what are a lawyer's responsibilities if a client wants to sell property with serious problems that the buyer has not, or could not have discovered?[15] What if one spouse in an acrimonious divorce case wants to threaten a custody battle to force a skewed financial

---

12. See Rhode & Luban, supra note 3, at 504–06; Stephen L. Pepper, "Counseling at the Edge of the Law: An Exercise in the Jurisprudence and Ethics of Lawyering," 104 Yale L. J. 1545 (1995).

13. Stephen Pepper, supra note 12, at 1570–75.

14. Compare Robert Gordon, "A New Role for Lawyers?: The Corporate Counselor after Enron," 35 Conn. L. Rev. 1185 (2003) and William Simon, "After Confidentiality: Rethinking the Professional Responsibilities of the Business Lawyer," Ford. L. Rev. (2006); with Steven L. Schwarcz, "The Limits of Lawyering: Legal Opinions in Structured Finance," 84 Tex. L. Rev. 1 (2005).

15. Rhode and Luban, supra note 3, at 469.

settlement that will cause substantial hardship for the children and custodial spouse?[16] How should lawyers in the executive branch respond if senior officials want a narrow interpretation of federal statutes and international conventions on torture to permit interrogation practices that the lawyers believe are inconsistent with widely recognized principles of human rights?[17] Such issues pose diverse concerns but raise a common question: Should lawyers ever refuse to assist conduct that complies with the letter of the law but that frustrate its objectives?

The Case for Moral Counseling

In a widely publicized speech at a Securities and Exchange Commission Conference, the Commission's chair, Harvey L. Pitt addressed some of these counseling issues. His remarks endorsed a view of lawyers' ethical obligations consistent with the ABA–AALS report quoted earlier. According to Pitt:

> Lawyers are paid, and are professionally obligated, to advocate legitimate views and interests of their clients, with emphasis on the word "legitimate".... [E]xperience teaches it is inappropriate for corporate lawyers to assist clients in finding ways to evade legal requirements, or disserve the public interest, even if those results can be achieved in a manner arguably within the literal letter of the law.[18]

This statement provoked immediate controversy. Critics wondered what "experience" Mr. Pitt was referring to, what "disserve the public interest" really meant, and how lawyers were supposed to know. If in doubt, who should they ask? "Their rabbi?" "Harvey Pitt"?[19] In critics' view, clients are entitled to information about the letter of the law and to decide for themselves whether to press its limits. If lawyers believe that such conduct would be unwise, they are "free to share that advice." But if the public is ill served when clients comply only with the letter of the law, then critics believe

---

16. For the classic account, see Richard Neely, "The Primary Caretaker Parent Rules: Child Custody and the Dynamics of Greed," 3 Yale Law & Pol'y Rev. 168 (1984). See also Eleanor Macoby and Robert Mnookin, Dividing the Child 154–59 (1992).

17. David Luban, "Liberalism, Torture, and the Ticking Bomb," in The Torture Debate in America 35 (Karen J. Greenberg, ed. 2006); Robert K. Vischer, "Legal Advice as Moral Perspective," 19 Geo. J. Legal Ethics 225 (2006); W. Bradley Wendel, Legal Ethics and the Separation of Law and Morals, 91 Cor-

nell L. Rev. 67 (2006); and the discussion in Chapter VIII of the government lawyer's role.

18. Harvey L. Pitt, Remarks at SEC Speaker Conference (Feb. 22, 2002). See also Harvey L. Pitt, Remarks before the American Bar Association, Aug. 12, 2002.

19. Lawrence J. Fox, "The Fallout from Enron: Media Frenzy and Misguided Notions of Public Relations Are No Reason to Abandon Our Commitment to Our Clients," 2003 U. Ill. L. Rev. 1243, 1250 (2003).

that "the answer is to change the letter, not to change the professional responsibility foundations of lawyering."[20]

A serious difficulty, of course, is that changing the law may require information and political leverage that are unlikely to be forthcoming in time to avert serious harm. Related difficulties arise when lawyers believe that the client, or the managers who normally speak for the client, are not well-positioned to make appropriate ethical judgments. The question then becomes under what, if any, circumstances do lawyers have the responsibility to make their own ethical assessments and to attempt either to persuade the client or to withdraw from representation.

One cluster of problems emerges when the stress, acrimony, and financial pressures that can accompany legal disputes compromises clients' ability to perceive their own long-term interests or the ethical implications of self-serving behavior.[21] As Elihu Root famously put it, "about half the practice of a decent lawyer consists in telling would-be clients that they are damned fools and should stop."[22] At the very least, lawyers can provide a useful reality check for individuals whose judgment is skewed by self-interest or cognitive biases. One such bias involves cognitive dissonance; individuals tend to suppress or reconstrue information that casts doubt on a prior belief or action.[23] These tendencies may lead clients to discount or devalue evidence of the harms of their conduct or the extent of their own responsibility. Such skewed assessments are particularly likely where the victims are distant and diffuse—shareholders and consumers, not identifiable persons.[24] Self-serving biases compound the problem. Social psychology research confirms what common sense and common experience suggest. People have a natural inclination to conflate what is personally advantageous with what is socially just and ethically justifiable.[25]

20. Id., p. 1250.

21. For examples, see Rhode & Luban, supra note 3, at 515–21, 553–37, 539–41,708–727; and Deborah L. Rhode, "Moral Counseling," Ford. L. Rev. (2006).

22. Philip C. Jessup, 1 Elihu Root 133 (1930).

23. The classic account is Leon Festinger, Theory of Cognitive Dissonance 128–34 (1957). See generally, Cognitive Dissonance: Progress on a Pivotal Theory in Social Psychology (Eddie Harmon–Jones and Judson Mills, eds., 1999).

24. Sung Hui Kim, "The Banality of Fraud: Re–Situating the Inside Counsel

as Gatekeeper," 74 Ford. L. Rev. 983, 1033 (2005); Don A. Moore & George Lowenstein, "Self–Interest, Automaticity, and the Psychology of Conflict of Interest," 17 Social Just. Res. 89, 197 (2004).

25. Kim, supra note 24, at 1030–31; Ziva Kunda, "The Case for Motivated Reasoning," 108 Psychol. Bull. 480, 485 (1990); Michael B. Metzger, "Bridging the Gaps: Cognitive Constraints on Corporate Control and Ethics Education," 16 U. Fla. J. Law & Pub. Pol'y., 435, 499 (2005).

Organizational structures can also compromise moral judgment. Countless studies document the influence of authority figures, peer pressure and group loyalty in producing actions that individuals find unacceptable under other circumstances.[26] A related set of distortions emerge from "principal-agent" conflicts. These occur in organizational settings where managers' desire to maximize their own income, power, or status encourages decisions inconsistent with the interest of owners and other stakeholders. The problem is particularly apparent where compensation and advancement are too closely tied to short term profits.[27] Such skewed reward structures help explain the moral meltdowns on display in cases like Enron and its predecessors during the Savings and Loan crisis of the 1990s.[28]

Bar ethical rules, reflecting basic corporation law, respond to principle-agent difficulties by making clear that the lawyer represents the entity not any of its constituent members. As discussion in Chapter VIII notes, in cases of unlawful conduct by corporate personnel, that obligation may sometimes entail seeking reconsideration of managerial decisions by the organization's highest authority. See Model Rule 1.13 and the Sarbanes–Oxley Act of 2002. However, ethical rules and legal requirements leave lawyers with considerable discretion when the conduct is not clearly illegal or when the highest authority acts in ways that the lawyer believes will compromise important societal or third-party interests.

Identifying the Public Interest: Cost/Safety Tradeoffs as a Case Study

In considering that issue, the first question is whether lawyers in a particular context can come to a satisfactory determination of what else, beyond legal requirements, fairness to others or concern for the public interest in fact requires. That in turn will often depend on the clarity of information available and the nature and importance of the values at stake. Consider, for example, how

26. For examples, see Rhode, "Moral Counseling," supra note 18.

27. Deborah L. Rhode, "Where Is the Leadership in Moral Leadership?," in Moral Leadership: The Theory and Practice of Power, Judgment, and Policy (2006); David Skeel, Icarus in the Boardroom: The Fundamental Flaws in Corporate America and Where They Came From 152–155 (2005).

28. Ronald R. Sims and Johannes Brinkmann, "Enron Ethics (Or: Culture Matters More than Codes)," 45 J. Bus. Ethics 243, 247 (2003); John R. Kroger, "Enron, Fraud, and Securities Reform: An Enron Prosecutor's Perspective," 76 Col. L. Rev. 57 (2003); See also Langevoort, The Organizational Psychology of Hyper–Competition. For discussion of the savings and loan crisis, see sources cited in Rhode & Luban, supra note 3, at 287–297. For a general discussion, see Donald C. Langevoort, "Where Were the Lawyers? A Behavioral Inquiry into Lawyers' Responsibility for Clients' Fraud," 46 Vanderbilt L. Rev. 75 (1993).

lawyers could assess the appropriate level of safety for client products, working conditions, or industrial pollutants. Modifications that would increase safety are frequently available, but at a significant cost. One conventional way to analyze the issue is from a utilitarian standpoint, weighing the full costs and benefits of plausible alternatives. Although clear in principle, this approach is generally indeterminate in practice, given the ambiguities inherent in estimating and valuing benefits and risks. For example, should the safety of an automobile be assessed in terms of a particularly risky feature, or the overall performance of the car compared with its competitors? In some celebrated cases involving automobile gas tanks that exploded in low speed collisions, the subcompact cars at issue had generally good safety records in comparison with other cars in the same price range but performed much worse in the relatively infrequent circumstances of rear end collisions.[29]

A related problem involves quantifying consequences. For example, if particular safety decisions impose some increased risk of fatalities, what price should be placed on human life? Federal agencies operate with widely varying figures ranging from under $100,000 to over $100 million.[30] Jury verdicts also reflect significant variations that partly depend on the age, gender, race, and earning potential of the victim. A very different measure comes from the value that individuals place on their own lives, estimated by the salary premiums that they demand for dangerous working conditions.[31]

Further indeterminacies arise in quantifying other consequences that may result from unsafe products, working conditions, or industrial pollutants. Such consequences may include impaired reputation from high visibility litigation, or diminished quality of life for workers and community residents. By the same token, the long-term price of safety improvements may be equally hard to predict. That price would need to take into account not only the direct costs of modification, but also the indirect costs associated with lower profits and higher prices, such as lost sales, jobs, and stock value. Those outcomes may have further ripple effects that are even harder to assess, such as loss of pension savings and increased risks of plant closings, with all their attendant costs for workers, their families, and their communities.

29. Gary T. Schwartz, "The Myth of the Ford Pinto Case," 43 Rutgers L. Rev. 1013, 1032 (1992).

30. Marianne Lavalle, "Placing a Price on Human Life," Nat'l L. J., Oct. 10, 1988, at 26–28 (comparing for example, a decision on space heaters by the Consumer Protection Safety Commission with a pesticide ban by the Food and Drug Administration).

31. See Rhode & Luban, supra note 3, at 396–99.

Another difficulty in applying a cost-benefit analysis involves the distance between those who make the calculation and those whose welfare is at issue. Responsibility for such calculations always rests with someone in authority, typically business managers or public officials. Most individuals whose welfare is at stake usually are far lower down the socioeconomic scale. The discrepancy between public and professional views is often reflected in public officials' extreme reluctance to address such issues explicitly. These individuals include those who hold office by vote of ordinary people but who often take substantial campaign contributions from business leaders, and who often see little to gain from direct confrontation with cost/safety tradeoffs. The result is a high degree of abstraction, or euphemisms about "adequate" protection.

Given the indeterminacies of cost-benefit calculations, many situations raising these tradeoffs will not yield any single "right" answer. But some answers will be better than others—more respectful of the available evidence and more responsive to all the values at issue. Lawyers have assisted client actions that many disinterested decision makers have found difficult to reconcile with accepted ethical principles or any coherent notion of public interests. Commonly cited examples involve the attorneys who were active, sometimes "cheerful abettors" of conduct such as: the distribution of hazardous Dalkon shields; the suppression of information related to tobacco and asbestos health risks; the abusive interrogation techniques for international prisoners; and the financially irresponsible transactions of many savings and loans institutions and corporate giants like Enron.[32] The question that these cases raise is whether lawyers who would find such conduct morally repugnant or problematic have some obligation to withhold their assistance.

Declining and Withdrawing From Representation

Bar ethical rules recognize lawyers' right to decline representation or to withdraw from cases that they find "repugnant" or "with which [they have] a fundamental disagreement." Model Rule 1.16, Comment; See DR 1–110(c). Whether they have a moral responsibility to do so is a more difficult question on which the profession has long been divided. American legal ethics commentators in the

---

32. See Deborah L. Rhode, In the Interests of Justice 57 (2002); Bruce A. Green, "Thoughts About Corporate Lawyers After Reading the Cigarette Papers: The Wise Counselor Gives Way to the Hired Gun," 51 DePaul L. Rev. 407 (2001); Robert Gordon, "Portrait of a Profession in Paralysis," 54 Stan. L. Rev. 1425 (2002); Rhode, Moral Counseling, supra note 21; See also Vischer, supra note 17 (discussing the nondisclosure of child sexual abuse by catholic priests).

first half of the nineteenth century maintained that lawyers had an obligation to refrain from pursuing unjust causes at least in certain contexts.[33] Some contemporary commentators take a similar position.[34] In making the case for "compliance counseling," Professor Robert Gordon notes:

> Suppose the legal rule is clear, yet the chance of detecting violations low, the penalties small in relation to the gains from noncompliance, or the terrorizing of regulators into settlement by a deluge of paper predictably easy. The mass of lawyers who advise and then assist with noncompliance in such a situation could, in the vigorous pursuit of their clients' interests, effectively nullify the laws. The only justification for their doing so would have to be their confidence that the system was self-equilibrating, so that some countervailing force would operate to offset their efforts. But such confidence is unfounded....
>
> [T]he critic then says: all right, lawyers play legitimate roles in [encouraging legal compliance but they] have no right to intrude their opinions, their influence, their political values. They are neither elected officials nor their agents; lawyers have no special authority to go around telling people how they should behave.
>
> The traditional response to this is simple: lawyers do indeed have an official status as licensed fiduciaries for the public interest, charged with encouraging compliance with legal norms. In contexts like counseling, where there is no official third party like a judge to oversee the interaction between the client and the state, the lawyer is not only supposed to predict the empirical consequences of certain behavior, but also to represent the viewpoint of the legal system to the client. Lawyers can't coerce anyone; they can only advise and persuade, sometimes only under the threat of resignation rather than disclosure. Surely the right of the lawyer to encourage compliance with the law's purposes through persuasion is at least as clear as the client's right to demand the lawyer's help in exploiting the law's ambiguities and procedural opportunities and in engaging in strategic behavior designed to evade the law. The other and even better response to the critic is that even conceding that lawyers have no special authority to guide

---

33. David Hoffman, Fifty Resolutions in Regard to Professional Deportment in A Course of Legal Study (2d ed. 1836). George Sharswood, Essay on Professional Ethics (1854).

34. David Luban, Lawyers and Justice: An Ethical Study (1988); William H. Simon, The Practice of Justice: A Theory of Lawyers' Ethics (1998); Rhode, supra note 32.

their clients, neither do they have any special immunity from responsibility for the things they help their clients do....[35]

The debates often ignore gradients between unquestioning assistance to a client and resignation in protest. Situations that are morally repugnant to a conscientious lawyer are often at least legally debatable, in which case the lawyer has an obligation to give advice that takes the debatable dimension into account. On the other hand, many situations that are morally uncertain are also within the realm of "reasonable business judgment" for the client—for example, how much to spend on safety measures not required by legal regulation.

An extreme version of ethical obligation would require lawyers to refuse assistance in any matter that was inconsistent with their personal moral values, quite apart from legality. In the view of most commentators, such an assumption of power is unwarranted. If lawyers threaten to withdraw from representation when their ethical advice is not taken, the result may be "a reversal of the underlying structure of responsibility for the ... conduct. The adviser becomes the ultimate arbiter and the client a subordinate."[36] And if lawyers do withdraw, there is always the risk that their successors will be worse. Yet as Chapter VI also suggested, unless the lawyer is the last in town, his or her advice may not preempt client action. Rather, it may simply require a client to reassess the conduct at issue or to assume the financial and psychological costs of finding alternative counsel. And as philosophers note, the risk of a less ethical replacement may be relevant but certainly is not determinative of an individual's own moral assessments. For example, we would not exonerate those who assisted Nazi genocide efforts or the recent terrorist attacks on the ground that their successors would have been worse.

Withdrawal from representation is, of course, an unpalatable prospect for all concerned, and it should come as no surprise that lawyers rarely report refusing a matter on ethical grounds.[37] One reason is that a publicized withdrawal on such a basis might

---

35. Robert W. Gordon, "The Independence of Lawyers," 68 B.U. L. Rev. 1, 72–73 (1988); see also Robert W. Gordon, Why Lawyers Can't Just be Hired Guns, in Ethics in Practice, supra note 11, at 42.

36. Geoffrey C. Hazard, Jr., Ethics in the Practice of Law, 136, 143–45 (1978). For similar views, see Lee A. Casey & David B. Rivkin, Jr., "Devil's Advocate: The Danger of Judging Law-

yers by their Clients," Policy Rev., Feb.-March 2002, at 15; Ted Schneyer, "Reforming Law Practice in the Pursuit of Justice: The Perils of Privileging 'Public' Over Professional Values," 70 Fordham L. Rev. 1831 (2002); Monroe H. Freedman, "How Lawyers Act in the Interests of Justice," 70 Fordham. L. Rev. 1717 (2002).

37. Nelson, supra note 10, at 535–37.

frequently compromise the duty of confidentiality. Moreover, lawyers generally choose clients and practice settings that are likely to minimize moral conflicts. Economic and psychological pressures also encourage practitioners to evaluate information and arguments in ways that avoid such conflicts. As social science research makes clear, individuals who are assigned a particular position become more likely to believe in its validity, and those who have a self-interest in a given practice become more likely to interpret and recall facts in a manner that supports their position.[38] Yet by the same token, lawyers who have less personal stake in a particular decision than their clients will be able to evaluate its ethical implications from a more neutral perspective. And where important values are at issue, lawyers have the right, and many argue the responsibility, to act in accordance with their own convictions.

D. Paternalism

Some of the most difficult ethical dilemmas in counseling involve paternalism. Here the problem arises not because lawyers' values are inconsistent with clients' interests, but because lawyers believe that clients misperceive their own interests. How should an attorney respond when a client's decision making appears seriously impaired or highly imprudent? Clearly lawyers can and should share their views about the wisdom of the client's proposed decision. The hard question is determining the point at which advice becomes unacceptably paternalistic, i.e., inappropriately manipulative or coercive. That, in turn, may depend on how impaired the client's decision appears to be, which may also be difficult to determine.

At some point, a lawyer may withdraw from a representation if the client proposes a course of conduct that the lawyer regards as unacceptable. Model Rule 1.16 as originally drafted used the term "imprudent" to justify withdrawal on this basis, but the revised version adopts the term "fundamental disagreement." The precise formulation is, however, less important than the way it is interpreted in specific circumstances. Relevant facts include not only financial implications but also moral and psychological concerns, including the attitudes of both clients and lawyers. A common example is a client who wants to refuse a generous settlement out of an

---

38. See sources cited in Rhode, supra note 21; Thomas Gilovich, How We Know What Isn't So: The Fallibility of Reason in Everyday Life 80 (1991). For discussion of how lawyers' cognitive biases implicate them in unethical conduct, see David Luban, "The Ethics of Wrongful Obedience," in Ethics in Practice, supra note 11, at 95; and Douglas C. Langevoort, "Where Were the Lawyers? A Behavioral Inquiry into Lawyers' Responsibility for Client Fraud," 46 Vand. L. Rev. 75 (1993).

unrealistic desire for total vindication, and a lawyer who does not want to incur the costs in time and credibility of getting bogged down in a hopeless cause. The problems are compounded when the client is not paying any or all of the costs of representation, as in a typical contingent fee case.

Bar ethical codes include a number of provisions that address this issue. Some rules seek to protect clients from decisions that are likely to prove prejudicial or susceptible to improper lawyer influence. So, for example, clients may not prospectively waive rights to sue for malpractice unless they have independent representation, and lawyers may not prepare certain documents that unduly favor their own interests. Model Rule 1.8(h) and (c). As Chapter VIII's discussion of conflicts of interest notes, the point of such rules is not only to protect clients but also to preserve public confidence in the profession.

Another ethical rule, Model Rule 1.14, provides protection and guidance where clients have "diminished capacity." Under its terms:

(a) When a client's capacity to make adequately considered decisions in connection with a representation is diminished, whether because of minority, mental impairment or for some other reason, the lawyer shall, as far as reasonably possible, maintain a normal client-lawyer relationship with the client.

(b) When the lawyer reasonably believes that the client has diminished capacity, is at risk of substantial physical, financial or other harm unless action is taken and cannot adequately act in the client's own interest, the lawyer may take reasonably necessary protective action, including consulting with individuals or entities that have the ability to take action to protect the client and, in appropriate cases, seeking the appointment of a guardian ad litem, conservator, or guardian.

Yet what constitutes a "considered decision" or appropriate "protective action" is often uncertain. Since such issues cannot be resolved in the abstract, it is helpful to consider several concrete examples. How should a lawyer handle the following situations?

- In a capital case, a defendant who has been declared competent wants to forego a valid appeal because he believes that he should atone for another crime he committed in an earlier life, and because he believes that he will be reincarnated after his execution.

- An elderly man with incurable cancer wants to rewrite his will and leave his entire estate to a faith healer who has been supportive but who does not appear to have exercised "undue influence."

- An employee with serious but intermittent mental health difficulties will not accept disability leave or insurance coverage because he believes that it will imply that he is "crazy."

- A sixteen-year-old girl wants to remain in an abusive family situation because she believes that she can handle the abuse by her stepfather, and that, if she discloses it, either her mother won't believe her or it will break up the family and force her into an institution or a foster care situation that would be worse.

- Parents of a severely depressed sixteen year old boy reject doctors' recommendations that he take medication and receive family therapy because they believe that his participation in a church youth group is a better way of handling his "attitude" problems.[39]

The literature on paternalism suggests a number of approaches to these issues. Moral theorist Dennis Thompson proposes a three part test for justifiable interference with an individual's choices: "First, the decision-making capacity of the person who is to be constrained must be *impaired.* . . . Second, the restriction is as *limited* as possible. . . . Finally, the restriction prevents serious and irreversible *harm.*"[40] Yet each of the highlighted terms—*impaired* decision, *limited* restriction, and *serious irreversible harm*— is clearly open to dispute across a wide range of situations. Moreover, even where individuals' decision making capacities are generally unimpaired, their ability to make a particular choice may be clouded. Additional difficulties arise when the client is mature but underage, or is a family member whose questionable decisions may adversely affect a child, an elderly parent, or a disabled spouse who is legally incapable of consent.

Another way to approach these situation-specific incapacities is what theorists sometimes describe as "hypothetical consent."

---

39. All of these hypotheticals are based on actual cases. For discussion of Gary Gilmore, who attempted to fire his attorneys after they filed an appeal over his objection, see Norman Mailer, The Executioner's Song 482, 505–06 (1979). See also State v. Berry, 706 N.E.2d 1273 (Ohio 1999) (denying defense attorney's motion to review the competency of a death row inmate who desired abandonment of all appeals). For other examples, see Rhode & Luban, supra note 3, at 673–75, and Jan C. Costello,

" 'The Trouble is They're Growing, The Trouble is They're Grown': Therapeutic Jurisprudence and Adolescents' Participation in Mental Health Care Decisions," 29 Ohio Northern U. L. Rev. 607, 609–611 (2003).

40. Dennis Thompson, "Paternalism in Modern Law and Public Policy," in Ethics Teaching in Higher Education 246, 250–51 (Dennis Callahan & Sissela Bok eds., 1980).

[S]ince we are all aware of our irrational propensities, deficiencies in cognitive and emotive capacities, and avoidable and unavoidable ignorance it is rational and prudent for us to in effect take out "social insurance policies." We may argue for and against proposed paternalistic measures in terms of what fully rational individuals would accept as forms of protection.[41]

That is, we ask what people *would* consent to if they were fully rational. Under this approach, hypothetical consent becomes the touchstone of justifiable paternalism. The difficulty here, of course, is that we do not know exactly what "fully rational individuals" would consent to. None of us, after all, is fully rational under all circumstances.[42]

Accordingly, some theorists propose a third approach, a contextual, ad hoc paternalism, that attempts to determine whether a particular choice is consistent with the individuals' core commitments and concerns. So for example, Professor David Luban argues that paternalism is justified to protect clients' long term values or objective interests (such as money or freedom) against momentary wants or whims. However, paternalism is not justified if choices that are seemingly contrary to clients' objective interests are rooted in their deeply held values.[43] Of course, this approach still requires lawyers to make a decision that is inevitably influenced by their own values and life experience. It also entails knowledge about clients' values. Clearly, lawyers need some criteria for assessing decision-making capacity apart from the perceived merits of the decision at issue. Otherwise, the inquiry will become circular: a client who made a seemingly "irrational" judgment could be deemed incompetent, and an incompetent client could be deemed incapable of rational judgment.[44]

Practitioners who work with clients under some disability have identified a number of criteria for assessing their decision making capabilities and the need for paternalistic intervention. For exam-

41. Gerald Dworkin, "Paternalism," in Morality and the Law 120 (Richard A. Wasserstrom, ed., 1971).

42. For a critique of hypothetical consent, see David Luban, "Paternalism and the Legal Profession," 1981 Wis. L. Rev. 454, 463–67. For discussion of the paternalism reflected in bar ethics rules, see Fred C. Zacharias, "Limits on Client Autonomy in Legal Ethics Regulation," 81 Boston U. L. Rev. 198 (2001). For discussion of cognitive biases that encourage individuals to make overly optimistic assessments of their own circumstances and capabilities, see Jeffrey J. Rachlinski, "The Uncertain Psychological Case for Paternalism," 97 N.W. L. Rev. 1165, 1772, 1192 (2003).

43. Luban, supra note 42, at 467–74.

44. Rhode & Luban, supra note 3, at 601; Thompson, supra note 40, at 252; Paul R. Tremblay, "On Persuasion and Paternalism: Lawyer Decisionmaking and the Questionably Competent Client," 3 Utah L. Rev. 515, 533–38 (1987).

ple, lawyers representing elderly patients should consider factors such as: clients' ability to articulate the reasons behind a decision; the variability in their mental states; their appreciation of the consequences of a particular decision; the substantive fairness of the outcome; and its consistency with their lifetime commitments.[45] Lawyers representing juveniles should similarly take into account issues such as the risks of a "wrong" decision and the minor's age, mental capacity, psychological stability, strength of preferences, and ability to make rational, consistent judgments without undue influence by others.[46]

Certain factors may be more important than others, depending on the context. The ABA Standards of Practice for Lawyers who Represent Children in Abuse and Neglect Cases (1996) recognize as much. Standard B–4 provides that the attorney generally should "respect the child's expressed preference and follow the child's directions throughout the course of litigation." However, Standard B–4(3) adds:

> If the child's attorney determines that the child's expressed preference would be seriously injurious to the child (as opposed to merely being contrary to the lawyer's opinion of what would be in the child's interest), the lawyer may request appointment of a separate guardian ad litem and continue to represent the child's expressed preference ... The child's attorney shall not reveal the basis of the request for appointment of a guardian ad litem which would compromise the client's position.

The Comment to this provision notes that one of the "most difficult ethical issues for lawyers representing children occurs when the child is able to express a position ... that could result in serious injury." This is particularly likely when the child desires to "live in a dangerous situation ... rather than risk the unknown world of a foster home or other out-of-home placement." The difficulty will not be resolved by appointment of a guardian ad litem if the child chooses not to disclose the dangerous situation. Under such circumstances, a conscientious counselor might take

---

45. Peter Margulies, "Access, Connection and Voice: A Contextual Approach to Representing Senior Citizens of Questionable Capacity," 62 Fordham L. Rev. 1073, 1084–85 (1994). See also Jan Ellen Rein, "Clients With Destructive and Socially Harmful Choices—What's an Attorney To Do? Within and Beyond the Competency Construct," 62 Fordham L. Rev. 1101, 1108 (1994).

46. Peter Margulies, "The Lawyer as Caregiver: Child Clients' Competence in

Context," 64 Fordham L. Rev. 1473, 1487–93 (1996); David R. Katner, "Coming to Praise, Not to Bury, the New ABA Standards of Practice for Lawyers Who Represent Children in Abuse and Neglect Cases," 14 Geo. J. Legal Ethics 103, 113 (2000); Jean Koh Peters, Representing Children in Child Protective Proceedings: Ethical and Practical Dimensions (2d ed. 2001).

advantage of the discretion provided under Model Rule 1.14 and pursue other "protective action" reasonably necessary to protect the child as well as any siblings exposed to an abusive environment.

As these examples suggest, effective counseling for clients under a disability may sometimes require therapeutic skills and knowledge about a client that are beyond what many lawyers can supply.[47] One of the most important characteristics of conscientious advisors is an understanding of their own limitations and a willingness to seek assistance from others, such as family members, friends, colleagues, mental health professionals, and social workers who can advance the legal system's therapeutic function.[48] Such assistance may also be important to protect lawyers' own interests; there is always the risk of later recriminations, sometimes litigation, if the lawyer attempts to challenge client decisions. Practitioners who represent an individual with diminished capacity have a special obligation to ensure that they have adequate expertise, or that they affiliate with other professionals who do.

E. Negotiation

Few areas are more central in legal practice than negotiation. Bargaining is a mainstay not only in dispute resolution and transactional planning on behalf of clients, but also in lawyers' own workplace relationships. Legal practice requires negotiation not just with opposing counsel, but also with clients, colleagues, supervisors, support staff, and court personnel. Because so much bargaining takes place in contexts that lack formal structures of accountability, lawyers' own ethical norms play a critical role.

These norms vary among individuals and across practice settings. The following factors are especially relevant.

- *Relationships between the Participants*

   Do the parties have ongoing business or personal relationships, or is the negotiation a one-shot transaction? Do the lawyers have a continuing relationship? How will particular bargaining tactics affect their reputations and future dealings?

---

47. See Jean Koh Peters, "The Roles and Content of Best Interests in Client–Directed Lawyering for Children in Child Protective Proceedings," 64 Fordham L. Rev. 1505 (1996); Bruce A. Green and Bernadine Dohrn, "Foreword: Children and the Ethical Practice of Law," 64 Fordham L. Rev. 1281 (1996).

48. For discussion of "therapeutic jurisprudence," namely the role of the law in enhancing clients' psychological well being, see Law in a Therapeutic Key: Developments in Therapeutic Jurisprudence (David B. Wexler and Bruce J. Winick, eds., 1996).

- *Legal and Social Context*

  What are the legal and community norms that govern the transaction? Do they establish any substantive standards for fairness? Will the outcome be reviewed by a court or neutral third party? How accessible are remedies for negotiation abuses? What are the norms and expectations of the relevant legal culture?

- *Relative Bargaining Strength*

  What are the resources of the parties and their lawyers in terms of time, money, information, and expertise?

- *Issues and Constraints*

  What are the key issues and factors affecting their resolution? To what extent do they involve fixed financial trade-offs? What other less visible but "potentially explosive" concerns are at stake, such as "control, turf, ego and reputation"?[49]

- *Personal Characteristics*

  What are the ethical values, bargaining styles and tolerance for risk of the parties and their lawyers?

To take an obvious example, the level of candor and cooperation in divorce negotiations will be affected by the likelihood of significant future dealings between the parties and their lawyers; the need to comply with specific child support guidelines and obtain judicial approval of the settlement; the financial and non-financial stakes involved; the clients' capacities to subsidize protracted proceedings; the degree of acrimony and risk averseness among the participants; and the role orientation of the lawyers (whether they see themselves as "bombers" or as "problem solvers").

Not only are there substantial differences in negotiation contexts, there are also substantial differences over negotiation principles. As subsequent discussion indicates, surveys of both practitioners and legal ethics experts reveal sharp disagreements on issues such as disclosure of material information and fairness to other parties. These disagreements, in turn, help explain why ethical rules governing negotiation generally do not extend beyond civil law prohibitions on crime and fraud.

Model Rule 4.1 of the Model Rules of Professional Conduct provides the primary standard. It prohibits a lawyer from knowing-

---

49. G. Richard Shell, Bargaining for Advantage: Negotiation Strategies for Reasonable People 30 (1999).

ly making a "false statement of material fact or law," and from knowingly "fail[ing] to disclose a material fact when disclosure is necessary to avoid assisting a criminal or fraudulent act by a client" unless disclosure is prohibited by rules governing confidential information. See also DR 7–102(A)(5). On its face, this Rule apparently forbids lying to an adversary in a negotiation. However, the Comment to Rule 4.1 adds:

> Whether a particular statement should be regarded as one of fact can depend on the circumstances. Under generally accepted conventions in negotiation, certain types of statements ordinarily are not taken as statements of material fact. Estimates of price or value placed on the subject of a transaction and a party's intentions as to an acceptable settlement of a claim are ordinarily in this category. . . .

Formal Opinion 06–439 by the ABA Standing Committee on Ethics and Professional Responsibility (2006) similarly concluded that under Rule 4.1, "puffing" and "posturing" concerning settlement points and the strengths of parties' positions are not "ordinarily" considered factual statements on which opposing parties can justifiably rely.

An earlier version of Rule 4.1 would have provided a more demanding standard. It would have added requirements that "in conducting negotiations, a lawyer shall be fair in dealing with other participants" and that a lawyer must disclose a material fact "necessary to correct a manifest misapprehension of fact or law resulting from a previous representation made by the lawyer or known by the lawyer to have been made by the client. . . ."[50] This proposed disclosure requirement paralleled provisions in the Restatement (Second) of Contracts and the Restatement (Second) of Agency, which permit voiding the transaction or holding agents civilly liable for nondisclosure under similar circumstances. The early Model rule formulation also would have barred lawyers from negotiating agreements with clauses that had been held illegal or unconscionable, a provision later incorporated in the ABA Section of Litigation's Ethical Guidelines for Settlement Negotiations (2002) (§ 4–25).

The proposed Model Rule additions were withdrawn in response to overwhelming opposition from the organized bar. Underlying that opposition were several concerns. Some attorneys appeared reluctant to accept any regulation of their negotiation

---

50. ABA Model Rule Of Professional Conduct Rule 4.2, Discussion Draft (January 30, 1980).

behavior, at least by bar disciplinary rules.[51] Others objected to the general norms of fairness and disclosure reflected in the proposed draft. In their view, the provisions were set at "too high a level of generality" and failed to acknowledge wide variations in bargaining approaches across geographic locations, substantive fields, and practice settings.[52]

The Model Rules debate revealed not only different conventions concerning candor and disclosure, but also different expectations concerning substantive expertise and technical sophistication among the parties. Many practitioners worried that "[a] rule based on the premise that the legal profession is substantially homogeneous . . . would put the technically sophisticated lawyer in a hopeless dilemma when dealing with an unsophisticated opposing counsel."[53] If the sophisticated lawyer exploited his expertise or withheld information that his opponent overlooked, the transaction would be voidable and the lawyer could be subject to discipline. Conversely, if the lawyer supplied the information or tried to equalize the playing field, his client would end up subsidizing both sides of the transaction and adversaries would be allowed to free-load on others' work. According to some law and economics theory, the long term impact of such a rule might prove perverse, because neither side would have adequate incentives to prepare.[54] Sophisticated parties might be reluctant to invest effort on which they could not capitalize; unsophisticated parties might rely on the disclosure obligations of their adversaries rather than spend the effort necessary to duplicate their work.

Supporters of greater honesty and fairness in negotiations respond to such arguments on both practical and ethical grounds. As a practical matter, they invoke research that casts doubt on the efficiency of hard-ball strategies. According to this research, the paradigm case for competitive frameworks involves a "zero-sum" situation in which parties lack a continuing relationship, and are unlikely to detect deception. These circumstances are less typical than is commonly assumed. Most bargaining contexts present mutually advantageous "value-creating" opportunities, as well as win-

---

51. Geoffrey C. Hazard, Jr., "The Lawyer's Obligation to be Trustworthy When Dealing With Opposing Parties," 33 S.C. L. Rev. 181, 191–96 (1981).

52. James J. White, "Machiavelli at the Bar: Ethical Limitations on Lying in Negotiations," 1980 A.B. Found. Res. J. 926, 927 (1980). See also Hazard, supra note 51, at 192–96. For a summary of research on ethical attitudes about bluff-

ing and other competitive bargaining strategies, see Roy J. Lewicki, Joseph A. Litterer, John W. Minton, and David M. Saunders Negotiation 392–98 (2d ed. 1994).

53. Hazard, supra note 51, at 195.

54. Alan Strudler, "Moral Complexity in the Law of Nondisclosure," 45 UCLA L. Rev. 337, 374–75 (1997).

lose "value-claiming" opportunities. Misleading or exploitative approaches may preempt the realization of mutually advantageous solutions to joint problems. Classic game theory also verifies what common sense suggests, namely that negotiators who encounter each other repeatedly will penalize aggressive bargainers. Cooperation works better over the long run.[55]

Other commentators argue for cooperation, candor, and fairness on ethical grounds. They claim that individuals' own interests in preserving their honesty, integrity, and fairness deserve a central role in evaluating negotiating behavior. From this perspective, common excuses for deceptive or manipulative tactics are unpersuasive. To rely on rationalizations such as "everyone does it" or "the other side is doing it" presupposes an impoverished view of morality—a view generally rejected in other contexts. Moreover, when lawyers know that their adversary is being deceptive, retaliatory deception is not simply corrective justice; rather, it is an attempt to impose the kind of injury that the lawyers themselves have avoided by discovering the duplicity.

Cutting ethical corners may also involve selective evaluation of the consequences. Consciously or unconsciously, many individuals overvalue the short-term benefits from unethical tactics, and disregard the long-term personal and systemic costs. Deception adversely affects both the parties and the process. When misrepresentation is suspected or revealed, it compromises the lawyer's credibility, and may provoke retaliatory or defensive responses. Deception breeds deception, a point captured in the adage that it is easy to tell one lie but difficult to tell only one.[56] The result is often to diminish parties' level of trust, their capacity to reach fair agreements, their ability to exchange credible commitments, and their sense of personal integrity. Honesty and fairness are to some extent collective goods. The more that lawyers seek to become "free riders," the greater the profession's difficulty in maintaining a climate of trust, credibility, and fair dealing.

So too, an unqualified willingness to exploit an opponent's ignorance or mistake carries broader costs. Disparities in talent, resources, and information inevitably skew negotiation results. While it may be unrealistic to expect parties to forego all the

55. See What's Fair: Ethics for Negotiators (Carrie Menkel–Meadow & Michael Wheeler, eds. 2004); Roger Fisher & William Ury, Getting to Yes: Negotiations Agreement Without Giving In (1981).

56. Sissela Bok, Lying: Moral Choice in Public and Private Life (1978); Peter C. Cramton & J. Gregory Dees, "Promoting Honesty in Negotiation," in What's Fair, supra note 55, at 108, 111; Reed Elizabeth Loder, "Moral Truthseeking and the Virtuous Negotiator," 8 Geo. J. Legal Ethics 45 (1994).

advantages that arise from such inequalities, it may be reasonable to expect negotiators to forego some. Particularly where parties lack equal access to relevant facts, it will often be both equitable and efficient to impose reasonable disclosure obligations.

That is, in part, why contract and tort law requires parties to correct material misapprehensions. The prevailing caselaw summarized in § 161 of the Restatement (Second) of Contracts mandates disclosure when necessary to correct a previous assertion that is erroneous, or when the fact in question concerns a basic assumption of the negotiation and failure to disclose would violate "good faith and ... reasonable standards of fair dealing." The doctrine summarized in §§ 527 and 529 of the Restatement (Second) of Torts, is that an injured party can recover damages caused by materially misleading misrepresentations, including ambiguous statements made with reckless indifference for how they will be interpreted. Partially true statements can be materially misleading if they fail to state qualifying information. Section 551 of the Restatement similarly notes that nondisclosure can result in liability where the undisclosed fact is basic to the transaction and where one party, "because of the relationship [with the other party], the customs of the trade or other objective circumstances, would reasonably expect a disclosure...." Unlike Model Rule 4.1, the Restatement does not expressly distinguish between lies, "generally accepted" puffery, half-truths, and truthful-but-misleading statements. All are tortious frauds if other parties rely on them to their detriment. Lawyers may be civilly liable for statements that qualify as fraud under these circumstances.[57]

Professor Donald Langevoort offers an economic justification for this "half-truth doctrine."

> [T]he law of fraud is efficient. It allows the less informed party to forego the costly and duplicative process of factual investigation and information discovery, thereby reducing transaction costs. The law offers a credibility bond for the reliability of factual representations by the informed party. It is not at all hard to extend this same logic to the half-truth.... Language is inherently imprecise; it is not functional to force people to stop and analyze statements to see if there is some subtle limit or ambiguity that must be clarified....[58]

---

57. See Restatement (Third) of the Law Governing Lawyers § 98; ABA Section of Litigation, Ethical Guidelines for Settlement Negotiations 4.1.1 (2002).

58. Donald C. Langevoort, "Half–Truths: Protecting Mistaken Inferences by Investors and Others," 52 Stan. L. Rev. 87 (1999).

In evaluating these arguments for more or less regulation of negotiating ethics, it is again helpful to consider concrete cases. The following examples reflect common negotiating tactics. It is useful to consider not only what the lawyer should have done but also what, if any, consequences should follow from conduct held to be unethical. Possibilities include: setting aside the agreement, imposing sanctions on the party and/or lawyer under procedural rules; holding the party and/or lawyer civilly liable; and imposing disciplinary sanctions on the lawyer.

- In a dispute over a hotel's breach of contract to host an organization's conference, the attorney for the defendant hotel makes an initial settlement offer of $50,000. Counsel for the plaintiff organization maintains that his client's officers would never accept such an offer, that damages from the breach are likely to be much higher, and that any jury award would be more substantial. Counsel actually believes that if the case went to trial, his client would receive a substantially smaller sum. Based on that advice, the plaintiff's president had earlier authorized counsel to settle for any amount over $30,000.

  In responding to initial offer, the plaintiff's attorney also represents that it would be impossible for his client to find another suitable hotel under such short notice. When the attorney later contacts his client to report the settlement offer, he learns that another hotel has orally agreed to host the conference. When he then calls the defendant lawyer to accept the settlement, the lawyer opens the conversation by asking, "How are efforts to mitigate the damages coming along?" Plaintiff's counsel responds, "nothing definite yet." The settlement is then finalized at $50,000.[59]

- In negotiations over the property settlement in an uncontested divorce, the husband and wife disagree about the value of certain assets, including real estate and stock in a family corporation. When reviewing the wife's proposed settlement, the husband's lawyer notices a $50,000 calculation error by opposing counsel that understates her alleged interest in jointly owned real estate. The lawyer brings the matter to the attention of his client, who believes that the understated figure is a more accurate reflection of the property's true worth. Accordingly, the lawyer prepares a counteroffer repli-

59. The case is described in Monroe Freedman, "Lying: Is It Ethical?," Legal Times, Dec. 12, 1994, at 20; see also Monroe Freedman, "Acceptable Lies," Legal Times, Feb. 20, 1995, at 24.

cating the error in a way that minimizes the likelihood of its discovery. On the mistaken belief that the husband has surrendered his challenge to the value of the real estate, the wife abandons her challenge to the value and ownership of the stock. Both parties ultimately accept a version of the husband's counteroffer and sign a final agreement that recites the disposition of assets without specifying their value.[60]

- In a case involving a bank that inappropriately canceled a loan agreement, the plaintiff-borrowers describe themselves as quite "upbeat." Although they claim that their business was "ruined," they deny experiencing any severe emotional distress. In settlement negotiations, their lawyer nonetheless represents that they have greatly suffered as a result of the canceled agreement. During those discussions, counsel for the bank makes it clear that he thinks the plaintiffs have gone out of business. The plaintiff's lawyer did not make that claim. In fact, the business is continuing, and several important contracts are in the offing. The lawyer finalizes a settlement without correcting her opponent's misimpression.[61]

- In negotiations over the lease of space in a shopping center, the lawyer for the owner did not disclose that the center was about to go into foreclosure and the lessee's lawyer failed to discover that fact. After the lessees incurred costs in renovating the space, they were evicted by the company that bought the property at the foreclosure sale.[62]

In a survey of experts on legal ethics, participants considered hypothetical fact situations analogous to those above. With respect to cases like the first example, a majority of experts believed that it was impermissible for a lawyer directly to misrepresent whether a client had authorized settlement for a specific amount. Most of the others indicated that it was permissible but that they would not do it. One expert felt that lying was acceptable because an opponent didn't have a "right to the information."[63] Those who found the conduct unethical noted that experienced negotiators can generally sidestep a direct inquiry about settlement authority with responses such as "Are you able to offer more?," or "I'm authorized to get the best result I can."[64]

60. See Stare v. Tate, 98 Cal.Rptr. 264 (App.1971).

61. Larry Lempert, "In Settlement Talks, Does Telling the Truth Have Its Limits?," 2 Inside Litigation 1 (1988).

62. Davin v. Daham, 746 A.2d 1034 (N.J. Super. A. D. 2000).

63. See Lempert, supra note 61, at 16.

64. White, supra note 52, at 933 (suggesting evasive responses); Gerald

The actual case on which the hotel example is based arose during the 1960s, when the Washington, D.C. Mattachine Society planned what it billed as the first national conference to focus on gay and lesbian rights. The Manger Hotel agreed to host the conference with knowledge of its subject. Then, two weeks before the event, after publicity had begun and invitations had been mailed, management in the hotel's chain's home office ordered cancellation of the agreement. Professor Monroe Freedman, the Society's lawyer, later defended his nondisclosure of the client's successful efforts to find a new hotel.

> Was anything definite about mitigation at that point? Is anything ever definite in this life? After all, the Mattachine Society had thought that the deal with the Manger was definite, and it turned out that it wasn't.... The statement about mitigation wasn't a flat-out denial: it was equivocal—an evasion that a careful listener could have picked up on. "What do you mean 'nothing definite'?" he might have said.... [65]

According to Freedman, the new offer of a hotel site was confidential information and, as long as he did not make a false statement of material fact, he did not need to disclose it under Model Rule 4.1.

With respect to the bank loan agreement case, about two-thirds of the surveyed negotiation experts found the claims about the plaintiff's emotional distress unethical. Of the others, one reasoned that "obviously some [emotional] distress had occurred." If the clients "didn't care at all there wouldn't be a legal matter.... [The lawyer is just] embellishing the concern."[66] Another who agreed that the exaggeration was acceptable drew analogies to bargaining over the sale of a car. To him, the fundamental question was "what are your and my legitimate expectations" as opposing negotiators?[67] Professor Ronald Rotunda invoked the same analogy to arrive at a different conclusion. In his view: "If lawyers want to be like used car salesmen, this is a good place to start."[68]

Those who find "puffing" acceptable generally assume that others will recognize an exaggeration for what it is. But if that were always true, puffing would also be ineffective. The practice continues because sometimes it works and some opponents are deceived. To commentators such as Professor Rotunda and federal judge

Wetlaufer, "The Ethics of Lying in Negotiations," 75 Iowa L. Rev. 1219, 1237 (1990) (suggesting that lawyers can challenge the question as inappropriate or justify their preferred figure).

65. Freedman, "Lying: Is It Ethical?," supra note 59, at 20.

66. See Lempert, supra note 59, at 18 (quoting Charles Craver).

67. Id. (quoting James White).

68. Id. (quoting Ronald Rotunda).

Alvin Rubin, parties dealing with a lawyer should not need to exercise the same degree of caution as they would if trading at a Far Eastern bazaar.[69]

The divorce case "scrivner's error" example is based on *Stare v. Tate*, 98 Cal.Rptr. 264 (App.1971). There, the court noted:

> [t]he mistake might never have come to light had not [the husband] desired to have that exquisite last word. A few days after [the wife] had obtained the divorce he mailed her a copy of the offer which contained the errant computation. On top of the page he wrote with evident satisfaction: "PLEASE NOTE ... MISTAKE IN YOUR FIGURES."

98 Cal.Rptr. at 266.

The wife then filed suit to reform the agreement and the Court granted that motion under § 3399 of the California Code. In terms similar to caselaw in other jurisdictions, the Code provides: "When, through fraud or mutual mistake of the parties, or a mistake of one party, which the other at the time knew or suspected, a written contract does not truly express the intention of the parties, it may be revised on the application of a party aggrieved...."

The court did not consider the lawyers' obligation, but other bar ethics committees have done so. In Informal Opinion 86–1518 (Feb. 9, 1986), the ABA's Standing Committee on Ethics reviewed a situation in which a lawyer discovered that the final draft of a contract prepared by opposing counsel's office erroneously omitted a material provision. In the Committee's view, neither the Model Rules nor the Model Code required the lawyer to obtain the client's permission before correcting the mistake. Although the client had a right to know facts necessary for "informed decisions" on the matter, once he had accepted the provision, no further decision remained to be made. One could view this ABA Informal Opinion as a reflection of appropriate "paternalism," or perhaps mutual protectiveness among lawyers, to cover the kind of mistakes that are bound to occur in legal practice.

Similarly, in the shopping center case, the court held that lawyers for both sides might be liable. The lawyer for the lessee should have done a more thorough investigation. The lawyer for the lessor should have advised his client to disclose the impending foreclosure, and if the client had refused, the lawyer should have withdrawn. In the court's view, a lawyer "has a duty to represent

---

69. Alvin B. Rubin, "A Causerie on Lawyers' Ethics in Negotiations," 35 La. L. Rev. 577, 589 (1975).

his or her client effectively and vigorously," but also "to act fairly, and in good faith." The lawyer for the shopping center was in "a difficult position," but, the court added, "the practice of law is not easy."[70]

For negotiators who confront such issues, the ethical difficulties often resemble the prisoner's dilemma in game theory. As Professor Robert Condlin notes:

> When both bargainers cooperate they receive the benefits of joint action and produce an outcome that is favorable for both. When one cooperates and the other competes, the competitor usually exploits the cooperator and does better. When both compete, they waste resources in ego battles, leave money on the table out of exhaustion and polarization, and frequently end up with a mediocre outcome. In any single negotiation, choosing presents a [prisoner's] dilemma because the rational choice for each individual bargainer often leads to a mutually undesirable outcome. There are ways out of this dilemma in repeat bargaining.... But in any single negotiation, where there is no prospect for future dealing, it is usually irrational for individual bargainers to act cooperatively, and that is the bargainer's dilemma.[71]

In repetitive bargaining contexts, the "way out" is a "tit-for-tat" strategy. The most successful negotiators begin by cooperating; retaliate if the opponent engages in noncooperative or unethical practices; return to a cooperative stance if the opposing side ceases objectionable behavior; and clearly convey this intended course of action.[72] Another way that parties can escape the prisoner's dilemma is to hire attorneys who are committed to maintaining a reputation for cooperation, fairness, and candor.[73]

It might also be possible to increase the likelihood of candor and cooperation in negotiations through formal rules or informal reputational sanctions. In one large national survey of practitioners, about 40 percent believed that revising codified rules would be an effective way of improving negotiation conduct.[74] Judge Alvin Rubin has proposed such a revision:

70. Davin v. Daham, 746 A.2d 1034 (N.J. Super.A.D. 2000).

71. Robert J. Condlin, "Bargaining in the Dark: The Normative Incoherence of Lawyer's Dispute Bargaining Role," 51 Md. L. Rev. 1, 12 (1992).

72. See Fisher & Ury, supra note 55; What's Fair, supra note 55.

73. Ronald J. Gilson & Robert H. Mnookin, "Disputing Through Agents: Cooperation and Conflict Between Lawyers in Litigation," 94 Colum. L. Rev. 509 (1994).

74. Stephen Pepe, "Standards of Legal Negotiation," Interim Report for ABA Commission on Evaluation of Pro-

It is inherent in the concept of professionalism that the profession will regulate itself, adhering to an ethos that imposes standards higher than mere law observance. Client avarice and hostility neither control the lawyer's conscience nor measure his ethics. Surely if its practitioners are principled, a profession that dominates the legal process in our law-oriented society would not expect too much if it required its members to adhere to two simple principles when they negotiate as professionals: Negotiate honestly and in good faith; and do not take unfair advantage of another—regardless of his relative expertise or sophistication.[75]

Even in the absence of a codified rule, many lawyers practice under these principles. And in the long run, both they and the profession would benefit if those norms were more widely reinforced in practice. There is real "market value" in a reputation for candor and fair dealing. As one law firm partner told us: "Our firm's reputation for honesty and accuracy in dealings with the government agencies is one of the most valuable assets we have to sell on behalf of clients. There are many times when it would be difficult to prove some fact or other, but where an agency will take our word for it." Another partner reported giving advice along similar lines to a junior attorney: "If misleading text in your financial documents is not corrected immediately, you are not going to be in your firm for long, nor will you be elsewhere in practice in this town." Of course, these comments presupposed that the lawyers would be repeat players, which is what "reputation" is based on. But all lawyers are repeat players in some practice settings. And for most practitioners, reputation is one of their most crucial, and marketable, assets.

F. Lobbying

The importance of lobbying has increased dramatically over the last half century, and so also has the role of lawyer lobbyists. Before the 1950s, only a few corporations or public interest organizations and a few thousand unions and trade associations had offices in the nation's capitol. Today, over 500 corporations, 2000 public interest organizations, and 85,000 unions and trade associations have such offices.[76] Groups range in size and importance from the American

---

fessional Standards and ABA House of Delegates (1983).

75. Rubin, supra note 69, at 593.

76. Ronald G. Shaiko, "Lobbying in Washington: A Contemporary Perspective," in The Interest Group Connec-

tion: Electioneering, Lobbying, and Policymaking in Washington 3, 7–8 (Paul S. Hernson, Ronald G. Shaiko, & Clyde Wilcox eds., 1998). For an overview, see Congressional Research Service, Lobby-

Bar Association, with some 400,000 members, to the National Frozen Pizza Institute. Lobbying activities have similarly increased at the state and local level and in aggregate probably exceed those in Washington, D.C.

The number of lawyers assisting these groups has correspondingly escalated, as has the scope of their activities. "Governmental relations" work involves a broad variety of tasks, such as providing advice about political and legislative developments; preparing testimony for legislative and administrative hearings; drafting position papers and proposed statutes, regulations, and comments; negotiating government contracts; communicating a client's position to public officials and governmental bodies; and coordinating legal, political, and public relations strategies at local, state, and national levels.[77] Performing these functions effectively requires an equally wide array of capabilities, including substantive knowledge, technical expertise, personal contacts and credibility, and sound political judgment. Contrary to public image, lawyer lobbying is far less a matter of "glad handing" than of meticulous preparation.[78] Lawyers help to form an important bridge between public and private interests, and their lobbying efforts often significantly shape government policies.

This degree of influence imposes corresponding obligations. Leaders of the bar have long emphasized that when lawyers are advising on matters of public policy in a nonadversarial context, they have a special responsibility to consider public welfare. As law professor Paul Freund once put it, an attorney in this setting has a "wider scope and obligation to see around a problem unconstrained by what may be too parochial concerns of his clients, and to advise accordingly."[79] Lawyers' own reputational interests often push in similar directions. Many practitioners who specialize in governmental relations have invested a substantial part of their careers either in serving in public office or in establishing good working relations with those who do. Their effectiveness usually depends on maintaining a reputation for candor, fairness, integrity, and reasonable-

ist and Interest Groups: Sources of Information (June 10, 2005).

77. Id., at 9. For the expansion of lobbying activities, see Congressional Research Service, Lobbying Reform: Background and Legislative Proposals, 109th Congress (March 23, 2006). For the evolution of this role, see Mark J. Green, The Other Government: The Unseen Power of Washington Lawyers (1975); Edward O. Laumann, et al.,

"Washington Lawyers and Others: The Structure of Washington Representation," 37 Stan. L. Rev. 465 (1985).

78. Laumann, et al., supra note 77, at 495; Barbara Rabinovitz, "Another View of Lobbying Puts Emphasis on Public Interest and Legal Expertise," Kansas City Daily Record, May 3, 2006.

79. Green, supra note 77, at 12 (quoting Paul Freund).

ness among those with whom they will have continued dealings.[80] By the same token, government attorneys who move through the revolving door between public and private practice also have reputational concerns. The result is that governmental work generally is "characterized less by confrontation and conflict than by cooperation and compromise."[81]

Yet some issues involve intense conflict among interest groups, and between those groups and government regulators. In such contexts, the limited research available suggests that lawyer/lobbyists are no less partisan than advocates in other settings.[82] Prominent recent examples include attorneys for the tobacco industry and for now bankrupt corporations and failed savings and loan associations.[83] One legendary case history of the obstructionist abilities of Washington lawyers involved a Covington & Burling partner who fought FDA efforts to regulate the peanut content of peanut butter. The industry position was that the public was not all that concerned about what was in peanut butter as long as it tasted like peanuts. Although the government finally prevailed, its efforts required twelve years and entailed a 24,000 page hearing transcript and close to 75,000 pages of documents.[84] Such examples are a large part of what fuels widespread public distrust of lawyer/lobbyists. According to one media strategist for an attorney who had once worked in government relations before running for public office, nothing had ever "tested worse" on public image than "lawyer-lobbyist."[85]

If anything, that image has worsened after recent ethics scandals. The guilty plea by celebrated Washington lobbyist Jack Abramoff to fraud, tax evasion, and bribery charges, along with related investigations and Congressional hearings, fueled public distrust. Nearly 90 percent of surveyed Americans believe that there is a serious, or very serious, problem of political corruption in the nation's capitol.[86]

---

80. Laumann, et al., supra note 77, at 490–95.

81. Id., at 490.

82. Id.

83. See Rhode & Luban, supra note 3, at 258–61, 289–91; Ralph Nader & Wesley J. Smith, No Contest: Corporate Lawyers and the Perversion of Justice (Random House: 1998); Richard Zitrin & Carol Langford, "The Moral Compass of American Lawyers," in Truth, Justice, Power, and Greed (1999); William H. Simon, "The Kaye–Scholer Affair: The Lawyer's Duty of Candor and the Bar's

Temptations of Evasion and Apology," 23 Law & Soc. Inquiry 243, 269 (1998).

84. Green, supra note 75, at 133–39 (describing efforts of Thomas Austern).

85. Mike Soraghan, "Strickland Changes Tack on 'Lawyer Lobbyist' Label," Denver Post, Sep. 4, 2001, at A10 (quoting Bob Klein).

86. Edward Alden, "Abramoff Adds to Pressure For Clean–Up in Washington," The Financial Times (London), January 5, 2006, at 5 (citing AP–Ipos poll).

Unsurprisingly, lawyers have attempted to distance themselves from the lobbying label, and have preferred to cast themselves as "strategists" or "government relations" experts.[87] But some of these experts believe that the best way to improve popular perceptions is for attorneys to give greater consideration to the public interest in their policy work. Many highly successful government relations attorneys do so, and have withdrawn from representation when a client took a position they found unacceptable. A celebrated case involved the Washington D.C. firm that refused to assist a long-standing tobacco client in resisting requirements of warning labels on its products.

Of course, what constitutes the public interest will often be subject to dispute. On many contemporary issues involving financial, safety, and environmental regulation, there is no such agreement. Lawyer/lobbyists often take comfort from this fact and steer their work toward causes with which they are personally sympathetic. As a consequence, lobbyists are often sincere in asserting that their positions reflect the public interest.

Other ethical issues that arise in somewhat distinctive form for lawyer/lobbyists involve conflicts of interest. In order to prevent both the fact and appearance of impropriety, various federal, state, and local laws require detailed disclosure of lobbying activity; they also restrict the gifts, meals, and entertainment that lobbyists can provide to government officials.[88] Related laws regulate the revolving door between public office and private practice. One underlying concern is that government lawyers who wish to maximize their future employment options might avoid taking positions that could alienate potential clients or employers. A further concern is that when former government lawyers become lobbyists, they will inappropriately capitalize on their prior experience and relationships by gaining preferential access and exploiting confidential information.

To address such concerns, federal, state, and local legislation regulates the activities of former public officials. For example, the Ethics in Government Act, 18 U.S.C. § 207, permanently prohibits former executive branch employees (including lawyers) from representing any person on matters in which they participated "personally and substantially" while in office. The Act also provides for a two year "cooling off" period by prohibiting a former executive branch employee from making any communication to, or appearance before, a federal agency or court with the intent to influence a

87. Rabinovitz, supra note 78.

88. See Wright H. Andrews Jr., et al., New Federal Lobbying Disclosure, Gift, and Political Fund Raising Law and Rules: What You Need to Know to Do Business in Washington in 1996 (1996); Shaiko, supra note 76, at 13–15.

matter actually pending within a year preceding the employee's termination of employment. The Model Rules of Professional Conduct, Rule 1.11, like its predecessor DR 9–101(B) of the Code of Professional Responsibility, similarly bars former government lawyers from representing private clients on matters in which the lawyer had participated personally and substantially while serving in public office unless the appropriate agency gives informed written consent. However, the Model Rules permit other lawyers in the same firm to provide such representation, provided that the former government lawyer is screened from any participation and financial interest in the matter. Rule 1.11(c). These ethical provisions attempt to balance the need to prevent improper influence of public officials with the need to preserve the attractiveness of government employment for talented professionals who might later desire careers in the private sector.[89]

Another common ethical issue for lawyer/lobbyists arises in representation of trade associations. A key question is whether lawyers or firms who represent the association may undertake work adverse to one of its members. In essence, reported decisions and bar ethical opinions generally conclude that the lawyer or firm may accept such work as long as they are not deemed to represent the individual member as well as the association.[90] That is a factual question, which depends both on the member's reasonable expectations and on the likelihood that the lawyer acquired confidential information about the member during the course of representation.

A broader issue involves the ethics of representing special interest associations and coalitions that seek to mask the identity of members. The problem arises when such associations mount "stealth campaigns" to influence public policy without public accountability.[91] The problem is compounded when lawyer/lobbyists assert an attorney-client privilege to shield their activities, making it even harder for citizens, policy makers, and journalists to know who is funding the group's activities.

Whether the privilege applies to lawyers' lobbying efforts is itself a question that has gained increasing attention. In the relatively infrequent cases in which the issue has been litigated, courts

---

89. For an overview, see Rhode & Luban, supra note 3, at 616–20; Geoffrey C. Hazard, Jr., Susan P. Koniak, Roger C. Cramton, and George M. Cohen, The Law and Ethics of Lawyering 510 (4th ed., 2005).

90. D.C. Ethics Op. 305 (2001); Ernest T. Lindberg, "Representation of Trade Association," Wash. Lawyer, Feb.

2002, at 10; Westinghouse Electric Corp. v. Kerr–McGee Corp., 580 F.2d 1311 (7th Cir.1978).

91. Congressional Research Service, Lobbying Reform, supra note 77, at 3; Darrell M. West & Burdett A. Loomis, The Sound of Money: How Political Interests Get What They Want 69–70 (1998).

have generally held that political activities as such are not protected from disclosure.[92] However, when the activities may have legal significance, and advice in a matter is provided by a lawyer in a law firm (as distinct from a public relations firm), communications with the client generally are protected by the privilege. If a lawyer is engaged or acts as a public relations counselor, the issue becomes more complicated, although most attorneys have operated on the assumption that virtually all of their work is privileged.[93]

That assumption has, however, come under question as a result of two widely publicized rulings. One involved a decision by a federal district judge for the Southern District of New York that neither the attorney-client privilege nor the work-product doctrine protected documents and testimony relating to a presidential pardon request.[94] The case involved the fugitive American business executive Mark Rich, who obtained a pardon from President Clinton during his last days in office. According to the district court, Rich's lawyers were "acting principally as lobbyists and not primarily as lawyers."[95] The lead attorney who secured the pardon had been hired for his political not legal skills and his team was "being used principally to put legal trappings on what was essentially a lobbying and political effort."[96] Communications and materials connected with this effort were therefore not protected from government subpoena. In a similar ruling, a District of Columbia district judge permitted the Federal Deposit Insurance Corporation to subpoena records of Patton Boggs lawyers; their work involved political as well as legal activities on behalf of a Texas businessman implicated in the failure of a Houston Savings and Loan Association.[97]

The courts' analyses in these cases present obvious difficulties for lawyer/lobbyists, who are often hired to pursue both legal and political strategies. One possible result is that more firms will attempt to construct strong ethical screens between litigation and lobbying.[98] Another possibility is that clients will be less disposed to

92. Edna Selan Epstein, The Attorney–Client Privilege and the Work-Product Doctrine 231 (ABA Section on Litigation 2001).

93. Luke Mullins, "Open Secrets?: Some Worry About Threats to Lobbyists' Attorney–Client Privilege," Roll Call, July 27, 2005.

94. In re Grand Jury Subpoenas dated March 9, 2001, 179 F.Supp.2d 270 (S.D.N.Y. 2001).

95. Id., at 289.

96. Id., at 290.

97. James Grimaldi, "FDIC Case Against Texas Businessman Hurwitz Moves Forward with Approval of Subpoena," Washington Post, April 12, 2002, at E01.

98. Louis Jacobson, "Were They Lawyers or Lobbyists?," Nat. L J., Jan. 12, 2002, at 109.

hire lawyers for multifaceted governmental relations work, or to be less candid with those they do hire.[99] However, neither possibility appears to have occurred in the first several years following the decisions.[100] And a countervailing benefit is that prosecutors and the press will face fewer obstacles in discovering illegal conduct and in providing a credible deterrent for lawyers' involvement in such conduct. Yet in this context, the best deterrent may be lawyers' own internalized standards, reinforced by the profession's workplace norms and practices. The same may be true of other ethical issues involving transactional practice where the need for public trust often outstrips the capacity for effective regulation.

99. Id.   **100.** Mullins, supra note 93.

Chapter VIII

CONFLICTS OF INTEREST

A. Introduction

Basic to the client-lawyer relationship is the duty of loyalty. Conflicts of interest arise when lawyers have other professional or personal relationships that could compromise that loyalty. These conflicts are a common and increasingly contested feature of American legal practice. A rapid growth in the size of private firms and their organizational clients, together with the expansion of branch offices and corporate subsidiaries, has increased the possibility of actual, attenuated, or inadvertent conflicts. More client engagements of law firms involve short-term specific matters, rather than long-term retainers, so the typical "portfolio" of law firm clients is in constant turnover. So too, an increase in lateral mobility among lawyers has led to a corresponding turnover in personnel, so firms face an escalating need for conflicts checks and a growing risk of vicarious disqualification. Similarly, a growing specialization in legal practice within and among firms has generated greater potential for simultaneous or successive representation of competing interests. The more technically complex the matter, the greater the premium placed on prior expertise and the greater the likelihood that the client will seek an attorney who has had some previous involvement with the general subject-matter. That involvement can often provide a basis for disqualification.

Firms that enjoy geographic, substantive or "social network" monopolies are most likely to encounter demands for assistance from parties that have, or might have, conflicting concerns.[1] In response to a survey by Susan Shapiro of the American Bar Foundation, large firms estimated that they turn away anywhere from a third to a half of all potential cases because of conflicts of interest; small firms estimated that they decline five to ten percent of prospective business for that reason.[2]

As conflicts problems have grown more pervasive, so also have conflicts disputes, both within and across firms. In firms' internal dealings, the issue of which business to accept has become increasingly divisive. "Conflicts over conflicts" can often trigger major turf

---

1. Susan P. Shapiro, Tangled Loyalties: Conflict of Interest in Legal Practice (Ann Arbor: University of Michigan Press, 2002).

2. Id.

disputes and occasionally the defection of partners unable to take on matters that encroach on colleagues' clientele. Firms have also needed more elaborate oversight procedures to prevent opportunistic lawyers from accepting questionable matters in the hopes that potential conflicts will not materialize, will not be detected, or will not be protested.[3] In attorneys' external relationships, the conflicts issue now generates frequent disputes, primarily because of the disqualification remedy typically pursued. Unlike other ethical rules, which usually are enforced through bar disciplinary actions or malpractice proceedings after the fact, violations of conflicts rules can result in disqualification of the offending attorney before or during representation. If a court finds that a lawyer has misused confidential information, it may also prohibit the lawyer from turning over work products to successor counsel. Such disqualification remedies are a powerful strategic weapon for increasing an opponent's expense and delay. So too, when clients suffer substantial costs from disqualification or inadequate representation due to conflicts of interest, they are increasingly likely to sue for malpractice. These remedies help explain why conflicts doctrine has been so extensively litigated.

Conflicts of interest can arise in a wide variety of circumstances but generally take one of the following forms:

- Multiple representation: representing more than one client in the same matter when their interests may diverge;

- Successive representation: representing a current client against a former client in a related matter;

- "Personal" conflicts: representing clients in a context where their interests conflict with the attorney's own financial, professional, or other interests (including those of close family members);

- Positional conflicts: representing a client whose legal position could adversely affect another client in a factually unrelated matter;

- Vicarious conflicts: representing clients in a matter where another member of the lawyer's organization has one of the preceding non-personal conflicts.

---

3. Geoffrey C. Hazard, Jr. & Ted Schneyer, "Regulatory Controls in Large Law Firms," 44 Ariz. L. Rev. 593 (2002). Elizabeth Chambliss, "The Professionalization of Law Firm In–House Counsel," 84 N. Car. L. Rev. 1515, 563–66 (2006). For an example of how those procedures can fail in the face of strong attorney self-interest, see Milton C. Regon, Eat What You Kill: The Fall of a Walk Street Lawyer (2004).

The term "lawyer for the situation" was coined by Louis Brandeis in the 1916 Senate hearings on his proposed confirmation as a Justice of the United States Supreme Court. Brandeis' appointment had aroused considerable opposition partly on the unstated grounds that he was liberal and Jewish, and partly on the stated grounds that he had represented parties with conflicting interests. Critics objected to his representation of a family business after a dispute arose among family members, his oversight of a business transaction for several different parties, and his mediation of differences between owners and creditors of a business in order to keep it afloat. Although the clients had given their consent, dispute centered on whether Brandeis could adequately represent the conflicting interests involved and whether he had provided sufficient information to the parties concerning the risks of joint representation. While acknowledging that his disclosures may not always have been sufficient, Brandeis defended his practice of acting as "lawyer for the situation." Eventually, the ethical accusations subsided in the face of acknowledgements by other reputable lawyers that they had engaged in similar conduct.[4]

Brandeis' view of the lawyer's role has inspired continuing debate. Critics have objected that lawyers are not retained by a "situation," and that they and their clients may have very different views as to what a given context requires.[5] The interests of multiple clients are seldom, if ever, totally congruent, and if subsequent disputes arise, an advocate for "everyone" may look like an advocate for no one.

The key concept in bar ethical rules and the law of disqualification concerning multiple representation is "adversity" of interests. That concept refers both to the likelihood that a conflict will develop, and to the probable intensity of any that does. The issue is not only whether parties have divergent interests or inclinations, but also how far they are likely to pursue their differences.[6] That, in turn, often depends on legal advice, which sometimes threatens to make the conflict inquiry circular. The parties are asking the lawyer whether problems are likely to develop, while the lawyer should be asking the same question.

---

4. Geoffrey C. Hazard, Jr., Ethics in the Practice of Law 58–62 (1978); Richard W. Painter, Contracting Around Conflicts in a Family Representation: Louis Brandeis and the Warren Trust, 8 U. Chic. L. Sch. Roundtable 353 (2001).

5. John P. Frank, "The Legal Ethics of Louis D. Brandeis," 17 Stan. L. Rev.

683, 702 (1965); John S. Dzienkowski, "Lawyers as Intermediaries: The Representation of Multiple Clients in the Modern Legal Profession," 1992 U. Ill. L. Rev. 741, 784 (1992).

6. Hazard, supra note 4, at 69.

As a general matter, multiple representation carries both benefits and costs. For parties, it avoids the expense and possible acrimony involved in having separate counsel. For lawyers, serving all the parties may result in additional fees and less delay and divisiveness. The risk, however, is that if a conflict develops, parties can end up with even more costs and delays than if they had been separately represented from the outset. They will need to hire their own separate counsel, who typically will have to duplicate or even contest prior legal work. Under such circumstances, attorneys often become scapegoats for problems not necessarily of their making. In contexts of multiple representation, lawyers are expected both to be fair and to seem fair to everyone. They are also expected to foresee the likelihood of conflict at the outset. This is an inherently difficult task, since it will depend not only on the objective facts of a transaction but also on the subjective attitudes of parties, all of which can change over time.[7]

Like other professions, the bar's preferred method of dealing with most conflicts of interest is disclosure and informed consent. Here too, this strategy poses obvious advantages and costs. On its face, disclosure offers something to everyone. It increases the information available to affected parties but enables professionals to engage in lucrative activities.[8] Yet research on disclosure strategies reveal that they are highly imperfect responses to conflicts of interest. Various cognitive biases prevent individuals from adequately adjusting for misleading information even when conflicts are fully disclosed. Because so much self-serving bias operates at unconscious levels, neither those who give, nor those who receive, skewed advice may appreciate the extent of the problem. Moreover, people have difficulty ignoring or discounting information even when they are aware that it is inaccurate.[9] A further problem is that informed consent strategies may reduce professionals' feelings of concern about potentially misleading advice, and encourage them to merely disclose, rather than avoid, compromising influences. In some experiments, disclosure actually leads to more inaccurate decision making than non-disclosure.[10] In the context of lawyer-

---

7. Id. at 70–73.

8. Daylian M. Cain, George Loewenstein, & Don A. Moore, "The Dirt on Coming Clean: Perverse Effects of Disclosing Conflicts of Interest," 34 J. Legal Studies 1, 2 (2005) Paul M. Healy and Krishna G. Palepu, "Information Assymetry: Corporate Disclosure and the Capital Markets: A Review of the Empirical Disclosure Literature," 31 J. Accounting & Econ. 405 (2001).

9. Don A. Moore & George Loewenstein, "Self–Interest, Automaticity, and the Psychology of Conflict of Interest," 17 Social Justice Research 189 (2004); Cain, Loewenstein & Moore, "The Dirt on Coming Clean," supra note 8, at 3.

10. Cain, Loewenstein & Moore, "The Dirt on Coming Clean," supra note 8, at 3. In their experiment, subjects played one of two roles: estimators or advisors. Estimators attempted to

client relationships, such research underscores the need for rules preventing, as well as disclosing, serious risks of conflicting interests.

B. Simultaneous Representation of Multiple Interests

The primary ethical rule governing simultaneous representation is Model Rule 1.7. In terms generally similar to its predecessor, DR 5–105, Rule 1.7 prohibits representation that will be "directly adverse" to another client or that presents a "significant risk" of being "materially limited" by obligations to another client. The first of these restrictions prohibits a lawyer or law firm from representing opposing parties in litigation and in similar contentious proceedings. This restriction on directly adverse representation cannot be waived; clients cannot consent to such simultaneous representation because of the likely negative effects on their own interests and on the system of justice. Model Rule 1.7(b)(3). The second restriction, which applies both to litigation relationships and to transactional matters, prohibits a lawyer from representing a client when doing so is likely to be significantly constrained by responsibilities to another client. This restriction can be waived; clients who have full information can consent in writing to such simultaneous representation if lawyers "reasonably believe" that they will be able to provide "competent and diligent assistance to each affected client." Model Rule 1.7(b)(1).[11]

As the Restatement (Third) of the Law Governing Lawyers notes, another reason to prohibit joint representation of adverse parties in litigation involves the need to protect "the integrity of a proceeding."[12] A lawyer who attempted to present both sides of a dispute might fail to provide the forceful advocacy necessary for informed decisionmaking. Both the fact and appearance of justice would be at risk, and reported cases recognize as much.

---

gauge an uncertain quantity of coins in a jar and were rewarded for accuracy. Advisors were provided with a better view of the jar and were told to advise the estimators. In one variation of the experiment, advisors were paid more when the estimator gave a high, rather than accurate estimate, and this incentive was disclosed. In this variation of the experiment, estimators gave more inaccurate answers than when advisors had no such incentive or when their incentive was not disclosed. Id., at 16–22.

11. The Code provision, DR 5–105, is cast in somewhat different terms, but has essentially the same meaning in application. It provides that lawyers must decline representation if their professional judgment on behalf of another client will be "adversely affected," or if it is not "obvious" that they can "adequately represent the interests of each."

12. Restatement (Third) of the Law Governing Lawyers, § 201 (1991). See also Fred C. Zacharias, "Waiving Conflicts of Interest," 108 Yale L. J. 407, 413–415 (1998).

California is the only state with a significantly different ethical rule. It permits any joint representation where clients give informed consent. California Rule 3–310(B). However, California courts have declined to permit joint representation of clients with an actual (as opposed to potential) conflict during litigation, on the ground that any purported consent would be "neither intelligent nor informed."[13]

In assessing whether clients are in a position to give informed consent, courts and commentators stress several factors:

- the nature of client interests and services to be provided;
- the timing, extent, and intelligibility of lawyers' disclosures concerning issues such as loyalty, confidentiality and the attorney-client privilege;
- clients' capacity to assess the nature of their interests and the consequences of joint representation; and
- clients' ability to exercise uncoerced choice.

So, for example, in matters involving large stakes, unstable circumstances, and adversarial or coercive relationships, joint representation is far less likely to be appropriate than in matters involving smaller stakes, routine services, and cooperative, ongoing relationships. A factor of obvious importance, frequently noted in reported decisions, is whether the client was independently represented in considering and agreeing to a waiver. The most common situation of this kind is where an independent law firm seeks a waiver from a corporate client that is advised by its in-house law department. Conflict waivers obtained on this basis are, quite properly, difficult to invalidate.

The middle ground among these extremes is where most problems arise. Particularly when dealing with unsophisticated parties, prudent lawyers make sure to provide a realistic appraisal of the advantages as well as costs of separate counsel. Many individuals who are involved in coordinated projects are understandably inclined to take an optimistic view of their ventures and to discount the likelihood of later conflicts. Lawyers, who have their own interests in maximizing fees and minimizing transaction costs, may be similarly inclined. But as the Restatement (Third) of the Law Governing Lawyers, § 202 notes, informed consent requires that the client have "reasonably adequate information about the material risks [involved]." And all participants will be well served if the attorney attempts to be as candid as possible in projecting those risks.

---

13. Klemm v. Superior Court, 142 Cal. Rptr. 509, 512 (App. 1977).

Clients can waive future as well as current conflicts of interest. The ABA Ethics Committee in Formal Opinion 93–372 (Apr. 16, 1993), severely discouraged the practice, and warned that such a waiver must describe the conflict with sufficient clarity so that the client's consent is truly informed. A prospective waiver that does not identify either the potential opposing party or at least the class of potentially conflicting clients and interests would be unlikely to survive scrutiny. Id. However, as subsequent discussion notes, the ABA and the Restatement have since taken a more permissive position, particularly where the client is sophisticated and adequately informed. In-house counsel for businesses often advise them to waive present and future conflicts (sometimes on condition of appropriate screening), in order to obtain representation from a well-qualified outside lawyer. Less sophisticated individual clients are also highly likely to provide waivers, often based on lawyers' assurance that they can provide effective representation.[14]

Joint representation of multiple plaintiffs or defendants in litigation poses special concerns. The chief advantages to litigants from representation by the same lawyer are readily apparent. First, and most obviously, the clients save money. By pooling their resources, parties often obtain the services of an expert attorney who would otherwise be unaffordable. In some civil and white-collar criminal contexts, an employer may be willing to subsidize a unified defense but reluctant to pay for separate counsel for all employees as well as the organization, unless required to do so by an indemnification agreement. From the standpoint of both individuals and their employer, joint representation can facilitate mutually advantageous "stonewalling," in which the attorney is able to coordinate a "common front" by multiple litigants or targets of investigations.

However, each of these advantages of multiple representation carries corresponding disadvantages. Most obviously, the lawyer might forego opportunities to assist one client at the expense of another. Where a common front strategy is being subsidized by an employer (or by an organized crime conspiracy), counsel might refrain from negotiating a settlement or plea agreement that would be advantageous for one client in exchange for cooperation that would adversely affect others.

Joint representation can be a risky proposition even when the attorney attempts in good faith to advance the individual interests of multiple clients. If a common front does not work, hindsight may

---

14. Leonard E. Gross, "Are Differences Among the Attorney Conflict of Interest Rules Consistent with Principles of Behavioral Economics?," 19 Geo. J. Legal Ethics 111, 136 (2006).

show that one of the clients would have been better off with a separate deal. Professor Kenneth Mann's study of white collar criminal defense describes this fact-pattern: "[E]ach client holds inculpatory evidence against the other, and the government has just enough evidence to consider asking for an indictment against each, but not enough to dismiss the option of granting immunity to one client in order to get determinative evidence against the other." Mann concludes that "it is difficult for an attorney to act without compromising one of the client's interests. If he advises neither to make a deal because he believes that he may be able to win the case for both, he is sacrificing certain success for one of them. And he clearly cannot advise one to make a deal against the other's interest."[15]

This fact-pattern reflects the well-known "prisoner's dilemma" in game theory discussed in Chapter VII. If both clients refuse to cooperate, each may stand a better chance of escaping indictment than if both try to bargain where the prosecutor will immunize only one of them. But, from another point of view, each fares better trying for an immunity arrangement regardless of what the other one does. If his codefendant refuses to cooperate, the client who makes the deal obtains immunity while the stonewalling partner goes to jail. Conversely, if his codefendant strikes a bargain, the client's refusal to cooperate is a path to likely conviction. The prisoner's dilemma makes it rational for each client to seek immunity, even though both can foresee that the other will do the same, and that they would both be better off stonewalling. As two game theorists put it: "True, players will find themselves completely frustrated; nonetheless they have no real alternative."[16]

Lawyers advising clients under such circumstances confront a similar dilemma. Those who propose a common front strategy are asking the clients to trust each other, even though each client should know that the other has a strong incentive to deal with the prosecution. But is it prudent to counsel a client to trust someone who has such a powerful reason to violate that trust? Moreover, each client knows that the other knows about that reason. Each, therefore, has grounds to suspect that the other will undertake a "preemptive" deal. As a practical matter, the lawyer's role in such contexts may sometimes be to try to convince each client that the other is trustworthy. By breaking the spiral of mutual suspicion, the lawyer may be able to prevent bargains that are less desirable

---

15. Kenneth Mann, Defending White Collar Crime: A Portrait of Attorneys at Work 170 (1985).

16. Duncan Luce & Howard Raiffa, Games and Decisions 101 (1957).

than a united strategy. But this requires advising clients to follow a course that carries significant risks.

These risks are by no means unique to criminal proceedings. Similar dilemmas often arise in civil litigation. For example, codefendants may have common interests in opposing the plaintiff's claims but each may also have incentives to settle and to offer evidence shifting liability to the other. However, in criminal cases, multiple representation poses special concern because of the constitutional interests at issue. Supreme Court decisions have established standards for determining when conflicts of interest jeopardize a defendant's Sixth Amendment right to effective assistance of counsel. In Holloway v. Arkansas, 435 U.S. 475 (1978), the Court held that a conviction will be reversed when counsel is forced to represent codefendants over a timely objection unless the trial court finds that no conflict of interest existed. In Cuyler v. Sullivan, 446 U.S. 335 (1980), the Court declined to extend this reversal rule to circumstances in which no objection is made. In such cases, the conviction will be overturned only if the defendant can demonstrate that a conflict of interest adversely affected the lawyer's performance. And in Mickens v. Taylor, 535 U.S. 162 (2002), the Court adhered to that rule even in a capital murder case where the trial judge appointed a lawyer to represent the defendant who had also been counsel to the murder victim and where the court made no inquiry into possible conflicts of interest.

By the same token, the Supreme Court has sustained a trial court's grant of a prosecution motion to disqualify counsel over a defendant's objection. Wheat v. United States, 486 U.S. 153 (1988). The government's concern was that a defendant might, in a subsequent proceeding, assert the defense lawyer's conflict of interest in order to establish ineffective assistance of counsel. Of course, allowing the government to assert a conflict when the defendant has waived any such objection opens the possibility that the government's true motive is to remove a particularly effective adversary. However, the Court expressed confidence that trial judges can take that possibility into account when ruling on joint representation. Id. The underlying concept is that a conflict is, in effect, "unwaivable" if it is of "such a serious nature that no rational defendant would knowingly and intelligently desire that attorney's representation."[17]

The problems created by multiple representation in criminal cases, including the effects of successful stonewall defenses on the

---

17. United States v. Schwarz, 283 F.3d 76, 95 (2d Cir. 2002). See also United States v. Fulton, 5 F.3d 605 (2d Cir. 1993).

administration of justice, have led some countries' legal systems to require separate counsel.[18] Supporters of this approach point out that the tactical advantages of multiple representation could be accomplished with fewer risks through joint defense agreements among separately represented parties. Such agreements permit defendants to share confidential information without waiving the attorney-client privilege.[19] However, separate representation under these agreements still imposes the financial costs of duplicative work, which individual defendants and state-subsidized indigent defense systems are sometimes unable or unwilling to assume. In any event, as long as joint representation is a viable option, defense counsel have a special responsibility to ensure that clients are fully aware of the risks before accepting such arrangements.

In civil litigation, although conflicts doctrine generally prohibits lawyers from representing opposing parties, courts have occasionally carved out exceptions. One involves divorce. The rise of no-fault procedures and the public interest in reducing their financial and emotional costs have led to more permissive approaches. An increasing number of jurisdictions permit joint representation of both spouses in limited circumstances of uncontentious separations after full disclosure by the attorney and separate consent of each spouse. Other states maintain that the potential of conflicting interests and the problems of confidentiality are sufficient to bar dual representation.

Taken together, court decisions and expert commentary suggest several rules of thumb for lawyers in multiple representation contexts. Fully informed consent is necessary but not sufficient. An attorney may be unable to provide adequate assistance to both parties where they have substantially unequal bargaining power, where one spouse dominates the decision-making of the other, or where the attorney's special relationship with one party makes the fact or appearance of neutrality difficult to sustain.[20]

In most civil litigation contexts, if parties have given informed consent to a conflict, they will have great difficulty convincing a court to set aside a judgment on grounds that their representation was inadequate and that the lawyer improperly obtained a conflict waiver. However, if the facts are sufficiently compelling, judges will attempt to give teeth to bar ethical requirements. A celebrated case

---

18. Deborah L. Rhode & David Luban, Legal Ethics 465 (3d ed. 2001) (discussing West Germany's prohibition on joint representation).

19. See Amy Foote, Note, "Joint Defense Agreements in Criminal Prosecu-

tions: Tactical and Ethical Implications," 12 Geo. J. Legal Ethics 377 (1999).

20. See Rhode & Luban, supra note 18, at 579.

in point is Amchem Products, Inc. v. Windsor, 521 U.S. 591 (1997), which set aside a class action certification on the basis of class counsel's conflict of interest. A more common remedy if clients can establish an improper conflict that impaired their representation is a malpractice judgment against the lawyer along the lines discussed in Chapter XII.

C. Positional Conflicts of Interest

A "positional" conflict of interest arises when a lawyer for one client adopts a position that might have a negative impact on another client who is not directly involved in the matter. A familiar example is the assertion of a novel theory for protection of borrowers that is advanced by a lawyer who also represents commercial lenders, such as banks. A positional conflict arises when the theory, if accepted by the courts, could be disadvantageous to banks in the future.

Neither the Code nor the Model Rules categorically forbid positional conflicts of interest. Yet both codes include prohibitions that would encompass such conflicts in certain situations. First, if a positional conflict would compromise the lawyer's "independent professional judgment" on behalf of either client, it is impermissible under Model Rule 2.1 and its predecessor DR 5–105 of the Code. If the representation would be directly adverse to another client, it would be impermissible under Model Rule 1.7(a)(1). If a positional conflict risks the misuse of a client's confidences, it is impermissible under Model Rule 1.6 and its predecessor DR 4–101 of the Code.

With respect to influences on lawyers' judgment and performance, the Comment to Model Rule 1.7(b) states:

> Ordinarily a lawyer may take inconsistent legal positions in different tribunals at different times on behalf of different clients. The mere fact that advocating a legal position on behalf of one client might create precedent adverse to the interests of a client represented by the lawyer in an unrelated matter does not create a conflict of interest. A conflict of interest exists, however, if there is a significant risk that a lawyer's action on behalf of one client will materially limit the lawyer's effectiveness in representing another client in a different case; for example, when a decision favoring one client will create a precedent likely to seriously weaken the position taken on behalf of the other client. Factors relevant in determining whether the clients need to be advised of the risk include: where the cases are pending, whether the issue is substantive or procedural, the temporal relationship between the matters,

the significance of the issue to the immediate and long-term interests of the clients involved and the clients' reasonable expectations in retaining the lawyer. If there is significant risk of material limitation, then absent informed consent of the affected clients, the lawyer must refuse one of the representations or withdraw from one or both matters.[21]

Under that framework, the important questions are what constitutes a limitation on effectiveness and who should decide.

Significant positional conflicts clearly run the risk of antagonizing clients. Causing distress to a client (such as a bank in the example above) does not, and should not, amount to a violation of the ethics codes (although, of course, it might lead the client to employ other counsel). In practice, lawyers and firms frequently find themselves taking positions that run counter to the concerns of some client or other. That is particularly the case when lawyers are working pro bono at the same time as representing businesses dealing with the public or for paying clients in cases with broad societal consequences. Free expression of legal argument, with its corresponding public interest implications, gives life to the ideal of professional independence.[22]

Protecting the independence of lawyers is also important to ensuring their participation in law reform and related bar association efforts. Although such activity is sometimes undertaken for paying clients, it may also reflect disinterested judgments by well-informed professionals, who advocate views that their clients reject. The bar has long supported such advocacy. Ethical Consideration 8–1 of the ABA Code emphasizes that lawyers "should participate in proposing and supporting legislation and programs to improve the system, without regard to the general interests or desires of clients or former clients," EC 7–17 similarly insists that a lawyer "may take positions on public issues and espouse legal reforms he favors without regard to the individual views of any client." Model Rule 1.6 continues this tradition by providing that lawyers "may serve . . . an organization involved in reform of the law . . . notwithstanding that the reform may affect the interests of a client." Such professional independence is central to a well functioning democracy, which requires that individuals knowledgeable about the inadequacies of legal policy feel free to address it.

---

21. The American Law Institute's Restatement (Third) of The Law Governing Lawyers, § 128, Cmt. f, takes the same position.

22. See Ronald D. Rotunda, "Alleged Conflicts of Interest Because of the 'Appearance of Impropriety,' " 33 Hofstra L. Rev. 1141, 1143 (2005); Norman W. Spaulding, "The Prophet and the Bureaucrat: Positional Conflicts in Service Pro Bono Publico," 50 Stan. L. Rev. 1395 (1998).

In its Restatement (Third) of the Law Governing Lawyers, the American Law Institute amplifies these well settled principles. According to its summary of the law, attorneys may take a public position on a controversial issue that is contrary to the views of clients without obtaining their consent.[23] An alternative view would compromise both societal and professional interests. For example, "if tax lawyers advocating positions about tax reform were obliged to advocate only positions that would serve the positions of their present clients, the public would lose the objective contributions to policy making of some persons most able to help."[24]

A variation of positional conflicts involves what are often termed "ideological" conflicts. One such conflict arises when a lawyer's position in a particular matter antagonizes another client even though its interests are not directly implicated. These conflicts help explain why specialists in certain substantive areas typically represent only "one side of the street"; personal injury plaintiffs' lawyers generally do not take insurance defense cases, and union lawyers do not represent management.

Another type of ideological conflict involves political positions. These conflicts are particularly likely to arise when lawyers take pro bono cases or engage in other public service that is offensive to paying clients. In one national survey, about forty percent of lawyers reported that their organization discouraged pro bono work likely to advance positions inconsistent with client's interests or values.[25] Yet lawyers' willingness to take unpopular cases can also be a source of enormous pride, both for them and for the profession. Bar associations often confer their highest awards on lawyers who have risked alienating other clients or potential sources of business. Part of what distinguishes law as a profession is the willingness of its members to put principles above profit by engaging in pro bono work.

D. Successive Representation

Conflicts between a current and former client pose somewhat different concerns than conflicts among current clients. To current clients, lawyers owe obligations of loyalty and confidentiality. To former clients, the obligations of loyalty are far more circumscribed. Protecting former clients in perpetuity according to the same

---

23. Restatement, supra note 17, § 125 comment e (2000).

24. Id.

25. Deborah L. Rhode, Pro Bono in Principle and in Practice 146 (2004). See also Esther F. Lardent, "Positional Con-flicts in the Pro Bono Context: Ethical Considerations and Market Forces," 67 Fordham L. Rev. 2279 (1999); Spauld-ing, supra note 16; John S. Dzienkowski, "Positional Conflicts of Interest," 71 Tex. L. Rev. 457 (1993).

standard applicable to current clients would virtually destroy independent law practice: A lawyer who once served a client could never undertake a matter adverse to that client. As attorneys' careers progressed and their number of past clients increased, their ability to accept new cases would proportionately decrease. In effect, counsel would become forever identified with particular clients and causes.

However, although lawyers should be able to accept matters that are adverse to former clients, some obligations to those clients persist after representation is over. Lawyers may not use the confidences of former clients against them and may not directly attack work done for those clients. With respect to loyalty, the Restatement (Third) of the Law Governing Lawyers § 132, Comment b explains: "[A]t the time the lawyer represented the former client, the lawyer should have no incentive to lay the basis for subsequent representation against that client, such as by drafting provisions in a contract that could later be construed against the former client."

With respect to the protections involving confidentiality, courts and ethical codes have focused on whether there is a substantial relationship between a current and previous representation. Under Model Rule 1.9, "[a] lawyer who has formerly represented a client in a matter shall not thereafter represent another person in the same or a substantially related matter in which that person's interests are materially adverse to the interests of the former client unless the former client gives informed consent, confirmed in writing." Matters are considered substantially related if there is a "substantial risk that confidential factual information as would normally have been obtained in the prior representation would materially advance the client's position in the subsequent matter." Model Rule 1.9 comment.[26] When the previous and new matters are "substantially related," a presumption arises that the lawyer obtained relevant confidences and that a conflict of interest therefore exists. The rationale for that presumption is that former clients should not have to prove that confidences actually passed, which might require information impossible to obtain or disclosure of the very matters that were intended to remain secret.[27]

However, under the Model Rules, the presumption of disabling confidences does not apply if representation was provided by a firm

---

26. See also Restatement, supra note 17, § 132, Comment.

27. See T.C. Theatre Corp. v. Warner Bros. Pictures, 113 F.Supp. 265, 268 (S.D.N.Y. 1953); Analytica Inc. v. NPD Research Inc., 708 F.2d 1263, 1266 (7th Cir. 1983).

that the lawyer has left and the lawyer had no personal involvement with the prior matter. Model Rule 1.9(b) provides that where an attorney's former firm represented a client in the same or substantially related matter, the attorney may accept a new representation unless the interests of the current client are adverse and the attorney personally acquired relevant confidential information. Similarly, in cases where the representation involves matters that are not substantially related, Model Rule 1.9(c) requires simply that the attorney not use confidential information to the disadvantage of the former client. In addition, under Model Rule 1.10(b), lawyers remaining in a firm that a lawyer has left are not barred from taking matters adverse to the departing lawyer's client if none of the remaining lawyers were personally involved in the prior matter.

Somewhat more permissive rules apply to former government lawyers. The Code and Model Rules reflect the approach taken by most courts and bar ethics committees and codified in the Federal Ethics in Government Act.[28] Model Rule 1.11(a) provides that a lawyer who has formerly served as a public officer or employee of a government agency may not use confidential information to the disadvantage of the government and may not "represent a client in connection with a matter in which the lawyer participated personally and substantially as a public officer or employee, unless the appropriate government agency gives its informed consent, confirmed in writing, to the representation." Under Model Rule 1.11(b), when a government lawyer is disqualified from representation:

> no lawyer in a firm with which that lawyer is associated may knowingly undertake or continue representation in such a matter unless:
>
> (1) the disqualified lawyer is timely screened from any participation in the matter and is apportioned no part of the fee therefrom; and
>
> (2) written notice is promptly given to the appropriate government agency to enable it to ascertain compliance with the provisions of this rule.

See also DR 9–101(B).

The permissibility of screening for government lawyers reflects the fact that many of these lawyers do not plan on remaining permanently in public service. The American political system contemplates that governmental leadership, including high-level lawyers, will leave office if their political party loses. After such a loss,

28. 18 U.S.C. §§ 201–219. See ABA Formal Op. 342 (1976).

the lawyers then typically return to the private sector, and often hope for a later return to public service. Many lower ranking lawyers also take civil service jobs for a relatively short period with the hope of acquiring skills and contacts that will be useful to them in the private sector. These patterns are commonly described as a "revolving door." If conflict of interest rules for former public officials were too stringent, the revolving door would stop revolving, and the ability of government to recruit talented lawyers (especially at the relatively low salary levels now prevailing) would be seriously compromised. Undue restrictions on career mobility would also deprive the public sector of fresh perspectives, and would deprive the private sector of lawyers with valuable government experience. Civil servants who have alternative job possibilities may also be more able to challenge government positions that appear inconsistent with the public interest. And private lawyers who have held significant government positions may have more experience, stature, and credibility in counseling clients on legal compliance issues.[29]

Yet concerns for both the fact and appearance of integrity among former public officials make some regulation necessary. Screening has been the strategy of choice. Accordingly, as noted below, a screen around a former government lawyer prevents imputation of the lawyer's conflicts to others in the new practice situation. However, validation of the screening mechanism in this context has raised a fundamental question about conflicts rules more generally. If such a mechanism works for former government employees, why wouldn't it work for other lawyers as well?

E. Vicarious Disqualification, Screening, and Waivers

The [bar's] traditional position on conflicts of interest has been that the disqualification of one lawyer in a law firm or other legal organization is imputed to all its other members. Model Rule 1.10, DR 5—105(b). The only exceptions are for government lawyers and for conflicts that are "based on a personal interest of the prohibited lawyer and . . . [that do] not present a significant risk of materially limiting the representation of the client by the remaining lawyers in the firm." Model Rule 1.10(a); DR 9–101(B). The theory underlying vicarious disqualification is that colleagues share revenue, reputation and future prospects, as well as opportunities for exchange of confidences that are not readily detected. Professor Charles Wolfram summarizes the conventional objection to screening: "In the

---

29. Robert W. Gordon, "Private Career Building and Public Benefits: Reflections on 'Doing Well By Doing Good'," 41 Houston L. Rev. 113, 131–32 (2004).

end there is little but the self-serving assurance of the screening-lawyer foxes that they will carefully guard the screened-lawyer chickens."[30] One of the few efforts to test that proposition found that virtually all surveyed lawyers believed that an opponent's screen could be breached without detection.[31]

Yet strict vicarious disqualification rules have come to seem more and more problematic in an era of increasing size among law firms and increasing lateral mobility among their members. Particularly in large firms, which have hundreds of lawyers spread over multiple branch offices, a presumption of shared confidences appears anachronistic, and may unduly restrict clients' access to qualified counsel. The approach developed in accounting firms of "insulation walls" to segregate employees with conflicts of interest has accordingly gained support in the legal profession as well. A growing number of states have provided that screening is an adequate response for at least some conflicts.[32]

The ABA Ethics 2000 Commission recommended that screening be permitted, with notice to any affected clients, when a disqualified lawyer makes a lateral move to a new firm, as long as any confidential information is not likely to be significant in the future representation. The Commission based its recommendation on the absence of virtually any complaints of harm in the jurisdictions that have permitted screening, some of which have allowed the practice for over a decade. The Commission also heard substantial evidence concerning problems with the current rule: undue restraints on the mobility of lawyers, excessive costs to parties, unnecessary burdens on courts handling disqualification motions, and unreasonable assumptions that screening can work for former government lawyers but not for anyone else. Although the ABA House of Delegates rejected the Commission's proposed rule on screening, it is likely to remain a subject of ongoing debate and a model for adoption by some states.

30. Charles Wolfram, Modern Legal Ethics 402 (1986).

31. Lee A. Pizzimenti, "Screen Verite: Do Rules About Ethical Screens Reflect the Truth About Real–Life Law Firm Practice?," 52 U. Miami L. Rev. 305, 331–32 (1997).

32. A 2006 survey revealed that eleven states had rules permitting the screening of lateral lawyers regardless of the screened lawyers' level of knowledge or degree of involvement in the matter at the former firm. Most jurisdictions require notice to the former client and prohibit the screened lawyer from sharing in the fees generated by the matter. Seven other states have rules that permit screening in certain circumstances. Relevant factors include the degree of the lawyers' involvement in the former matter and the likelihood that information acquired previously would be relevant in the subsequent matter. Attorneys' Liability Assurance Society, Loss Prevention Manual (2006).

As matters now stand, firms take a variety of approaches in identifying conflicts of interest. Susan Shapiro's American Bar Foundation study found four primary strategies. A few lawyers, the "ostriches" of the group, do not specifically address the issue and hope for the best. A small minority, the "elephants," trust that they will never forget a matter that they have undertaken, and rely simply on the memories of lawyers and staff. This is seldom fully effective because recollections fade and institutional history disappears when lawyers retire or move to another firm. A third group of firms, the "squirrels," hold on to as much paper as possible, and pore over their records when a new case is proposed. In some firms, lawyers or staff simply consult a client-list to ensure that the adverse party in a potential new matter is not already a client. In others, lawyers scrutinize mailing lists and time, billing, or accounting records. A fourth group, "cybersquirrels," have developed electronic databases to manage conflicts of interest. These systems vary in sophistication, but are often highly complex and labor intensive. Experience has demonstrated that even the most sophisticated computer conflict checks require monitoring by legal staff. Some large firms employ as many as ten specialists whose sole responsibility is revising the database and conducting computerized conflicts searches, which are then reviewed by lawyers.[33] The limited empirical evidence available suggests that the procedures in many firms leave much to be desired in terms of the quality of information collected about conflicts, the frequency with which the information is updated, the notice provided to parties about screening, and the procedures for maintaining screens.[34]

The frequency of conflicts problems has led to a growing reliance on advance waivers and "contract screening." The latter term describes arrangements under which the client waives defined conflicts, present and sometimes future, and the law firm agrees to screen the lawyers serving adverse interests. It is likely that contract screening will become standard practice as firms grow larger and encounter new engagements under greater time pressure. Indeed, some law firms, whose services are regarded as unique or nearly so, now insist on broad conflicts waivers as a matter of course.

Advance waivers, while not unethical, are also not a wholly dependable way of preventing subsequent problems. The Comment to Model Rule 1.7 notes: "The effectiveness of such waivers is generally determined by the extent to which the client reasonably

---

33. Shapiro, supra note 1, at 9.   **34.** Pizzimenti, supra note 31, at 321–24.

understands the material risks that the waiver entails. The more comprehensive the explanation of the types of future representations that might arise and the actual and foreseeable adverse consequences of those representations, the greater the likelihood that the client will have the requisite understanding.... If the consent is general and open-ended, then the consent will be ineffective, because it not reasonably likely that the client will have understood the material risks involved." The Comment, like ABA Formal Opinion 05–436 (2005), also emphasizes that much may depend on the sophistication and prior legal experience of the client. And an advance waiver will be ineffective if a conflict materializes that would not be subject to consent under the general conflicts of interest provisions. Model Rule 1.7 Comment.

Waivers and screening are clearly on the rise and large firms may have a dozen or more "screens" in effect within a single office at any time. In states that have the most permissive rules on screening, the systems tend to be subject to greater regulation and supervision than in states that allow them only for former government employees, for lawyers with "personal" conflicts, or for lawyers who implement them voluntarily (often as a condition of a client's waiver).[35] Ironically enough, a liberal rule on screening thus appears to offer clients more protection than most jurisdictions' restrictive frameworks.

If current trends continue, the bar will face increasing challenges in developing cost-effective strategies concerning conflicts of interest. Already many firms face a daunting task in managing their data bases and preventing turf battles. Tens of thousands of otherwise billable hours are devoted to screening and infighting over new business.[36] Although much of the cost is inherent in an increasingly complex and competitive legal environment, minimizing conflicts over conflicts is an important priority for the profession.

F. Representing Organizations

In addition to conflicts of interest between past and present clients, conflicts can also arise within a client organization. In general, bar ethical rules and the law governing organizations instruct lawyers to represent the interests of the "entity" rather than any of its particular constituents. Model Rule 1.13 Comment. However, such instructions may be of limited assistance when the issue is what those interests are, and who should decide.

35. Id.   **36.** Shapiro, supra note 1, at 9–11.

In a substantial fraction of law practice, particularly transactional matters, lawyers represent organizations, and the individuals with whom the lawyers interact are not technically "clients." Officers, directors, and employees are all agents or trustees for the organizational client. The organization is the beneficiary of lawyers' duties of loyalty and confidentiality, and is the holder of the company's legal rights and attorney-client privilege. Lawyers owe allegiance to the entity and reasonable care in fulfilling the representation. Where they fall short, they are subject to discharge and malpractice liability. These consequences follow from the law of corporations, partnerships, and agency, as well as bar ethical rules. As a practical matter, however, an organization can only speak and act through its individual agents. In physical terms, these individuals embody the organization, but in legal doctrine they do not. This distinction is the source of special conflicts problems in corporate practice. When differences may arise between the interests of shareholders, managers, and boards of directors, lawyers often encounter problems in determining who represents the client and can act on its behalf.

Such conflicts of interest assume multiple forms. Common examples involve determining management compensation; defending the corporation and its officers in shareholder derivative actions; representing both the entity and its employees in suits brought by third parties; and investigating or litigating possible misconduct by employees that might also be imputed to the organization.

Model Rule 1.13 codifies the legal relationships involved. Rule 1.13(a) states the premise that the client is the organization and not its "constituents," such as officers, directors, and employees. This Rule reflects basic corporation law: the entity is a legal construct with an independent capacity to engage counsel. Model Rule 1.13(b) and (c) then address the implications of this premise. In general terms, if the lawyer confronts conduct by officers or employees that violates their duties to the corporation or that will likely subject the corporation to significant liability, the lawyer must pursue the organization's "best interests." Basically, the lawyer is obligated to advise, object, and, if necessary, take the matter to higher authority within the organization.

Under these circumstances, in-house counsel face greater difficulties than outside lawyers for the organization. Not only are they more personally accountable to the decision makers involved, they are professionally more vulnerable; they have only one client who is providing their salary and benefits, and who can fire them without cause. Moreover, inside lawyers usually have informal access to much more information about corporate operations, including ones that may be legally problematic. In short, in-house counsel have maximum responsibility and minimum job security.

In circumstances where the organization's interests may be adverse to those of constituents, the comment to Model Rule 1.13 provides that: "the lawyer should advise any constituent . . . of the conflict or potential conflict of interest. . . . Care must be taken to assure that the individual understands that, when there is such adversity of interest, the lawyer for the organization cannot provide legal representation for that constituent individual, and that discussions between the lawyer for the organization and the individual may not be privileged." As a practical matter, however, the more explicit the lawyer's warning, the less likely individuals are to cooperate with an inquiry or investigation that may expose compromising information but that may also be essential for an appropriate organizational response. In recognition of this obvious tradeoff, the Comment to Model Rule 1.13 obliquely provides: "[w]hether such a warning should be given by the lawyer for the organization to any constituent individual may turn on the facts of each case."

A related issue, whether a lawyer can jointly represent the organization and any of its constituents, will also depend on the facts of a particular case. The general considerations are those set forth above in the discussion of multiple representation and those in Model Rule 1.8(f) on third-party payments of legal fees. This Rule prohibits a lawyer from accepting compensation from another party unless: the client gives informed consent; there is no interference with lawyer's independent judgment or relationship with client; and confidential information is protected.

Joint representation under these circumstances has the obvious advantages of minimizing expenses and coordinating a unified defense with a consistent version of events. The obvious disadvantage with such arrangements is that the interests of the organization and the officer or employee may ultimately diverge. If both are vindicated, joint representation has been a benefit. But if they are not, the organization may want to repudiate the conduct of the employee and may seek indemnification on the theory that the employee was solely responsible. Differences can then arise as to whether employees were acting within the scope of their employment or under directions from a supervisor, or whether particular actions were within the scope of an insurance policy. In contexts of potential criminal liability, individual employees may also have opportunities to cooperate with the prosecution in exchange for leniency, which raises the issues associated with prisoners dilemmas noted earlier.

Typically, the risks of joint representation will be greater for individuals than for the organization, given the pressures employees typically face to consent to joint representation, and the biases created by the attorney's own employment relationship. Such concerns impose a special responsibility on corporate counsel to ensure that consent to joint representation is not only fully informed, but is also reasonable under the circumstances. If a conflict is likely, lawyers should not wait to withdraw from the representation until it surfaces, because by then the individual's interests may already be irreparably injured. And if lawyers have acquired compromising confidential information, they may be forced to withdraw from representing both the organization and the individual, an outcome especially problematic for in-house attorneys.[37]

Shareholder derivative suits can pose related issues. The Comment to Model Rule 1.13 views joint representation of the organization and its management and officers as presumptively valid:

> Most derivative actions are a normal incident of an organization's affairs, to be defended by the organization's lawyer, like any other suit. However, if the claim involves serious charges of wrongdoing by those in control of the organization, a conflict may arise between the lawyer's duty to the organization and the lawyer's relationship with the board. In those circumstances, Rule 1.7 [the general rule governing simultaneous representation] governs who should represent the directors and the organization.

By contrast, the Restatement (Third) of the Law Governing Lawyers § 219 follows recent case law and finds joint representation presumptively invalid. Unless the shareholders' claims clearly lack merit on their face, separate representation is generally thought advisable.[38] Because in-house counsel are closely identified with management, a standard practice is for the corporation to create an independent committee of outside directors not named as defendants to review the merits of the claim and, where appropriate, to select outside legal counsel for the organization.

G. Representing The Government

Related issues arise in identifying "the client" of the government lawyer. Theoretically, the client could be the public, the

---

37. Nancy J. Moore, "Conflicts of Interest for In House Counsel: Issues Emerging From the Expanding Role of the Attorney–Employee," 39 S. Tex. L. Rev. 497, 508 (1998). For the challenges facing in-house counsel, see Sung Hui Kim, "The Banality of Fraud Re-Situat-ing the Inside Counsel as Gatekeeper," 74 Ford. L. Rev. 983 (2005).

38. Geoffrey C. Hazard, Jr., Susan P. Koniak, & Roger C. Cramton & George M. Cohen, The Law and Ethics of Lawyering 537–38 (4th ed. 2005).

government as a whole, the branch of government in which the lawyer is employed, the agency in which the lawyer works, or the officials responsible for the lawyer's actions. Courts, commentators, and bar ethical codes have taken different views, although they all maintain that lawyers in public office owe special responsibilities to the public.[39] The difficulty lies in determining what constitutes the public's interest and what it requires when members of the government disagree.

That difficulty arises in a wide variety of factual settings. In some instances, lawyers in one agency are responsible for representing another agency's position but find that position inconsistent with applicable laws, policies, the position of other agencies, or societal concerns. In other contexts, higher authorities within the lawyers' own agency or the central administration may direct them to act in ways that they find similarly problematic. For example, a change in administration during the pendency of litigation may result in directives for a government lawyer to "switch sides," although the lawyer believes that the new position is unsupported by the law or facts. At another level, an unwillingness by the legislative or executive branch to provide adequate funding for government institutions, such as prisons or mental health facilities, may place attorneys in the position of defending conditions that they believe violate constitutional standards or individual rights. Another common dilemma arises when lawyers learn confidential information that they believe should be shared with other legislative, executive, or judicial decision makers or with the general public.

Very little law is available to help identify the "client" in such circumstances.[40] Commentators and bar ethics codes have taken three primary approaches. One position is that the client is normally the government agency that employs the lawyer. This "agency approach" is reflected in Rule 1.13 of the Federal Bar Association's Model Rules of Professional Conduct for Federal Lawyers. However, the Rule includes the caveat that a government lawyer may have "authority to question such conduct more extensively than

39. See Model Rule of Professional Conduct 1.13; Model Code of Professional Responsibility EC 7–13 (1969); Symposium on Government Lawyering, 61 J. Law & Contemp. Probs. 1 (1998); Steven K. Berenson, "Public Lawyers, Private Values: Can, Should, and Will Government Lawyers Serve the Public Interest?" 41 B. C. L. Rev. 789 (2000); Steven K. Berenson, "The Duty Defined: Specific Obligations that Follow From Government Lawyers' Duty to Serve the Public Interest," 42 Brandeis L. J. 13 (2003); Jack B. Weinstein & Gay A. Crosthwait, "Some Reflections on Conflicts Between Government Attorneys and Clients," 1 Touro L. Rev. 1 (1985).

40. For a summary, see Hazard, Koniak, Cramton, & Cohen, supra note 38, at 583–86.

... a lawyer for a private organization in similar circumstances." The Restatement (Third) of the Law Governing Lawyers reflects a variation of the agency approach. The Comment to § 156 suggests that in most cases, the client of the government lawyer is the agency involved in the underlying dispute, but that the lawyer's responsibility may vary depending on the circumstances.

The agency approach has several advantages. One is familiarity; it models the relationship between lawyers and clients in private practice. So too, some commentators have argued that an agency framework fosters political accountability. By limiting the government lawyer's discretion to make independent judgments of the public's interest, this approach vests decision-making authority with elected officials who are more directly responsible to the public.[41]

Yet the agency approach neither resolves all ambiguity nor responds adequately to limitations in the democratic system. One problem involves determining who speaks for the agency. Normally, this would be the officials responsible for its decisions. However, as courts and commentators have emphasized, the lawyer represents the organization, not the personal interests of the elected or politically appointed individuals temporarily serving as its leader.[42] Moreover, in at least some contexts, an agency framework reflects an unrealistic assumption of political accountability and an impoverished conception of the government lawyer's social responsibilities. After all, most government decisions are made by bureaucrats who are not in any direct sense subject to majoritarian control. Even senior agency officials have highly limited democratic accountability. High-ranking federal officials can owe their appointments to a single election where no candidate has even received a majority of the popular vote let alone a consensus on the issue pending before the government lawyer.[43] More fundamentally, the agency-as-client framework may unduly restrict the lawyer's obligation as a govern-

---

41. See, e.g., Catherine J. Lanctot, "The Duty of Zealous Advocacy and the Ethics of the Federal Government Lawyer: The Three Hardest Questions," 64 S. Cal. L. Rev. 951, 1012–17 (1991); Jonathan R. Macey & Geoffrey P. Miller, "Reflections on Professional Responsibility in a Regulatory State," 63 Geo. Wash. L. Rev. 1105, 1116 (1995); Geoffrey P. Miller, "Government Lawyers' Ethics in a System of Checks and Balances," 54 U. Chi. L. Rev. 1293, 1294–95 (1987); Michael Stokes Paulsen, "Hell, Handbaskets, and Government Lawyers: The Duty of Loyalty and Its Limits," 61 Law & Contemp. Probs., 83, 85–86 (1998).

42. Hazard, Koniak, Cramton, & Cohen, supra note 38, at 584; Michael Paulson, "Who 'Owns' the Government's Attorney–Client Privilege?," 83 Minn. L. Rev. 473, 486–87 (1998).

43. Note, "Rethinking the Professional Responsibilities of Federal Agency Lawyers," 115 Harv. L. Rev. 1170, 1175 (2002). See also Berenson, supra note 39, at 823.

ment employee to ensure that government policy is appropriately carried out. Where, for example, higher level officials are directing a lawyer to act in ways that defy applicable law, regulations, or well-established legal principles, some effort to challenge that decision is consistent with democratic values.

To that end, a second approach identifies the client of the government lawyer as the government as a whole. The Model Rules take that view. The Comment to Rule 1.13 notes:

> Defining precisely the identity of the client and prescribing the resulting obligations of such lawyers may be more difficult in the government context and is a matter beyond the scope of these Rules.... Although in some circumstances the client may be a specific agency, it may also be a branch of government, such as the executive branch, or the government as a whole. For example, if the action or failure to act involves the head of a bureau, either the department of which the bureau is a part or the relevant branch of government may be the client for purposes of this Rule. Moreover, in a matter involving the conduct of government officials, a government lawyer may have authority under applicable law to question such conduct more extensively than that of a lawyer for a private organization in similar circumstances....

This approach, however, raises as many questions as it answers. Indeed, the Rule itself recognizes as much, by placing beyond its scope the question of what concrete actions lawyers should take in the face of wrongful conduct.

A final approach, which views the public as the client, is plausible in principle but even more indeterminate in practice. Some efforts have been made to specify the implications of this approach in particular contexts. For example, Model Rule 3.8 and the ABA Standards Relating to the Administration of Criminal Justice: The Prosecution Function, elaborate the prosecutor's obligation to "seek justice," not simply convictions.[44] That obligation includes:

- filing only charges supported by probable cause;

- making timely disclosure of exculpatory or mitigating evidence; and

- ensuring that the accused has a reasonable opportunity to obtain counsel.

---

44. The phrase comes from Berger v. United States, 295 U.S. 78, 88 (1935).

Efforts to define the government lawyer's obligations in civil contexts have been more limited and less specific. For example, EC 7–14 of the Code states:

> A government lawyer in a civil action or administrative proceeding has the responsibility to seek justice and to develop a full and fair record, and he should not use his position or the economic power of the government to harass parties or to bring about unjust settlements or results.

Yet what constitutes an "unjust" settlement is often open to dispute. Agency lawyers have taken different views on such questions as whether the government should disclose adverse material facts, assert a statute of limitations, warn an unrepresented opponent of his risks of self-incrimination, or advise opposing counsel of impending procedural defects that might defeat an otherwise meritorious claim.[45] Lawyers in the United States Solicitor General's office have long agreed that it is sometimes appropriate for the government to "confess error" and to ask the Supreme Court to vacate a lower judgment in the government's favor. But Solicitor General lawyers have disagreed about which particular cases warrant such a request.[46]

A case study in the ethical obligations of government attorneys involves the highly publicized role of federal lawyers in drafting "torture memos" in the aftermath of the 9/11 terrorist attacks. Two of the most controversial memoranda came from the Office of Legal Counsel (OLC) and concluded that the Geneva Conventions do not cover Al Qaeda or Taliban captives. These set the stage for a statement by President George Bush affirming that conclusion and stating that treatment of these prisoners would comply with Geneva principles "to the extent appropriate and consistent with military necessity."[47]

An equally controversial memo, signed by OLC chief Jay S. Bybee, concluded that various harsh interrogation tactics did not

45. Bruce A. Green, "Must Government Lawyers 'Seek Justice' in Civil Litigation?," 9 Widener J. Public Law 235 (2000); N.Y. State Bar Association, Committee on Professional Ethics, Op. 728 (2000) (concluding that it was appropriate for a municipal lawyer to advise an unrepresented opponent that he faced risks of self-incrimination and might profit from the advice of counsel).

46. David A. Strauss, "The Solicitor General and the Interests of the United States," 61 Law & Contemp. Probs. 165, 169 (1998).

47. For discussion of these memos, see David Luban, "Liberalism, Torture, and the Ticking Bomb," in The Torture Debate in America 35, 52–53 (ed. Karen J. Greenberg, 2006); Hazard, Koniak, Cramton, & Cohen, supra note 38, at 587–90; W. Bradley Wendel, "Legal Ethics and the Separation of Law and Morals," 91 Cornell L. Rev. 67 (2005); Anthony Lewis, "Making Torture Legal," New York Review of Books, July 15, 2004.

violate United States obligations under the international Torture Convention and its implementing statutes. Among the memo's conclusions were that:

- the infliction of pain rises to the level of torture only if the pain is as "severe as that accompanying death, organ failure, or serious impairment of body functions";

- it would be unconstitutional to apply anti-torture laws to interrogations authorized by the president in the war on terror; and

- "under current circumstances, necessity or self-defense" may justify interrogation methods that violate criminal prohibitions on torture.[48]

In the wake of widespread criticism, the OLC repudiated the Bybee memo and replaced it with a more circumspect statement opposing torture, and rejecting the narrow definition of severe pain, but failing to condemn all but the most egregious methods of torture, and declining to discuss justifications of self-defense or necessity.[49]

These memos raise a number of broader questions about the role of government lawyers. First, does that role require what a statement of best practices for the OLC prescribes: that attorneys give advice that is "accurate and honest" even where it will "constrain the administration's pursuit of desired policies"?[50] Alternatively, can lawyers appropriately provide any colorable legal justification for what administration leaders believe is in the national interest? As law professor David Luban frames the issue, if the White House wants not candid advisors but loyal "absolvers," can government attorneys ethically comply?[51]

Law professors Eric Posner and Adrian Vemeule maintain that these attorneys can. In their view, to see OLC's function as "solely to supply disinterested advice or serve as a conscience for the government is to adopt a sentimental, distorted, and self-serving picture of a complex reality." Lawyers who drafted the memos on

48. Office of the Legal Counsel, Department of Justice, Memorandum for Alberto R. Gonzales, Counsel to the President Re: Standards of Conduct for Interrogation, Aug. 1, 2002, reprinted in the Torture Papers, supra note 47, 72 and discussed in Luban, supra note 47, at 53, Wendell, supra note 47, at 68; and Hazard, Koniak, Cramton, & Cohen, supra note 38, at 587.

49. Memo from Daniel Levin, for James. Comey, Deputy Attorney General, Re: Legal Standards Applicable Under 18 U.S.C. §§ 2340–2340A, December 30, 2004, discussed in Luban, supra note 47, at 72.

50. Walter E. Dellinger et al., Principles to Guide the Office of Legal Counsel (2004), quoted in Wendel, supra note 47, at 112. The statement was signed by several former heads of the Office, along with numerous deputies and attorney-advisors.

51. See Luban, supra note 47, at 68–72.

torture were not asked for an opinion about its morality, nor did they have any more insight on that question than their political superiors. Rather, these attorneys were asked about "legal limits on interrogation" and they provided "reasonable legal advice" on that issue.[52] By contrast, Luban argues that the advice was not reasonable, but contrary to well settled international and American law and accepted moral principles. In his view, the "lawyer as absolver" role is analogous to that of an "indulgence seller," and inconsistent with professional rules and principles.[53]

A related controversy involves what government lawyers should do if their advice is rejected and their superiors insist on taking a position that the lawyers believe is legally or morally unjustifiable. How high up the ladder may or should the lawyers go in challenging their supervisor's decision? If the administration's position authorizes actions that the lawyers believe are illegal, may or must they report them? To whom? Would it ever be appropriate to leak draft memos, or related classified material, as some administration officials did during the torture debates?[54] Or are the only options withdrawal, or in cases of fundamental importance, resignation? If the attorney chooses not to resign, would it ever be appropriate to issue a public statement registering disagreement with the position taken. A celebrated example involves Lawrence Wallace, a career government attorney serving as Acting Solicitor General, when he was defending the Internal Revenue Service's denial of a tax exemption to a university practicing racial discrimination. While the case was pending, there was a change of administration and its new leaders instructed the office to reverse its position and to support the university. Wallace filed a brief that complied with the instruction but included a statement that it did not reflect the views of the Acting Solicitor General.[55]

To the extent that such cases suggest generalizable principles, they imply some obligation on the part of attorneys to preserve governmental legitimacy by promoting compliance with applicable laws and ensuring fairness in substantive and procedural decisions. When a proposed governmental action appears inconsistent with these principles, attorneys have, at minimum, a responsibility to seek internal review and reconsideration. If such internal efforts are unsuccessful, lawyers should consider the need for disclosure of information to others, such as the legislature, the courts, or the

---

52. Eric Posner and Adrian Vemeule, Opinion, "A Torture Memo and the Torture Critics," Wall St. J. July 6, 2004, at A22.

53. Luban, supra note 47, at 68–72.

54. Hazard, Koniak, Cramton, & Cohen, supra note 38, at 588–89.

55. Philip B. Heymann & Lance Liebman, The Social Responsibilities of Lawyers: Case Studies, 139, 181 (1988).

public. These bodies may or may not secure reversal of the decision in the case at issue, but they may be able to alter future policy.

In contexts involving illegal activities by government officials, disclosure of relevant information may be mandatory or protected under federal and state law.[56] For example, federal employees are required to inform the Attorney General of possible criminal violations by federal officers. The Whistleblower Protection Act of 1989 also prohibits a federal agency from taking an adverse personnel action against an employee who discloses information that reveals a violation of law, rule or regulation; gross mismanagement; gross waste of funds; an abuse of authority; or a specific and substantial danger to public health and safety.[57] Whistleblowing is seldom a costless enterprise for government employees, but it can also result in enormous societal benefits and the personal satisfaction that comes from acting from moral principles in the service of public interests.

H. Class Action Representation

A final form of intra-group conflicts of interest arise in class action lawsuits. The interests of class members seldom fully coincide, the ideological and financial interests of lawyers and clients may diverge dramatically, and class members may be unaware of the conflicts or even that they are part of a lawsuit. With the rise of class actions as a distinctive feature of American legal processes, conflicts have emerged in a wide variety of settings, such as consumer suits, mass tort claims, employment discrimination cases, and public interest litigation. Although the structural features of these class actions somewhat differ, they also present certain common concerns.

The basic framework for these cases is Rule 23 of the Federal Rules of Civil Procedure and its state law analogues. Under Rule 23, class actions are appropriate if:

> (1) the class is so numerous that joinder of all members is impracticable, (2) there are questions of law or fact common to the class, (3) the claims or defenses of the representative parties are typical of the claims or defenses of the class, and (4) the representative parties will fairly and adequately protect the interests of the class.

---

56. See Hazard, Koniak, & Cramton, *supra* note 38, at 590; Roger C. Cramton, "The Lawyer as Whistleblower: Confidentiality and the Government Lawyer," 5 Geo. J. Legal Ethics 291 (1991).

57. 28 U.S.C. § 535; 5 U.S.C. § 3202(b).

Under the rules of civil procedure, bar ethical codes, and relevant caselaw, attorneys, as well as the named class representatives must "fairly and adequately protect the interests of the class." However, judicial and bar ethics decisions have provided insufficient guidance about lawyers' concrete responsibilities. Among the unanswered questions are whether "interests" can mean anything other than preferences, and what steps counsel must take to identify and address conflicts within a class.

The most serious threshold issue will be whether the proceeding is certified by the trial judge to be a proper class suit. After certification, almost all class suits are settled. Indeed, a growing procedural device is the "settlement-only" class action that ends when a proposed class and negotiated settlement are simultaneously approved by the court. Almost all class actions involve some conflicts of interest. Common disputes center around the distribution of monetary awards within the class, the tradeoffs between injunctive and financial remedies, and the amount of class counsel's fee.[58]

In public interest litigation, the remedial conflicts can be particularly complicated. School desegregation cases have repeatedly demonstrated these difficulties. For example, dispute has centered on the relative importance of integration, financial resources, curricular improvements, and minority control in remedying educational inequalities. Even constituencies that support school integration in principle have disputed its value in particular settings where long bus rides or white flight are likely results. So too, parents challenging the adequacy of bilingual or special education programs have differed over whether mainstreaming or upgrading separate classes represents the better solution. Suits involving mental health treatment have involved conflict over whether to demand improvement in residential facilities or creation of community care alternatives. In employment discrimination cases, controversy can arise on the tradeoffs between back-pay awards and prospective relief, the formulas for computing damages, and the means chosen to restructure hiring, promotion, and transfer systems.[59]

58. Rhode & Luban, Legal Ethics, supra note 18, at 624–62; Hazard, Koniak, Cramton, & Cohen, supra note 38, at 594–631; Symposium, Protecting Consumer Interests in Class Actions, 18 Geo. J. Legal Ethics 1161–1477 (2005); David J. Kahne, "Curbing the Abuser, Not the Abuse: A Call For Greater Professional Accountability and Stricter Ethical Guidelines for Class Action Attorneys," 71 Geo. J. Leg. Ethics 741 (2006).

59. For examples see Nancy Morawetz, "Bargaining, Class Representation, and Fairness," 54 Ohio St. L. J. 1, 37–38 (1993); Rhode & Luban, Legal Ethics, supra note 18, at 626–41.

Like other litigants, class members may also differ in their willingness to compromise or to assume the risks of protracted proceedings. Given the uncertainty of outcome and indeterminacy of relief in many class actions, risk-averse plaintiffs may be prepared to make substantial concessions. Other class members may prefer to fight, "if not to the death, at least until the Supreme Court denies certiorari."[60] The conflicts are compounded where the settlement provides generously only for class counsel, unduly rewards the named plaintiffs, or favors current over future class members.[61]

Although courts have the ultimate responsibility for ensuring substantive and procedural fairness in class action litigation, they often place corresponding obligations on lawyers. As one federal court of appeals put it, "class action counsel possess, in a very real sense, fiduciary obligations to those not before the court."[62] Principal among those duties is the responsibility to inform the trial judge of conflicting interests that may call for separate representation or other corrective measures.

This responsibility is straightforward in principle but difficult to enforce in practice. Although many attorneys make considerable efforts to identify and accommodate differences within a class, many also face significant pressures to present a united front. Most obviously, lawyers want to avoid laying foundations for opponents to challenge certification of the class. If such efforts prove successful, lawyers may lose a substantial investment that they cannot recover from the clients. At a minimum, controversy over certification results in expense and delay that divert resources from other essential pursuits. Highlighting conflicts of interest may also trigger involvement of additional lawyers, who will seek to share the limelight, the control over litigation decisions, and the resources available for attorneys' fees.

Exposing conflicts can also frustrate objectives that attorneys believe will serve the best interests of the class. A common example

60. Deborah L. Rhode, "Class Conflicts in Class Actions," 34 Stan. L. Rev. 1183, 1191 (1982).

61. For examples, see John C. Coffee, Jr., "Class Wars, The Dilemma of the Mass Tort Class Action," 95 Colum. L. Rev. 1343 (1995); Amchem Products, Inc. v. Windsor 521 U.S. 591 (1997); Julie Creswell & Jonathan D. Glater, "For Law Firm, Serial Plaintiff Had Midas Touch," N.Y. Times, June 6, 2006, A1; and "The Trial Lawyers' Enron,"

Wall St. J., July 7, 2005, A12 (describing alleged practice of Milberg Weis to generously reward the same named plaintiffs in multiple securities class actions that often yielded lucrative fees for class counsel and nominal remedies for class members).

62. Greenfield v. Villager Indus., Inc., 483 F.2d 824, 832 (3d Cir. 1973). See generally Rhode, supra note 60, at 1204–05.

involves institutional reform proposals that offer generous settlement terms for current class members but little protection or
precedential value for future members or victims.[63] Such proposals
may also pose conflicts between clients and lawyers' own interests
that are difficult to prevent or address. These concerns make
judicial oversight crucial, however difficult to institutionalize in
practice.

Part of the difficulty is that the main remedies courts have
employed to deal with conflicts of interest is to deny certification of
the class or overturn a judgment that resulted from inadequate
representation of certain subclasses. However, these remedies often
penalize innocent plaintiffs, whose recoveries are delayed or diminished, without adequately sanctioning lawyers who are responsible
for the problem.[64] Frustration with counsel's performance and the
absence of effective responses has led some disaffected class members to sue for malpractice.[65] Yet that remedy will also prove
inadequate for the vast majority of clients, who will lack sufficient
information or incentives to file civil liability claims. For that
reason, most experts recommend more oversight by courts and
disciplinary authorities, particularly where lawyers' own interests
conflict with those of their clients.

I. Lawyers' Personal Interests

Fiduciary law and bar ethical rules prohibit lawyers from
representation that will be "materially limited" by their own personal interests unless they reasonably believe that they will be able
to provide "competent and diligent" assistance and the client gives
informed consent. Model Rule 1.7. See also DR 5–101. Both the
Model Rules and Code also regulate specific conduct likely to pose
conflicts, such as lawyer-client business transactions, gifts, financial
assistance, and sexual relationships. Model Rule 1.8; DR 5–104.
Underlying these regulations are certain principles designed to
prevent exploitation of client ignorance, vulnerability, or lack of
bargaining power. So, for example, lawyers may not enter into
business transactions with clients unless the terms are fair, reasonable, and fully disclosed, and the client gives informed written

---

63. For recent cases in which the
Supreme Court was critical of class action attorneys who failed adequately to
represent the interests of future class
members, see Amchem Products, Inc. v.
Windsor, 521 U.S. 591 (1997), and Ortiz
v. Fibreboard Corp., 527 U.S. 815
(1999).

64. See Kahne, supra note 58, and
Susan P. Koniak & George M. Cohen,
"In Hell There Will be Lawyers Without
Clients or Law," in Ethics in the Prac-
tice of Law 177 (Deborah L. Rhode, ed.
2000).

65. David Wessel, "Now Being Sued:
Class–Action Lawyers," Wall St. J.
March 24, 2005, A2.

consent after being advised to seek independent legal advice. Model Rule 1.8(a). See also DR 5–104. Some conduct is so fraught with the potential for abuse that it is categorically prohibited, such as preparation of wills with testamentary gifts to the preparers, prospective limitations on malpractice liability to clients who lack independent counsel, or sexual relationships with clients that do not predate the legal representation. Model Rule 1.8(c), (h) and (j).

The primary objective of such rules is protection of clients, but some restrictions on conflicts of interest also seek to protect the public and to preserve confidence in the profession. For example, the prohibition on "maintenance"—i.e., financial assistance to clients for personal expenses—is partly designed to prevent "encourag[ing] clients to pursue lawsuits that might not otherwise be brought." Model Rule 1.8 Comment. The Rule also seeks to prevent lawyers from competing for clients though monetary inducements and from having such a stake in the outcome that it might compromise their ethical obligations. Id.

Whether all of these provisions in fact serve the public, however, is open to debate. The prohibition on maintenance has been subject to particular criticism. According to some courts and commentators, a categorical restriction on loans to needy clients too often prevents suits that should be brought; it forces litigants with meritorious claims to accept inadequate settlements instead of holding out for an appropriate judgment.[66] Such concerns underlie the more permissive approach of The Restatement of the Law Governing Lawyers. Section 48 allows a lawyer to make a loan on "fair terms" if it is necessary "to enable the client to withstand delay in litigation that might unjustly induce the client to settle or dismiss a case because of financial hardship rather than on the merits; and if the lawyer does not promise or offer the loan before being retained."

Other potential lawyer/client conflicts are regulated less by ethical rules and legal doctrine than by organizational policies and malpractice insurance requirements. For example, neither the Model Rules nor the Code prohibits lawyers from sitting on the board of directors of a client, although the Comment to Model Rule 1.7 cautions against such a dual role under circumstances where it would "compromise the lawyer's independence of professional judgment." Many ethics experts believe that the risks of such circum-

---

66. See Jack P. Sahl, "The Cost of Humanitarian Assistance: Ethical Rules and the First Amendment," 34 St. Mary's L. J. 795 (2003); Fred C. Zachari- as, "Limits on Client Autonomy in Legal Ethics Regulation," 81 Boston U. L. Rev. 198, 236–37 (2001).

stances are always present.[67] Accordingly, some law firms have policies against lawyers serving on client boards and some legal malpractice insurance policies exclude coverage for lawyers in that role. By contrast, other firms are willing to assume some risk of conflicts in exchange for the advantages that come with lawyers' board service, such as enhanced prestige, credibility, and personal relationships with corporate decision makers.[68]

Similar differences in organizational policy have emerged concerning lawyers' investment in clients. During the boom in internet and other high-technology companies in the late 1990s, many prominent law firms pioneered fee arrangements in which cash-strapped entrepreneurs compensated lawyers with shares or investments in their start-up companies. This practice has a long history. For example, lawyers in real estate development have often taken a share in the proceeds as part of their fee. The practice has, however always been somewhat controversial within the bar, both because it threatens to compromise lawyers' independent judgment and because lawyers sometimes receive windfall payouts that seem grossly disproportionate to the services provided.

In response to such concerns, ABA Formal Opinion 00–418 (2000) concluded that compensation in the form of client shares does not violate either the Model Rules or the Code if the terms were reasonable under circumstances ascertainable at the time of the transaction. To minimize disputes over what was reasonable, some experts and bar ethics committees advise lawyers to retain an investment professional who can estimate the value of the interests at issue. To minimize the risk that lawyers' professional judgment will be skewed by a desire to protect their investment, some firms have created common fund arrangements. In these firms, securities from any client go into a single fund in which firm members may invest. The result of these arrangements is to dilute the impact that legal advice to a particular client might have on a lawyer's personal investments. Whether such arrangements are sufficient protections against conflicts of interest is likely to remain an issue of ongoing debate in the bar.[69]

---

67. See Wolfram, supra note 30, at 739; Craig C. Albert, "The Lawyer–Director: An Oxymoron?," 9 Geo. J. Legal Ethics 413, 426 (1996).

68. For an overview of the debate, see SEC Staff Report on Corporate Accountability F2G–F31 (1980); Dean Starkman, "Lawyers Debate Ethics of Role in Boardrooms," Wall St. J., Aug. 5, 1996, at B1. Samuel C. Stretton, "Law-

yers Serving as Corporate Directors May Have a Conflict If They Represent the Company," 25 Pa. L. Wky. 244 (2002); Susanna M. Kim, "Dual Identities and Dueling Obligations: Preserving Independence in Corporate Representation," 68 Tenn. L. Rev. 179 (2001).

69. For an overview see Brian J. Redding, "Investing In or Doing Business With Clients: Some Thoughts on

These investment arrangements are, however, not the only, or even the primary, sources of lawyer-client conflicts concerning legal fees. As discussion in Chapter X indicates, almost all forms of payment pose some risk that lawyers' financial interests will depart from those of their clients. An hourly fee arrangement creates incentives to expand work to fit the budget available.[70] By contrast, a contingent fee agreement can create the opposite incentive. In these cases, clients are not paying for the attorneys' time so their interest centers solely on the result attained. Attorneys, by contrast, need also to consider the efforts necessary to achieve a good result and the competing claims on their resources.

The potential for attorney-client conflicts is compounded when a proposed settlement includes a provision for legal fees that is extremely generous or totally inadequate. These difficulties are also common when the litigation is governed by a fee-shifting rule, which provides attorneys' fees to a prevailing plaintiff. A dilemma then arises if the opposing party offers a generous settlement to the client but a paltry fee—or none at all—for counsel. Decisions of the Supreme Court permit the opposing party either to condition settlement on a waiver of attorney's fees or to avoid statutory fee awards by settling without a judgment on the merits.[71] The opposite problem arises with settlements that make lawyers the major beneficiaries; they receive millions for minimal work while class members recover only nominal damages or largely worthless coupons for the defendant's products.[72] Plaintiffs' attorneys generally argue that such cases serve a valuable function in deterring misconduct where the individual injuries are too small to justify litigation. However, commentators often question whether the amount of fees is proportionate to the results achieved or to the effort expended. In theory, judicial oversight of class action settlements and contingent fees is designed to prevent such abuses. In practice, however, trial

Lawyer Liability and Legal Ethics Issues," *Professional Lawyer* 113 (Fall 2000); Debra Baker, "Who Wants to Be a Millionaire?," ABA J., Feb. 2000, at 36; Edward H. Cohen, "Lawyers Investing in Their Clients: The Rules of Professional Responsibility," 14 Insights 2 (2000); John S. Dzienkowski & Robert J. Peroni, "The Decline in Lawyer Independence: Lawyer Equity Investments in Clients," 81 Tex. L. Rev. 405 (2002).

70. Deborah L. Rhode, In the Interests of Justice: Reforming the Legal Profession 61 (2000).

71. Evans v. Jeff D., 475 U.S. 717 (1986); Buckhannon Bd. and Care Home, Inc. v. West Virginia Dept. of Health & Human Resources, 532 U.S. 598 (2001).

72. See examples cited in Rhode & Luban, supra note 18, at 553–54; Rhode, supra note 51, at 176; Susan P. Koniak & George M. Cohen, "In Hell There Will Be Lawyers Without Clients or Law," in Ethics in Practice 177–204 (Deborah L. Rhode, ed. 2000).

courts are often reluctant to disturb agreements that clear their dockets and impose no risk of appeal.[73]

A specific case of conflict between lawyer and class has concerned "coupon settlements." Claims against businesses can be settled by payments not only in money but also in coupons for purchasing the business's goods or services at a discount. As a practical matter, these coupon payments can be worthless to class members because the amounts are too small to justify the costs of redemption or because the members will not need or want to buy another of the defendants' products during the time specified. The problems with coupon settlements became sufficiently visible that Congress ultimately responded. The Class Action Fairness Act of 2005 requires that in these cases, a lawyers' fee should be based on the value to the class of coupons that are redeemed or the amount of time reasonably expended on the case. How best to deal with other fee-related problems is likely to be a matter of increasing legislative, judicial, and bar regulatory concern.

Nonfinancial conflicts of interest are even harder for courts, clients, and bar disciplinary authorities to address. Lawyers often have career concerns that compete with fiduciary obligations. For example, they may be interested in attracting publicity, establishing their organization's reputation, or gaining trial experience.[74] Lawyers also have long-term interests in maintaining good relationships with courts, opposing counsel, potential clients, and other participants in the legal system such as insurance adjusters, regulatory agency personnel, and law enforcement officials. These interests may sometimes conflict with a particular client's objectives. So too, in contexts involving public interest or governmental litigation, attorneys may have ideological commitments that diverge from those of the class or agency that they represent. In commenting on such conflicts, Professor Derrick Bell has observed that concerns of principle, "though rarer than greed" are harder to control.[75] There are obvious limits in the ability of formal rules and enforcement structures to cope with personal interests that are present to some extent in every professional relationship.

73. Judith Resnik, Dennis Curtis, & Deborah R. Hensler, "Individuals Within the Aggregate: Relations, Representation, and Fees," 71 N.Y. U. L. Rev. 296 (1996); Rhode, supra note 60.

74. See Berenson, supra note 39, at 808–11. Macey & Miller, supra note 41, at 1117–19; Michael Selmi, "Public vs. Private Enforcement of Civil Rights: The Case of Housing and Employment," 45 UCLA L. Rev. 1401 (1998).

75. Derrick A. Bell, "Serving Two Masters: Integration Ideals and Client Interests in School Desegregation Litigation," 85 Yale L. J. 470, 504 (1976). For other examples, see Rhode, supra note 60.

That example points up a broader general point about conflicts of interest in general. Where formal mechanisms of accountability are lacking, lawyers have a special responsibility to ensure that their own concerns do not supplant those of parties who will have to live with the results.

Chapter IX

ACCESS TO JUSTICE

A. The Nature of the Problem

It is widely perceived that America has too much law and too little justice—too much litigation for those who can afford it and too little access to legal remedies for those who cannot. A majority of Americans believe that the nation has too many lawyers and four fifths agree that they file too many meritless lawsuits.[1] A majority also think that wealth matters in the kind of justice people receive.[2] There is, however, considerably less agreement about what, if anything, should be done about those problems. Part of the difficulty is that many individuals are poorly informed or deeply ambivalent about access to justice. They underestimate the true costs of legal process, overestimate the extent of litigiousness among the "haves," and are reluctant to subsidize adequate services for the "have-nots."

Litigiousness

Most complaints about litigiousness rest on three assumptions: that the nation has an excessive number of lawyers, that they file too many lawsuits, and that legal proceedings cost too much. The factual basis for each of these claims deserves closer exploration.

Since the Colonial era, Americans have complained about the number of lawyers, and early settlers made some efforts to exclude them entirely or at least to limit their role.[3] During the late eighteenth century, there were mob uprisings against the "cursed hungry Caterpillars" preying on the Commonwealth.[4] The contemporary tort reform movement often builds on similar sentiments, acerbically expressed in antilawyer humor.[5] Such criticisms typical-

---

1. See sources cited in Deborah L. Rhode, Access to Justice 26, 29 (2004); Deborah L. Rhode, In the Interests of Justice: Reforming the Legal Profession 117 (2000); ABA Section of Litigation, Public Perceptions of Lawyers Consumer Research Findings 7 (2002).

2. Marc Galanter, "Farther Along," 33 Law & Soc'y Rev. 1113 (1999); ABA, Perceptions of the U.S. Justice System 5 (1999) (finding that only a third of surveyed Americans believe that the justice system tries to treat wealthy and poor alike).

3. See Lawrence M. Friedman, A History of American Law 45–46 (1985); Terence C. Halliday, "Six Score Years and Ten: Demographic Transitions in the American Legal Profession, 1850–1980," 20 Law & Soc'y Rev. 53 (1986).

4. Friedman, supra note 3, at 96.

5. See Rhode, In the Interests of Justice, supra note 1, at 119; Rhode, Access to Justice, supra note 1, at 26–29; Marc Galanter, Lowering the Bar: Lawyer Jokes and Legal Culture (2005).

ly presuppose, but rarely defend, some evaluative standard by which America's legal profession looks too big. The implicit assumption is that this nation has a disproportionate number of lawyers compared to other societies.

Many critics, however, have key facts wrong. For example, although some politicians have asserted that America has seventy percent of the world's lawyers, informed estimates put the figure somewhere between a quarter and a third, which is roughly the United States' share of the world's combined Gross National Product.[6] Cross-cultural comparisons also can be misleading since they fail to reveal the number of practitioners in other countries who are not licensed members of the bar but who receive legal training and perform tasks that in this country are largely reserved for lawyers. In Germany, for example, in-house corporate counsel do not belong to the bar and are not counted as members of the legal profession, but provide the same services as American lawyers. In Japan, the number of individuals who are certified to act as courtroom advocates represents only a small fraction of those who receive legal education in universities and who give legal advice and prepare legal documents. The reason for Japan's disparity between licensed professionals and law-trained specialists is that pass rates on bar exams are kept at artificially low levels, under five percent.

Claims about America's oversupply of lawsuits are equally in need of qualification. Experts generally agree that current litigation rates in the United States are not exceptionally high, either in comparison with rates in prior historical eras or with those in many other Western industrial nations not known for contentiousness. More lawsuits per capita occurred in some American communities in the colonial era and in the nineteenth and early twentieth centuries.[7] Contemporary court filings in the United States are in the same range as in Canada, Australia, New Zealand, England, and Denmark, and the percentage that require costly trials is in decline.[8] In any event, litigation rates are not necessarily a barometer of cultural contentiousness. Over ninety-eight percent of American lawsuits are filed in the state courts, where uncontested mat-

---

6. Herbert M. Kritzer, "Lawyer Fees and Lawyer Behavior in Litigation: What Does the Empirical Literature Really Say?," 80 Tex. L. Rev. 1943, 1981 (2002); Marc Galanter, "The Vanishing Trial: An Examination of Trials and Related Matters in Federal and State Courts," 1 J. Empirical Leg. Studies 459 (2004).

7. See Marc S. Galanter, "Reading the Landscape of Disputes: What We Know and Don't Know (and Think We Know) About Our Allegedly Contentious and Litigious Society," 31 UCLA L. Rev. 4, 55–58 (1983).

8. Marc Galanter, "The Life and Times of the Big Six; or, the Federal Courts Since the Good Old Days," 1988 Wis. L. Rev. 921, 942–45 (1988).

ters such as divorces and probate account for a large proportion of the caseload.[9]

The other most frequently cited evidence for America's undue litigiousness relies on argument by anecdote: examples of seemingly avaricious lawyers who flood the system with frivolous claims. Yet what constitutes frivolity is in the eye of the beholder, and the portraits in tort reform commentary and the popular press can be highly misleading.[10] A textbook illustration involves a multimillion dollar verdict against the McDonalds fast-food chain. The conventional description of the case was that summarized by the national Chamber of Commerce: "Is it fair to get a couple of million dollars from a restaurant just because you spilled hot coffee on yourself?"[11] On closer examination, however, that description is highly misleading. The plaintiff, a 79–year–old woman, suffered acutely painful third-degree burns from 180–degree coffee. Only after McDonalds refused to reimburse her eight days of hospital expenses did she bring suit. At trial, jurors learned of 700 other burn cases involving McDonalds' coffee during the preceding decade, and warnings by medical experts that the beverage temperatures were causing serious injuries. The jury's verdict of $2.3 million included punitive damages reflecting two days of coffee sales revenues, and the judge reduced the judgment to $640,000. To avoid an appeal, the plaintiff then settled the case for a smaller amount. McDonalds put up warning signs and other fast-food chains adopted similar measures. While evaluations of this final result may vary, it was not the patently "ridiculous" travesty that media critics described.[12]

So too, other cases where the individual losses are small can serve as a useful deterrent to corporate negligence or misconduct. And for cases that are truly without merit, an appropriate response is the kind of sanctions that Chapter VI proposed, not a categorical indictment of lawyers and lawsuits. A more productive debate over litigiousness requires deeper analysis of fundamental questions. How much are we prepared to pay for legal remedies? How does access to the legal system compare with other demands on our social resources? What are the alternatives to litigation? Are law and lawyers handling public needs in the most cost-effective man-

9. National Center for State Courts, Examining the Work of State Courts, 10, 13 (2001).

10. William Halton & Michael McCann, Distorting the Law: Politics, Media, and the Litigation Crisis (2004); Deborah L. Rhode, "Frivolous Litigation and Civil Justice Reform," 54 Duke L. J. 447, 450–56 (2004).

11. See Rhode, In the Interests of Justice, supra note 1, at 122.

12. Id. See also Ralph Nader & Wesly J. Smith, No Contest 267–72 (1996). The McDonald's case has figured prominently in legislative debates over civil justice reform. Halton & McCann, supra note 10 at 279.

ner? Would tighter limitations on expensive discovery processes be desirable, or should losers pay their opponents' attorneys' fees?

On most of these issues, the public is divided, but concerns about the price of legal process are widely shared. Over four-fifths of surveyed Americans believe that litigation takes too long and costs too much; about three-quarters believe that it is damaging the country's economy.[13] Yet here again, the factual basis for the latter assumptions is weaker than commonly supposed. Although we lack reliable assessments of the total costs of civil liability, the best available calculations for the tort system do not reveal a substantial adverse effect on economic productivity. In tort cases, which attract the primary criticism, trials have declined considerably over the last two decades, and the average recovery in the small fraction of cases that actually go to trial is much smaller than media coverage would suggest; it is under $40,000 and the large judgments attracting public concern are often reduced on appeal.[14] Brookings Institution research estimates that tort liability could represent no more than two percent of the total price of United States goods and services, an amount "highly unlikely" to have a substantial impact on American competitiveness. Other estimates similarly suggest that businesses' total liability for all legal claims, including torts, is about 25 cents for every 100 dollars in revenue.[15] To be sure, the growth of large awards in some fields, such as medical malpractice, and the corresponding rise of insurance premiums, is a matter of legitimate concern. But the causes and remedies are often more complicated than public debate acknowledges.

There is a deeper political question as well: Compared to what? Presumably the objective is not a complete absence of effective legal regulation. In Europe, for example, there is much less personal injury litigation than in this country, but much more general taxation to provide broad medical and disability for everyone injured. There is much less regulatory litigation against business, but much more government direction of business conduct. Cost comparison of these very different legal regimes is difficult, but it is not obvious that our system is more burdensome.

13. See Rhode, Access to Justice, supra note 3, at 32.

14. Rhode, "Frivolous Litigation," supra note 10, at 457, 463; Rhode, Access to Justice, supra note 1, at 30; Myron Levin, "Coverage of Big Awards for Plaintiffs Helps Distort View of Legal System," L.A. Times, August 15, 2005, at C1.

15. Robert E. Litan, "The Liability Explosion and American Trade Performance: Myths and Realities," in Tort Law and the Public Interest: Competition, Innovation, and Consumer Welfare 127–28 (Peter H. Schuck ed., 1991); Nader & Smith, supra note 12, at 279.

There is a parallel problem in protection of the interests of ordinary citizens. In the European tradition, the government excises broad "paternalist" authority in matters of employee and consumer relationships. In our system, those relationships are more generally left to private arrangements, enforceable by private initiatives, including lawsuits.

Many Americans, including some prominent critics of the legal profession, seriously underestimate the need for legal assistance in enforcing individual rights and the factors that make such assistance inherently expensive to provide. To function effectively, this nation's adversary system generally requires parties to have competent lawyers with sufficient resources to present their case before a neutral judge. Such a process requires multiple professionals, facilities, and supporting administrative staff. Transactional practice, as distinct from litigation, generally requires fewer professionals, and can often prevent expensive legal problems, but it too can involve substantial costs.

Part of the reason is that legal skills, particularly in the United States, command a substantial market price. American lawyers have abilities that are highly valued, both within and outside the legal system. Practitioners are not only knowledgeable about the law, they also tend to be astute problem solvers, policy analysts, and financial planners. These skills enable many lawyers to move into other well-paid occupations if legal work is insufficiently rewarded. Many attorneys have a broad range of options: government, finance, real estate, insurance, intellectual property, corporate management, lobbying, and so forth, all of which may provide compensation in the same target range as law. About a quarter of all law school graduates eventually end up in these alternative markets.[16] Such is the price structure of legal services, and in a culture that highly values individual rights, they are bound to come at considerable cost.

Any fair minded evaluation of American "litigiousness" needs also to consider the benefits as well as the costs. To take a commonly cited example, the expenses attributable to product liability lawsuits have significantly increased the price of a football helmet. But they have also significantly reduced the frequency of serious head injuries.[17] Whether such precautions are worth the price involves complex contextual judgments. As Professor Law-

---

16. Joe G. Baker, "Employment Pattern of Law School Graduates," The Law School Admission Council Research Report 00–01 1 (2001).

17. Compare John Stossel, "Protect Us From Legal Vultures," Wall St. J., Jan. 2, 1996, at A8 with Rhode, In the Interests of Justice, supra note 1, at 127–28.

rence Friedman points out, the benefits of legal claims are "often quite intangible and immeasurable: expanded opportunities for women and minorities, expansion of civil liberties, fair procedures within institutions, limits on government. Who would deny that these are significant gains?"[18] Americans also turn to private lawsuits for remedies that other countries provide through direct government regulation, and for needs that others meet through centralized administrative measures such as guaranteed health benefits for injured parties.[19] An entrepreneurial bar has ensured accountability for hazardous products, fraudulent practices, discriminatory conduct and other violations of legal rights. Litigation that is financed by counsel and losing parties avoids the need to spend taxpayer dollars in enforcing legal standards and compensating victims. As long as this nation relies so heavily on private lawsuits to serve public interests, litigation is likely to remain at substantial levels, and to impose substantial expenses.

The real issue, then, is not whether the current system "costs too much" in some abstract sense. Rather, the critical question is "compared to what." Is the current process the most cost-effective means of protecting legal rights? For example, a wide array of research suggests that the current tort system undercompensates victims and overcompensates intermediaries, including lawyers. Almost all major studies indicate that a large number of victims fail to recover adequate compensation, and that legal expenses consume a grossly disproportionate share of payouts by defendants. For example, the most systematic research finds that only about 10–12 percent of accident and malpractice victims file claims and a much smaller percent receive compensation.[20] Errors run in the direction of too little compensation rather than too much.[21]

Moreover, transaction costs have been extremely high. Plaintiffs lawyers collect an estimated $30 billion in legal fees annually, some of which could otherwise be spent compensating or preventing injuries.[22] Of the amounts paid by insurance companies in surveyed tort cases, victims have received only about forty to fifty percent; in mass tort cases like those involving asbestos cases, two thirds of the

18. Lawrence M. Friedman, "Litigation and Society," 15 Ann. Rev. Soc. 17, 26–27 (1989).

19. Robert Kagan, Adversarial Legalism: The American Way of Law (2001); Thomas Burke, Lawyers, Lawsuits, and Legal Rights (2000); Rhode, Access to Justice, supra note 1, at 37–38.

20. Rhode, "Frivolous Cases," supra note 10, at 459–60.

21. David M. Studdert, et al., "Claims, Errors, and Compensation Payments in Medical Malpractice Litigation," 354 New England J. Med. 2024 (2006).

22. Rhode, "Frivolous Cases," supra note 10, at 464.

payouts have gone to lawyers and experts.[23] Those costs are not inevitable. Many countries save substantial amounts by relying on official investigations and alternative dispute resolution procedures to resolve accident and tort claims. In Japan, for example, legal fees claim only about two percent of payouts.[24] Those systems may, of course, create other problems of undercompensation. But these problems plague the American litigation process as well, which makes modest claims too expensive to pursue and imposes excessive transaction costs on the others.

Despite these flaws, over four-fifths of Americans believe that they have the best system of justice in the world. Part of the reasons for that confidence is that the vast majority of the population is poorly educated about what passes for justice among the have-nots. About four-fifths of Americans also believe, incorrectly, that the poor are entitled to counsel in civil cases; only a third think that low-income individuals would have difficulty finding legal assistance, a perception totally at odds with reality.[25] For the vast majority of consumers of limited or modest means, the problem is not too much law but too little.

Legal Needs

Bar association and government surveys generally reveal substantial levels of unmet legal need. They estimate that about four-fifths of the civil needs of the poor, and two- to three-fifths of the needs of middle-income individuals, are not addressed.[26] It is likely that these surveys understate the extent of the problem, since they typically rely on individuals' own perceptions of their needs, and individuals are not always aware of matters that would justify legal remedies. For example, parties may not know that they are entitled to certain benefits, that their consumer loans fail to meet legal requirements, or that their apartments violate housing code standards. Most legal needs surveys also exclude collective public interest concerns such as environmental risks, racial discrimination in school financing, or political redistricting plans.

Moreover, counting problems does not of itself provide an adequate profile of unmet needs because such an approach makes

23. Rhode, Access to Justice, supra note 1, at 34; James S. Kakalik et al., Costs of Asbestos Litigation vi, viii (1983); James S. Kakalik & Nicholas M. Pace, Costs and Compensation Paid in Tort Litigation xiii (Rand Institute for Civil Justice, 1986).

24. Kagan, Adversarial Legalism, supra note 17, at 136–37; Rhode, Access to Justice, supra note 1, at 34.

25. Id., at ABA, Public Perceptions, supra note 1, at 26.

26. Legal Services Corporation, Documenting the Justice Gap in America (2005); Rhode, Access to Justice, supra note 1, at 3.

no distinctions between urgent concerns and minor grievances; between matters that require extensive assistance and those that demand only minimal help; or between problems that call for attorney expertise and those that could be addressed through less expensive means, such as aid from lay specialists and self-help materials. The best solution to law-related needs is not always more law, lawyers, and legal proceedings. Professor Marc Galanter puts the relevant question, presumably rhetorically: "is the utopia of access to justice a condition in which all disputes are fully adjudicated?"[27] After all, access to the justice system does not guarantee justice in a substantive sense. As Chapter VI notes, the "haves" are still likely to come out ahead, given other advantages apart from lawyers, such as the resources for investigation and expert testimony, the capacity to withstand delay, and the ability to appeal or to lobby for reversal of unfavorable legal decisions.[28]

Americans like to believe that "social justice" (i.e. fairer distribution of societal resources) can be realized through "civil justice" (i.e., access to courts).[29] But as a political matter, it is a very dubious proposition. Distributive justice can be achieved only partly through a legal system, and only through very substantial public subsidies of legal assistance. Indeed, much of the political opposition to subsidized legal services is based on objections to using litigation as a redistributive strategy—as a means of allocating resources such as housing, education, and health care. Many Americans believe that these distributive issues should be resolved through democratic political processes, and not through countermajoritarian judicial proceedings. As discussion below notes, this view has severely constrained the kinds of legal aid that publicly-funded programs can supply.

The problem of unmet need is further compounded by considering the quality of assistance necessary to ensure that access to the legal system is truly meaningful. "Equal justice under law" is a common slogan on courthouse doors, but it does not describe what goes on behind those doors or what guides the nation's funding priorities. Except in a few limited contexts, parties with civil legal needs have no right to any legal assistance, let alone equal assistance. In Lassiter v. Department of Social Services, 452 U.S. 18 (1981), the Supreme Court held that the Constitution required

---

27. Marc Galanter, "Justice in Many Rooms," in Access to Justice and the Welfare State 147, 150–151 (Mauro Cappelletti ed. 1981).

28. Marc Galanter, "Farther Along," 33 Law & Soc'y Rev. 1113, 1114 (1999); Marc Galanter, "Why the Haves Come Out Ahead: Speculations on the Limits of Legal Change," 9 Law & Soc'y Rev. 95 (1974).

29. Geoffrey C. Hazard, Jr., "Social Justice Through Civil Justice," 36 U. Chi. L. Rev. 699 (1969).

provision of counsel in civil cases only where the proceedings would otherwise prove fundamentally unfair, a standard that is almost never met in practice.[30] Other countries' standards are more inclusive. The European Court of Human Rights, for example, recognizes a right to appointed counsel in cases with important interests at stake if an unrepresented litigant "cannot represent himself or herself effectively." Steel and Morris v. United Kingdom, 41 E.H.R.R. 22 (2005).

Even in the criminal law system, where indigent defendants have a constitutional right to effective assistance of counsel, that right is nowhere close to being realized.[31] Public defender caseloads and reimbursement rates for court-appointed counsel are set at grossly unrealistic levels, which make adequate preparation for most defendants a statistical impossibility. Caseloads can range as high as 3500 misdemeanors and 900 felonies per lawyer per year, and $1000 to $1500 limits for counsel fees in felony matters are common.[32] Resources for training, investigation and experts are grossly inadequate, and national expenditures for prosecution are over twice that for defense.[33]

Despite the poor quality of representation that inevitably results, trial judges have declined to find ineffective assistance of counsel in all but a tiny fraction of cases; one study found that 99 percent of such claims were unsuccessful.[34] Convictions, even in death penalty cases, have been sustained where attorneys were asleep, drunk, on drugs, suffering from severe mental illness, or parking their car during key parts of the prosecution's case.[35] Some lawyers have spent less time preparing for a felony trial than the average American spends showering before work; others even in capital cases have been ignorant of key procedural and substantive law.[36] Yet challenges to inadequate statutory fees for private attorneys and excessive assignments for public defenders have too sel-

---

30. See Rhode, supra note 1, at 9.

31. See American Bar Association (ABA), Gideon's Broken Promise: America's Continuing Quest for Equal Justice (2004).

32. Rhode, supra note 1, at 12; ABA, supra note 27, at 17; Vivian Berger, "Time for a Real Raise," Nat'l L. J. Sept. 13, 2004, at 27.

33. ABA, supra note 27, at 13; Rhode, Access to Justice, supra note 1, at 12, 129.

34. Victor E. Flango & Patricia Mckenna, "Federal Habeas Corpus Re-

view of State Court Convictions," 31 Cal. W. L. Rev. 237, 259–60 (1995).

35. Stephen B. Bright, Statement Before the Senate Committee on the Judiciary on the Innocence Protection Act of 2001, Federal News Service, June 27, 2001; Texas Defender Service, Lethal Indifference (2002); David Cole, No Equal Justice: Race and Class in the American Criminal Justice System 87 (1999); Stephen B. Bright, "Sleeping on the Job," Nat'l L. J., Dec. 4, 2000, at A26.

36. Bright, "Sleeping on the Job," supra note 31, at A26; Rhode, supra note 1, at 13; ABA, supra note 27, at 16.

dom been successful.[37] Indeed, judges, who face crushing caseloads of their own, often have been reluctant to encourage effective advocacy that would result in more time-consuming trials and pretrial proceedings.[38]

B. An Overview of Possible Responses

Law, of course, is not the only context in which basic needs remain unmet and the "have-nots" are at a significant disadvantage. Yet the gap between the aspiration and the operation of our legal system is of special concern. Access to justice is critical to the legitimacy of legal and democratic processes. As the Supreme Court has recognized, the right to "sue and defend" is a right "conservative of all other rights, and lies at the foundation of orderly government."[39] For most individuals, in most contexts, that right of access will not be meaningful without some legal assistance.

Yet providing sufficient assistance poses both practical and theoretical difficulties. As a practical matter, guaranteeing a right to civil legal representation for all those who cannot realistically afford counsel could prove quite expensive. To be sure, the right could be limited along the lines that some European countries have developed; subsidies could be available to parties on a sliding scale for cases involving significant interests and a plausible chance of prevailing. Still, such guarantees would entail large increases not only in legal aid budgets, but also in legal costs of opposing parties and in remedies that legal proceedings could secure. If Americans of limited means became able to assert all their entitlements under common law and government programs, the financial implications would be dramatic. In the current political climate, the prospects for such a reform agenda are unpromising, to say the least.

However, it by no means follows that we have done all that is feasible to address unmet needs and to reduce inequalities in legal representation. Many less wealthy nations do a better job than the United States along these dimensions, and promising reform strategies for the American system are readily available. Those strategies

---

37. Rhode, supra note 1, at 128, 132. For examples of efforts to challenge indigent defense systems see ABA, supra note 27, at 33–34. For an ABA ethics opinion maintaining that court-appointed lawyers for indigents should refuse assignments or withdraw from representation if their workload precludes adequate assistance, see ABA Standing Committee on Ethics and Professional Responsibility, Formal Opinion 06–441 (2006).

38. See James L. Kelley, Lawyers Crossing Lines: Nine Stories 171–72 (2001); Rhode, supra note 1, at 128, 132. For examples of efforts to challenge indigent defense systems see ABA, supra note 27, at 33–34.

39. Chambers v. Baltimore & Ohio R.R., 207 U.S. 142, 148 (1907). See David Luban, Lawyers and Justice: An Ethical Study, 263–64 (1988).

take three primary forms: reducing the need for legal intervention and assistance; minimizing the costs of legal procedures and services; and increasing access to subsidized legal representation.

The first approach involves simplification or modification of legal rules and processes to enable parties to avoid legal assistance. Examples include small-claims courts, plain-English statutes, no-fault insurance schemes, standardized forms for simple wills and uncontested divorces, courthouse services for self-represented parties, and automatic wage garnishment for obligations such as child support payments. A second approach is to reduce the cost of such assistance through greater reliance on computer programs, on-line aid, alternative dispute resolution procedures, and nonlawyer experts. A third approach is to expand access to lawyers through publicly subsidized legal aid programs and pro bono contributions by the private bar.

C. Court Reform and Non–Lawyer Services

In "poor peoples' courts" that handle housing, bankruptcy, small claims, and family matters, parties without lawyers are less the exception than the rule. Cases in which at least one side is unrepresented are far more common than those in which both have counsel. In some of these courts, over four-fifths of the proceedings involve pro se litigants.[40] Yet most systems in which these parties operate have been designed by lawyers for the functions of lawyers. A challenge for societies committed to access to justice is to make those systems effective for those who cannot afford counsel.

To that end, a growing number of jurisdictions have developed pro se assistance programs involving procedural simplification, expanded small claims courts, standardized forms, educational publications, on-line materials, self-help centers with interactive kiosks for information and document preparation, and free in-person advice from volunteer lawyers or court personnel.[41] Yet many court systems still have no formal pro se services and many of the services that are available are unusable by those who need help most: uneducated litigants with limited computer competence and English language skills. All too often, these unassisted parties are expected to prepare forms and navigate procedures of bewildering

---

40. Pamela A. MacLean, "Self–Help Centers Meet Pro Se Flood," Nat'l. L. J., June 26, 2006, at 1, 15; Russell Engler, "And Justice For All—Including the Unrepresented Poor: Revisiting the Roles of the Judges, Mediators, and Clerks," 67 Fordham L. Rev. 1987 (1999); Jona Goldschmidt, "How Are Courts Handling Pro Se Litigants?," 82 Judicature 13, 14 (1998).

41. For an overview, see Rhode, Access to Justice, supra note 1, at 84–86; Goldschmidt, supra note 40, at 29–34; Engler, supra note 40, at 2049.

complexity. Court clerks and mediators are instructed not to give legal advice, since that, technically, would constitute a violation of statutes prohibiting "unauthorized practice of law".[42] Further assistance is obviously critical to make "equal justice under law" a realistic aspiration.

More jurisdictions could also follow the lead of justice systems that include "holistic," "therapeutic," and specialized community courts. These courts partner with nonlegal experts, including mental health professionals and social service providers, to address problems such as domestic violence, homelessness, and misdemeanor offenses involving prostitution, drugs, and juveniles. This approach seeks to deal with underlying causes, not simply their legal symptoms. The research available suggests that many of these approaches have been successful in reducing repeat offenses and designing effective remedial plans.[43]

Reforms are also necessary concerning nonlawyer services outside the courthouse. Every state imposes criminal penalties for engaging in the unauthorized "practice of law" by individuals who are not licensed members of the bar. What falls within this prohibition varies across jurisdictions, but the dominant approach is to ban any personalized legal advice. In general, lay practitioners may type documents, but may not answer even the simplest law-related questions or correct obvious errors. Internet providers may supply information and generic documents, but not specific advice.[44] Bar ethical rules also prohibit lawyers from assisting the unauthorized practice of law. Model Rule 5.5; DR 3–101(1).

These ethical and statutory prohibitions have been subject to increasing criticism. During the last decade, courts and legislatures in over half the states have considered proposals involving nonlawyer specialists and a few jurisdictions have liberalized rules regarding lay document providers. Such proposals are in part a response to simplification of certain legal processes, and the increasing availability of computer software, standardized forms, and alternative dispute resolution proceedings that facilitate alternatives to lawyers. The push for nonlawyer assistance also comes from re-

---

42. Engler, supra note 33, at 2056, 2060, 2064; Tina L. Rasnow, "Traveling Justice: Providing Court–Based Pro Se Assistance to Limited Access Communities," 20 Fordham Urban L. J. 1281, 1293 (2002).

43. Rhode, Access to Justice, supra note 1, at 86; Greg Berman & John Feinblat, Problem Solving Courts: A Brief Primer (2001).

44. See Rhode, In the Interests of Justice, supra note 1, at 136; ABA, Consumer's Guide to Legal Help on the Internet; Self–Help, available at http://abanet.org/legalservices/publicdiv.html; Model Rules of Professional Conduct, Rule 5.5, Comment. (2002).

search surveying their performance here and abroad, which finds that lay specialists are generally at least as qualified as lawyers to provide assistance on routine matters where legal needs are greatest.[45] That is not entirely surprising since law schools do not usually teach, and bar exams do not test, the specialized information involved in dealing with divorces, landlord-tenant disputes, bankruptcy, immigration, welfare, and similar claims.

Accordingly, most scholars and bar association commissions that have systematically studied the issue believe that unauthorized practice rules should be reconsidered and that alternative forms of regulation be developed.[46] For example, states could develop licensing systems for nonlawyers and Internet services and enforce more narrowly drawn prohibitions against unethical or unqualified providers. Lay practitioners and services could also be required to carry malpractice insurance, contribute to compensation funds for defrauded clients, and observe the same ethical obligations as lawyers concerning confidentiality, competence, and conflicts of interest. Responsibility for enforcement of such regulatory systems could rest with local prosecutors and consumer protection authorities rather than with the organized bar, which has an obvious economic stake in restricting nonlawyer competitors.

D. Subsidized Legal Services

The first American legal aid society was founded in 1876 as part of an organization to assist German immigrants. Within the next several decades, legal services programs were established in various urban areas through private charity and municipal subsidies. In 1919, Reginald Heber Smith published a landmark study, Justice and the Poor, which reported a total of only about 40 organizations throughout the country, with woefully inadequate resources. The ABA subsequently appointed Smith to head its Standing Committee on Legal Aid, which began providing modest support to local offices. However, as late as 1963, the United States had only about 250 legal services offices with a combined annual budget of approximately four million dollars.[47] Many bar associa-

---

45. See sources cited in Rhode, Interests of Justice, supra note 1, at 136–38; Herbert Kritzer, Legal Advocacy: Lawyers and Nonlawyers at Work 193–203 (1998).

46. See sources cited in Rhode, In the Interests of Justice, supra note 1, at 136–38; Kritzer, supra note 45; ABA Commission on Nonlawyer Practice, Nonlawyer Activity in Law–Related Situations: A Report with Recommendations (1995).

47. Bryant G. Garth, Neighborhood Law Firms for the Poor: A Comparative Study of Recent Developments in Legal Aid and in the Legal Profession 19–20 (1980). For accounts of the earlier development of legal aid programs, see Ronald Pipkin, "Legal Aid and Elitism in the American Legal Profession," in Be-

tions initially opposed expansion of legal services organizations out of concern that they would compete for clients with private practitioners and pave the way to greater state and federal control of the profession (the legal analogue to "socialized medicine"). According to one ABA president, "the entry of the government into the field of providing legal services is too dangerous to be permitted ... in our free America."[48]

In the 1960s, a liberal political climate, with its "War on Poverty" brought a massive influx of federal aid, widespread bar association support, and a new reformist ethos to civil legal aid programs. The consequences were quickly apparent, as poverty law offices achieved significant victories in consumer, welfare, housing, health, and related legal areas. However, these victories also resulted in political backlash, which translated into curtailment of funds and restrictions on the kinds of cases and activities that lawyers could pursue. To provide somewhat greater political insulation for poverty law offices, in 1974, Congress established the Legal Services Corporation, with board members appointed by the President and confirmed by the Senate. Although the Corporation has supervisory authority over legal services programs, Congress has the power to curtail their efforts by cutting the budget for legal assistance and by preventing federally-subsidized programs from pursuing controversial activities. At current funding levels, legal aid programs can serve less than a fifth of their target population; their combined annual budget works out to less than $10 for every person officially classified as poor. Prohibited activities include lobbying, community organizing, class action lawsuits, and cases involving prisoners, undocumented aliens, abortion, homosexual rights, school desegregation, and housing for accused drug dealers.[49] Although the Supreme Court has struck down one restriction on welfare reform litigation as unconstitutional viewpoint discrimination, lower courts have consistently upheld the other limitations as permissible conditions on federal funding.[50]

Despite strong support from the organized bar, efforts to expand the budgets and activities of legal service providers have encountered substantial resistance. Criticism of these programs comes from all points on the ideological spectrum. Critics from the

fore the Law: An Introduction to the Legal Process 185 (John J. Bonsignore et al., eds. 2d ed. 1979).

48. Jerold S. Auerbach, Unequal Justice: Lawyers and Social Change in Modern America 236 (1976) (quoting Harold J. Gallagher); Alan W. Houseman, "Political Lessons: Legal Services

for the Poor—A Commentary," 83 Geo. L. J. 1669, 1678 (1995).

49. See U.S.C. § 2996 et seq.

50. Legal Services Corporation v. Velazquez, 531 U.S. 533 (2001); Legal Aid Society of Hawaii v. Legal Services Corporation, 145 F.3d 1017 (9th Cir.1998).

right have often denounced poverty lawyers as ideological vigilantes who have attempted to mastermind social change without public accountability.[51] Other commentators have questioned the effectiveness of legal services in redistributing income and power. In their view, when poverty lawyers defend "deadbeat" consumers or tenants, opponents' additional legal costs will be passed on to other low-income individuals in the form of higher prices.[52] Alternatively, recognition of formal rights may have little concrete effect, given the post-judgment relations of the parties, the difficulties of enforcement, and the possibility of legislative reversal. Some critics also question whether providing legal services is a more cost-effective means of transferring goods and services to the poor than subsidizing those goods directly, for example, through housing grants, community redevelopment programs, or broader coverage of medical needs.[53]

Critics from the left raise other concerns. One is that publicly subsidized legal assistance may sometimes work against fundamental change by channeling disputes into individualized grievances that exact small scale remedies but do not challenge systemic problems or basic power relations. Because congressional restrictions prevent lobbying, class actions, and community organizing, it is difficult for legal aid lawyers to address the structural causes of poverty-related needs. Another concern is that federally-funded programs, in order to appease legislative critics and avoid further budgetary cutbacks, have been forced to focus on maximizing the number of individuals assisted in noncontroversial matters. The result is to compromise the quality of representation provided and to leave the most politically vulnerable causes with no legal protections. Another longstanding concern is that some poverty lawyers are insufficiently sensitive to class, racial, and ethnic concerns, and have failed to empower clients, individually or collectively, to address their own problems.[54]

By contrast, defenders of civil legal aid view it as a vital means of securing basic rights, challenging government and corporate

---

51. Kenneth F. Boehm, "The Legal Service Program: Unaccountable Political, Anti–Poor, Beyond Repair and Unnecessary," 17 St. Louis Publ. L. Rev. 321, 327–34, 340–51 (1998); Patrick J. Kiger, An Unsolved Mystery: Why Are Rogue Politicians Trying to Kill a Program that Helps Their Neediest Constituents? 2 (Brennan Center for Justice, 2000).

52. Hazard, supra note 29, at 737.

53. Richard Posner, Economic Analysis of the Law 479–481 (6th ed. 2003).

54. For concerns, see Gerald Lopez, Rebellious Lawyering (1992); Marc Feldman, "Political Lessons: Legal Services for the Poor," 83 Geo. L.J. 1529, 1537–41, 1552–56 (1995); for challenges, see Alan W. Houseman, "Racial Justice: The Role of Civil Legal Assistance," 36 Clearinghouse Review: Journal of Poverty Law & Policy 5 (1992) at 5.

misconduct, and empowering low-income constituencies. For many impoverished clients, legal services may be the only way to address fundamental needs in areas involving health, housing, welfare, education, family law, or related matters. Also, since courts, unlike legislatures, are open as of right, they are often the most accessible, if not always the most effective, forums in which to seek redress. To withhold legal services in the hopes of channeling frustrations into more fundamental change seems to many commentators strategically dubious and morally objectionable. So also, to assume that cash transfers for the poor would be more effective than direct provision of services ignores the political obstacles to achieving such transfers and the importance of meeting nonquantifiable or collective needs. Providing every poor person the cash equivalent of legal aid subsidies—currently about ten dollars per year—would scarcely do much to protect basic needs. By contrast, legal services programs can at least deter or redress some serious injustices and help some clients develop the capacity to help themselves.

To that end, most poverty law experts advocate targeting resources to widely shared problems and collaborative, community-based responses. By focusing some resources on educational projects, self-help programs, representation of local organizations, and partnering with other social service providers, legal services offices can aid low-income clients not only in resolving individual problems, but also in challenging certain underlying causes of subordination.[55]

Given the chronic underfunding of legal aid programs, many experts also advocate additional sources of financial support. Proposals include increases in court filing fees and taxes on law-related revenues. Related possibilities include more public interest programs and greater pro bono contributions from the private bar, along the lines discussed below.

E.   Public Interest Law and "Cause Lawyering"

Although the terms "public interest law" and "cause lawyering" are relatively recent, the concepts have their roots in earlier civil liberties and civil rights initiatives. The growth of an organized civil liberties movement began during World War I, when a small group of pacifists founded an organization that evolved into the

---

55. López, supra note 54; Rhode, Access to Justice, supra note 1, at 117–19; National Association of Legal Aid and Defender Association, Leaders for Justice: A National Leadership Development Initiative for the Legal Aid Community and the Equal Justice Movement (2002); Matthew Diller, "Lawyering for Poor Communities in the Twenty–First Century," 25 Fordham Urb. L. J. 673, 678 (1998).

American Civil Liberties Union. Its activities eventually broadened to include not only free speech and association but also equal rights and reproductive choice. America's first major civil rights organization, the National Association for the Advancement of Colored People, also emerged in the early twentieth century. In the late 1930s, the NAACP Legal Defense Fund spun off as a separate organization to orchestrate a systematic legal campaign against racial injustice.[56] Other smaller organizations joined these efforts and served as models for many contemporary public interest organizations.

During the late 1960s and early 1970s, a rise in political activism, together with a large increase in foundation funding, gave birth to new forms of cause lawyering. Judicial and legislative initiatives further encouraged this development. Test-case litigation became a more effective strategy as courts began liberalizing doctrines regarding ripeness, standing, and sovereign immunity, and as Congress began authorizing fee awards to "prevailing parties" in various civil rights, consumer, environmental, and analogous cases. By the 1990s, some 200 centers with some 1,000 lawyers met the definition of a public interest legal organization developed by the Council for Public Interest Law: a tax-exempt non-profit entity that employs at least one attorney and devotes at least thirty percent of its total resources to the legal representation of previously unrepresented interests on matters of public policy.[57] The National Association for Law Placement has a broader definition that includes "positions funded by the Legal Services Corporation and others providing civil legal services as well as positions with private non-profit advocacy or cause oriented organizations ... non-profit policy analysts and research organizations and public defenders." By this definition, slightly under 3 percent of law graduates now take jobs with public interest organizations.[58] In addition, a substantial number of private firms that do not qualify for non profit tax-exempt status devote a major portion of their work to public interest representation.

When the term public interest legal organization first appeared in the late 1960s, it was associated with liberal causes. By the mid 1970s, a growing number of conservative advocacy organizations began emerging. Those groups increased dramatically in size and

---

56. See Richard Kluger, Simple Justice: The History of Brown v Board of Education and Black America's Struggle for Equality (1976); Mark V. Tushnet, The NAACP's Legal Strategy Against Segregated Education, 1925–1950 (1987).

57. Id.

58. National Association for Law Placement, Jobs & J.D.s: Employment and Salaries of New Law Graduates— Class of 2005 (2006).

influence during the next two decades, building on coalitions with the religious right, libertarians, and corporations.[59] Some of these organizations fall outside the National Council's definition of public interest lawyering because they take positions that are already well-represented by their corporate funders.

The Council's definition raises long-standing questions about the role and meaning of "public interest" organizations. The conventional justification for public interest law rests on the failure of current political and market structures to take adequate account of the concerns of unorganized or subordinate groups. Where transaction costs in organizing are high, and parties have limited resources or individual stakes in representation, the rationale for public interest advocacy is greatest. Yet this rationale leaves key definitional issues unresolved. Clearly "underrepresentation" and nonprofit status do not of themselves qualify a legal position as being "in the public interest." For example, few individuals would apply the public-interest label to an organization of adults who sought to eliminate prohibitions on sexual relations with children. Yet, if the concept of public interest presupposes some widely shared values or socially defensible criteria, how should these be determined? And who should decide? On many of the most important social issues facing the court, legal advocacy organizations are on both sides of the controversy, each claiming to represent the public interest.

Much cause lawyering raises a broad range of concerns analogous to those involving subsidized legal services. Critics from the right have traditionally complained that the public interest movement vests too much influence in non-majoritarian judicial processes, while critics from the left have complained that such influence is too limited to produce lasting social change. Conservative objections build on a long tradition of challenges to judicial activism. Litigation that avowedly aims at restructuring institutions or redistributing resources has drawn criticism on the ground that courts lack the competence or accountability for such a role. According to critics, such cases invite rule by judges who lack the necessary training, institutional familiarity, and enforcement mechanisms.[60] However, over the last decades, as appointments to the federal bench have become increasingly conservative, this traditional critique has become more qualified; judicial activism on behalf of

---

59. Ann Southworth, "Conservative Lawyers and the Contest Over the Meaning of 'Public Interest Law'," 52 UCLA L. Rev. 1223 (2005).

60. Ross Sandler & David Schoenbrod, Democracy by Decree: What Happens When Courts Run Government (2003); Gerald N. Rosenberg, The Hollow Hope: Can Courts Bring About Social Change? (1991).

conservative causes is precisely what conservative legal groups often advocate.[61]

The traditional critiques of public interest law have prompted responses on several levels. Defenders note that it is not inconsistent with democratic principles for the public to delegate certain functions to non-majoritarian processes. Such a delegation is particularly appropriate to protect the needs of "discrete and insular minorities," or diffuse majorities that lack resources to organize in a political system unavoidably shaped by well-financed interests.[62] Courts can play a critical role in enforcing constitutional principles that other branches of government fail to vindicate. And public interest organizations play an equally critical role in bringing the cases that make such judicial oversight possible.

Moreover, public interest work often focuses on lobbying or on legal strategies designed to further, not subvert, legislative intent. Examples include suits seeking compliance with environmental, occupational safety, and consumer regulation. In many contexts, public interest organizations increase accountability in governmental policy making by providing review that is otherwise absent. Elected representatives may lack the time, information, and technical expertise to monitor implementation of statutory mandates. Where courts face similar limitations, they can rely on special masters or broker settlements that involve stakeholders who have the necessary skills and knowledge.[63]

While critics from the right often worry that cause lawyering has too much influence, critics from the left worry that it has too little. From their perspective, public interest attorneys have overly relied on litigation and formal rights, which have diverted efforts from the political organizing necessary to make rights meaningful. Too often, public interest lawyers lack resources to monitor compliance with test-case decrees, and some defendants—particularly governmental institutions (such as prisons, schools, or mental hospitals)—lack funds for adequately implementing judicial remedies. Decisions that lack public support are also vulnerable to statutory reversal or administrative agency resistance. Critics claim that public interest lawyers place undue reliance on litigation because their credibility and professional reputations depend on such visible

---

61. Southworth, supra note 59.

62. United States v. Carolene Products Co., 304 U.S. 144, 152 (1938); Luban, supra note 39, at 358–70; Stuart Scheingold & Austin Sarat, Something to Believe In: Professionalism, Politics, and Cause Lawyers (2004).

63. Charles F. Sabel & William H. Simon, "Destabilization Rights: How Public Law Litigation Succeeds," 117 Harv. L. Rev. 1015 (2004).

achievements, and because their backgrounds often ill-equip them for other roles such as grass roots organizing. The result is not to empower clients to challenge their subordination but instead only to alleviate its symptoms.[64]

Such concerns, together with broader cultural trends, have led many public interest legal organizations to focus less on litigation and more on lobbying, education, research, outreach, counseling, and related programs.[65] The increasing conservatism of federal courts, together with stricter notice and standing requirements, has prompted liberal public interest groups to use test cases less often and more strategically. In some instances, litigation is filed or threatened simply to gain bargaining leverage in out-of-court settings. In other contexts, lawsuits serve primarily as catalysts for political action and organizing efforts. Even when public interest groups "lose" in court, they may win outside in the wider struggle for public support, community empowerment, and policy reforms.

A final set of concerns raised by public interest law involves issues of accountability and conflicts of interest. As the discussion of class actions in Chapter VIII noted, the more unorganized the clients, the fewer the constraints on counsel. And public interest lawyers by definition have political and moral commitments that transcend client interests.[66] In critics' view, lawyers who lack accountability are no more likely to speak for the public than the government officials whose actions are at issue. In what sense can these lawyers claim to be more representative of the public than elected or executive officials?

In response to such criticisms, public interest lawyers note that they are not without some forms of accountability. Their influence depends on credibility with various constituencies: clients, funders, courts, policy makers, commentators, peers, and community organizations. In the long run, the effectiveness of any public interest organization depends on its accountability—its ability to express widely shared values, vindicate critical principles, and justify a need for its continued advocacy.

F. Pro Bono Representation

The "learned professions," including law and medicine, distinguish themselves from business occupations by emphasizing their

64. López, supra note 54; Anthony Alfieri, "Practicing Community," 107 Harv. L. Rev. 1747 (1994).

65. Laura Beth Nielsen & Catherine R. Albiston, "The Organization of Public Interest Practice: 1975–2004," 84 N. Car. L. Rev. 1591, 1612 (2006). A signifi-cant proportion of public interest legal organizations focus on direct provision of services to individual clients. Id., at 1593.

66. Scheingold and Sarat, supra note 62; Nielsen & Albiston, supra note 65.

collective commitment to public service. The bar in this country has a long-standing tradition of service *pro bono publico:* legal services "for the public good," provided at no cost or at a reduced fee. This concept encompasses a wide range of activities, including law reform efforts, participation in bar associations and civic organizations, and individual or group representation. Clients who receive such assistance also span a broad range including: low-income individuals; nonprofit organizations; ideological or political causes; and friends, relatives, or employees of the lawyer.

Although the bar has long supported pro bono in principle, its commitment in practice has been more qualified. The Model Code of Professional Responsibility included only aspirational references to lawyers' "basic responsibility" to assist those unable to pay for legal services. Ethical Consideration 2–25. No Disciplinary Rule reinforced this responsibility, and the bar's internalized commitments were uneven at best. One representative mid–1970s study found that lawyers' average contribution was under 6 percent of billable hours and only about 5 percent of this work went to assist the poor; the vast majority of pro bono assistance went to friends, relatives, employees, bar associations, and organizations serving middle or upper-income constituencies, such as Jaycees, Little Leagues, and symphonies.[67]

In 1980, in an effort to inspire greater levels of service, the Commission that drafted the Model Rules initially proposed a requirement that lawyers devote 40 hours of work at no fee or a reduced fee, or offer an equivalent financial contribution, to persons of limited means or to organizations assisting them. That proposal prompted overwhelming opposition, as did a requirement that lawyers report their voluntary contributions. Accordingly, the Rules as originally adopted included only an aspirational provision, which a series of amendments gradually strengthened. As currently formulated, Model Rule 6.1 states that a lawyer "should aspire to render at least (50) hours of pro bono publico legal services per year" and should provide a "substantial majority" of such services to "persons of limited means" or to organizations that are designed primarily to assist such individuals. The Comment to this Rule makes clear that it "is not intended to be enforced through disciplinary process."

Over the past two decades, many bar associations and state courts have rejected mandatory pro bono proposals, but a few jurisdictions have imposed limited requirements. According to ABA

---

67. Joel F. Handler, et al., "The Public Interest Activities of Private Practice Lawyers," 68 ABA J. 1388, 1389 (1975).

Standing Committee on Pro Bono and Public Service, five states require members of the bar to report their contributions to a voluntary program. Eleven states have voluntary reporting provisions. New Jersey appoints unpaid counsel for indigents, and other jurisdictions require pro bono assistance by attorneys who wish to be considered for appointments in paying cases.[68] Although the Supreme Court has never issued a full opinion on the constitutionality of requiring uncompensated service, it has suggested in dicta and in a summary dismissal of an appeal that such requirements are permissible.[69]

Full information about lawyers' pro bono contributions is unavailable. Only three states mandate reporting of contribution levels, and many lawyers take liberties with the definition of "pro bono" to include bar association involvement and any uncompensated or undercompensated client service, even if performed with the expectation of payment.[70] In the ABA's most recent national survey, about two-thirds of lawyers report some pro bono contributions, broadly defined.[71] However, levels of service appear quite modest in the states that collect such data, ranging from about 20 to 40 hours.[72] Fewer than ten percent of practitioners accept referrals from federally-funded legal aid offices or bar-sponsored poverty-related programs.[73] Most lawyers are not more charitable with their money than their time. In short, the best available research finds that the American legal profession averages less than

68. See ABA Standing Committee on Pro Bono and Public Service Responsibilities, summarized in 22 ABA/BNA Manual on Professional Conduct 321 (2006); Deborah L Rhode, Pro Bono in Principle and in Practice 17 (2005). The Florida program, developed by the state bar, states an expectation that every Florida attorney will perform at least 20 hours annually of direct pro bono legal services to the poor or make a $350 cash contribution. Each lawyer must report whether the expectation was met, but failure to do so will not result in any disciplinary sanctions. Talbot D'Alemberte, "Tributaries of Justice: The Search for Full Access," Florida Bar J., April, 1999, at 12. New Jersey exempts from its requirements practitioners in certain categories, such as public defenders, legal aid lawyers, and private practitioners who volunteer at least 25 hours of assistance to the poor through qualifying legal aid organizations. Madden v. Township of Delran, 601 A.2d 211 (N.J. 1992); "Exemptions from Madden v.

Delran Pro Bono Assignments for 2002," N.J. Bar J. March 11, 2002, at 1.

69. Sparks v. Parker, 368 So.2d 528 (Ala.1979), appeal dismissed, 444 U.S. 803 (1979); Powell v. Alabama, 287 U.S. 45, 73 (1932).

70. See Carroll Seron, The Business of Practicing Law: The Work Lives of Solo and Small–Firm Attorneys 129–33 (1996); see also sources cited in Rhode, Pro Bono, supra note 68, at 19–20.

71. ABA, Supporting Justice: A Report on the Pro Bono Work of America's Lawyers (2005). Under the ABA's definition, bar association involvement would qualify, even though such work is often primarily undertaken for the lawyer's professional benefit and is unrelated to the needs of underserved communities.

72. Rhode, Pro Bono, supra note 68, at 20.

73. LSC Statistics: Private Attorney Involvement, All Programs, available at http://www.lsc.gov/pressr/pr_pai.htm.

half an hour of work per week and under half a dollar per day in support of pro bono legal services.[74] The record for the profession's most affluent members is not significantly better. Only about a third of the nation's large law firms have committed themselves to meet the ABA's Pro Bono Challenge, which requires contributions equivalent to three to five percent of gross revenues and only slightly over a third of the lawyers at the nation's 200 largest firms devote at least 20 hours a year to pro bono work.[75]

Efforts to increase the profession's public service commitments through mandatory obligations have met with both moral and practical objections. As a matter of principle, many lawyers believe that compulsory charity is a contradiction in terms. From their perspective, requiring service would undermine its moral significance and infringe lawyers' own rights. To some practitioners, such an obligation seems tantamount to "involuntary servitude."[76] If access to justice is a societal value, then society as a whole should bear its cost. The poor have fundamental needs for food and medical care, but we do not require grocers or physicians to donate their help in meeting those needs. Why should lawyers' responsibilities be greater?

Supporters of pro bono obligations offer several answers. Lawyers have special privileges that entail special obligations, and access to legal services justice is critical not only to individual well being but to the legitimacy of the justice system. America's highly legalized culture makes legal assistance "essential to virtually all projects of social import[ance]."[77] Attorneys in this nation have a much more extensive and exclusive right to provide legal assistance than attorneys in other countries, and a greater monopoly than other professions in providing essential services.[78] The American bar has long guarded those prerogatives and severely restricted lay competition. Under these circumstances, supporters of pro bono work believe that it is not unreasonable to expect lawyers to provide some charitable assistance in return for their privileged status. The ABA's proposed standard of 50 hours per year, roughly

---

74. Rhode, Pro Bono, supra note 68, at 20.

75. Id. Michael Aneiro, "Room To Improve," The American Lawyer, July 2006, at 100.

76. Tigran W. Eldred & Thomas Schoenherr, "The Lawyer's Duty of Public Service: More Than Charity?," 96 W. Va. L. Rev. 367, 391 n. 97 (1993–94); and sources quoted in Rhode, Pro Bono, supra note 68, at 37–38.

77. Harry T. Edwards, "A Lawyer's Duty to Serve the Public Good," 65 N.Y.U. L. Rev. 1148, 1156 (1990).

78. Andrew Boon & Jennifer Levin, The Ethics and Conduct of Lawyers in England and Wales 55–59, 402 (1999); see also Christine Parker, Just Lawyers: Regulation and Access to Justice 1–9 (1999).

an hour per week of uncompensated assistance, scarcely seems the functional equivalent of slavery.

Yet many lawyers who support pro bono in principle believe that mandatory obligations would be unworkable in practice. Defining what would qualify as pro bono and monitoring compliance pose significant challenges. If the primary objective is, as the ABA's Model Rules suggest, to assist persons of limited means, then requiring contributions of lawyers with no interest or expertise in poverty law scarcely seems a cost-effective way of providing services. But to supporters of pro bono requirements, the question again is, "Compared to what?" For many low-income groups, some assistance would be better than none, which is their current alternative. Experience with bar-supported voluntary programs suggests that concerns of cost-effectiveness can be addressed by two strategies: offering a diverse range of opportunities for participation, coupled with educational programs and support structures; and allowing lawyers unwilling or unable to provide direct service the option of substituting cash assistance to legal aid providers. Even if full compliance with pro bono requirements could not be assured, these measures would at least support attorneys who would like to participate in such public service but who work in organizations that have discouraged participation.

However the debate over mandatory pro bono is resolved, the bar has strong reasons to encourage greater voluntary involvement. For many lawyers, such involvement provides crucial opportunities to develop new skills, obtain valuable trial experience, and enhance their contacts and reputations in the community. Such opportunities, in the context of causes to which attorneys are committed, are also a way of connecting many practitioners to the concerns that sent them to law school in the first instance. That is a connection that too many attorneys find lacking in their current practice. Indeed, bar surveys consistently report that lawyers' greatest source of dissatisfaction with their careers is the lack of contribution to the social good.[79] Pro bono work not only provides such opportunities, it also gives participants a better understanding of how the justice system functions, or fails to function, for the have-nots.[80] Such exposure may build support for reform, and make increased access to justice a greater professional priority.

---

79. ABA Young Lawyers Division Survey: Career Satisfaction 11 (2000).

80. Steven Lubet & Cathryn Stewart, "A 'Public Assets' Theory of Lawyers' Pro Bono Obligations," 145 U. Pa. L. Rev. 1245, 1299 (1997); Rhode, Pro Bono, supra note 68, at 29.

Chapter X

REGULATING THE MARKET
FOR LEGAL SERVICES

The standard justification for regulating how lawyers promote, structure, and price their services rests on imperfections in the market for legal assistance. These imperfections include what economists describe as information barriers, free riders, and externalities.

The information problems arise from many consumers' inability to make knowledgeable assessments about the services they receive, either before or after purchase. Most individual (as opposed to organizational) clients are one-shot purchasers; many will not consult an attorney more than once or twice in a lifetime, and of those who do, a majority will select different lawyers each time. This lack of experience, coupled with the expense and difficulties of comparative shopping for professional services, makes it hard for consumers to make cost-effective choices. In the absence of external regulation, some clients may suffer significant losses from incompetent or unethical practitioners. When consumers cannot accurately differentiate among the services available, lawyers may lack adequate incentives to provide quality representation and a "market for lemons" may develop.

An additional difficulty involves "free riders"—i.e., those who gain benefits without contributing to collective goods. For example, the bar collectively has an interest in securing the public's trust, and in having lawyers conduct themselves as fiduciaries in such a way as to maintain that trust. However, without effective regulatory structures, individual attorneys may have inadequate economic incentives to avoid cheating; they can benefit as free riders from the bar's general reputation without adhering to basic ethical mandates themselves.

A final category of problems calling for regulatory responses involves external costs to society and third parties from conduct that may be advantageous to particular clients and their lawyers. For example, the public generally has an interest in promoting just and expeditious resolution of disputes and discouraging non-meritorious claims, but in some circumstances, a litigant's or attorney's economic interests may be to the contrary.

184

Although commentators on the legal profession generally agr
that these problems call for regulation, there is considerable di
pute about the forms it should take, and how much control the
profession should exercise over the regulatory process. The following materials explore these issues.

A. Advertising

Although many lawyers view advertising of legal services as a
recent and regrettable development, it is restrictions on advertising
that are recent. Practitioners in ancient Greece and Rome were not
hesitant to hawk their services. Nor was there any such reluctance
among some of this country's most distinguished nineteenth century attorneys, including Abraham Lincoln and David Hoffman, the
author of one of the first legal ethics treatises.

However, as the materials in Chapter II indicate, bar leaders at
the turn of the twentieth century became increasingly concerned
about promotional practices. The ABA's 1908 Canons of Ethics
maintained that it was "unprofessional to solicit professional employment" through advertisements. Even indirect promotional
methods, such as comments to newspapers, were considered inappropriate. According to Canon 2.1, "self-laudation" of any form
would "offend the traditions and lower the tone of our profession."
Canon 2.1. By and large, that remained the bar's position until the
1970s. For most of the twentieth century, legal ethics committees
spent more time on refining and enforcing restrictions on advertising and solicitation than on any other subject.[1] Impermissible
practices included distributing calendars, embossed matchbooks, or
Christmas cards with a lawyer's name and profession; displaying
office signs with ostentatiously large lettering; cooperating with a
magazine profile of "blue chip firms"; wearing jewelry with the
state bar insignia; and using boldface type in telephone books.[2]

The seemingly trivial preoccupations of some ethics opinions
should not, however, obscure the serious concerns at issue. To

---

1. James Willard Hurst, The Growth
of American Law: The Law Makers 331
(1950); Philip Shuchman, Ethics and Legal Ethics: The Propriety of the Canons
as a Group Moral Code, 37 Geo. Wash.
L. Rev. 244, 255–56 (1968).

2. Geoffrey C. Hazard, Jr., Susan P.
Koniak, Roger C. Cramton, & George M.
Cohen, The Law and Ethics of Lawyering 930 (4th ed. 2005) (discussing magazine profile and calendars); In re Maltby,
202 P. 2d 902 (Ariz. 1949) (matchbooks);
ABA Comm. on Prof. Ethics, Formal Op.

309 (1963) (Christmas cards); In re Duf-
fy, 242 N.Y.S. 2d 665 (App. Div.1963)
(neon sign); Henry S. Drinker, Legal
Ethics 289, app. A., at 289 (1953) (size of
sign); Belli v. State Bar, 519 P. 2d 575
(Cal. 1974) (Scotch); ABA Comm. on
Prof. Ethics, Informal Op. C–747 (1964)
(state bar jewelry); ABA Comm. on
Prof'l. Ethics, Formal Op. 184 (1951)
(phone book); but see ABA Comm. On
Prof'l. Ethics, Informal Op. 1222 (1972)
(jewelry with ABA insignia permissible).

leaders of the organized bar, the prohibitions on advertising and solicitation expressed deeply felt understandings about law as a profession rather than a business. From their perspective, allowing overt self-promotion would erode professionalism, invite deception, and diminish lawyers' public image and reputation.

Ethical Rules

Beginning in the late 1960s, broad prohibitions on advertising were coming under increased challenge. Various factors fueled criticism of the bar's anti-competitive policies: the rise of a consumer movement, the growing acceptance of advertising by other professionals; the emergence of high-volume low-cost legal clinics; and the heightened concerns about unmet legal needs among groups of limited income. Many lawyers viewed these policies as anachronistic. They seemed premised on the model of a small-town legal practice in which professional reputation was a matter of common knowledge and information about the cost and quality of services was readily accessible. In addition, critics objected to the elitist biases underpinning bar policy. Lawyers representing wealthy individuals and corporations had various opportunities for genteel self-promotion among potential clients; their firms not only subsidized social events and memberships in private clubs, they also purchased listings in bar-approved law directories available to major businesses. By contrast, attorneys representing poor and middle income individuals had fewer chances to publicize their services, and their potential clients were less likely to have other channels of information.

These concerns set the stage for legal challenges that eventually reached the Supreme Court. The first of these suits, Bates v. State Bar of Arizona, 433 U.S. 350 (1977), involved a somewhat colorless advertisement for a legal clinic offering "legal services at very reasonable fees." The ad also listed charges for certain routine services such as uncontested divorces, adoptions, and simple personal bankruptcies. The Supreme Court held that lawyer advertising could not be subjected to blanket suppression, and that the advertisement at issue fell within First Amendment protections.

In a subsequent decision, In re R.M.J., 455 U.S. 191 (1982), the Court again struck down content restrictions on non-misleading advertising claims. Drawing on general commercial speech doctrine as set forth in Central Hudson Gas & Electric Corp. v. Public Service Comm., 447 U.S. 557 (1980), the Court summarized its approach as follows:

> Truthful advertising related to lawful activities is entitled to the protections of the First Amendment. But when the particu-

lar content or method of the advertising suggests that it is inherently misleading or when experience has proved that in fact such advertising is subject to abuse, the States may impose appropriate restrictions. Misleading advertising may be prohibited entirely. But the States may not place an absolute prohibition on certain types of potentially misleading information, e.g., a listing of areas of practice, if the information also may be presented in a way that is not deceptive. . . . Although the potential for deception and confusion is particularly strong in the context of advertising professional services, restrictions upon such advertising may be no broader than reasonably necessary to prevent the deception.

Even when a communication is not misleading, the State retains some authority to regulate. But the State must assert a substantial interest and the interference with speech must be in proportion to the interest served. Restrictions must be narrowly drawn, and the State lawfully may regulate only to the extent regulation furthers the State's substantial interest. In re R.M.J., 455 U.S. at 203.

Subsequent cases held that states could not prohibit nondeceptive graphic illustrations or descriptions of ongoing litigation, Zauderer v. Office of Disciplinary Counsel, 471 U.S. 626 (1985); mailings targeted to a specific recipient rather than members of the general public, Shapero v. Kentucky Bar Ass'n, 486 U.S. 466 (1988); or accurate identification of an attorney as a certified trial specialist, Peel v. Attorney Registration and Disciplinary Comm'n, 496 U.S. 91 (1990).

All of these decisions provoked strong dissent within the Court and dissension within the bar. Although advertising is now a billion dollar industry, and almost all lawyers engage in some promotional activity, only a small minority place commercials in mass media television and radio markets.[3] Most rely on brochures, yellow pages, websites, and outreach activities involving professional, civic, and social functions.[4] Surveys have generally found that most lawyers oppose mass media advertising.[5] By contrast, most consumers find

---

3. For the industry estimates, see William Hornsby, Jr., "Clashes of Class and Cash: Battles from the 150 Years War To Govern Client Development," 37 Ariz. St. L. J. 255 (2005). For mass media estimates, see sources cited in Deborah L. Rhode & David Luban, Legal Ethics 739 (4th ed. 2004).

4. Rhode & Luban, supra note 3 at 739; Geoffrey C. Hazard, Jr., "Advertis-

ing and Intermediaries in Provision of Legal Services: *Bates* in Retrospect and Prospect," 37 Ariz. St. L. J. 307, 313 (2005).

5. Archer W. Honeycutt & Elizabeth A. Wibker, "Consumers' Perceptions of Selected Issues Relating to Advertising by Lawyers," 7 J. of Prof. Services Marketing 119, 120 (1991) (finding that al-

such advertising acceptable.[6] The challenge of reconciling public and professional concerns is reflected in continuing revisions to bar ethical rules.

The Model Rules on advertising provide:

Rule 7.1: Communications Concerning a Lawyer's Services

A lawyer shall not make a false or misleading communication about the lawyer or the lawyer's services. A communication is false or misleading if it contains a material misrepresentation of fact or law, or omits a fact necessary to make the statement considered as a whole not materially misleading.

Comment

[2] ... A truthful statement is misleading if it omits a fact necessary to make the lawyer's communication considered as a whole not materially misleading. A truthful statement is also misleading if there is a substantial likelihood that it will lead a reasonable person to formulate a specific conclusion about the lawyer or the lawyer's services for which there is no reasonable factual foundation.

Rule 7.2: Advertising

(a) Subject to the requirements of Rules 7.1 and 7.3, a lawyer may advertise services through ... written, recorded or electronic communication, including public media.

Comment

[3] ... Questions of effectiveness and taste in advertising are matters of speculation and subjective judgment. Some jurisdictions have had extensive prohibitions against television advertising, against advertising going beyond specified facts about a lawyer, or against "undignified" advertising. Television is now one of the most powerful media for getting information to the public, particularly persons of low and moderate income; prohibiting television advertising, therefore, would impede the flow of information about legal services to many sectors of the public. Limiting the information that may be advertised has a similar effect and assumes that the bar can accurately forecast

---

most ninety percent of surveyed ABA members believe that advertising harms the profession's image). See Mary Hladky, "High Court Case to Test Limits on Lawyer Ads," Legal Times, Jan. 9, 1995, at 1.

6. William E. Hornsby, Jr., "Ad Rules Infinitum: The Need for Alterna-

tives to State–Based Ethics Governing Legal Services Marketing," 36 U. Rich. L. Rev. 49, 87–88 (2002); ABA Commission on Advertising, Lawyer Advertising at the Crossroads: Professional Policy Considerations (1995).

the kind of information that the public would regard as relevant.

These rules incorporate significant revisions made in 2002, in response to recommendations by the Ethics 2000 Commission. The revisions generally reflect a more permissive approach to advertising than the prior standards, and most states have retained more stringent approaches than the Model Rules.[7]

Current Controversies

One central difference has involved claims about performance. Many states prohibit testimonials, endorsements, specialty designations, or "self-laudatory" assertions, or require that they be accompanied by disclaimers. The mandatory disclaimers are often cumbersome or unfeasible in many advertising formats. Other jurisdictions provide that lawyers who advertise a specialty certification by organizations other than the state bar must include disclaimers that their state does not recognize or require such certification.[8] Many legal ethics commentators and consumer protection experts raise concerns about such rules. In a submission to the ABA Commission on Advertising, the staff of the Federal Trade Commission noted:

> To be sure, testimonials and endorsements can be used in ways that mislead about likely outcomes, and it may be both appropriate and necessary to take action against those that do. But some aspects of professional services, unrelated to particular outcomes, might well be communicated truthfully and usefully by a report of a client's actual experience. Rather than a conclusive ban, an approach might be taken similar to that of the [FTC] Commission's guides on this subject, that seeks to ensure that client testimonials are truthful and not misleading. . . .
>
> Disclaimer and other disclosure prohibitions, which many jurisdictions require, tend to increase advertising costs, by requiring that messages be longer or by forcing advertisers to displace other information. Disclosure obligations may also discourage advertising if advertisers believe consumers will take the disclosure to reflect negatively on the advertiser, regardless of whether that imputation is justified. Because of

---

7. Louise L. Hill, "Change Is in the Air: Lawyer Advertising and the Internet," 36 U. Rich. L. Rev. 21, 22 (2002).

8. For online links to the specific state ethics provisions governing the communications of legal services, see ABA Comm'n. On Responsibility in Client Dev., Links to State Ethics Rules Governing Lawyer Advertising, Solicitation, and Marketing, ABA Network, at htttp://www.abanet.org/legalservices/clientdevelopment/adrules.

these effects, disclosure requirements that are unnecessary can reduce the amount of useful information available to consumers. Disclosures and disclaimers can sometimes be necessary to prevent deception. It is important in evaluating disclosure requirements to weigh the costs against the expected benefits.[9]

A related area of controversy and inconsistency in state regulation involves prohibitions on "undignified" advertising techniques such as lyrics, jingles, animations, and dramatizations. To many judges and bar leaders, such techniques undermine lawyers' professionalism and cheapen their public image. According to Justice O'Connor, "fairly severe constraints on attorney advertising" are appropriate because they "act as a concrete day-to-day reminder to the practicing attorney of why it is improper for any member of this profession to regard it as a trade or occupation like any other." Shapero v. Kentucky Bar Association, 486 U.S. 466, 490–91 (1988) (O'Connor J., dissenting). Then Chief Justice Warren Burger put the point more emphatically. Selling law like laxatives was, in his view, " 'sheer shysterism,' and an outrageous breach of professional conduct." He personally would have preferred to "dig ditches" before placing an advertisement and he advised consumers "never, never, never, engage the services of a lawyer who finds it necessary to advertise in order to get clients."[10]

Yet most research, including ABA national surveys, finds that advertising is not a major factor in shaping public impressions of the legal profession.[11] Entertaining television commercials of the kind that some states prohibit have a positive effect on viewers' perceptions of lawyers. Indeed, in one study, even sensational or cartoonish commercials improved audience evaluations of attorneys' professionalism, knowledge, helpfulness, and effectiveness.[12] Although a large minority of consumers believe that changing the way that lawyers advertise might improve the profession's reputa-

---

9. Federal Trade Commission, Submission of the Staff of the Federal Trade Commission to the ABA Commission on Advertising 12 (June 24, 1994). See also Hornsby, supra note 6, at 66–69. Anthony E. Davis, "The Proposed New Rules Governing Lawyer Advertising," N.Y.L.J. July 3, 2006, at 3 (criticizing proposed changes in New York's advertising rules.)

10. David Margolick, "Burger Criticism Prompts Defense of Lawyer Ads," N.Y. Times, July 9, 1985, at A3; Warren E. Burger, "The Decline of Professionalism," 63 Fordham L. Rev. 949, 953, 956 (1995).

11. See surveys cited in Hazard, Koniak, Cramton, & Cohen, supra note 2, at 945; ABA Commission on Advertising, supra note 4, at 3; Hornsby, supra note 4, at 55; Richard J. Cebula, "Does Lawyer Advertising Adversely Influence the Image of Lawyers in the United States? An Alternative Perspective and New Empirical Evidence," 27 J. Legal Studies 503 (1998); Wiese Research Associates, Attorney Advertising Perception Study 10–11 (ABA 1994).

12. Hazard, Koniak, Cramton, & Cohen, supra note 2, at 1033.

tion, most consider it the least important of various reform strategies.[13] Most experts agree that advertising has far less impact on
public perceptions than portrayals of lawyers in books, televisions,
and films, and reports by friends, family and colleagues.[14]

From a purely consumer protection standpoint, many states'
restrictions on lawyer advertising are difficult to justify. Empirical
research finds that advertising generally increases competition and
reduces prices without diluting quality in professional services.
Lower prices tend to heighten demand, expand volume, and encourage economies of scale. In a country where the average consumer
receives close to a thousand messages a day, effective mass media
advertising may depend on attention-getting devices of the sort that
bar rules often condemn.

To a large extent, the debate over dignity in advertising involves a tradeoff between the public's interest in access to information and the bar's interest in maintaining decorum, status, and
professional identity. That tradeoff emerged clearly in a dialogue
published by the ABA Journal between Jeffrey Zuckerman, then
director of the FTC Bureau of Competition, Consumer Protection,
and Economics, and Adrian Foley, former Chair of the ABA Commission on Advertising. According to Zuckerman, requirements of
dignity reflected a "bias against advertising" that restricted competition and the free flow of information.[15] By contrast, Foley considered such requirements to be crucial to the profession's self-image
and acceptance of advertising. A Journal reporter then asked, "Is
anyone really harmed if [a lawyer] pops out of a swimming pool in a
television ad and asks 'if you're having trouble keeping your head
above water?' Does this merely prick the profession's pomposity?"
Foley responded, "To an extent, yes. But it also demeans the
dedication of a great many lawyers whose professionalism is the
result of years of study and hard work."[16]

Enforcement Structures

To the extent that advertising regulation poses a conflict
between professional and public interests, it also raises a more
fundamental question: who should decide where to strike the balance. Should the organized bar play the dominant role, particularly
given the low percentage of members with a personal stake in mass

---

13. ABA Section of Litigation, Public
Perceptions of Lawyers: Consumer Research Findings 32 (April 2002).

14. Fred Zacharias, "What Direction
Should Legal Advertising Regulation
Take," Professional Lawyer 45, 52–53
(2006).

15. "At Issue: Is Dignity Important
in Legal Advertising?" 73 ABA J., Aug.
1987, at 52, 53.

16. Id.

media communication and the high percentage of complaints about advertising, typically around 90 percent, that come from other lawyers?[17] Some commentators believe that current restrictions reflect class biases and make it harder to reach consumers of limited means.[18] One proposed alternative would be to place oversight responsibility in more neutral authorities such as consumer protection agencies.[19] Other reform possibilities involve increasing the sources of information available to potential clients. For example, state or national bodies could create electronic data bases with basic facts about lawyers comparable to the clearinghouses available for physicians.[20] States could also liberalize rules on referrals from organizations that match potential clients with qualified providers.[21]

A related issue involves the extent of discretion that regulatory agencies should exercise. Recent research suggests that advertising rules are grossly underenforced. Since *Bates*, surveyed jurisdictions have averaged fewer than one reported disciplinary case per year for advertising violations.[22] Formal enforcement actions are rare even in jurisdictions where noncompliance with specific rules is common.[23] A number of factors may account for this pattern:

- a lack of resources within disciplinary agencies;

- a lack of client complaints and demonstrable harm from violations;

17. Deborah L. Rhode, In the Interests of Justice: Reforming the Legal Profession 148 (2001).

18. Hornsby, supra note 3. According to Van O'Steen, one of the parties in Bates v. Arizona State Bar, "For those in lower income and less well connected classes, however, advertising is fresh information about serious legal needs.... Stifling lawyer advertising is class legislation in the name of professional dignity." Van O'Steen, "Bates v. State Bar of Arizona: The Personal Account of a Party and the Consumer Benefits of Lawyer Advertising," 37 Ariz. L. J. 245 (2005).

19. Rhode, supra note 17, at 144–49; Linda Morton, "Finding a Suitable Lawyer: Why Consumers Can't Always Get What They Want and What the Legal Profession Should Do About It," 25 U.C. Davis L. Rev. 283, 303 (1992).

20. Rhode & Luban, supra note 3, at 739.

21. Current rules permit lawyers to pay the "usual charges" of a non-profit or "qualified lawyer referral service" that has been approved "by an appropriate regulatory authority." Model Rule 7.2(b)(2). Relatively few services not run by bar associations have been approved, and relatively few consumers consult bar services. For discussion of the inadequacy of current approaches, see Hazard, supra note 4, at 316–17, and Hornsby, supra note 3, at 300–01.

22. Fred C. Zacharias, "What Lawyers Do When Nobody's Watching: Legal Advertising As a Case Study of the Impact of Underenforced Professional Rules," 87 Iowa L. Rev. 971, 992 (2002).

23. In San Diego during a one year period, there were 257 cases of actual or presumptive noncompliance. In the entire state of California, there were only 3 disciplinary cases involving predominantly advertising violations. Id., at 978–88.

- a lack of consensus within the bar about the appropriateness of advertising restrictions; and

- a lack of confidence among regulatory officials that rules can be fully and fairly enforced.

Yet however persuasive these explanations, the high visibility of unsanctioned rule violations raises obvious concerns. Flagrant failure to enforce ethical standards prevents predictability, erodes respect for bar regulatory processes, and shields judgments about commercial speech from open debate and review. At the very least, some commentators argue, disciplinary authorities should define and defend their enforcement policies, and work to bring formal rules in line with actual practices.

Regulation and the Internet

A final area of controversy involves how to monitor advertising on the internet. The number of attorneys with website listings and promotional materials has been growing rapidly and bar regulatory efforts have been unable to keep pace. These efforts have been limited by inadequacies in enforcement resources and authority over out-of-state lawyers.[24] In an era of increasingly multijurisdictional practice, state-based regulatory structures with inconsistent standards present obvious problems. Full compliance with every jurisdiction's advertising requirements would unduly hamper promotional efforts and limit firms' ability to compete. For example, what happens if a website includes self-laudatory and testimonial material that is permissible in the state where the firm has its principle office, but not in states where potential clients read the material or states where a case arising from the advertisement is filed?[25] Bar regulatory bodies are just beginning to grapple with a host of internet-related issues, involving not just advertising, but also solicitation, unauthorized practice of law, and formation of lawyer-client relationships. Designing appropriate rules for new technologies and multijurisdictional practice is a central challenge for the contemporary legal profession.

24. R.J. Westermeier, "Ethics and the Internet," 17 Geo. J. Legal Ethics 267 (2004); Richard B. Schmitt, "Lowering the Bar: Lawyers Flood Web, But Many Ads Fail to Tell Whole Truth," Wall St. J. Jan. 15, 2001, at A1; ABA Commission on Advertising, White Paper: A Reexamination of the ABA Model Rules of Professional Conduct Pertaining to Client Development in Light of Emerging Technologies (July 1998); Hill, supra note 7.

25. Westermeier, supra note 24; Jill Schachner Chanen, "Watch What You Say," ABA J., October, 2005, at 59, 62. For the ABA's best practices guidelines for websites, see Elawyering Task Force, ABA Law Practice Management Section and ABA Standing Committee on the Delivery of Legal Services, Best Practice Guidelines for Legal Information Web Site Providers, available at www.elawyering.org/tools/practices.html. For resources on elawyering generally, see www.legalethics.com.

B. Solicitation

Prohibitions on lawyers' personal solicitation of clients date to medieval England. During a time when tribunals were all too easily corrupted, the profession sought to discourage various practices associated with solicitation: maintenance (assisting others to prosecute or defend a suit without just cause); champerty (helping to maintain a suit in return for a share of the recovery); and barratry (stirring up quarrels and litigation).

In this country, solicitation has been linked with similar practices and with invasions of the privacy of accident victims and their families. However, personal contact by lawyers has also had positive consequences in informing individuals of their legal rights, preventing exploitation by defendants, and enlisting plaintiffs in public interest litigation.[26]

Ethical Rules

Model Rule 7.3 attempts to strike a balance reflecting this mixed experience. It provides:

> (a) A lawyer shall not by in-person, live telephone or real-time electronic contact solicit professional employment from a prospective client when a significant motive for the lawyer's doing so is the lawyer's pecuniary gain, unless the person contacted:
>
>> (1) is a lawyer; or
>>
>> (2) has a family, close personal, or prior professional relationship with the lawyer.
>
> (b) A lawyer shall not solicit professional employment from a prospective client ... if:
>
>> (1) the prospective client has made known to the lawyer a desire not to be solicited by the lawyer; or
>>
>> (2) the solicitation involves coercion, duress or harassment.
>
> (c) Every written, recorded or electronic communication from a lawyer soliciting professional employment from a prospective client ... shall include the words "Advertising Material" on the outside envelope, if any, and at the beginning and ending of any recorded or electronic communication, unless the recipient of the communication is a person specified in paragraphs (a)(1) or (a)(2).

---

26. See Charles W. Wolfram, Modern Legal Ethics 786 (1986) (discussing, for example Abraham Lincoln, the Aaron Burr litigation, and the Dred Scott Case); Deborah L. Rhode, "Solicitation," 36 J. Legal Ed. 317, 325–29 (1986) (discussing Brown v. Board of Education).

This Rule is consistent with the approach of two companion Supreme Court decisions: Ohralik v. Ohio State Bar Association, 436 U.S. 447 (1978), and In re Primus, 436 U.S. 412 (1978). *Ohralik* upheld the imposition of disciplinary sanctions on a lawyer who had personally solicited employment from a hospitalized accident victim and her family. *Primus* reversed the imposition of sanctions on a lawyer for the American Civil Liberties Union who had provided free legal advice and had written a letter offering pro bono representation to victims of abusive sterilization practices. In the Court's view, the potential for overreaching was sufficiently great to justify prohibitions on in-person solicitation in contexts involving potential financial gain for the lawyer. By contrast, a written solicitation by a lawyer with no monetary interest in the case posed far fewer risks. The Court did, however, leave open the possibility that states could fashion reasonable time, place, and manner restrictions on any form of solicitation.

In Florida Bar v. Went For It, 515 U.S. 618 (1995), the Court sustained one such restriction—a prohibition on targeted mail by plaintiffs' lawyers to accident victims and their families within thirty days of the accident. According to the majority, the state has a substantial interest in improving the "flagging reputations" of lawyers and in preventing the "erosion of confidence in the profession that such repeated invasions [of privacy have fostered]." Id. at 625, 635. Yet, as critics of that ruling noted, the Court has not permitted such restrictions on truthful speech to prevent overreaching or to salvage the reputation of other occupational groups. For example, in Edenfield v. Fane, 507 U.S. 761 (1993), the Court struck down a ban on personal solicitation by certified public accountants. Moreover, the main study supporting the Florida bar's concerns in *Went For It* found that only a quarter of consumers reported a lower regard for the legal profession as a result of such targeted solicitations. Although the state has a legitimate interest in protecting victims' privacy, many commentators agree with the dissenting Justices in *Went For It*, that such protection can be accomplished by narrower means. In the dissent's view, it is enough for states to follow the approach of Model Rule 7.3 and require disclosure on the outside of envelopes indicating that they contain a commercial solicitation.

Current Challenges and Alternative Strategies

The problem with broader thirty-day prohibitions on targeted mail by lawyers is that these bans generally do not apply to insurance company investigators as well. The result is that accident victims and their families may be pressured into accepting inadequate settlements before they have obtained legal advice. Victims who negotiate directly with an insurance company tend to receive substantially lower recoveries than those who are represented by lawyers.[27]

In order to address such problems, some legislators have enacted prohibitions on communications with victims by all potential litigants, including insurance companies, for a prescribed period. A representative example is the 1996 Federal Aviation Reauthorization Act, which bans unsolicited communication concerning legal action within thirty days of an air crash. Drawing on such examples, some commentators advocate solicitation rules that apply to a wider group of individuals than current prohibitions, but that cover a narrower range of conduct. So, for example, states could make all unsolicited communications to accident victims concerning potential litigation subject to reasonable time, place, and manner restrictions. Both the profession and the public have an interest in preventing the kind of bare-faced ambulance chasing that has too often accompanied personal injuries. Commonly proposed restrictions would prohibit in-person solicitation that:

- involves harassment, coercion, or undue influence;

- involves communication with persons who have expressed a desire not to be contacted; or

- occurs when a potential client is unable to exercise reasonable, considered judgment.[28]

Unlike the Model Rules, this approach would focus solely on harm to the potential recipient, not on the motives of the solicitor. Such a shift in emphasis would recognize that personal contact by a lawyer can sometimes be beneficial even if not disinterested. Indeed, some potential for financial gain is present even in most "public interest" litigation, given the possibility of enhanced reputation and statutory fee awards for prevailing parties.

Another way of meeting individual needs for legal advice while preventing abusive conduct is to maintain bans on personal solicitation but increase pro bono assistance. A growing number of bar associations have established mass disaster aid programs in which volunteer lawyers offer free advice or representation, and the presence of clearly identified bar response teams at disaster sites

---

27. Peter A. Bell & Jeffrey O'Connell, Accidental Justice: The Dilemma of Tort Law 165–66 (1997); Richard Zitrin & Carol M. Langford, The Moral Compass of the American Lawyer, 129, 135–39 (1999).

28. FTC, supra note 9, at 151; James L. Kelley, Lawyers Crossing Lines: Nine Stories 157–58 (2001); Rhode, supra note 17, at 149.

deters exploitation by other attorneys.[29] For example, in the aftermath of the 9/11 terrorist attacks, thousands of attorneys volunteered free legal services for victims and their families. The Association of Trial Lawyers of America also asked attorneys representing those individuals to observe a temporary moratorium on filing suits. Widespread compliance with that request protected victims' privacy and gave them time to determine whether to seek compensation from a federal fund that required waiver of other legal remedies.[30] Similarly, in the aftermath of Hurricane Katrina, bar associations established pro bono assistance programs and made clear that volunteer lawyers could not use their participation to solicit paying clients.[31] In the long run, such combinations of pro bono assistance and voluntary restraint may be among the best means of countering the problems traditionally associated with solicitation.

C. Multijurisdictional Practice

The Traditional Approach

As the preceding discussion indicated, one of the greatest challenges in regulating the contemporary market for legal services involves multijurisdictional practice. The bar's longstanding position, codified in the Model Rules of Professional Conduct and the Code of Professional Responsibility, is that a "lawyer shall not . . . practice law in a jurisdiction where doing so violates the regulation of the legal profession in that jurisdiction." Model Rule 5.5. Accord DR 3–101(b). Under Model Rule 8.5, lawyers are subject to discipline in any jurisdiction where they provide legal services in violation of local ethics rules.

Attorneys who wish to represent a client outside of the jurisdiction where they are licensed generally must either limit themselves to extremely brief and occasional instances, affiliate local counsel, or, if the matter involves litigation, request the court to admit them temporarily, *pro hoc vice.* Although courts are not constitutionally obligated to extend *pro hoc vice* admission, they often do so, typically on the condition that the out of state lawyer affiliates local counsel.[32] A few jurisdictions permit in-house lawyers to provide

---

29. Solomon Moore, "Lawyers Seek Out Victims of Crash," Los Angeles Times, February 7, 2005, at B3.

30. William Glaberson, "4 Suits Filed, Despite Calls for Restraint by Lawyers," N.Y. Times, Jan. 15, 2002, at A13.

31. Louisiana State Bar Association Rules of Professional Conduct Comm.

Op. 005–RPPC–005 (September 27, 2005).

32. Leis v. Flynt, 441 U.S. 956 (1979); Hazard, Koniak, Cramton, & Cohen, supra note 2, at 1125.

legal services on behalf of their employer from an office outside of the state if they register and submit to the local bar's regulatory authority.[33] Many states also allow members of a foreign bar to obtain licenses as legal consultants. Typically this status is available without passage of a bar examination but practice is limited to advice on the law of the consultant's home jurisdiction.[34] About half of all jurisdictions also allow foreign lawyers to take the bar exam without graduating from an accredited American law school.[35]

The Prevalence of Multijurisdictional Practice and the Rationale for Reform

The narrow exceptions to prevailing unauthorized practice rules do not, however, address the needs of most lawyers with multijurisdictional practices. For these lawyers, the traditional state-based licensing structure has become increasingly unworkable and unenforceable. Many legal matters and fields of specialization do not observe state boundaries. Nor do many attorney communications by phone, email, fax, and internet websites remain within states where the attorneys are licensed to practice law. In an era in which the law of other jurisdictions is readily accessible electronically, and organizational clients increasingly have needs in multiple locations, the pressure to reduce geographic constraints on practice has intensified. ABA Commission on Multijurisdictional Practice notes:

> Testimony before the Commission was unanimous in recognizing that lawyers commonly engage in cross-border legal practice. Further, there was general consensus that such practice is on the increase and that this trend is not only inevitable, but necessary. The explosion of technology and the increasing complexity of legal practice have resulted in the need for lawyers to cross state borders to afford clients competent representation....

> The existing system of lawyer regulation is and should be a matter of serious concern for many lawyers. Even in contexts where jurisdictional restrictions clearly apply, as in state-court proceedings, problems are caused by the lack of uniformity

---

33. ABA Report of the Commission on Multijurisdictional Practice (Aug. 2002) available at http://www.abanet. org/cpr/mjp/final_mjp_rpt_5-13.pdf.

34. See ABA Model Rule for the Licensing of Legal Consultants (1993); American Law Institute, Restatement of the Law Governing Lawyers (Third) § 2 Comment g.

35. Hazard, Koniak, Cramton & Cohen, supra note 2, at 135, n. 118. Some jurisdictions impose special requirements, such as one year of an American law school for lawyers whose legal education was not in English in a common law jurisdiction or whose legal education is not deemed sufficiently comparable to that available in an American law school. Id.

among the *pro hoc vice* provisions of different states, unpredictability about how some of the provisions will be applied by the courts in individual cases, and, in some cases, the provisions' excessive restrictiveness. Of even greater concern, however, is that, outside the context of litigation, the reach of the jurisdictional restrictions is vastly uncertain as well as, potentially, far too restrictive. Lawyers may recognize that UPL [unauthorized practice of law] enforcement proceedings are infrequent, and that when UPL laws are invoked, courts have the ability to interpret them realistically to accommodate the interests of clients with interstate or multi-state legal problems. Nevertheless, some lawyers will turn down clients or take other steps to avoid or reduce the risk of having to defend against UPL charges or of appearing to violate rules of professional conduct.

The existing system of lawyer regulation has costs for clients. For example, out of concern for jurisdictional restrictions, lawyers may decline to provide services that they are able to render skillfully and ethically.... Further, even if lawyers felt free to ignore UPL laws in areas where there is a professional consensus that the laws are outmoded and there appears to be a tacit understanding that they will not be enforced, it is undesirable to retain the laws as written, rather than amending them to accord with contemporary understandings and practices that serve clients well. Keeping antiquated laws on the books breeds public disrespect for the law, and this is especially so where the laws relate to the conduct of lawyers, for whom there is a professional imperative to uphold the law.[36]

The problems inherent in prevailing unauthorized practice rules are illustrated by a widely publicized California Supreme Court decision, Birbrower, Montalbano, Condon & Frank v. Superior Court, 949 P.2d 1 (Cal.1998). There, a New York lawyer represented a family corporation that had branches in New York and California in a dispute with a New York software manufacturer. The lawyer made several trips to California to confer with corporate officers, to negotiate with software representatives, and to initiate arbitration proceedings. The dispute was settled before arbitration but the client then sued the attorney for malpractice. The attorney cross claimed to recover his fee. In rejecting the cross claim, the California Supreme Court reasoned that the fee agreement was unenforceable because the attorney had engaged in the unauthorized practice of law. Under the court's analysis, the "primary inquiry is whether the unlicensed lawyer engaged in sufficient

36. ABA Report, supra note 33, at 10–12.

activities in the state, or created a continuing relationship with the California client that included legal duties and obligations." Id. at 5. Physical presence, according to the court, was a relevant but not conclusive factor. Lawyers could engage in unauthorized practice by providing legal advice by telephone, fax, or other means.

The Revised Model Rules Approach

The *Birbrower* decision attracted widespread criticism. The California legislature partially addressed the concerns by creating a statutory exemption from unauthorized practice prohibitions for arbitration proceedings. But the broader problem of geographic limitations on the delivery of legal services calls for more fundamental solutions. After *Birbrower*, the ABA appointed its Commission on Multijurisdictional Practice and adopted its recommended revisions to the Model Rules of Professional Conduct. In essence, the modifications create "safe havens" from unauthorized practice prohibitions. Model Rule 5.5 (c) enables an out-of-state lawyer to provide legal services on a temporary basis that:

(1) are undertaken in association with a lawyer who is admitted to practice in this jurisdiction and who actively participates in the matter;

(2) are in or reasonably related to a pending or potential proceeding before a tribunal in this or another jurisdiction, if the lawyer, or a person the lawyer is assisting, is authorized by law or order to appear in such proceeding or reasonably expects to be so authorized;

(3) are in or reasonably related to a pending or potential arbitration, mediation, or other alternate dispute resolution proceeding in [the] . . . jurisdiction, if the services arise out of or are reasonably related to the lawyer's practice in a jurisdiction in which the lawyer is admitted to practice and are not services for which the forum requires *pro hoc vice* admission;

. . .

(4) are not within paragraph (c)(2) or (c)(3) and arise out of or are reasonably related to the lawyer's practice in a jurisdiction in which the lawyer is admitted to practice.

Under Model Rule 5.5(d), a lawyer may also provide legal services that

(1) are provided to the lawyer's employer or its organizational affiliates and are not services for which the forum requires *pro hoc vice* admission; or

(2) are services that the lawyer is authorized by federal or other law to provide in this jurisdiction.

Alternative Proposals

How workable this approach will prove in practice is not yet clear.[37] Some commentators believe that it is unduly complex and restrictive. A variety of other possibilities have been proposed. Options include: a national system of bar admission, discussed in Chapter XI; more permissive state-based reciprocity rules modeled on the European Union system; and a national license to provide "cyber advice."[38] Under a national bar admission system, a license to practice law would be similar to a driver's license; the attorney's state of residence would test for competence, and other jurisdictions would honor its judgment as long as the non-resident attorney's presence was temporary. Alternatively, the federal government could administer a national exam that would serve as the basic qualification for all attorneys or attorneys who limit their practice to federal law. Under a system like the European Union, lawyers could provide legal services in another jurisdiction if they registered to do so, limited their practice to occasional activity, agreed to comply with local ethics rules and enforcement processes, and maintained legal malpractice insurance.[39] Under a cyber licensing system, lawyers could offer electronic advice in jurisdictions where they demonstrated some basic familiarity with the local laws.[40]

All of these options pose difficult tradeoffs. At issue are concerns not only of competence and efficiency, but also of economic self-interest by local practitioners. In states with large retirement populations, many lawyers are particularly worried about competition from émigrés from other states who would like to engage in some part time practice if they could avoid retaking a bar examination. A national admission system raises additional questions about federalism, and the ability to protect the independence of the profession under a centralized structure.

Although lawyers disagree about which approach to multijurisdictional practice makes most sense, there is broad agreement on

37. Although only a few states have adopted the ABA's Model Rule, a substantial number are reviewing possible responses. See Mark Hansen, "MJP Picks Up Steam: More States Are Looking at ABA Proposals to Ease Rules on Mutijurisdictional Practice," ABA Journal, Jan., 2004, 42.

38. Martha Neil, "Easing Up," ABA J., Feb. 2002, at 47, 49; Lance J. Rogers, "ABA Commission Hears Proposals, Concerns Over Expanded Multijurisdictional Law Practice," 17 ABA/BNA Lawyer's Manual on Professional Conduct

133 (2001). See also Anthony E. Davis, "Multijurisdictional Practice By Transactional Lawyers–Why the Sky Really Is Falling," 11 Prof. Law 1 (Winter 2000).

39. See Geoffrey C. Hazard Jr., "New Shape of Lawyering," Nat'l. L. J., July 23, 2001, at A21; Stephen Gillers, "Protecting Their Own," American Lawyer, Nov. 1998, at 118.

40. Katy Ellen Deady, Note, "Cyberadvice: The Ethical Implications of Giving Professional Advice Over the Internet," 14 Geo. J. Legal Ethics 891 (2001).

two general points. First, as the ABA Commission has noted, multijurisdictional practice is an inevitable and necessary response to clients' needs in a multijurisdictional social-economy. Second, current unauthorized practice rules require reform in order to take account of those needs and permit more effective service.[41] At present, the most acceptable response appears to be a prohibition on out-of-state lawyers "setting up shop" where they are not admitted, but permission or acquiescence in out-of-state lawyers carrying through locally on representation originated out of state.

D. Multidisciplinary Practice

Many of the same socioeconomic forces that have challenged the geographic boundaries of legal practice have also called into question its disciplinary boundaries, namely the barrier between law and other professional services. The bar's traditional approach, reflected in Model Rule 5.4 and DR 3–102(A), is that lawyers may not share fees or control over their practice with nonlawyers. Although attorneys have been allowed to employ non-lawyer professionals and work in-house for organizations owned by nonlawyers, they have not been permitted to form partnerships with nonlawyers to deliver legal services. The rationale for such prohibitions is that protection of the independence of lawyers is necessary to preserve the core values of the profession.

Over the last decade, that prohibition has become the focus of growing controversy. Faced with increasing competition for clients and increasing needs for cross-disciplinary expertise, many lawyers have sought to forge closer relationships with providers of other professional services. Disputes over how to structure such relationships have involved two organizational forms: (1) ancillary businesses, which are separate entities that work in collaboration with lawyers, such as firms offering financial, lobbying, and real estate services; and (2) multidisciplinary partnerships (MDPs), such as law-and-accounting firms, which offer multiple professional services under one roof.

Ancillary Businesses

The current controversy began with ancillary businesses. It came to a head in the early 1990s when the District of Columbia adopted a rule allowing lawyers to own such businesses and permitting nonlawyers to become partners under specified circumstances.[42] This rule, and the broader trends it reflected, prompted

41. ABA Commission, supra note 33, at 1.

42. D.C. Rules of Professional Conduct, Rule 5.4 provides that lawyers may practice with nonlawyer partners who

considerable dispute and many reform proposals within other bar organizations. The American Bar Association's House of Delegates first voted to prohibit lawyers' ownership of ancillary non-legal businesses, then repealed the ban, and finally adopted Model Rule 5.4. It permits such lawyer-owned businesses but does not allow nonlawyers to be partners. Only a few jurisdictions have adopted that Rule.[43] However, lawyers have always been free to own or operate a business unrelated to their law practice, for example, a real estate management company. By contrast, some European countries prohibit lawyers from engaging in unrelated business which is thought "incompatible" with law practice.

Underlying the controversy in this nation are a range of issues about quality, efficiency, commercialization, and professionalism. Proponents of lawyer-owned ancillary businesses argue that they encourage cost-effective collaborations between legal and nonlegal experts; decrease search costs in hiring such experts; and give lawyers incentives to monitor the performance of ancillary service providers. By contrast, critics worry that diversification into other business activity distracts lawyers from the practice of law; impairs their objectivity in recommending other professionals; invites misuse of confidential information; introduces too much profit-oriented, nonlawyer influence into law firm management; and erodes the distinctiveness of law as a profession rather than a business.

The Evolution of Multidisciplinary Practice

Similar issues underpin the current debate over multidisciplinary partnerships. That debate has attracted increasing attention largely due to increasing competition from accounting firms. Other western industrialized nations generally permit nonlawyers to provide some law-related services, to employ lawyers, to form partnerships with lawyers, or to hold ownership interests in law firms. As a consequence, the major accounting firms have a strong position in the global legal market. They have a presence in 138 countries and some employ over 60,000 workers.[44]

assist the organization in providing legal services, provided that these individuals abide by bar ethical rules and that lawyers undertake the same responsibility for these activities as if the participants were lawyers.

43. Hazard, Koniak, Cramton, & Cohen, supra note 2, at 1119; Mary C. Daly, "What the MDP Debate Can Teach Us about Law Practice in the New Millennium and the Need for Curricular Reform," 50 J. Leg. Ed. 521 (2000).

44. See generally Rees M. Hawkins, "Not 'If' but 'When' and 'How': A Look at Existing De Facto Multidisciplinary Practices and What They Can Teach Us About the Ongoing Debate," 83 N. Car. L. Rev. 481, 493–97 (2005); Charles W. Wolfram, "MDP Partnerships in the Law Practice of European and American Lawyers," in Lawyers' Practice and Ideals: A Comparative View 301–50 (John

These accounting firms are also making increased inroads in the American market. Federal law provides that federal tax advice and representation in federal tax court does not constitute the practice of law. This exception to traditional unauthorized practice prohibitions enables lawyers to provide services for clients of accounting firms as long as the work can be defined as tax, not legal, assistance. Lawyers may also provide legal advice to a professional who is giving nonlegal advice to a client. Over the past decade, the major accounting firms have pushed these boundaries between legal and nonlegal work, and have expanded their in-house legal staff to provide much the same services as law firms on matters such as tax, financial, and estate planning, intellectual property, ADR, and litigation support. The American legal profession faces growing difficulties in competing with these accounting organizations, which frequently offer a wider range of services, more international networks and name recognition, greater economies of scale, and more effective marketing, information technology, and managerial capacities. Although bar leaders believe that many multidisciplinary organizations are violating unauthorized practice statutes, a lack of resources and public support has inhibited enforcement efforts.[45]

Current Controversies

Supporters of liberalized rules on multidisciplinary practice stress the advantages to clients of "one stop" shopping, and the advantages to lawyers of being able to compete more effectively with other service providers. The benefits would extend not just to large firms and business clients, but also to small firms and solo practitioners with individual clients, such as senior citizens needing a range of legal, medical, and social services. Permitting nonlawyers to hold ownerships in legal organizations would also diversify sources of capital investment and could encourage more cost-effective delivery structures.

By contrast, opponents worry that lawyers will become accountable to supervisors from a different tradition with less rigorous standards governing confidentiality, conflicts of interest, and pro bono service. Particular concerns center on accounting firms' unwillingness to impute conflicts of interest; they rely rather on client consent and ethical screens. In critics' view, such safeguards are often ineffective, and allowing lawyers to become participants in these organizations will compromise core principles and blur the

Barcelo & Roger C. Cramton, eds., 1998).

45. Daly, supra note 43, at 536; Philip S. Anderson, "Facing Up to Multidis-

ciplinary Practice," 50 J. Leg. Educ. 473, 480 (2000).

boundaries between law and business. Clients will reportedly pay the price as professional judgments are driven by the bottom line.[46]

In 1999, an ABA Commission on Multidisciplinary Practice issued a report acknowledging these ethical concerns but proposing strategies short of prohibition. The Commission recommended holding nonlawyers in multidisciplinary firms to the same ethical standards governing conflicts and confidentiality as those applicable to the bar generally. In addition, the Commission proposed special audit provisions to prevent nonlawyers from interfering with lawyers' professional judgments. Under this framework, the attorney-client privilege could be extended to cover nonlawyers, or clients could be warned about its unavailability.[47] An alternative approach, proposed by accounting firms, would be to follow their less stringent conflict of interest procedures. According to these firms, experience demonstrates the adequacy of this approach; sophisticated clients appear satisfied and have not pressed for reforms or alternatives.

The ABA House of Delegates overwhelmingly rejected the Commission's recommendations and declined to consider any less restrictive alternative. House members voted against relaxing prohibitions on multidisciplinary partnerships in the absence of evidence that they would serve the public interest and would not compromise lawyers' independence or loyalty to clients. Evidence to this effect was foreseeably unattainable. The Commission responded by reconsidering and supplementing the evidence that it had received from a broad range of professional and client groups. In the Commission's view, it would be impossible to measure the public interest in such arrangements until the "taint of illegality" was removed. In the interim, the support expressed by consumer groups and the market demand for lawyers in multidisciplinary settings was, from the Commission's perspective, evidence of the perceived social value of these arrangements.[48] Accordingly, the Commission submitted a revised proposal authorizing multidisciplinary partnerships under specified circumstances. The House of Delegates again rejected the Commission's recommendations.[49]

46. For an overview of these arguments, see David Luban, "Asking The Right Questions," 72 Temple L. Rev. 839 (1999).

47. ABA Commission on Multidisciplinary Practice, "Report of the Commission on Multidisciplinary Practice to the ABA House of Delegates," reprinted in 10 Professional Lawyer 1 (Spring 1999).

48. "MDP Rides Again," ABA J., Feb. 2000, at 96.

49. House of Delegates Resolution 10F (2000), reprinted in Daly, supra note 43, at 532.

Controversy then shifted to the states, and by the turn of the twenty-first century, virtually every jurisdiction was considering the issue.[50] A cottage industry of commentary also emerged. Analysis centered not simply on how to structure professional services, but also on how to define and pursue professional values in an increasingly competitive global market.[51] Recent scandals involving accounting practices fueled further disputes. To some commentators, the misconduct in cases like Enron reflected conflicts of interest between accountants' audit and consulting functions and demonstrated why lawyers should keep their distance.[52] To other commentators, these conflicts of interest underscored the need for tighter regulation of competing professionals who were employing a growing number of lawyers and supplying an increasing volume of law-related services. Congress partly responded to that need with the Sarbanes–Oxley Act of 2002, which prohibits registered public accounting firms that perform audits for securities issuers from simultaneously providing legal services unrelated to the audit.[53] However, many other issues involving potential conflicts of interest in MDPs remain subject to dispute.

Part of the difficulty in resolving these controversies involves the lack of systematic information about the extent of ethical problems in multidisciplinary organizations and the likely effectiveness of proposed responses. Lawyers who have worked in both law firms and MDPs testified before the Commission that there were not significant differences in the ethical cultures of the two kinds of organizations, apart from the rules about imputed conflicts. Many of the MDPs that presented testimony also pointed to records of public service that rivaled those of law firms.[54] In any event, even if

50. John B. Attanasio, "The Brave New World of Multidisciplinary Practice: Foreword," 50 J. Leg. Ed. 469, 470 (2000). See also Daly, supra note 35, at 527. For an overview see ABA, Center for Professional Responsibility, Status of Multidisciplinary Practice Studies by State (and some local bars), Feb. 11, 2002, available at http://www.abanet.org/cpr/mdp-state_action.html

51. Symposia on the subject include: "The Brave New World of Multidisciplinary Practice," 50 J. Leg. Ed. 469 (2000); "Future of the Profession: A Symposium on Multidisciplinary Practice," 84 Minn. L. Rev. 1083 (2000); "New Roles, No Rules? Redefining Lawyers Work," 72 Temp. L. Rev. 773 (1999). For other overviews, see Mary C. Daly, "Choosing Wise Men Wisely: The

Risks and Rewards of Purchasing Legal Services from Lawyers in a Multidisciplinary Partnership," 13 Geo. J. Legal Ethics 217 (2000); and Report of the N.Y. State Bar Association Special Committee on the Law Governing Firm Structure and Operation (2000).

52. Geanne Rosenberg, "Scandal Seen as Blow to Outlook for MDP," Nat'l. L. J., Jan 21, 2002, at A1; Steven C. Krane, "Let Lawyers Practice Law," Nat'l. L. J., Jan. 28, 2002, at A16.

53. Sarbanes–Oxley Act of 2002, § 201(a), amending § 10A of the Securities and Exchange Act of 1933, 15 U.S.C. § 78j–1.

54. Phoebe A. Haddon, "The MDP Controversy: What Legal Educators Should Know," 50 J. Leg. Ed. 504, 511–12 (2000).

it could be established that conflicts and confidentiality problems were somewhat more likely to arise in multidisciplinary firms, and that those firms were somewhat less likely to provide institutional support for public service than law firms, it would not be self-evident that total prohibition is the best response. Many experts believe that clients should have the option of weighing the risks and benefits of MDPs, and that ethical restrictions should be narrowly tailored to address demonstrated abuses.

However these issues are resolved, multidisciplinary collaborations of some form are obviously here to stay. There is a strong market demand and legitimate societal need for integrated legal and nonlegal advice. Where state bars prohibit multidisciplinary partnerships, multidisciplinary practice will take other forms. For example, New York now permits, and some American law firms are developing, "strategic alliances" with professional services firms. Under these arrangements, the firms agree to share clients and sometimes costs and marketing capacities.[55] Whether these arrangements can address client needs as effectively as "one stop shopping" MDPs remains to be seen. If experience is any guide, the only viable long term strategy for regulating the legal services market is one that can adequately adapt to competitive forces.

E. Attorneys' Fees

Of all the public's complaints about lawyers, expense is at the top of the list. Most Americans believe that legal assistance costs too much, and fewer than five percent believe that they get good value for the price of lawyers' services.[56] Such perceptions are longstanding. Virtually all societies have, at least intermittently, made efforts to restrict attorneys' fees.[57] Many countries now set these fees by detailed statutes that graduate the amount of payment for specified services. America's regulatory structure reveals a more complicated combination of bar oversight, deference to market forces, and sporadic legislative and judicial intervention.

Practices involving legal fees have long aroused discomfort among both lawyers and clients. In England, early tradition had it that gentlemen did not pay other gentlemen for their services, so

55. Daly, supra note 43, at 542; Hazard, Koniak, Cramton, & Cohen, supra note 2, at 1122; Hawkins, supra note 44, at 498.

56. Public Perceptions of Lawyers, supra note 13, at 14 (2002); Gary A. Hengstler, "Vox Populi: The Public Perception of Lawyers," ABA J., Sept. 1993, at 63.

57. William Howard Taft, Ethics in Service 4–8, 15 (1915); Charles Warren, A History of the American Bar 112–13 (1911); Dennis R. Nolan, Readings in the History of the American Legal Profession 103–05 (1980).

more discrete forms of remuneration were required. Barristers, the elite of the profession, never discussed fees with their clients; all matters of compensation were handled through solicitors and clerks.[58] In this country, many attorneys also attempted to avoid "haggling" over money by adherence to bar-established minimum fee schedules. The Canons of Ethics encouraged this practice and condemned any form of "underbidding."[59] In 1975, the Supreme Court struck down minimum fee schedules as a restraint of trade in violation of the Sherman Antitrust Act.[60] However, some information concerning standard charges has remained accessible through various publications for practitioners.

Lawyers have also looked for other ways to avoid fee disputes. In cases where they anticipate or experience reluctance by clients to settle accounts, practitioners can employ a variety of measures apart from litigation: substantial non-refundable retainers, refusal to complete work or relinquish client papers, informal modifications of their bills, or threats to reveal confidential information in the course of suing to recover payment.

Four types of fee arrangements are now common. The predominant billing method is the hourly fee. Other options are a flat fee for a particular matter; a proportional fee (such as a percentage of an estate or property involved in a transaction); or a contingent fee, which gives the lawyer a flat fee or a proportion of the recovery if the matter is successfully resolved. Such billing methods can also be used in combination, such as a flat fee with a bonus contingent on a particular result.

Regulation of these fees takes several forms. Rule 1.5 of the Model Rules of Professional Conduct prohibits lawyers from charging "unreasonable" fees, and DR 2–106 of the Code prohibits fees that are "clearly excessive." However, bar ethics committees and disciplinary authorities generally have not enforced these rules in individual cases unless the amount charged is so excessive as to be unconscionable or equivalent to a misappropriation of funds.[61] Rather, bar authorities have largely confined their focus to the general propriety of certain billing practices. For example, in Formal Opinion 93–379 (1993), the ABA Ethics Committee ruled that a lawyer should not double bill by charging more than one client for

---

58. W. J. Reader, Professional Men: The Rise of the Professional Classes in Nineteenth–Century England 36–37 (1966); R. E. Megarry, Lawyer and Litigant in England 56–60 (1962).

59. ABA Canons of Ethics, Canons 27 and 28.

60. Goldfarb v. Virginia State Bar, 421 U.S. 773, 787 (1975).

61. Hazard, Koniak, Cramton, & Cohen, supra note 2, at 771; Rhode, supra note 17, at 172.

the same hours or work product; should not bill a client for overhead expenses generally associated with equipping an office; and should not impose surcharges on services such as photocopying beyond the costs actually incurred.

On the whole, however, bar regulatory authorities have viewed the appropriate remedy for unreasonable charges to be nonpayment of fees, malpractice claims, or breach of contract actions. To most disciplinary committees, the criteria for deciding what constitutes an excessive fee are too indeterminate to justify disciplinary proceedings except in egregious cases, and bar disciplinary systems generally lack sufficient resources to handle ordinary fee disputes.

However, as Chapter XII notes, malpractice and contractual litigation is often an inadequate means of deterring or remedying excessive fees. For individuals with fee-related grievances, paying a second attorney to challenge the charges of the first is seldom an appealing option, particularly if the amount at issue is modest. Although corporate clients may have sufficient knowledge, experience, and leverage to protect themselves from excessive charges, many individual clients do not. And even sophisticated clients may not always have adequate information to insure fairness, as is clear from the frequency of problems concerning excessive charges, nonrefundable retainers, and contingent fees noted below.

Excessive Charges

Model Rule 1.5 lists the following factors as relevant in determining the reasonableness of a fee:

(1) the time and labor required, the novelty and difficulty of the questions involved, and the skill requisite to perform the legal service properly;

(2) the likelihood, if apparent to the client, that the acceptance of the particular employment will preclude other employment by the lawyer;

(3) the fee customarily charged in the locality for similar legal services;

(4) the amount involved and the results obtained;

(5) the time limitations imposed by the client or by the circumstances;

(6) the nature and length of the professional relationship with the client;

(7) the experience, reputation, and ability of the lawyer or lawyers performing the services; and

(8) whether the fee is fixed or contingent.

Courts and commentators generally agree with this list, although some would add the client's ability to pay and two further considerations set forth in the Restatement (Third) of Law Governing Lawyers: "when the agreement was made, did the lawyer afford the client a free and informed choice?; [and] . . . was there a subsequent change in circumstances that made the fee agreement unreasonable?"[62]

Although there is widespread consensus about the relevant standards in assessing a fee, there is widespread difficulty in applying them in particular cases. Fee-related abuses fall across a spectrum, reflecting everything from flagrant fraud and "creative timekeeping" to sloppy accounting and inefficient staffing. The frequency of such abuses is difficult to gauge, since many constitute the "perfect crime." Although sophisticated business clients have become increasingly adept at monitoring charges, it is often impossible to verify whether certain tasks were essential and whether they required, or actually consumed, the time that lawyers charged for completing them. Auditors find demonstrable fraud in about five to ten percent of the bills they review and questionable practices in another twenty-five to thirty-five percent. Such practices include inflating hours, overstaffing cases, performing unnecessary work, and double billing multiple clients for the same task or time. Forty percent of surveyed lawyers acknowledge that some of their work is influenced by a desire to bill additional hours.[63]

The basic problem arises from the obvious divergence in lawyers' and clients' interests. In purely economic terms, an attorney's goal, so far as compensation is concerned, is to maximize profits; a client's goal is to maximize value and minimize costs. If lawyers are charging by the hour and lack other equally profitable uses for their time, they have an incentive to prolong projects or to accept matters beyond their expertise that will require substantial learning at clients' expense. The problem is compounded by the amount of billable work that firms increasingly demand, and its importance in determining lawyers' status, promotion, and compensation. Current billable hour quotas generally range between 1800 and 2000 a year, and the averages are higher in many firms. Most estimates

---

62. Restatement (Third) of Law Governing Lawyers § 46 Comment. For a summary of cases finding clients' lack of resources relevant, see Wolfram, supra note 26, at 518–22. See also former Canon 12 of the ABA Canons of Ethics, which provided that a client's ability to pay could not justify charges in "excess of the value of . . . services," but that poverty could justify lower charges.

63. William G. Ross, The Honest Hour: The Ethics of Time–Based Billing by Attorneys 65 (1996); Rhode, supra note 17, at 171–72. Lisa G. Lerman, "Blue–Chip Bilking: Regulation of Billing and Expense Fraud by Lawyers," 12 Geo. J. Legal Ethics 205 (1999). Some lawyers have double billed for the same time if, for example, while traveling for one client they do work for another.

indicate that about a third of lawyers' office time cannot be billed honestly to clients; administrative matters, firm meetings, personal needs, and keeping current with legal developments all occupy a substantial chunk of time. To generate 2000 billable hours, attorneys typically need to work ten hours a day, six days a week. As Chief Justice Rehnquist has noted, if lawyers are expected to bill at current levels, "there are bound to be temptations to exaggerate the hours actually put in."[64]

In the face of such pressures, rationalizations for padding hours and relabeling expenses come readily to hand. Studies of billing abuses find that lawyers often insist that their work really was "worth more" than the time that it required. Others use upward "adjustments" to compensate for hours and expenses that they assume they have forgotten to claim or for tasks that clients will not reimburse. In egregious cases, lawyers have billed over 6,000 hours a year, have charged running shoes as "ground transportation," and have classified dry cleaning for a toupee as a litigation expense.[65] Such forms of fee-related deception erode client trust and attorney integrity. They also deflect attention from the problems that contribute to overbilling, such as poor time management or excessive overhead expenses.

Bar disciplinary processes are not well structured to police fee-related misconduct. As noted earlier, most enforcement agencies are unwilling to intervene except in extreme cases, and even these may be difficult for clients to prove. Most lawyers are reluctant to second-guess their colleagues' charges, or to support a regulatory approach that might subject everyone's fees to more frequent oversight. Only a minority of jurisdictions have arbitration systems for fee disputes. Even fewer require lawyers to participate.[66] The Model Rules provide only that lawyers should "conscientiously consider" submitting to arbitration programs.[67] Most of these programs also exclude issues regarding the quality of services, even though such issues underlie many fee disputes.

The absence of alternative dispute resolution procedures compromises lawyers' interests as well as those of clients. Sophisticated clients can be very aggressive, indeed exploitive in responding to lawyers' charges. Some insurance companies, for example, routinely

---

64. William H. Rehnquist, "The Legal Profession Today: Dedicatory Address," 62 Ind. L. J. 151, 153 (1987). See Ross, *supra* note 63, at 3, 27.

65. Hazard, Koniak, Cramton, & Cohen, *supra* note 2, at 775; Lerman, *supra* note 63; Barbara A. Serrano, "Lawyers Who Flouted Ethics Rules Escape Repri-

mand," Seattle Times, March 31, 1996, at A1; Gerald F. Phillips, "Reviewing a Law Firm's Billing Practices," Professional Lawyer 2 (2001).

66. Rhode, *supra* note 17, at 181.

67. Model Rule 1.5 Comment 9.

review and meticulously challenge lawyer statements. Some also delay payment, keeping the accruing interest for themselves. By contrast, billing arrangements between lawyers and clients who have continuing relationships typically are friendly, although subject to discussion where either is dissatisfied or uneasy. However, when disputes arise, litigation is seldom a desirable strategy for collecting unpaid fees; it is likely to prove highly unpleasant, impose significant financial and reputational costs, and encourage malpractice counterclaims. Particularly where the unpaid bills are modest and clients' assets are limited, attorneys may end up providing services pro bono, but not by choice.

An obvious way to improve fee-related enforcement structures is for all states to establish alternative dispute resolution programs and to require that lawyers participate on clients' request. These programs should address issues of performance as well as charges, and should be as independent as possible of the organized bar. They should include qualified nonlawyer representatives and should be publicized through media outreach and disclosure requirements. Bar ethical codes should require that lawyers provide clients with a standard "bill of rights," including information about fee-related rules and remedies. Systematic efforts to assess participants' evaluation of alternative dispute resolution processes should also be a high priority, because the limited evidence available reveals substantial client dissatisfaction with current programs.[68]

Not only do we need better remedies for consumers, we also need better responses from law firms. Studies of attorneys convicted of billing fraud illustrate common patterns of institutional indifference. When the issue is padding or meter running, supervising lawyers often look the other way or fail to look at all. And when significant misconduct comes to light, significant responses too seldom follow. Studies of fraudulent billing find that firms typically fail to report criminal conduct of their members to bar disciplinary authorities or prosecutors, and sanctions rarely follow for non-reporting.[69] In most cases, the only penalty for excessive fees is a reduction of charges or reimbursement for overpayments, coupled with a loss of future business from the client. Given the low probability of detection, such sanctions provide inadequate deterrence.

To change these incentive structures, more severe penalties are necessary. In cases of serious ethical abuses, legal fees as a matter

---

68. Id.

69. Lisa Lerman, "A Double Standard for Lawyer Dishonesty: Billing Fraud vs. Misappropriation," 34 Hofstra L. Rev. 847, 891 (2006); Kelly, supra note 28, at 182; Lerman, supra note 63, at 278; Ross, supra note 63, at 199–219.

of law can be subject to forfeiture, including fees that have already been paid. Lawyers should more readily be required to forfeit fees and should be subject to discipline for failure to report fraud by other attorneys. Firms in which significant billing abuses occur should be required to develop appropriate oversight procedures, including internal training programs and random audits.[70]

Alternative Billing Structures

Finally, the profession could encourage more realistic billable hour quotas and more alternatives to hourly rates. Over the last decade, interest in innovative billing structures has substantially increased. Common alternatives include fixed fees for routine tasks, reduced hourly fees plus a contingency bonus based on results, and blended fees, involving flat rates with adjustments based on hours or results. Such arrangements can accommodate client concerns such as the desire to increase predictability, encourage efficiency, compare risks, or share risks.[71]

Of course, these alternative structures also carry certain disadvantages. If flat fees are set too high, clients may decide to look elsewhere for legal services. If flat fees are set too low, lawyers have an incentive to cut quality. The risk of insufficient preparation is especially pronounced for unsophisticated clients or for those who are not paying for the lawyers' services. For example, inadequate quality has been a chronic problem in the context of indigent criminal defense contracts, where lawyers submit competitive bids to cover a jurisdiction's entire caseload for a fixed fee.[72] However, in matters involving experienced corporate clients, where attorneys have a strong economic interest in maintaining their reputation for quality, a fixed fee or blended fee can be an attractive option.[73] Still, for most practitioners, time-based billing seems to offer advantages of predictability, familiarity, objectivity, and profitability. Only greater experience with alternatives is likely to help reduce the uncertainties that now deter most lawyers and clients from experi-

---

70. Lerman, supra note 63, at 297–300; Erin White, "More Law Firms Are Auditing Themselves to Catch Billing Errors," Wall St. J., July 14, 1998, at B8.

71. ABA Commission on Billable Hours Report to the House of Delegates (2002), available at http://www.abanet.org/careercounsel/billable/toolkit/bib.html. See also Donald C. Massey & Christopher A. D'Amour, "The Ethical Considerations of Alternative Fee Bill-

ing," 28 S. U. L. Rev. 111 (2001); The Committee on Lawyer Business Ethics, "Business and Ethics Implications of Alternative Billing Practices: Report on Alternative Billing Arrangements," 54 Bus. Law. 175 (1998).

72. See Rhode, supra note 17, at 61.

73. See Robert E. Litan & Steven C. Salop, "Reforming the Lawyer–Client Relationship Through Alternative Billing Methods," 77 Judicature 191 (1994).

menting with potentially cost-effective approaches.[74]

Nonrefundable Retainer Fees

Nonrefundable retainer fees generally take two forms. One is an "engagement" fee or "general retainer." An engagement fee is earned when attorneys lend their names to the case, and it bears no relation to the charge for hours spent on the matter. Such a fee is intended to compensate for the attorney's reputation, commitment to a specific client, unavailability to an opponent, and reservation of future time to be spent on that client. A second type of non-refundable fee is a "special" retainer; services are billed against that initial amount but at the conclusion of the case, the attorney keeps any part of the retainer that has not yet been charged.

Some jurisdictions prohibit use of certain types of non-refundable fees. For example, the New York Court of Appeals disallowed "special retainer" agreements in a case in which a divorce lawyer had attempted to collect substantial sums for little or no work. In the court's view, if such agreements were "allowed to flourish, clients would be relegated to hostage status," because they would find it prohibitively expensive to fire their counsel.[75] That same logic argues for broader bans on nonrefundable fees, or for modifications of the original agreement if the attorney-client relationship ends before the object of representation is completed.

Contingent Fees

Fees that are conditional on a successful outcome are a matter of longstanding controversy. Contingent fees are now virtually universal in personal injury litigation, and widespread in other areas such as professional malpractice, tax refunds, employment discrimination, eminent domain, debt collection, shareholders' derivative claims, and private antitrust actions. The size of the fee varies, but one-third of the total client recovery is a common rate.

Such arrangements have prompted continuing criticism and intermittent restrictions. Early English common law banned con-

---

74. Surveys indicate that the vast majority of business clients use hourly fees for the vast majority of work. Daniel Lee Jacobs, "Is the Billable Hour Running Out of Time?", California Lawyer, April, 2006, at 68 (in a survey by the Association of American Corporate Counsel, over four-fifths of in-house counsel relied on the hourly rate for a median of three-quarters of the work sent to outside firms). See also ABA Commission on Billable Hours, supra note 72, 7–10 (documenting resistance to alternatives).

75. In re Cooperman, 633 N.E. 2d 1069, 1072 (N.Y. 1994). The court did not, however, prohibit general retainer agreements. Section 34 of the Restatement (Third) of the Law Governing Lawyers views engagement retainer fees as legitimate to the extent that they bear a reasonable relationship to income that lawyers sacrifice or expenses that they incur.

tingent fees entirely as a form of unlawful maintenance, barratry, and champerty (i.e., selling shares in the subject matter of a lawsuit and stirring up frivolous litigation). Although some American jurisdictions initially replicated such prohibitions, by the early twentieth century, contingency arrangements subject to judicial supervision were generally permissible.[76] By contrast, many other countries have banned contingent fees, not only because of concerns about non-meritorious suits but also because of potential lawyer-client conflicts of interest. However, the current tendency is to permit contingent fees in some form in some categories of cases, in recognition that the ordinary citizen cannot afford litigation if required to bear the cost of an unsuccessful outcome.

Defenders of contingent fees generally emphasize three main advantages of America's more permissive rules. Such arrangements:

- give lawyers an incentive to pursue a case vigorously in contexts where clients would have difficulty evaluating the quality of professional services;

- allow clients with limited financial resources to afford competent legal assistance by trading upon the value of their claims; and

- enable clients to shift most of the risk of an unsuccessful suit to attorneys, who can spread the costs among other claimants.

Critics of prevailing contingency agreements, however, object to the conflict of interest that they create between lawyers and clients. Attorneys' economic interest lies in maximizing the return on their work; clients' interest lies in gaining the highest possible settlement. Depending on the amount of effort and expense that lawyers invest in preparing a case, the alternative uses of their time, and their attitude toward risk, they may be more or less inclined to settle than their clients. Most commentators have concluded that for claims with low or modest stakes, contingent fee lawyers have inadequate incentives to prepare a case thoroughly and to hold out for the highest possible settlement. Conversely, in high-stakes cases, once lawyers have spent substantial time in preparation, they may be more inclined than their economically-pressed clients to gamble for a large recovery.

---

76. After heated debate, the ABA adopted that position in its 1908 Canons of Ethics. For a critical analysis of the organized bar's hostility toward contingent fees, and the class, religious, and ethnic biases that helped explain such animosity, see Jerold Auerbach, Unequal Justice: Lawyers and Social Change in Modern America 45–51 (1976).

In addition, critics of contingency arrangements object to fee structures in which a lawyer's return bears no necessary relationship to the amount of work performed or to the risk actually assumed. In cases with easy facts and large damages, a standard one-third percentage recovery will provide windfalls for the attorney. In some widely publicized examples, the amount of work done was so insignificant that it would amount to hourly returns estimated at between $12,500 and $30,000 an hour. Mass tort litigation has, on occasion, yielded even higher rates; tobacco cases have sometimes produced over $150,000 an hour.[77]

Lawyers defend such recoveries as essential to subsidize other cases with higher risks. Evidence on this point is mixed. One study of California litigation found that personal injury plaintiffs were successful in only about one-third of the cases, as compared with an average plaintiff success rate of about one-half. The authors of the study observe that this is precisely what one would expect if personal injury plaintiffs' lawyers, who generally use contingency fees, were accepting the riskier cases that justify contingency arrangements.[78] At least some evidence also suggests that outside the large metropolitan areas where most high-stakes litigation occurs, the average earnings of contingent-fee attorneys are not significantly higher than those of counsel who bill hourly.[79] But as critics also note, in too many cases, lawyers' windfall recoveries may far exceed a reasonable return and a necessary incentive to bring socially useful lawsuits.[80] And too many clients are presented with standard contingent fee contracts on a take-it-or-leave-it basis, without information about possible alternatives.

The potential for abuse is especially great in class action litigation because most members of large plaintiff classes lack sufficient information or incentive to monitor lawyers' fees. The

77. Lester Brickman, Michael Horowitz, & Jeffrey O'Connell, Rethinking Contingency Fees: A Proposal to Align the Contingency Fee System with Its Policy Roots and Ethical Mandates 20–23 (1994); Marcia Coyle, "Bill Targets Class Action Fees Sparked by Ire Over Tobacco Money," Nat'l Law Journal, May 19, 2003, at A1.

78. Samuel R. Gross & Kent D. Syverud, "Getting to No: A Study of Settlement Negotiations and the Selection of Cases for Trial," 90 Mich. L. Rev. 319, 337 (1991).

79. Herbert M. Kritzer, "The Wages of Risk: The Returns of Contingency Fee Legal Practice," 47 DePaul L. Rev. 267,

302 (1998); Lester Brickman, "Contingency Fee Abuses, Ethical Mandates and the Disciplinary System: The Case Against Case-by-Case Enforcement," 53 Wash. & Lee L. Rev. 1339, 1345 (1996).

80. Alison Frankel, "Why People Hate the System: Greedy, Greedy, Greedy," American Lawyer Nov. 1996, at 71; Lester Brickman, "Lawyers' Ethics and Fiduciary Obligation in the Brave New World of Aggregative Litigation," 26 Wm & Mary Envtl. L. & Pol'y Rev. 243 (2001); Brickman, supra note 79; and Brickman, Horowitz, & O'Connell, supra note 77.

same deficiency of information hampers trial judges, despite their formal responsibility to ensure the fairness of settlements and the reasonableness of fees. Effective oversight of compensation often requires more time-consuming review than overburdened judges can readily supply. Many courts face staggering caseloads, and the prospect of prolonging a case by overturning a fee agreement is seldom appealing.[81] Adequate judicial review is particularly difficult when defense counsel agree to fee requests. Although defendants sometimes have an interest in challenging such requests in order to discourage nonmeritorious claims, the path of least resistance in other contexts is a cheap settlement with generous fees. Where mass torts are at issue, the judgments are so enormous that a standard contingency arrangement may deliver returns out of all proportion to the work performed or the risks assumed.

To address the problem of windfall fees, a number of approaches are possible. One strategy is to set statutory caps on fees, with advancing percentage formulas. Under this approach, lawyers receive a larger portion of the total recovery as the case progresses and presumably becomes more time consuming. So, for example, in a matter settled without filing suit, the lawyer receives twenty-five percent of the recovery; in a case settled after filing, thirty-three percent, in a case that goes to trial, forty percent; and in a case won on appeal, fifty percent. An obvious problem with such a formula, however, is that it may encourage lawyers to prolong proceedings where the stakes are sufficiently high. An alternative that some jurisdictions have adopted sets a graduated scale giving lawyers a smaller percentage of recovery as clients' claims grow larger. This approach prevents windfall fees, but at the cost of discouraging lawyers from accepting large, complex claims. Another increasingly popular strategy is to cap contingency fees in certain contexts, such as medical malpractice litigation, where large recoveries have dramatically affected insurance premiums and led to strong political opposition.[82] How these caps affect injured plaintiff's access to legal services remains unclear.

An alternative, widely discussed strategy for curbing windfall recovery has been the "settlement offer" approach developed by the

---

81. Jonathan Molot, "An Old Judicial Role for a New Litigation Era," 113 Yale L. J. 27, 52–3 (2003); John C. Coffee, Jr., "The Corruption of the Class Action: The New Technology of Collusion," 80 Cornell L. Rev. 851, 855 (1995); Samuel Issacharoff, "Class Action Conflicts," 30 U.C. Davis L. Rev. 805, 829 (1997).

82. Leonard Gross, "Are Differences Among the Attorney Conflict of Interest Rules Consistent with Principles of Behavioral Economics?," 19 Geo. J. Legal Ethics 111, 136 (2006); David Horrigan, "Lawyers, Doctors, Clash on Fee Caps," Nat'l Law Journal, Aug. 8, 2005, at A5.

Manhattan Institute. Under its proposal, a defendant in a civil suit would have an opportunity to make an early settlement offer within sixty days of a plaintiff's demand for such an offer. If the defendant chooses not to make an offer, the proposal would not apply and the plaintiff's lawyer would be free to negotiate a contingent fee, subject to general requirements of reasonableness. However, if an offer was made and accepted, the compensation to the plaintiff's attorney would be limited to a reasonable hourly rate or a modest share of the recovery, such as ten percent of the first $100,000 and five percent of any greater amounts. If a settlement offer was made and refused, that offer would set a baseline for later assessing the reasonableness of contingency fees.[83]

Opponents of this approach claim that it would prove both under- and over-inclusive; it would offer no protection in the absence of a settlement offer, and it could deny lawyers a reasonable recovery in some settled cases. The ultimate effect might be to reduce attorneys' willingness to take contingent cases, restrict clients' access to legal services, and decrease the deterrent value of liability claims. But only through experience with such a formula can these concerns be accurately assessed. The effects may differ across different categories of cases. However, the limited evidence now available indicates that some lawyers already take lower contingent fees in cases that settle early and nonetheless manage a reasonable return. If the approach restricted windfall fees and had only marginal effect on attorneys' ability to subsidize speculative cases, the trade-off might still be worthwhile.[84]

Courts and bar associations could also do more to protect clients, and to enable clients to protect themselves in class action proceedings. Steering committees that are representative of the entire class can help select attorneys and negotiate competitive fee arrangements. Greater reliance on special masters to review compensation agreements could also prove useful. For individual cases, requiring lawyers to disclose the effective hourly return might help deter and remedy the worst abuses.[85] Still another approach would permit a form of "privatization" now prohibited by the unauthorized practice rules: "lay intermediaries," such as labor unions and employers, could be secondarily involved in the lawyer-client relationship, and could monitor the fee arrangements.

83. Brickman, Horowitz, & O'Connell, supra note 77.

84. Id. For debates over the proposal, see Peter Passell, "Contingency Fees in Injury Cases under Attack by Legal Scholars," N.Y. Times, Feb. 11, 1994, at 1; Lawrence Fox, "Contingent Fees," ABA J., July 1995, at 44; Kritzer, supra note 78.

85. Gross, supra note 82, at 144.

A related reform proposal worth consideration involves contingent fees for expert witnesses. DR 7–109(C) of the Code explicitly bans such payments, and Model Rule 3.4(b) bans any "inducement ... prohibited by law", which often covers witness compensation beyond expenses. In rejecting constitutional challenges to such bans, the Second Circuit Court of Appeals nonetheless noted that there might be sound policy reasons for changing these rules:

> Cross-examination would reveal whatever financial stake a witness has in the outcome of litigation. . . . [Moreover] experts often have ongoing business relationships with the parties who retain them and therefore, in an indirect sense, frequently have a stake in the outcome of litigation although their fee is not contingent and thus not covered by DR 7–109(C). Other experts, although retained on a "fixed fee" basis, often do not expect to receive payment unless the party for whom they testify is successful.[86]

The prevailing system not only disadvantages litigants of limited means, it also does a poor job of exposing expert bias because it may encourage de facto rather than explicit contingency arrangements. Such tacit understandings are harder to discover and to expose in cross examination, which suggests reasons for modifying current rules.[87]

Another common reform proposal is to permit lawyers to advance plaintiffs' medical and living expenses with repayment contingent on the outcome of the lawsuit. Model Rule 1.8 now prohibits such financial assistance. The reason, according to Comment 10, is that such aid "would encourage clients to pursue lawsuits that might not otherwise be brought and ... gives lawyers too great a financial stake in the litigation." By contrast, many commentators believe that such "humanitarian assistance" would pose no greater threat of lawyer self-interest than the current contingent fee structure, and that cash advances would enable meritorious, not frivolous cases to be brought. Under the current system, plaintiffs with greatest needs for recovery are too often forced to accept inadequate settlements in order to meet urgent living expenses.[88] An alternative approach, adopted by a small number of jurisdictions, is to permit lawyers to advance funds or

---

86. Person v. Association of Bar of City of New York, 554 F.2d 534, 539 (2d Cir. 1977).

87. Jeffrey J. Parker, Note, "Contingent Expert Witness Fees: Access and Legitimacy," 64 S. Cal. L. Rev. 1363, 1387 (1991).

88. Jack P. Sahl, "The Cost of Humanitarian Assistance: Ethical Rules and the First Amendment," 34 St. Mary's L. J. 795 (2003); Gross, supra note 82.

guarantee loans for reasonably necessary living expenses provided that the advances or guarantees are not promised as "an inducement to obtain professional employment" before the lawyer is retained.[89]

On similar reasoning, some commentators propose reforms that would allow third parties to help finance lawsuits in exchange for a share of the recovery. Such investment in litigation, long condemned as "champerty" at common law, remains impermissible in many jurisdictions.[90] Advocates of reform argue that permitting such financial arrangements would increase access to the courts and enable litigants of modest means to obtain adequate recoveries. The current system, by allowing investment only by lawyers under contingent fee arrangements, limits the investment market and permits lawyers to earn an inflated "economic rent."[91] Because third party funding companies will have no incentive to invest in claims with little chance of recovery, permitting such financial arrangements appears unlikely to encourage frivolous litigation.

Protection for Sophisticated Clients

A final area of debate concerning compensation arrangements involves the degree of protection appropriate for sophisticated clients. The traditional rationale for regulating fee arrangements is that many consumers "do not bargain effectively because of need and inexperience. The services required are often unclear beforehand and difficulty to monitor as a lawyer provides them."[92] The more sophisticated the client, the less compelling the rationale for judicial oversight.

That was, in effect, the court's view in one of the most celebrated cases involving a fee dispute in corporate practice. In Brobeck, Phleger & Harrison v. Telex Corporation, the court enforced a $1 million fee for services that turned out to involve only filing one petition for *certiorari*.[93] The case arose from antitrust

---

89. Louisiana State Bar Association v. Edwins, 329 So.2d 437, 446 (La. 1976). *Edwins* is the leading precedent. The Restatement of the Law Governing Lawyers (Third) § 48 similarly permits humanitarian assistance. For other state court rules and decisions, see Sahl, supra note 88, at 822–23, and Danielle Z. Cohen, "Advancing Funds, Advancing Justice: Adopting the Louisiana Approach," 19 Geo. J. Legal Ethics 613 (2006).

90. Saladini v. Righellis, 687 N.E.2d 1224 (1997); Douglas R. Richmond, "Litigation Funding: Investing, Lending, or Loan Sharking?," Professional Lawyer 17 (2005); Susan Lorde Martin, "Financing Plaintiffs' Lawsuits: An Increasingly Popular (and Legal) Business," 33 U. Mich. J. L. Reform 57 (2000).

91. Rudy Santore and Alan D. Viard, "Legal Fee Restrictions, Moral Hazard and Attorney Rents," 44 J. L. & Econ. 549 (2001).

92. American Law Institute, Restatement of the Law Governing Lawyers (Third) § 34, Comment b.

93. Brobeck, Phleger & Harrison v. Telex Corp., 602 F.2d 866 (9th Cir. 1979).

proceedings in which Telex obtained a $259 million judgment against IBM, but lost an $18 million counterclaim. On appeal, IBM won reversal of the judgment and affirmance of its counterclaim. In the face of liability substantial enough to bankrupt the company, Telex sought the best available lawyer for its petition to the Supreme Court. The company settled on a partner at Brobeck Phleger & Harrison, and agreed to a complicated contract specifying different fees contingent on different outcomes. After the Supreme Court granted certiorari, Telex and IBM reached a settlement in which each dropped their claims. In rejecting Telex's claim that the $1 million fee was unconscionable, the court concluded that the contract must be reviewed "with reference to the time [it was made] and cannot be resolved by hindsight."[94]

As a practical matter, such fee-related litigation with sophisticated clients is rare. These clients take the relevant risk factors into account if they resort to contingency arrangements, and lawyers frequently adjust their bills to avoid charges that become unreasonable in light of the results obtained. But where unanticipated circumstances arise and lawyers fail to reduce excessive fees, even sophisticated clients may need protection. In the long run, neither the profession nor the public is well served by a system that overlooks serious overcharging, whatever the reason.

94. Id., at 875.

Chapter XI

QUALIFICATIONS FOR THE BAR

A. Introduction

For much of its history, the American bar made relatively little effort to ensure adequate qualifications among its members. As Chapter III noted, the courts traditionally asserted inherent power to regulate the practice of law. However, until the twentieth century, formal admission standards were lax. Courts required applicants to demonstrate "fitness to practice" law, but generally required only perfunctory oral exams and some limited period of preparation. What occurred during that period generally left much to be desired. The dominant method of qualification was through "reading law" independently and serving as an apprentice. Under the conventional apprenticeship arrangement, aspiring attorneys offered their services plus a fee to established lawyers in exchange for "instruction" and the right to use the lawyers' legal forms later in practice. In an era before typewriting, preprinted forms, and duplicating services, students often spent much of their apprenticeships copying documents.[1]

During the late nineteenth century, the growth of bar associations and the general cultural trend toward heightened occupational standards encouraged a corresponding formalization of qualifications for legal practice. Ever since, the structure of legal education and bar admission has been a matter of continuing attention and periodic reform.

B. Legal Education

During the late eighteenth and early nineteenth centuries, formal legal education typically centered in small for-profit schools. Although a few applicants to the bar traveled to England for instruction in the Inns of Court, or took some undergraduate legal courses at an American university, the most accessible training was in one of about twenty specialized institutions run by practitioners.[2] However, these independent schools, along with university law

---

1. See generally Charles R. McKirdy, "The Lawyer as Apprentice: Legal Education in Eighteenth Century Massachusetts," 28 J. Legal Educ. 124 (1976); Lawrence M. Friedman, A History of American Law 97–98 (3d ed. 2005). The arrangement in Europe was much the same. See Geoffrey Hazard and Angelo Dondi, Legal Ethics: A Comparative Study, ch. 2 (2004).

2. J. Willard Hurst, The Growth of American Law: The Law Makers, 277–93 (1950); Robert Stevens, Law School: Legal Education in America from the 1850s to the 1980s 7–10 (1983).

courses, dwindled during the populist Jacksonian era, when admission standards were exceptionally lax.[3]

The characteristic features of modern legal education emerged at Harvard Law School after the Civil War. The impetus came largely from Dean Christopher Columbus Langdell, who, like many of his academic colleagues, had great faith in scientific methodology. In their view, law was a science that could be taught through the Socratic case method. Just as rules of nature could be discovered from examining biological specimens, legal principles could be deduced from parsing judicial decisions. Yet the seeming "objectivity" of this case method was achieved only by excluding a broad array of other critical issues, such as legislation, lawyering skills, and the operation of the justice system in practice. Proponents of this approach, however, viewed it as a means of making the educational curricula more "rigorous." To that end, they also attempted to extend its duration into a three-year post-graduate program.

This effort coincided with a period of increased support for higher educational standards within most professions, including law. The American Bar Association, formed in 1870, soon recommended tighter admission requirements. As Chapter II noted, much of the organized bar's concern was driven by an influx of new applicants from lower class and immigrant backgrounds, who were graduating in increasing numbers from for-profit night programs.[4] Similar reform recommendations emerged from the Association of American Law Schools (AALS), which formed in 1900 to support and strengthen legal education.

This campaign for heightened academic standards was not without its critics. Among the most prominent was sociologist Thorstein Veblen, who argued that "vocational" schools like law "belong[ed] in the modern university no more than a school of fencing or dancing."[5] Other commentators, although sympathetic towards efforts to make legal education more rigorous, were concerned about changes that would reduce its accessibility. During the early 1900s, about a third of the nation's law students were enrolled in night programs. A requirement of three years of full-time training would exclude many of these individuals. And such an

3. Stevens, supra note 2, at 7–8. In 1860, only nine of thirty-nine states required any specific period of legal study. Id.

4. Jerold S. Aurbach, Unequal Justice: Lawyers and Social Change in Modern America 62–87 (1976); Herb D. Vest,

"Felling the Giant: Breaking the ABA's Stranglehold on Legal Education in America," 50 J. Legal Educ. 494 (2000).

5. Thorstein Veblen, The Higher Learning in America: A Memorandum on the Conduct of Universities by Businessmen 211 (1918).

extended period of study was not self-evidently necessary for the routine matters that dominated most lawyers' practice. These concerns were reflected in an influential 1921 Report for the Carnegie Foundation, Training for the Public Profession of Law. It recommended a divided bar with different exams and educational requirements. The more highly trained graduates could serve business and government clients, and the graduates of night and part time programs could remain available to meet more routine individual needs.

Both the ABA and the AALS flatly rejected that recommendation. Rather, they pushed for more stringent admission requirements for all lawyers and more demanding accreditation standards for all law schools. These efforts were largely successful, but controversies persist over the appropriate form of education for an increasingly diverse profession. Who should teach what, to whom, for how long, and by what methods, all remain matters of dispute. Discussion here focuses on the most contested issues: educational structure; law school curricula, methodology, and climate; professional responsibility and pro bono service; and diversity in student admissions, faculty appointments, and institutional culture.

Educational Structure

Law schools are subject to multiple regulatory systems. The United States Department of Education recognizes the ABA's Council of the Section of Legal Education and Admission to the Bar as the nation's accrediting authority for professional training in law. Under that authority, the Council has developed detailed accreditation standards governing matters such as classroom hours, student-faculty ratios, library resources, and so forth. Once a school has established its compliance with these standards, it is subject to a site visit every seven years to insure its continued adherence to accreditation requirements. Forty-five states and the District of Columbia require applicants to the bar to graduate from an ABA accredited school. The other states have developed their own accreditation systems, and California also permits practice by graduates of unaccredited schools who pass the bar exam.

Current accreditation requirements have been subject to frequent criticism. Many commentators believe that the diversity of legal practice should be matched by diversity in educational structure. The day-to-day work of a Wall Street securities specialist bears little resemblance to that of a solo practitioner handling matrimonial cases, and it is not obvious that they should be trained in the same way. Nor is it clear that the time and expense of a three year program is necessary for all fields of practice. Federal judge and law professor Richard Posner puts the case for more diversity in law school structures. As he notes:

> We have no experimental or otherwise empirical basis ... for believing that law school has to take so long, at enormous cost.... Graduate schools of business grant an M.B.A. after only two years, and the business world seems not to be suffering as a result of the "abbreviated" education that their students receive.... It will be argued that law students can't make a judgment whether they need a third year of law school; they are too immature and too ignorant about law. Maybe so. But employers know whether a third year of law school is necessary. If they think it is, they will not hire students who have not completed a third year of law school, or they will pay students who leave earlier much less.... There is no need for government to do the insisting.
>
> I am willing to concede the case for some paternalism. Some newly graduated lawyers hang out their own shingle rather than going to work for a law firm or other knowledgeable employer.... If consumer protection is needed in this area, it can be provided by stiffening the bar exam, or perhaps by giving a special bar exam to students who don't complete the third year, or perhaps by confining the title "lawyer" to the three-year graduate and assigning another title, such as "legal advocate" or "legal counselor," to practitioners who have not had three years of law school.
>
> Courts, too, need protection from lawyers who lack the skills or experience to handle a trial. But the necessary protection can be obtained by court rules requiring demonstrated skills and experience, not completion of an artificially determined period of schooling.[6]

Debates over the appropriate length and focus of law school are longstanding. The three-year curriculum was initially envisioned as covering everything a new lawyer needed to know. But since 1900, and particularly in the last half century, the subject matters of practice have grown exponentially and specialization within legal fields has intensified. A three-year curriculum cannot include everything that all lawyers need to know over the course of their careers. Dean William Prosser, of torts fame, once reviewed all the demands

6. Richard A. Posner, "Let Employers Insist if Three Years of Law School Is Necessary," Los Angeles Daily J., Dec. 15, 1999, at A6. See also Stephanie Shaffer, "The First Question on Third Year: Why?," Nat'l Law J., Aug. 22, 2006, at A6.

that legal education was expected to satisfy and sardonically suggested that a 10–year curriculum might be adequate.[7]

Yet the logic of this analysis might argue for a shorter rather than longer required course of study. Law school can aspire only to serve as an introduction to basic legal skills and information, and that might well be accomplished in under three years. For example, a two or two-and-a-half year program could leave room for some electives, interdisciplinary courses and skills training, along with coverage of basic subjects, such as Property, Contracts, Torts, Civil Procedure, Tax, Criminal Law, Constitutional Law, Administrative or Regulatory Law, and Corporate Law.

More specialized course work often would be most useful later in lawyers' careers, after they have established fields of concentration. For many practitioners, specialization in practice is determined partly by design but mostly by fortuity. Early job placement, assignments and opportunities shape careers in ways that individuals cannot fully anticipate while in law school. So too, a basic survey course taken while a student will not provide practitioners with all that is necessary for competent representation in that area many years later. As a consequence, many lawyers could benefit from short intensive post-graduate courses in their specialty. This is, in fact, the format of some of the most successful Continuing Legal Education programs, such as one sponsored by the National Institute of Trial Advocacy. In any event, it is only through greater experimentation with alternatives that the relative merits of the current three-year curriculum can be assessed. A competitive process might well produce effective two-year programs, as it has in other professional and business contents.

A similar argument has been advanced in the courts as well as in the broader educational community. In the late 1990s, the Massachusetts School of Law failed to satisfy accreditation requirements and subsequently sued the ABA and the AALS on antitrust grounds. According to the MSL complaint, the current accreditation system functioned as a cartel by setting unnecessary and burdensome standards that unjustifiably raise the cost of legal education.[8] Although courts rejected the MSL claims on both procedural and

---

7. The demands included instruction not only in basic doctrine and legal skills but also in jurisprudence, philosophy, ethics, legal history, political science, economics, sociology, psychology, international and comparative law, and the legal profession. William I. Prosser, "The Ten Year Curriculum," 6 J. Legal Educ. 149, 152–55 (1953).

8. Margo Slade, "A Little Law School Does Battle with the ABA," N.Y. Times, Feb. 4, 1994, at A19; Courtney Leatherman, "Rebellion Brews in Tight–Knit World of Law Accreditation," Chron. of Higher Educ., June 1, 1994, at A14, A16.

substantive grounds, similar concerns about accreditation authority have emerged from mainstream educators.[9] In 2006, the American Law Deans Association requested the Department of Education to remove the ABA's authority to control tenure requirements for clinicians, library directors, and writing instructors. According to the Deans, the ABA's requirement of tenure or long term contracts for these law school staff leads to fewer appointments and limits program development.[10]

Underlying such disputes are broader arguments about the accreditation process. In the view of many experts, the current system is overly intrusive and inflexible, and stifles innovation in favor of a "one size fits all" model of legal education.[11] The high costs of complying with accreditation requirements inflates tuition and limits access to the profession, particularly by students from low-income groups. These entry barriers, in turn, raise the cost of legal services and help price law out of reach for consumers of limited means.[12] Moreover, the high debt burden which students acquire in order to finance their legal education limits career options after graduation and makes it harder for many new attorneys to take lower paying jobs that serve underrepresented causes and communities.[13] Critics would like to see more variation and competition in legal education, either through relaxing accreditation standards, or eliminating the requirement of graduation from an accredited law school. Under the latter approach, schools would be forced to demonstrate to students and employers that their programs added sufficient value to justify the expense.

9. Massachusetts School of Law at Andover v. ABA, 107 F.3d 1026 (3d Cir. 1997).

10. Leigh Jones, "ABA's Tenure Power is Disputed," Nat'l Law Journal, April 3, 2006, at A1, A12.

11. Deborah L. Rhode, In the Interests of Justice: Reforming the Legal Profession, 190–91 (2000); Leatherman, supra note 8, at A14, A16 (quoting a letter from deans of fourteen law schools); Vest, supra note 4, at 497–501.

12. George B. Shepherd, "Make it Optional: Why Are Accreditation, Three Years of School, and the Bar Exam Such a Big Deal," Legal Times, September 5, 2005, p. 32; George B. Shepherd, "No African–American Lawyers Allowed: The Inefficient Racism of the ABA's Accreditation of Law Schools," 53 J. of Legal Educ. 103, 105 (2003).

13. A majority of students rely on loans and the median debt burden among surveyed graduates is $60,000 to $70,000. Ronit Dinovitzer, After the J.D.: First Results of a National Study of Legal Careers 71–72, The NALP Foundation for Law Career Research and Education and the American Bar Foundation (2004); George Kuh, Bryant Garth, et al., Student Engagement in Law Schools: A First Look (LESSE, Indiana University 2004). Debt is of course only one factor that affects career choices, and the most comprehensive study to date did not find variations in debt levels of recent law school graduates across different practice settings. Low-paid public interest attorneys had the same average burdens as lawyers in higher-paying private practice settings. After the J.D., supra, at 72.

By contrast, defenders of the current structure typically respond that at a time when the law is becoming "more complex than ever before and occupying more areas of economic and social life, we should [not] acquiesce in the notion that lawyers can be trained in two-thirds of the time."[14] Many bar leaders would like to tighten, not loosen, educational standards in certain areas involving fundamental skills and values. An influential 1992 report by an ABA Task Force on Law Schools and The Profession, Narrowing the Gap (the MacCrate Report), identified ten core skills and four central values necessary for any "well-trained generalist to practice law competently and professionally." The "Fundamental Lawyering Skills" describe functions common to nearly all areas of practice: (1) problem solving; (2) legal analysis and reasoning; (3) legal research; (4) factual investigation; (5) communication; (6) counseling; (7) negotiation; (8) litigation and alternative dispute-resolution procedures; (9) organization and management of legal work; and (10) recognition and resolution of ethical dilemmas. The "Fundamental Values of the Profession" formulate norms of ethical lawyering that call upon lawyers to: (1) provide competent representation; (2) strive to promote justice, fairness, and morality; (3) improve the profession; and (4) undertake professional self-development.[15] This ambitious agenda contemplates enriching, not shortening, current educational requirements. Dean Prosser's ten-year curriculum redux.

So too, law school administrators face pressures that cut against a less expensive, more streamlined course of study. The economic pressures of contemporary practice have decreased the availability of mentoring for new entrants, and increased the responsibility of law schools to provide skills-based training.[16] Tougher bar examination standards, coupled with the substantial costs for both students and their institutions of high exam failure rates, has also led many schools to add multiple "bar prep" courses to the curriculum.[17] The importance of prestige, measured partly by *U.S. News and World Report* rankings, also encourages expensive investment in areas that will boost the schools' reputation among peers and prospective students. Many law school professors would like even more time for research instead of teaching, thereby requiring

14. Preble Stolz, "The Two Year Law School: The Day The Music Died," 25 J. Legal Educ. 37, 42–44 (1973).

15. American Bar Association Section of Legal Education and Admissions to the Bar, Legal Education and Professional Development—An Educational Continuum, Report of the Task Force on Law Schools and the Profession: Narrowing the Gap (1992) [MacCrate Report].

16. Richard Matasar, "The Rise and Fall of American Legal Education," 49 N.Y. L. Rev. 465, 472–73 (2005).

17. Id.

more faculty to staff the courses. Those financial demands in turn encourage legal educators to support an accreditation system that can maintain their leverage in resource negotiations with central university decision makers. Historically, many universities have viewed law schools as "cash cows"—money makers with relatively low costs and high tuitions, which can subsidize other educational programs that are less well endowed. Law schools' need to comply with accreditation requirements governing libraries, faculty size, and so forth has enabled them to hold onto resources that might otherwise go to poorer academic cousins.

Consensus in this area is difficult because legal education has multiple constituencies with competing agendas. Law schools are expected to produce both "Pericles and plumbers"—lawyer statesmen and legal scriveners.[18] The most direct consumers—students— have interests that are not identical with those of the ultimate consumers—clients and the public. Education is one of the rare contexts where many buyers want less for their money.[19] Some students would like to earn a degree with the minimal effort required to pass a bar examination and land a job; others find too much of law school classwork impractical or irrelevant. In the absence of strict accreditation standards, law schools might need to reduce costs and quality standards in order to compete for applicants who view "less as more." By contrast, for many practitioners and professors, "less is more" has different and far less appealing connotations. Less rigorous educational standards means more graduates competing for business and more difficulties generating funds for law school facilities, salaries and support services.

Not only are there competing concerns within the profession, there are competing demands from the clientele served by the bar. The constituencies directly affected—students, faculty, and practitioners—all have interests that are not entirely consistent with those of the public. Ordinary Americans' overriding concern is access to reasonably competent assistance at a price they can afford. Clients at different income levels with different needs are likely to make different cost/quality tradeoffs. A central challenge for legal education lies in striking an appropriate balance among these competing public and professional concerns. A structure that permitted more variation and innovation in educational structure might at least provide a more informed basis for finding that balance.

18. William Twining, "Pericles and the Plumber," 83 L. Q. Rev. 396 (1967).

19. Rhode, supra note 11, at 188–92.

Educational Content, Climate, and Methodology

Questions concerning the structure of legal education are related to other issues about curricula, teaching, scholarship, and climate, all of which have been equally controversial. According to many critics, law schools offer too little practice and too little theory. They provide too little training in basic skills and too little grounding in related disciplines such as philosophy, psychology, history, finance, and management. Other criticisms focus on the dominant instructional methods of casebooks and Socratic dialogue; the lack of support for legal ethics and public service; and the allegedly overly competitive, stressful aspects of law school culture.

Although modern legal education has largely rejected Langdell's assumptions about law as a science, his approach is often said to "rule us from the grave." A diluted case method and quasi-Socratic style remain common in many law school classrooms. The reasons have less to do with educational quality than with the adaptability of this method to large classes, its corresponding low costs, its lively interactive format, and its perceived ability to maintain analytic rigor while accommodating different intellectual approaches.

Yet the case approach is of limited value and somewhat of a misnomer. It does not in fact require study of actual cases. It relies rather on published judicial opinions, which leave out much of the living process of the law: the translation of a dispute into a legal grievance; the investigation and presentation of parties' claims; the unstated factors influencing judicial decisions; the consequences of those decisions on the individuals involved; and the social, political, and economic implications of the legal process. In effect, students often get law without lawyering, perhaps a legal analogue of "geology without the rocks."[20]

Also absent in some law school curricula is any sustained effort to address the practical skills and interpersonal dimensions of lawyers' work. These capabilities are largely relegated to clinical courses, which are still treated as poor relations in some academic communities.[21] Between two-thirds and four-fifths of surveyed graduates believe that skills such as negotiation, fact gathering, and document preparation could be taught effectively in law school, but only about a quarter feel that those subjects receive sufficient attention. Similar disparities are reported for problem solving, oral

20. Lawrence Friedman, quoted in Rhode, *supra* note 11, at 198.

21. ABA Section of Legal Education and Admissions to the Bar, *supra* note 15; see also Rhode, *supra* note 11, at 197–98.

communication, counseling, and litigation.[22] So too, despite recognition of the importance of cross-cultural and cross-disciplinary perspectives, the core curriculum stubbornly resists intruders. With the exception of law and economics approaches, which have managed to influence many law school courses, interdisciplinary materials generally remain at the margins of law school curricula. At most schools, a "bit of borrowed intellectual finery dresses up the standard legal wardrobe, but the fashion remains the same."[23] The consequence is to deprive students of approaches that could prove useful in their future work, from fields such as finance, management, psychology, organizational behavior, and international relations. In an era of increasing multidisciplinary and global practice, future lawyers need exposure to insights from a broad range of fields.[24]

Corresponding limitations are apparent in legal scholarship. Law schools' curricular focus on reported cases and inadequate support for interdisciplinary or empirical work have constrained research agendas. Legal academics write increasingly for each other, too often in forms insufficiently informed by other fields and insufficiently intelligible to practitioners, judges, and policy makers.[25]

The quasi-Socratic style of law school teaching also has limitations. When Langdell first pioneered his approach, most students could "see nothing in [the] system but mental confusion and social humiliation."[26] Contemporary quasi-Socratic approaches are more humane. But according to critics like Ralph Nader, they still offer students only freedom to "roam in an intellectual cage."[27] At its best, the Socratic method promotes critical reflection and facility in oral argument.[28] At its worst, it can lead to a controlled dialogue in which the professor first invites the student to "guess what I'm thinking," and then finds the response inevitably lacking. The system rewards "quick answers, and to admit to being puzzled—a

22. Joanne Martin & Bryant G. Garth, "Clinical Education as a Bridge Between Law School and Practice: Mitigating the Misery," 1 Clinical L. Rev. 443, 448 (1994).

23. Rhode, supra note 11, at 198.

24. Mary C. Daly, "What the MDP Debate Can Teach Us About Law Practice in the New Millennium and the Need for Curricular Reform," 50 J. Legal Educ. 521, 543–44 (2000); Judith Welch Wegner, "The Curriculum: Patterns and Possibilities," 51 J. Legal Educ. 431 (2001).

25. Deborah L. Rhode, "Legal Scholarship," 115 Harv. L. Rev. 1327 (2002); Harry T. Edwards, "The Growing Disjunction Between Legal Education and the Legal Profession," 91 Mich. L. Rev. 34 (1992).

26. Charles Warren, 2 History of the Harvard Law School 372–73 (1908).

27. Ralph Nader, "Law Schools and Law Firms," New Republic, Oct. 11, 1969, at 20–21, 23.

28. Phillip Areeda, "The Socratic Method," 109 Harv. L. Rev. 917 (1996).

key Socratic virtue—will not get a student very far."[29] Too often, the system silences the least assertive students and leads to what Professor Anthony Amsterdam once labeled MOPIE: Maximum Obtainable Passivity in Education.[30] Critics argue that such an atmosphere can diminish students' self-confidence, erode conviction, and encourage corrosive skepticism. By depersonalizing and decontextualizing inquiry, it may also foster an impoverished understanding of the lawyer's role.[31]

A related concern is the effect of law school culture on student values and career choices. A frequent critique is that legal education undermines the commitments that attract students to law in the first instance: they enter law school talking of justice but leave talking of jobs.[32] Probably the primary negative influence is the weak public support for meeting the legal needs of the poor. Law school students quickly learn that there are few positions available in legal services, and that the pay and career prospects are limited. However, critics believe that several aspects of the educational experience contribute to the decline in interest in public interest and legal service positions. First, the high tuition and limited financial aid and loan forgiveness programs at most law schools discourage students from taking such poorly-paid positions. Although some research suggests that the core problem is not debt levels but pay disparities between public interest and private practice careers, debt burdens obviously heighten the significance of those disparities.[33] In addition, as subsequent discussion suggests, law school culture often provides relatively little support for public interest work through pro bono programs, placement priorities, or other initiatives.[34]

---

29. Martha C. Nussbaum, "Cultivating Humanity in Legal Education," 70 U. Chi. L. Rev. 265, 272–73 (2003).

30. Anthony Amsterdam, Address Before the Society of American Law Teachers, quoted in Geoffrey C. Hazard, Jr., Susan P. Koniak, & Roger C. Cramton, The Law and Ethics of Lawyering 972 (3d ed., 1999).

31. Rhode, supra note 11, at 197; Roger C. Cramton, "The Ordinary Religion of the Law School Classroom," 29 J. Legal Ed. 247 (1978).

32. See Robert Granfield, Making Elite Lawyers: Visions of Law at Harvard and Beyond 38–39 (1992); Robert V. Stover, Making It and Breaking It: The Fate of Public Interest Commit-

ment During Law School (Howard S. Erlanger ed., 1989).

33. See Lewis A. Kornhauser & Richard L. Revesz, "Legal Education and Entry into the Legal Profession: The Role of Race, Gender, and Educational Debt," 70 N.Y.U. L. Rev. 829 (1995); Bruce Buckley, "Public Interest Honor Roll," 9 National Jurist, Jan./Feb. 2000, at 28 (In the late 1990s, the median public interest job paid half as much as the median private practice position).

34. See Granfield, supra note 32, at 8; Deborah L. Rhode, Pro Bono in Practice and in Principle 161–62 (2004); and text accompanying note 30, infra.

However, most empirical research finds that law school does not have a large measurable effect on attitudes, including attitudes toward public interest law, and that market forces are a much stronger influence.[35] For example, an in-depth study of Harvard Law students found that they reported becoming more interested in public interest and social justice issues while in law school, although only a tiny percentage ended up taking jobs in this area. What appeared to account for the disparity between interest and employment was the comparatively low salary and prestige associated with most public interest options available.[36]

Empirical research does, however, suggest that law school has a significant impact on other aspects of student life. Of greatest concern is its link with stress-related dysfunctions including obsessive-compulsive behavior, depression, severe anxiety, and isolation. Between twenty and forty percent of students in any given law school class report such symptoms. Another significant proportion develop substance abuse problems.[37] The most systematic research available indicates that the problem lies partly with the law school experience, not simply with the characteristics of students who choose law.[38]

Although the exact causes of stress-related dysfunctions are difficult to measure, most research identifies the following factors:

- excessive workloads and lack of assistance with time-management problems;

- high student-faculty ratios leading to limited interactions and feedback;

- overly competitive reward structures with too much emphasis on grades as the measure of status and self-worth;

35. See See J.D. Droddy and C. Scott Peters, "The Effect of Law School on Political Attitudes: Evidence from the Class of 2000," 53 J. Legal Educ. 33 (2003); surveys discussed in Hazard, Koniak, Cramton, & Cohen, supra note 30, at 1019.

36. Granfield, supra note 32, at 38–48, 88–90. See also Kornhauser & Revesz, supra note 33.

37. Mariam Alikhan, Note, "The ADA is Narrowing Mental Health Inquiries on Bar Applications: Looking to the Medical Profession to Decide Where to Go from Here," 14 Geo. J. Legal Ethics 159 (2000); See Susan Daicoff, "Lawyer Know Thyself: A Review of Empirical Research on Attorney Attributes Bear-

ing on Professionalism," 46 Am. U. L. Rev. 1378, 1380 (1997); Ann L. Iijima, "Lessons Learned, Legal Education and Law Student Dysfunction," 48 J. Legal Educ. 524 (1998); Lawrence S. Krieger, "What We're Not Telling Law Students—and Lawyers—That They Really Need to Know: Some Thoughts–In–Action Toward Revitalizing the Profession from its Roots," 13 J. L. & Health 15 (1998–99); "Report of the AALS Special Committee on Problems of Substance Abuse in Law Schools," 44 J. Legal Educ. 35, 44 (1994).

38. Daicoff, supra note 37, at 1380; Alikhan, supra note 37, at 159.

- inadequate information, counseling, and treatment programs concerning psychological and substance abuse problems; and

- inadequate assurances of confidentiality for students who would benefit from counseling and treatment.[39]

None of these issues are readily resolved. As commentators have often noted, innovation in legal education comes hard and dies young.[40] Talk is cheap and many educationally desirable initiatives are not. There are obvious limits to how much time-intensive or specialized training can be provided without increasing tuition, which may further restrict access and raise student debt burdens to intolerable levels. The competitive aspects of law school culture are difficult to alter, given that practice itself is highly competitive, beginning in the graduates' quest for their first job. Yet not all curricular initiatives require extensive additional resources. Many of the inadequacies noted above could be ameliorated through greater use of adjuncts, interdisciplinary collaboration, on-line technology, interactive exercises, and cooperative student projects. More support should be available for curricular development as well as empirical and cross disciplinary research. Students should receive multiple forms of feedback and greater access to confidential support services.

The problem with many of these strategies is not that they are unaffordable but rather that they are insufficiently rewarded. Improvements in the curriculum and support structures for students are not adequately reflected in law school rankings and guides for applicants. Nor is excellence in teaching the path to greatest recognition for individual faculty. Significant changes in law school curricula and climate will require significant changes in law school incentive structures. A crucial first step is to develop more systematic ways of assessing educational effectiveness and holding institutions accountable. At a minimum, more information needs to be available comparing and monitoring law schools on teaching and the quality of student life. Educators need more prodding to educate themselves about how to improve the learning environment and to respond accordingly.

Professional Responsibility and Pro Bono Service

A further limitation in legal education involves its treatment of professional responsibility. In 1974, largely in response to lawyers' involvement in illegal Watergate activities, the ABA mandated that

---

39. Report of the AALS Special Committee, supra note 37, Krieger, supra note 37, at 18.

40. Thomas Shaffer & Robert S. Redmount, Lawyers, Law Students, and People 24 (1977).

accredited schools provide some instruction in professional responsibility. A growing number of states also began to require such instruction as a condition of admission to practice, and bar examinations increased their coverage of ethical issues.

Although these initiatives resulted in substantial improvements, current approaches still fall short. Most law schools relegate professional responsibility to a single required course, which focuses largely on rules of conduct. This approach often leaves out crucial issues, such as those concerning access to justice, the conditions of practice, and the adequacy of bar regulatory processes. Moreover, ethical issues arise in every legal field, and the failure to address them throughout the curricula sends a negative message that no single course can counteract. Faculty who treat professional responsibility as someone else's responsibility encourage future practitioners to do the same.[41]

Part of the resistance to more extensive legal ethics coverage rests on an assumption that moral conduct cannot be effectively taught in professional schools. Many faculty and students assume that ethics instruction at the graduate level offers too little too late; a few classroom hours are unlikely to reshape values that individuals have acquired over long periods from family, friends, schools, churches, and other cultural influences. Moreover, even if course exposure has some impact on moral views, it is by no means clear how much effect it will have on moral conduct. Both historical experience and psychological research make clear that ethical behavior is highly contextual, and that situational pressures often undermine individuals' professed principles.[42]

Such evidence reveals important limits on the potential contributions of professional responsibility courses, but it is not a reason to avoid integrated coverage of the subject in law school curricula. Most psychological research finds that, despite the importance of situational pressures, moral judgment has some impact on moral behavior.[43] How individuals evaluate the consequences of their

41. Deborah L. Rhode, "The Professional Responsibilities of Professors," 51 J. Legal Educ. 158, 165 (2001); Deborah L. Rhode, "Ethics by the Pervasive Method," 42 J. Legal Educ. 31 (1992).

42. See research surveyed in Deborah L. Rhode, "Moral Counseling," Ford. L Rev. (forthcoming); David M. Messick & John M. Darley, How Organizations Socialize Individuals into Evildoing, in Codes of Conduct: Behavioral Research into Business Ethics 13, 16–25

(David M. Messick & Ann E. Tenbrunsel, eds. 1996); Deborah L. Rhode, "Where is the Leadership in Moral Leadership?," in Moral Leadership: The Theory and Practice of Power, Judgment, and Policy 1, 20–33 (2006); David Luban, Making Sense of Moral Meltdowns, in Moral Leadership, supra, at 57–77.

43. See sources cited in Rhode, "Where is the Leadership," supra note 42, at 22–24; Rhode, "Ethics By the

actions can be critical in shaping conduct, and education can affect those evaluative processes. It can also make individuals aware of how economic and peer pressures, structures of authority, and diffusion of responsibility skew moral judgment.

So too, a substantial body of evidence suggests that ethical values are by no means as fixed as is often assumed. Psychological research indicates that during early adulthood, significant changes occur in people's basic strategies for dealing with moral issues.[44] Studies evaluating ethics courses find that well-designed curricula can significantly improve capacities for moral reasoning.[45] So too, many issues in professional ethics and regulation call for the same skills of legal and policy analysis that are standard fare throughout the curriculum. Although the classroom experience cannot fully simulate, or insulate, individuals from the pressures that lead to unethical practices, it can provide a setting to explore their causes and appropriate institutional responses.

Similar points can be made about public service. In 1996, the American Bar Association amended its accreditation standards to call on schools to "encourage students to participate in pro bono activities and to provide opportunities for them to do so." The revised ABA standards also encourage schools to address the obligations of faculty to the public, including participation in pro bono activities. However, only a fifth of schools require pro bono work by students, and almost none impose such obligations on faculty.[46] Even at schools with mandatory pro bono programs, the amounts required are sometimes very modest: some demand fewer than eight hours per year. Although most institutions offer voluntary public service programs, only a minority of students are involved. In short, most law students graduate without pro bono legal work as part of their educational experience. So too, pro bono service is largely ignored in curricular coverage and public interest opportu-

Pervasive Method," supra note 41, at 45 n. 67.

44. James R. Rest, "Can Ethics Be Taught in Professional Schools? The Psychological Research," Easier Said Than Done, Winter 1988, at 22, 23–24; James R. Rest, Muriel Bebeau, & Joseph Volker, "An Overview of the Psychology of Morality," in Moral Development: Advances in Research and Theory 3, 14 (James R. Rest, et al. eds. 1986).

45. Rest, supra note 44; M. Neil Browne, Carrie L. Williamson, & Linda L. Barkacs, "The Purported Rigidity of an Attorney's Personality: Can Legal Ethics be Acquired?," 30 J. Legal Prof. 55 (2006); Steven Hartwell, "Promoting Moral Development Through Experiential Teaching," 1 Clinical L. Rev. 505 (1995).

46. Cynthia F. Adcock, Fact Sheet on Law School Pro Bono Programs (AALS: Feb. 20, 2003); AALS Commission on Pro Bono and Public Service Opportunities in Law School, Learning to Serve: A Summary of the Findings and Recommendations of the Commission on Pro Bono and Public Service Opportunities in Law Schools 4 (1999).

nities in clinics are often inadequate to fill the gap.[47] As a report by the Association of American Law Schools Commission on Public Service and Pro Bono Opportunities succinctly concluded: "law schools should do more."[48]

The inadequacy of support for pro bono and public interest work is a missed opportunity for both the profession and the public. Such work offers law professors and students a range of practical benefits, including trial experience, problem solving skills, and professional contacts. For many participants, this involvement provides their most direct exposure to what passes for justice for the poor and to the need for legal reforms. In addition to these educational benefits, positive experiences doing public interest work in law school may also inspire long-term personal commitments that will continue throughout practitioners' legal careers.[49] For these reasons, the AALS Commission recommended that schools seek to make available for every law student at least one well-supervised, law-related pro bono opportunity, and either require student participation or find ways to attract the great majority of students to volunteer.[50] Providing more rewards and recognition for public service could encourage more faculty and students to connect with the values of social justice that brought many of them to law in the first instance.

Diversity

A final challenge for legal education is to ensure diversity among law faculties and student bodies, and to foster values of equal opportunity and mutual respect within the law school com-

---

47. For findings that over half of students have not participated in pro bono work in law schools, see Law School Survey of Student Engagement, Annual Survey Results, Student Engagement in Law Schools 8 (2004); AALS Commission, supra note 46. In one large national sample, only 1 percent of law school graduates reported that pro bono service received coverage in their orientation program or professional responsibility courses. Only 3 percent observed visible faculty support for pro bono service or felt that their schools provided adequate clinical opportunities for pro bono work. Deborah L. Rhode, Pro Bono in Principle and in Practice 161–62 (2004).

48. AALS Commission, supra note 46 at 2.

49. These experiences need not come in a pro bono program, as opposed to a clinic, and mandatory programs do not always insure a positive experience. Research to date does not find that participants in mandatory programs are more likely to provide pro bono work after graduation. See Rhode, supra note 47, at 160–65; Robert Granville, The Pedagogy of Public Service: Assessing the Impact of Mandatory Pro Bono on Young Lawyers 82, 90 (Law School Admission Council Report, 2005). Such research suggests reasons for improving not abandoning pro bono programs.

50. AALS Commission, supra note 46.

munity. Here again, great progress has been made over the last quarter century, but substantial progress also remains to be made.

As Chapter II indicated, most law schools long discriminated on the basis of sex, race, ethnicity, and religion. Part of the impetus for tighter educational standards during the late nineteenth and early twentieth centuries reflected such biases. For example, Columbia Law School was urged to require that applicants have a college diploma or pass an examination including Latin as a way to "keep out the little scrubs whom the school now promotes from grocery counters...."[51] Discrimination against immigrants and Jewish students continued throughout the early twentieth century; racial barriers were still more enduring. Although the first black graduated from law school in 1869 and some black institutions formed graduate programs in law around the same period, few of these programs survived after the Reconstruction era. Those that did had grossly inadequate resources.

The barriers confronting racial minorities are apparent from the Supreme Court's landmark decision in Sweatt v. Painter, 339 U.S. 629 (1950), which held Texas' racially segregated law schools unconstitutional. At the time of the litigation, the Texas legal profession included approximately 7500 white attorneys and 22 blacks. When a qualified black applicant sought admission at the University of Texas Law School, the state responded first by adding law classes at Prairie View University, an impoverished black institution that offered college credit for mattress and broommaking. Two of the three law classrooms lacked chairs and desks. Yet, in the *Sweatt* litigation, the state court had concluded that the Prairie View facility was "substantially equal" to the University of Texas Law School.[52] After the Supreme Court's reversal of that decision, the AALS passed a resolution designed to encourage, but not to require, member schools to abolish racially discriminatory practices. It was only in 1964 that all schools did so. Even after removal of formal prohibitions against non-white applicants, the absence of financial aid, affirmative action, active recruiting strategies, and supportive academic environments worked against minori-

51. D. Kelly Weisberg, "Barred from the Bar: Women and Legal Education in the United States 1870–1890," in 2 Women and the Law 231, 252 (D. Kelly Weisberg ed., 1982); Stevens, supra note 2, at 100–101.

52. Douglas L. Jones, "The Sweatt Case and the Development of Legal Education for Negroes in Texas," 47 Tex. L. Rev. 677, 678–85 (1969); Richard Kluger, Simple Justice: The History of Brown v. Board of Education and Black Americas' Struggle for Equality, 261 (1975); Edward J. Littlejohn & Leonard S. Rubinowitz, "Black Enrollment in Law Schools: Forward to the Past?," 12 T. Marshall L. Rev. 415, 431 n. 81 (1987).

ties. Until the 1960s, they represented under two percent of the profession.[53]

For white women, the situation was better, but even the most intellectually qualified and economically privileged applicants faced significant discrimination. Throughout the first half of the twentieth century, female students never constituted more than three percent of law school classes except during World War II. Not until 1972 did all ABA-accredited schools remove bans on women students. Sol Linowitz, a prominent Washington practitioner, recalls that "[t]here were only two women in my class at Cornell Law School, and to tell the truth we felt somewhat uncomfortable when they were around. It never occurred to us to wonder whether *they* felt uncomfortable."[54]

Beginning in the 1960s, formal racial, ethnic and gender barriers declined, partly in response to the civil rights and women's movements. Increased financial aid packages, expanded recruitment strategies, and efforts to improve the law school experience for underrepresented groups also encouraged greater diversity. Women now account for about half of entering classes and twenty percent of full professors. Racial and ethnic minorities, which accounted for about thirty percent of the nation's population, constituted about twenty percent of law schools' student population and ten percent of full professors.[55]

However, despite substantial improvements, significant barriers to full inclusion persist. One involves minorities' underrepresentation in the eligible applicant pool of college graduates, in part because of inadequate financial assistance and educational preparation. A second major hurdle involves law schools' heavy reliance on objective admission criteria such as grades and LSAT scores, which are lower for most racial and ethnic minorities. A final barrier to full inclusiveness involves the climate for traditionally underrepresented groups, and its adverse affect on performance.

How law schools should respond to these problems has been a matter of continuing controversy. ABA accreditation standards, as recently strengthened, require law schools to demonstrate "by concrete action," a commitment to having a faculty and student

53. See Geraldine Segal, Blacks in the Law: Philadelphia and the Nation, 212–13 (1983); Karen Berger Morello, The Invisible Bar: The Woman Lawyer in America, 1638 to the Present 143–47 (1986).

54. Sol M. Linowitz with Martin Mayer, The Betrayed Profession: Lawyering at the End of the Twentieth Century 6 (1994).

55. Elizabeth Chambliss, Miles to Go: Progress of Minorities in the Legal Profession 8 (ABA Commission on Racial and Ethnic Diversity in the Legal Profession, 2005).

body "that is diverse with respect to gender, race, and ethnicity."
Compliance with that standard is to be assessed in light of the
"totality of the law school's actions and the results achieved."[56] The
most widely accepted strategies to increase racial and ethnic diversity are proactive recruitment and retention programs. These programs identify talented candidates from under-represented groups
and provide adequate financial aid and educational support services. A more controversial approach involves affirmative action
policies that give preferential treatment to applicants of color. In
Regents of the University of California v. Bakke, 438 U.S. 265
(1978), the Supreme Court held that educational institutions may
consider ethnicity and race in order to achieve a diverse student
body as long as they do not employ rigid quotas. Subsequent
challenges to law school admission processes involved the exclusion
of white applicants with GPAs and test scores higher than those of
racial and ethnic minorities, and federal appellate courts divided on
the constitutionality of racially-based preferential treatment.

In two highly publicized decisions, the Supreme Court gave
guidance on that issue. In Grutter v. Bollinger, 539 U.S. 306 (2003),
five Justices joined a majority opinion holding that the University
of Michigan Law School's admission process did not violate the
Equal Protection Clause by considering the race and ethnicity of
applicants along with other diversity-related factors. Six Justices
also joined the majority in a companion case that struck down the
undergraduate admissions program at the University of Michigan
because it awarded a substantial and fixed number of points toward
admission to members of targeted racial and ethnic minority
groups. Gratz v. Bollinger, 539 U.S. 244 (2003).

These cases attracted a record number of amicus briefs. Support for the law school's program came from virtually all higher
education associations, including the AALS, and a wide range of
business organizations, as well as a group of highly distinguished
military leaders. These defenders of affirmative action made several
claims. The first is that institutions of higher education, including
professional schools, have a compelling state interest in taking
racial and ethnic diversity into account in the admission process. In
supporters' view, it is essential to educate lawyers who will adequately reflect the diverse make-up of the population they will
serve. Writing for the majority in *Grutter*, Justice O'Conner agreed:
"In order to cultivate a set of leaders with legitimacy in the eyes of
the citizenry, it is necessary that the path to leadership be visibly
open to talented and qualified individuals of every race and ethnici-

---

56.   ABA Accreditation Standard 211
and Interpretation 211–3 (2006).

ty. All members of our heterogeneous society must have confidence in the openness and integrity of the educational institutions that provide this training." 539 U.S., at 332.

In addition, the *Grutter* majority stressed the wide range of research introduced in the court below and in amicus briefs indicating that a student body with varied backgrounds and perspectives enriches the learning environment for all participants. This research finds that students who experience racial diversity in education show less prejudice, more ability to deal with conflict, better cognitive skills, clearer understanding of multiple perspectives, and greater satisfaction with their academic experience. In one survey of some 1800 students at two leading law schools, some 90 percent reported positive effects of diversity on their educational experience.[57]

Proponents of affirmative action also argued, and the *Grutter* majority agreed, that the law school's admission system was narrowly tailored to achieve these compelling interests. That program neither established a fixed quota for minority admissions, nor restricted diversity considerations to those of race and ethnicity. Rather, the school considered candidates' whole file, and sought to achieve a "critical mass" of students of color. The number of African–American, Latino, and Native American students in each class varied between 14 and 20 percent during a previous seven year period, "a range inconsistent with a quota." 539 U.S at 330. Although the school had considered alternative systems, it could identify none that would be effective in both maintaining the school's high educational qualifications and ensuring a critical mass of minority students.

As proponents also argued, and the Court found, law schools were justified in taking into account factors other than quantitative measurements such as test and grade point averages. Although formulas based on these quantitative measures help predict first-year law school performance, many experts believe that such

57. American Council on Education and American Association of University Professors, Does Diversity Make a Difference? (2000); William G. Bowen & Derek Bok, The Shape of the River: Long–Term Consequences of Considering Race in College and University Admissions (1998); Richard O. Lempert, David L. Chambers & Terry K. Adams, "Michigan's Minority Graduates in Practice: The River Runs Through Law School," 25 Law & Soc. Inq. 395 (2000); Gary Orfield and Dean Whitla, Diversity and Legal Education: Student Experiences in Leading Law Schools, 14–16 (1999). But see Stanley Rothman, Seymour Martin Lipset, and Neil Nevitte, "Does Enrollment Diversity Improve University Education?," 15 Internat'l J. Public Op. Res. 8 (2002) (describing survey findings that universities with higher black enrollment reported less satisfaction with the quality of education and work ethic of students and more experiences of discrimination).

screening devices have assumed too much importance in the admission process. As they note, such formulas account for only 16–36% of the variance in law school grades, and grades measure only some of the skills necessary for effective legal practice.[58] The most systematic attempt to follow students after graduation has not found a significant correlation between law school grades and later achievements. In a longitudinal survey by Michigan Law School, LSATs, and GPAs did not correlate with graduates' earned income, career satisfaction, or contributions to the community. Minorities admitted under affirmative action criteria did as well on these measures as other graduates.[59] Supporters of affirmative action for law students generally include similar diversity concerns to justify affirmative action in faculty hiring. In addition, supporters emphasize the importance of providing mentors and role models for students of color.

Opponents of preferential treatment, while not necessarily disagreeing about the value of diversity, worry that differential standards for minorities will reinforce the stereotypes of inferiority that the legal profession should be seeking to challenge. Many opponents believe that affirmative action violates a moral principle of color-blindness. As Justice Thomas put it in his dissent in *Grutter*, "The Constitution abhors classifications based on race, not only because those classifications can harm favored races or are based on illegitimate motives, but also because every time the government places citizens on racial registers and makes race relevant to the provision of burdens or benefits, it demeans us all. . . ." 539 U.S. at 363 (Thomas, J., dissenting).

Critics of preferential treatment further argue that race is not a good proxy for diversity in experience, that the distinction between quotas and holistic review encourages hypocrisy, and that preferential treatment masks rather than addresses the core problem, which is inadequate educational preparation for law school.[60] According to Clint Bolick, director of litigation at the Institute of

---

58. The correlation between law school grades and undergraduate test scores and GPAs is a strong one in terms of what social scientists consider statistically significant. However, its predictive power is still quite limited, which points up the risks in admission systems that give almost conclusive importance to such formulas in admitting or excluding some group of applicants. *See* Law School Admission Council, New Models to Assure Diversity Fairness and Appropriate Test Use in Law School Admissions (1999); Jess Bravin, "Law School Admission Counsel Aims to Quash Overreliance on LSAT," Wall St. J. March 29, 2001, at B1; Chambliss, supra note 55.

59. Lani Guinier, "Confirmative Action," 25 *Law & Soc. Inq.* 565, 568 (2000); Lempert, Chambers, and Adams, supra note 57.

60. Charles W. Collier, "Affirmative Action and the Decline of Intellectual Culture," 55 J. Legal Educ. 3 (2005).

Justice, "So long as we have a regime of racial preferences that problem is not going to be addressed head-on. . . . When affirmative action is practiced that way it does not have any impact in expanding the pool of qualified applicants, which is what the goal should be. The way affirmative action is practiced today is cosmetic and superficial. It does not offer a systemic cure for serious social problems. It simply reshuffles the deck [among applicants]." In his view, current policies simply enable the most privileged nonwhite candidates to obtain better positions, and to attend better law schools than their credentials justify.[61]

UCLA Law Professor Richard Sander has raised similar concerns. In a widely publicized article, Sander claimed that affirmative action was counterproductive for African Americans because it enabled them to attend law schools beyond what their credentials justified. This in turn, led them to have lower grades, graduation rates, and bar exam pass rates than if they had attended lower ranked schools. By Sander's calculation, elimination of affirmative action would actually increase the number of black practitioners.[62] The article attracted extensive criticism. Looking at a wider data set than Sander, experts generally agreed that eliminating affirmative action would significantly decrease the number of African American lawyers, particularly those in leadership positions. Many commentators also questioned his assumption that if affirmative action were eliminated, African–American applicants would go to lesser ranked law schools, as opposed to pursuing other educational or employment opportunities.[63]

These controversies over affirmative action are likely to persist. Voter initiatives in three states, California, Florida, and Washington, have prohibited race-based preferences by state schools and other states have considered such initiatives. Critics of affirmative action have also brought legal challenges to various race-based policies that are allegedly inconsistent with *Grutter,* such as minority scholarships and supplemental educational programs.[64] These disputes over preferential treatment raise broader issues about what qualities are most important for membership in the bar and

61. Tim Wells, "Affirmative Action in Law Schools: Is It Necessary?," *Washington Lawyer*, Jan./Feb. 2000, at 48 (quoting Clint Bolick).

62. Richard Sander, "A Systematic Analysis of Affirmative Action in Law Schools," 57 Stan. L. Rev. 367 (2004).

63. See the symposium devoted to responses to Sanders' article in 57 Stan. L. Rev. 1807 et seq. (2005) and Cheryl Harris & William Kidder, "The Black Student Mismatch Myth in Legal Education: The Systemic Flaws in Richard Sander's Affirmative Action Study," J. Blacks in Higher Education, Winter, 2004/2005, at 102.

64. See Rachel Moran, "Of Doubt and Diversity: The Future of Affirmative Action in Higher Education," 67 Ohio St. L. J. 201, 228–33 (2006).

how they can be assessed. Many schools are experimenting with reduced reliance on quantitative measures and greater emphasis on other characteristics such as leadership ability, employment experience, community service, and persistence in the face of economic or other disadvantages. Whether giving weight to such factors can insure adequate diversity without producing unduly subjective and idiosyncratic decisions is a matter of ongoing evaluation.

In the interim, however, both sides in the debate over affirmative action have a stake in improving the law school environment for students of color. A wide variety of studies indicate that many racial and ethnic minorities, including African–Americans, underperform in law school relative to their entry credentials and that experiences of alienation, isolation, and marginalization remain common.[65] More curricular integration of materials on race and ethnicity, along with more proactive steps to combat bias and intolerance, and more appointments of faculty of color, should be educational priorities. Most important, law schools need to create formal structures for collecting information about diversity concerns and the adequacy of efforts to address them.

Similar initiatives are necessary for women. Although gender disparities in admissions have been largely eliminated, similar progress has not been made in faculty, administrative, and student leadership positions. Only twenty percent of full professors and ten percent of law school deans are female, and only about three percent of those in either position are women of color.[66] Women faculty are still clustered in the least prestigious academic specialties and positions, such as librarians, research and writing instructors, and non-tenured clinicians.[67] These sex-based disparities cannot be entirely explained by objective factors such as academic credentials or experience.[68] Legal education appears to share the general problems for women in the profession noted in Chapter III, such as unconscious gender biases and lack of accommodation of women's disproportionate family obligations.[69] Failure to address

---

65. Kevin R. Johnson & Angela Onwuachi–Willig, "Cry Me a River: The Limits of A Systemic Analysis of Affirmative Action in American Law Schools," 7 Afr.–Am. L. & Pol'y Rep. 1, 15–20; Nancy Dowd et al., "Diversity Matters: Race, Gender and Ethnicity in Legal Education," 15 J. L. & Pub. Pol'y. 11 (2003).

66. Association of American Law Schools, Statistical Report on Law School Faculty and Candidates for Law Faculty Positions (2004–2005), at http://www.aals.org/statistics/0405/html/0405.

67. Id.; Deborah L. Rhode "Midcourse Corrections: Women in Legal Education," 53 J. Legal Educ. 475, 481 (2003).

68. Rhode, supra note 67, at 482.

69. For example, two thirds of surveyed female faculty cite work/family conflicts as a significant problem. Catalyst, Women in Law: Making the Case 60 (2001).

these gender-related barriers in law school not only compromises equal opportunity for individual women, it also deprives the academic community of valuable role models, scholars, and classroom perspectives.

Equal opportunity for female students will also require broader changes in the educational culture. Research over the last decade consistently finds that women, particularly women of color, are more likely than men to be silenced in the classroom. Female students are less likely to volunteer, and their comments are more likely to be overlooked, devalued, or misattributed.[70] The highly competitive atmosphere of many law school classrooms also tends to silence students with lower self-confidence, who are disproportionately women. The marginalization of women's classroom participation is compounded by the marginalization of issues concerning gender and sexual orientation in core curricula, as well as the disparaging treatment of students and faculty who introduce such concerns. As Law Professor Catharine MacKinnon notes, "Focusing on women and gender is seen as narrow. Excluding women and gender is not."[71] These patterns help explain why women express less self-confidence, and greater dissatisfaction and disengagement with the law school experience than men.[72]

To address these concerns, commentators propose reforms along several dimensions. As with other matters relating to diversity, a crucial first step is to create a structure for identifying and responding to gender issues. For example, schools need to know if their family policies and complaint channels are adequate, if women are participating equally in the classroom, if they are represented equally in leadership positions, and if the curricula has appropriately integrated gender-related materials. Efforts should also focus on monitoring reform strategies, such as those noted earlier that seek to build more cooperative, less competitive learning environments. Legal education is, after all, responsible for training professionals who enforce our nation's commitment to equal opportunity. That responsibility imposes a corresponding obligation to model the practices on which true equality depends.

---

70. See e.g., Adam Neufeld, "Costs of an Outdated Pedagogy?: Study on Gender at Harvard Law School," 13 J. Gender, Social Policy & L. 511, 517, 531–32 (2005); Linda F. Wightman, Law School Admission Council Research Report Series, Women in Legal Education: A Comparison of the Law School Performance and Law School Experience of Women and Men 25, 36, 72–74 (1996); Elizabeth Mertz, Wamucii Njogu & Su-

san Gooding, "What Difference Does Difference Make? The Challenge for Legal Education," 48 J. Legal Educ. 1, 6–7 (1998).

71. Catharine A. MacKinnon, "Mainstreaming Feminist Theory," 53 J. Legal Educ. 199, 200 (2003).

72. Wightman, supra note 69, at 25, 36, 72–74. Women of color report the greatest alienation. Id.

This is not a modest agenda. But whatever the flaws in current educational programs, it is also important to acknowledge their strengths. Over the last half century, law schools have grown considerably in terms of applicants, resources, prestige, and diversity. Their graduates are among the nation's most influential leaders in both the public and private sector. If legal education is this successful by conventional measures, it must be doing something right.

C. **Admission to the Bar**

Competence

Bar examinations have an extended history, but their early forms bear little resemblance to their modern versions. Before the Civil War, exams were typically oral, and were administered by state judges or attorneys appointed by the court on an ad hoc basis. The process was often quite informal, as the following description of an examination by Abraham Lincoln suggests. The candidate, Jonathan Birch, encountered his examiner in a hotel room, in the process of taking a bath, which continued during the interview. According to Birch,

> [Lincoln] asked in a desultory way the definition of a contract, and two or three other fundamental questions, all of which I answered readily, and I thought, correctly. Beyond these meager inquiries, as I now recall the incident, he asked nothing more. Meanwhile, sitting on the edge of the bed he began to entertain me with recollections—many of them characteristically vivid and racy—of his own practice and the various incidents and adventures that attended his start in the profession. The whole proceeding was interesting yet so unusual, if not grotesque, that I was at a loss to determine whether I was really being examined or not.[73]

Eventually Lincoln sent Birch off with a note to the other member of the bar examining committee, who admitted him without further inquiry. The note read: "The bearer of this is a young man who thinks he can be a lawyer. Examine him if you want to. I have done so and am satisfied. He's a good deal smarter than he looks to be. Yours, Lincoln."[74]

In the late nineteenth century, states attempted to upgrade standards by establishing boards of bar examiners and requiring written exams. However, most early examiners were part-time or

---

73. Len Young Smith, "Abraham Lincoln as a Bar Examiner," B. Examiner, Aug. 1982, at 35, 37.

74. Id.

short-term employees, with limited expertise. The tests that they devised usually demanded only rote learning and basic literacy skills. What limited information is available leaves doubt that these examinations effectively measured competence. Almost all candidates ultimately passed.[75] Moreover, in many jurisdictions, the major impetus for screening candidates had less to do with ensuring competence than with enhancing public image and preventing overcrowding. Elite members of the bar often saw examinations as a means of stemming the tide of lower-class applicants, particularly religious and ethnic minorities, whose admission might threaten the profession's status.[76] Other practitioners favored barriers to entry that would reduce competition by new entrants.[77]

In 1931, a National Conference of Bar Examiners formed to upgrade standards and to promote more uniformity among state examinations. The later development of a multi-state, multiple choice test in core subjects reflected and accelerated this trend. Yet whether current bar exams are an appropriate means of assessing competence remains a matter of considerable dispute.

The rationale for these examinations rests on several grounds. According to proponents, the tests measure basic analytic and writing skills as well as knowledge of core subjects that are necessary for competent practice of law.[78] Bar exams provide incentives for students to synthesize their knowledge and to gain "at least passing familiarity with bodies of law and particular legal rules that the student may not have studied while in law school."[79] Unlike other skill-based assessments, standardized tests provide an objective, and relatively inexpensive form of evaluation that minimizes chances of bias based on applicants' personal characteristics.[80]

75. See e.g., Esther Lucile Brown, Lawyers and the Promotion of Justice 117 (1938) (80–90% of applicants passed); Hurst, supra note 2, at 292–93 (90% passed).

76. See Auerbach, supra note 4, at 49, 112–14 (1976); Randall Collins, The Credential Society: An Historical Sociology of Education and Stratification 149–56 (1979).

77. William C. Kidder, "The Bar Examination and the Dream Deferred: A Critical Analysis of MBE, Social Closure, and Racial and Ethnic Stratification," 29 Law & Soc. Inquiry 547, 555–556 (2004). Not coincidentally, bar passage rates were lowered during the Depres-

sion. Richard L. Abel, "The Contradictions of Professionalism," in Lawyers in Society Volume One: The Common Law World 186, 195 (Richard L. Abel and Philip S. C. Lewis, ed., 1988).

78. Suzanne Darrow–Kleinhaus, "A Response to the Society of American Law Teachers Statement on the Bar Exam," 54 J. Legal Educ. 442, 444 (2004).

79. Restatement of the Law Governing Lawyers (Third) § 2, Comment e. See also ABA Report of the Task Force on Law Schools and the Profession, supra note at 27.

80. Susan Case, "Licensure in My Ideal World," Bar Examiner, Nov. 2005, at 26, 27.

Finally, proponents fear that the likely alternative to bar exams would be worse. If, for example, all graduates of accredited law schools were entitled to practice, states might interfere more extensively with those schools' curricular offerings, graduation requirements, or admission standards. Given the current unwillingness of most faculty to fail students or to require mastery of all core subjects, elimination of the bar exam might leave no significant screening device for minimal competence.[81] Nor would an apprenticeship program be a better solution. The systems that most other countries employ vary considerably in quality and objectivity, and their history in this country offers little basis for optimism that they would prove successful in insuring basic competence. To the extent that current bar exams fall short in meeting their objectives, supporters wish to improve, not eliminate, testing procedures.

Opponents of bar examinations find these defenses unconvincing. The first and most fundamental criticism is that the skills that existing exams measure do not adequately predict performance as a lawyer. As critics have long noted, standardized testing procedures place a high premium on rote memorization, which is likely to be less critical in practice than various other untested skills such as research, negotiation, interviewing, drafting, counseling, oral advocacy, and working effectively with others.[82] A little knowledge can be a dangerous thing, and that is what bar examinations demand. This screening method is both over- and under-inclusive. It excludes individuals with experience and skills adequate for some areas of practice, while providing no assurance that candidates who pass are, or will, remain competent in their chosen fields. The result, according to opponents, is to encourage a superficial acquaintance with a broad span of substantive areas, which creates a false sense of assurance to the profession and to the general public.

A second problem involves grading procedures.

Although bar exams do measure some relevant skills, the current grading system does not capture relevant distinctions. No effort has been made to correlate performance on admission exams with performance in practice. The most that bar officials can establish is a correlation between examination scores and

---

81. Erwin Griswold, "In Praise of Bar Examinations," 42 B. Examiner 136 (1973).

82. Society of American Law Teachers [SALT], "SALT Statement on the Bar Exam," 52 J. Legal Educ. 446 (2002); Rhode, supra note 11, at 150; Kristin Booth Glen, "When and Where We Enter: Rethinking Admission to the Legal Profession," 102 Colum. L. Rev. 1646 (2002); Chief Justices Committee on Professionalism and Lawyer Competence, A National Action Plan on Lawyer Conduct and Professionalism 15 (1998); See ABA, Report of the Task Force on Law Schools and the Profession, supra note 15, at 273, 277–82.

law school grades. That relationship is scarcely surprising, since both measure similar skills. How well either predicts success as a lawyer is something else again, and has yet to be demonstrated. Charles Evans Hughes failed the New York bar exam six times and later became Chief Justice of the United States Supreme Court, and the list of less celebrated failures is extensive.

The inadequate link between exam and job performance is of special concern because minority applicants have disproportionately low passage rates. Part of the problem is that these applicants are least able to afford the time and expense of bar review courses and multiple attempts at passing. Although courts have rejected claims that the exam process is racially discriminatory and insufficiently predictive of competence in practice, their reasoning has relied on evidence that they have found deficient in other occupational contexts: unsupported testimony by administrators who believe that their questions are unbiased and relevant. . . . The selection of passing scores raises further difficulties. States that use the same multiple choice tests vary considerably in their selection of passing scores and in their ratios of successful to unsuccessful applicants. The percentage of candidates who pass ranges from the 30s to the 90s. Unsurprisingly, success rates tend to be lowest in the states with the greatest concentrations of lawyers, where new competitors are particularly unwelcome. By contrast, other jurisdictions pass a high proportion of candidates. . . . No evidence suggest that these states experience exceptional problems with lawyer performance. If states swapped cut-off scores, the majority of applicants passing the bar in permissive jurisdictions would fail, and the majority of those failing in stringent jurisdictions would pass. So too, as statisticians point out, higher grading standards do not guarantee higher competence in a system where about 95 percent of candidates who keep taking the exam eventually pass. In states with low success rates, students simply "study harder" and more applicants have to take the test multiple times.[83]

The problems of justifying state passing scores and ratios emerged clearly in an antitrust suit against the Arizona Board of Bar Examiners. In Hoover v. Ronwin, 466 U.S. 558 (1984), an

---

83. Rhode, supra note 11, at 151–52 (2000). For similar concerns, see Kidder, supra note 77, at 569–77; Glen, supra note 82; Deborah J. Merritt, Lowell L. Hargens, & Barbara F. Reskin, "Raising the Bar: A Social Science Critique of Recent Increases to Passing Scores on the Bar Exam," 69 U. Cincinnati L. Rev. 929 (2001).

unsuccessful bar applicant claimed that the Board's practice of setting passing scores after exams were graded constituted an anticompetitive effort to limit the number of licensed attorneys in violation of the Sherman Antitrust Act. The United States Supreme Court rejected that claim. In the majority's view, because bar admission occurred under Arizona Supreme Court auspices, it fell within the state action exemption to the Sherman Act. However, the majority also acknowledged the subjectivity involved in the choice of passing scores: "By its very nature, therefore, grading examinations does not necessarily separate the competent from the incompetent or—except very roughly—identify those qualified to practice and those not qualified. At best, a bar examination can identify those applicants who are more qualified to practice law than those less qualified." 466 U.S. at 578 n. 31.

A third and final criticism of bar exams involves their costs. Critics point to the disproportionate exclusion of minority candidates, the time and effort spent on cram courses, the inadequate accommodation of students with learning disabilities, and the reluctance of many students to take courses and professors to offer material that would be useful for practice but not for exam preparation.[84] Requiring out-of-state lawyers to retake the exam also imposes substantial barriers to practitioners' mobility across state lines, which carries a cost to the public as well as the profession. Those barriers are difficult to justify on competence-related grounds, particularly in states with reciprocity rules that waive exam requirements only for lawyers from states that extend the same privilege.[85] If a New York lawyer is sufficiently qualified to obtain admittance in Connecticut without retaking the multistate bar exam, it should not matter whether New York takes the same view of Connecticut lawyers.

84. For racial and ethnic differences in bar pass rates, see Kidder, supra note 77, at 569–77; Law School Admission Council, National Longitudinal Bar Passage Study (Newtown, Pennsylvania: National Law School Admission Council, 1998). For cases rejecting challenges to bar exams as racially discriminatory, see Delgado v. McTighe, 522 F.Supp. 886 (E.D. Pa. 1981); Richardson v. McFadden, 540 F.2d 744 (4th Cir. 1976); Parrish v. Board of Commissioners of Alabama State Bar, 533 F.2d 942 (5th Cir. 1976); Harper v. District of Columbia Comm. on Admissions, 375 A.2d 25 (D.C. App. 1977). For a critique, see Cecil J. Hunt II, "Guests in Another's House: An Analysis of Racially Disparate Bar Performance," 23 Fla. St. U. L. Rev. 721 (1996). For cases involving students with learning disabilities, see Geoffrey C. Hazard, Jr., Susan P. Koniak, Roger C. Cramton, & George F. Cohen, The Law and Ethics of Lawyering 1052–53 (4th ed., 2004).

85. Andrew M. Perlman, "A Bar Against Competition: The Unconstitutionality of Admission Rules for Out-of-State Lawyers," 18 Geo. J. Legal Ethics 135, 150 (2004).

These critiques have prompted some modest reform efforts. A few states, including California and Maine, have sought ways to expand the range of skills tested. Wisconsin has waived exam requirements for graduates of in-state law schools. Bar leaders and judges in Vermont, Maine, and New Hampshire have formed a Tri–State Task Force on Bar Admissions that has recommended a pilot program that would replace the bar exam. Instead, applicants would complete a comprehensive educational program designed to improve lawyer competence through in-depth skills training and evaluation.[86] New Hampshire has implemented a pilot version of that program for a small number of students, whose performance will be assessed on a continuing basis during law school by a committee of judges, bar examiners and faculty.[87] Another recent proposal involves supervised post-graduate pro bono work as an alternative to the exam.[88]

The prospects for such reform efforts remain unclear. The organized bar has shown little interest in reducing or rethinking standards for new entrants. Rather, recent trends have been toward raising exam passing scores.[89] Greater support may be available for reforming the system for out-of-state attorneys. As Chapter X noted, the ABA has recently approved a new Model Rule that permits limited multijurisdictional practice, and if this proves inadequate to the need, more fundamental changes might become politically feasible. The bar has also become increasingly supportive of outreach strategies to increase the diversity of the applicant pool. Efforts have included workshops, summer institutes, mentoring, and development of law-related curricula for colleges and secondary schools with large minority enrollments.[90]

The hard fact is that the traditional bar exam is relatively cheap to administer and thus "efficient" as a rough means of quality control, particularly in populous states dealing with thousands of applicants each year. It is also probably true that no exam format directly correlates with "success in practice," however that might be defined. Thus, debate will continue and so will the bar exams.

86. Chief Justices Committee on Professionalism and Lawyer Competence, supra note 15.

87. Hon. Linda S. Dalianis & Sophie M. Sparrow, "New Hampshire's Performance–Based Variant of the Bar Examination: The Daniel Webster Scholar Program," Bar Examiner, November 2004, at 23–26.

88. Glen, supra note 82.

89. Kidder, supra note 77, at 547–48.

90. Elizabeth Rindskopf Parker & Sarah E. Redfield, "The Educational Pipeline from Preschool to Professional School: Working to Increase Diversity in the Profession," Bar Examiner, May, 2006, at 7–20.

Character and Fitness

Every bar in this country makes moral fitness a prerequisite for practice. Such requirements have an extended history; similar standards were applicable in ancient Rome and thirteenth-century England.[91] Yet what qualifies as moral character and how it should be assessed have been matters of equally longstanding dispute. Eighteenth and nineteenth century American courts took different views. Some required affidavits from ministers or judges; others relied on applicant interviews.[92] However implemented, the requirement served to exclude a diverse and changing constituency, including immigrants and racial minorities as well as former felons, adulterers, political radicals, and bankrupts.[93] In what may have been the high water mark of exclusivity, one 1929 Pennsylvania board rejected candidates deemed "dull," "colorless," "subnormal," "unprepossessing," "shifty," "smooth," "keen," "shrewd," "arrogant," "conceited," "surly," and "slovenly." Also rejected were those who lacked "well defined ideas on religion," or who had family members with "unsavory" backgrounds or a "poor business reputation."[94]

During the Cold War and Vietnam eras, the exclusion of applicants with leftist political views led to a series of Supreme Court decisions imposing some constitutional constraints on character requirements. In Schware v. Board of Bar Examiners of New Mexico, 353 U.S. 232 (1957), the Court reversed the rejection of a candidate based on his membership in the Communist Party thirteen years before his application. Under the governing standard of *Schware*, which remains applicable to current proceedings, "any qualification must have a rational connection with the applicant's fitness or capacity to practice law." Id. at 246–47. In subsequent cases, the Court held that character committees could question applicants about whether they were "knowing member[s]" of organizations advocating violent overthrow of the government, and could exclude applicants who refused to answer.[95] Committees could not, however, ask about all organizations that an applicant had

91. Deborah L. Rhode, "Moral Character as a Professional Credential," 94 Yale L. J. 491 (1985). See also Geoffrey Hazard and Angelo Dondi, Legal Ethics: A Comparative Study, ch. 2 (2004).

92. Gerard W. Gawalt, The Promise of Power: The Emergence of the Legal Profession in Massachusetts 1760–1840 10 (1979); 2 Anton–Herman Chroust, The Rise of the Legal Profession in America 247–48, 267–68 (1965).

93. Rhode, supra note 91, at 500–03.

94. Walter C. Douglas, Jr., "The Pennsylvania System Governing Admission to the Bar," 54 Rep. ABA 701, 703–05 (1929).

95. Konigsberg v. State Bar of California, 366 U.S. 36 (1961); In re Anastaplo, 366 U.S. 82 (1961); Baird v. State Bar of Arizona, 401 U.S. 1 (1971); Application of Stolar, 401 U.S. 23 (1971).

joined since becoming a law student.[96] Since the early 1970s, the United States Supreme Court has issued no further rulings on issues of moral character. In the absence of such guidance, some state courts and committees have interpreted requirements in an inconsistent or intrusive fashion.

In principle, moral character requirements make perfect sense; the public has an obvious interest in protection from unethical lawyers. And some evidence suggests that attorneys who are disciplined are more likely to have had histories of problematic conduct than the applicant pool generally.[97] In practice, however, bar screening processes are highly limited in their ability to screen out unethical candidates. An inherent problem involves timing; the current process comes both too early and too late. Screening takes place before most applicants have faced circumstances comparable to those arising in practice, but after candidates have invested so much time and money in legal training that examiners are reluctant to deny admission. The most systematic research available suggests that about ninety-nine percent of bar applicants eventually gain entrance.[98] However, the process also imposes substantial burdens on candidates, and a significant number are delayed or deterred. Some evidence also suggests that Ivy League graduates receive more cursory investigation than other applicants, and that candidates of color receive more stringent review than white counterparts.[99]

States generally have lengthy questionnaires concerning any incidents of dishonesty, disrespect for law, mental health difficulties, or "dishonorable," "immoral," or "improper" conduct. Bar inquiry frequently extends to juvenile offenses, parking violations, child support payments, and civil disobedience. Violation of a fishing license statute ten years before application was sufficient to cause one local Michigan committee to decline certification. But in the same state at about the same time, other examiners admitted individuals convicted of child molesting and conspiracy to bomb a public building.[100] Decisions have been particularly inconsistent

96. Law Students Civil Rights Research Council, Inc. v. Wadmond, 401 U.S. 154 (1971).

97. Carl Baer & Peg Corneille, "Character and Fitness Inquiry: From Bar Admission to Professional Discipline," Bar Examiner, November 1992, at 5.

98. Rhode, supra note 91, at 516.

99. Mike Allen, "Beyond the Bar Exam," N.Y. Times, July 11, 1999 § 4, at 3; Abdon M. Pollasch, "Screening Process May Become Screaming Process for Bar Applicants," Chicago Lawyer, Sept. 1997, at 4; M. A. Cunningham, Comment, "The Professional Image Standard: An Untold Standard of Admission to the Bar," 66 Tul. L. Rev. 1015, 1037–39 (1992).

100. Rhode, supra note 91, at 538.

concerning bankruptcy, drug and alcohol offenses, sexual misconduct, and mental health treatment.[101]

There are, of course, some cases clearly justifying denial or deferral of admission, particularly where applicants make a bad situation worse by trivializing prior misconduct. Recent examples from California involve a candidate who explained theft while a bank teller as a "youthful indiscretion" (she thought the bank would "never miss the money"), and a candidate with half a dozen undisclosed convictions who could not be bothered to recount such "ancient history."[102] But in other cases, the degree of culpability and the appropriate response are subject to dispute.

One of the most controversial contemporary rulings involved Illinois' denial of admission to white supremacist Mathew Hale. Hale was the leader of World Church of the Creator, and was responsible for a Church web site that demonized Jews and "other mud races," and claimed that Hitler had the right idea.[103] Although some members of his organization had been convicted of violent hate crimes, Hale stated that he did not advocate violence, and his only criminal convictions involved minor charges in connection with protest activities like burning an Israeli flag. According to the Illinois committee panel, Hale was free

> to incite as much racial hatred as he desires and to attempt to carry out his life's mission of depriving those he dislikes of their legal rights, but in our view, he cannot do this as an officer of the court. Under any civilized standards of decency, the incitement of racial hatred for the ultimate purpose of depriving selected groups of their legal rights shows a gross deficiency in moral character, particularly for lawyers who have a special responsibility to uphold the rule of law for all persons.[104]

By contrast, many other bar leaders and examiners believe that excluding individuals on the basis of their moral beliefs compromises the principles that the system is designed to serve.[105] Hale,

---

101. Id. at 537–542, 574; Rhode & Luban, supra note 27, at 788–92.

102. Debra Murphy Lawson, "Tales From the Character and Fitness Trenches," The Bar Examiner, May, 2002, at 31, 33–34.

103. Pam Bellick, "Avowed Racist Banned from Practicing Law," N.Y. Times, Feb. 10, 1999, at A12.

104. Committee on Character and Fitness for the Third Appellate District

of the Supreme Court of Illinois (1998). The Montana bar also denied admission. See Montana Human Rights Network Newsletter, March, 2001, at 1.

105. George Anastaplo, "Lawyers, First Principles, and Contemporary Challenges: Explorations," 19 N. Ill. U. L. Rev. 353 (1999).

however, turned out not to be a clean example of a principled applicant wrongfully excluded. He was subsequently convicted of obstruction of justice and solicitation of murder of a federal judge who had ruled against him on a trademark infringement claim involving his organization's title.[106]

Taken together, these admission decisions raise concerns not only of inconsistency but also of inaccuracy. Psychological research makes clear that moral behavior is highly situational. While individuals differ in their responses to temptation, contextual pressures have a substantial impact on moral conduct. Attorneys' compliance with ethical rules depends heavily on factors that cannot be anticipated at the time of admission, such as client pressures, collegial practices, and health or family difficulties. Prior behavior is relevant but also sometimes misleading; it is necessary to know a good deal about how and why individuals responded to earlier situations in order to predict how they will react in somewhat different future circumstances. Examiners often lack that degree of knowledge.[107]

The same is true for predictions based on mental health and related difficulties. Many jurisdictions include broad questions about almost any mental health treatment and require applicants to release all medical records.[108] These requirements have been subject to increasing challenge under the Americans with Disabilities Act, which requires occupational licensing bodies to treat disabled individuals as "qualified" if they can meet the essential eligibility requirements for practice.[109] In these cases, bar examiners have been unable to show that past mental health assistance predicts future professional problems.[110] In general, about half of all individuals who seek such assistance do not have a diagnosable illness. Those who do may pose fewer risks than candidates with undisclosed and untreated problems.[111] Except in extreme cases,

---

106. See Hazard, Koniak, Cramton, & Cohen, supra note 84, at 1047 n. 16.

107. Rhode, supra note 91, at 556–62; Walter Mischel & Yuichi Shoda, "A Cognitive–Affective System, Theory of Personality: Reconceptualizing Situations, Dispositions, Dynamics, and Invariance in Personality Structure," 102 Psychol. Rev. 246 (1995).

108. Alikhan, supra note 37.

109. Department of Justice Analysis, 28 C.F.R. § 35.104 (1991), interpreting 42 U.S.C. § 12132 (1991).

110. Rhode, supra note 11, at 156; Stanley S. Herr, "Questioning the Ques-

tionnaires: Bar Admissions and Candidates with Disabilities," 42 Vill. L. Rev., 635, 669–674, 721, nn. 65–69 (1997); Hilary Duke, "The Narrowing of State Bar Examiner Inquiries into the Mental Health of Bar Applicants: Bar Examiner Objectives Are Met Better Through Attorney Education, Rehabilitation, and Discipline," 11 Geo. J. L. Ethics 101, 105–07 (1997); Clark v. Virginia Bd. of Bar Examiners, 880 F.Supp. 430, 436 (E.D.Va.1995).

111. Phyllis Coleman & Ronald A. Shellow, "Ask About Conduct, Not Mental Illness: A Proposal for Bar Examiners and Medical Boards to Comply with the ADA and Constitution," 20 J. Legis.

even mental health experts cannot reliably predict future difficulties based on past treatment. Untrained bar examiners are scarcely likely to do better. Their intrusive, often ill-informed inquiries during character proceedings have proved highly humiliating to applicants.[112] The potential psychological and financial costs of these proceedings, and the risk of being delayed or denied admission, also discourages many students from seeking appropriate professional services.[113]

A comparison of bar admission and disciplinary processes raises a final set of doubts about current character requirements. Bar disciplinary officials do not require practicing lawyers to report their parking violations, overdue child support payments, or mental health treatment. Yet if such conduct is relevant for applicants, why is it not even more relevant for licensed attorneys? Even more to the point, why doesn't the bar devote more of its resources to sanctioning misconduct involving clients? Behavior occurring after individuals become officers of the court surely is a more relevant indication of fitness to practice than behavior occurring before admission to practice. Yet the reverse double standard now prevails: applicants must satisfy higher requirements than practicing attorneys.[114] This disparity in standards is difficult to justify in terms of the stated rationale of bar admission processes: protection of the public.

How best to respond to these concerns is a matter of dispute. Defenders of the current process argue that a high percentage of lawyer disciplinary violations are linked to moral turpitude, mental health difficulties, and substance abuse.[115] Given the costs of detecting and remedying such violations after the fact, examiners believe that the public has a legitimate interest in character screening processes, however imperfect their implementation. Many experts argue, however, that this interest could be served by a narrower range of inquiries, in a system that is less idiosyncratic and intrusive. In the view of these commentators, applicants should have earlier and clearer notice about the conduct that could justify denial

---

147, 162 n. 83 (1994); see also Duke, supra note 110, and Herr supra note 110.

112. Jon Bauer, "The Character of the Questions and Fitness of the Process: Mental Health, Bar Admissions and the Americans With Disabilities Act," 49 UCLA L. Rev. 93, 164 (2001).

113. See Coleman & Shellow, supra note 11; Bauer, supra note 112; and Herr, supra note 110.

114. Frasher v. West Virginia Bd. of Law Examiners, 408 S.E.2d 675 (W.Va. 1991) (holding that higher standard of conduct for bar applicants than admitted attorneys is permissible).

115. Erica Moeser, "Personal Matters: Should Bar Applicants be Asked About Treatment for Mental Health? Yes: The Public Has the Right to Know About Instability," ABA J., Oct. 1994, at 36.

or deferral. Inquiry should be limited to recent histories of serious misconduct or current mental health impairments, and should avoid overbroad questions, particularly on matters such as psychological counseling and political beliefs. For example, with respect to mental health treatment, some jurisdictions make no inquiries or ask only about hospitalization. Other states limit their questions to a specific time period such as two or five years, or decline to act on disclosures unless the record reveals related facts—such as financial mismanagement or commission of a crime—indicating that the applicant would present a threat to clients.[116]

Whatever approach states choose, it would make sense to rely less on efforts to predict misconduct and focus more on disciplinary programs that could deter or remedy it. Only a more constrained and consistent administration of moral character requirements can avoid compromising the values at issue.

116. Mary Elizabeth Cisneros, "A Proposal to Eliminate Broad Mental Health Inquiries on Bar Examination Applications; Assessing an Applicant's Fitness to Practice Law By Alternative Means," 8 Geo. J. Legal Ethics 401 (1995); Herr, supra note 110, at 641–42; Duke, supra note 110, at 107.

Chapter XII

COMPETENCE AND DISCIPLINE

A. Introduction

Lawyers' conduct is subject to multiple forms of regulation. The most significant are informal: they flow from the rights of clients to select a lawyer of their choice, to discharge a lawyer with or without cause, and to share opinions about a lawyer with others. These influences on professional reputation help determine a lawyer's or law firm's success in the market place for legal services. More formal regulation includes: sanctions by courts and administrative agencies for misconduct in proceedings under their supervision; sanctions by disciplinary agencies acting under judicial authority; internal oversight by employers; civil liability for malpractice or breach of contract; and standards established by insurance companies as conditions of malpractice coverage. This chapter focuses primarily on discipline and malpractice proceedings because these oversight structures are the most official, the most criticized, and the most readily reformed. However, as the following discussion makes clear, the limitations of these proceedings make other forms of control equally critical.

Courts have long asserted authority to discipline lawyers as part of their inherent power to regulate the practice of law. The tradition of disbarment has its roots in thirteenth century England, where attorneys guilty of misconduct were literally cast out of the "bar," a wooden barrier separating judges from lawyers, litigants, and witnesses.

In this country, eighteenth and nineteenth century courts seldom exercised their disciplinary power. Community disapproval was the primary sanction for professional misconduct, and the perceived inadequacy of this approach was a major impetus for the formation of bar associations during the early twentieth century. Most associations responded to this concern by establishing grievance committees to handle attorney misconduct. However, these committees proved inadequate for the task. As part of a voluntary governance system, the committees lacked power to compel attendance of witnesses or to impose sanctions. The committees could recommend discipline to the court, but their members were often reluctant to incur the animosity that such recommendations could trigger. Given the infrequency of bar action, few attorneys or clients made efforts to file complaints.[1]

As the early twentieth century progressed, bar associations gradually acquired authority to investigate misconduct and to impose sanctions, subject to judicial review. The procedures now governing lawyer discipline vary from state to state, although they all must meet constitutional requirements. Because disciplinary proceedings are "quasi-criminal" in nature, they must incorporate basic due process safeguards, such as the opportunity of an accused lawyer to confront evidence and cross-examine witnesses, and the privilege against self-incrimination. However, lawyers granted immunity from criminal proceedings may be obligated to supply information to disciplinary authorities concerning possible misconduct; failure to do so may give rise to adverse inferences. So too, incriminating testimony given by an attorney under a grant of immunity from criminal prosecution is admissible in disciplinary proceedings.[2] Other procedural requirements are set forth in state statutes, rules of court, and bar ethical codes. A majority of jurisdictions require that disciplinary charges be proven by clear and convincing evidence; a minority require a fair preponderance of the evidence.

According to the ABA Standards for Lawyer Discipline and Disability Proceedings, Standard 1.1:

> [t]he purpose of lawyer discipline and disability proceedings is to maintain appropriate standards of professional conduct in order to protect the public and the administration of justice from lawyers who have demonstrated by their conduct that they are unable or are likely to be unable to properly discharge their professional duties.[3]

Another remedy for professional misconduct is a civil malpractice action by the injured party. An essential element of a malpractice claim is the lawyer's noncompliance with recognized standards of professional conduct. Those standards are largely reflected in ethical codes. As noted below, the terms of the codes are therefore

---

1. See generally James Willard Hurst, The Growth of American Law: The Law Makers 286–93 (1950); George Martin, Causes and Conflicts: The Centennial History of the Association of the Bar of the City of New York 1870–1970 (1970).

2. Willner v. Committee on Character and Fitness, 373 U.S. 96 (1963); Spevack v. Klein, 385 U.S. 511 (1967); In re Ruffalo, 390 U.S. 544 (1968). See Geoffrey C. Hazard, Jr. & Cameron Beard, "A Lawyer's Privilege Against Self–Incrimination in Professional Disciplinary Proceedings," 96 Yale L.J. 1060 (1987).

3. The most current standards are in the Model Rules for Lawyer Disciplinary Enforcement (1999).

centrally significant in malpractice litigation, even though the violation of an ethical rule is not, of itself, a basis for civil liability.

Neither disciplinary nor malpractice proceedings are fully effective in upholding professional standards. The same is, of course, true of all law enforcement, and as with other regulatory systems, the limitations of oversight procedures are matters of longstanding concern. Only about a quarter of surveyed Americans believe that the legal profession does a good job of disciplining its members.[4] "Too slow, too secret, too soft, and too self-regulated" is how the public views the disciplinary system.[5] Lawyers also have reservations about the current process, although their dominant concerns are the opposite of those of the public. According to ABA studies, lawyers generally see the process as too severe and too responsive to frivolous complaints.[6] Moreover, even attorneys who are critical of the current system oppose fundamental changes in its structure.[7]

This disjuncture between the public's and the profession's view of disciplinary processes raises broader questions about self-regulation such as those addressed in Chapter III. Are there inherent problems in a regulatory structure controlled by the group to be regulated? If so, what follows from that fact? As commentators have often noted, lawyers have interests that overlap but are not coextensive with those of the public. Most attorneys want a process that can protect clients and the profession's public image, as well as forestall more intrusive state regulation. But few lawyers have supported a system that would require major increases in their own bar dues, significantly expand oversight of their own conduct, or expose them to substantial risks of serious sanctions. This tension between professional and public interests accounts for many of the limitations in oversight structures identified below. The challenge remaining is how to design appropriate correctives without compromising the independence of the bar.

B. Disciplinary Standards and Structures

The Definition of Misconduct

Rule 8.4 of the Model Rules of Professional Conduct sets forth the basic standard on lawyer misconduct.

---

4. ABA, Perceptions of the U.S. Justice System 77 (1999).

5. ABA Commission on Evaluation of Disciplinary Enforcement, Lawyer Regulation for a New Century 12–16 (1992). See also "Lawyer Disciplinary Hearings," ABA J., Jan. 1990, at 109.

6. "Lawyer Disciplinary Hearings," supra note 5, at 109.

7. For example, only twenty percent of California lawyers think that the disciplinary system is effective, but some ninety percent want the bar to continue its disciplinary activities. Nancy McCarthy, "Pessimism for the Future," Calif. B. J., Nov. 1994, at 1.

It is professional misconduct for a lawyer to:

(a) violate or attempt to violate the Rules of Professional Conduct, knowingly assist or induce another to do so, or do so through the acts of another;

(b) commit a criminal act that reflects adversely on the lawyer's honesty, trustworthiness or fitness as a lawyer in other respects;

(c) engage in conduct involving dishonesty, fraud, deceit or misrepresentation;

(d) engage in conduct that is prejudicial to the administration of justice. . . .

DR 1–102 of the Code imposes similar prohibitions.

Reporting Requirements

Because law is intended to be a self-regulating profession and lawyers are often the only individuals with knowledge of other lawyers' misconduct, both the Model Rules and the Code include reporting requirements. Model Rule 8.3 provides: "A lawyer who knows that another lawyer has committed a violation of the Rules of Professional Conduct that raises a substantial question as to that lawyer's honesty, trustworthiness or fitness as a lawyer in other respects, shall inform the appropriate professional authority," unless the information is protected as a client confidence. DR 1–103 of the Code is more comprehensive: it requires reporting by lawyers with unprivileged knowledge of any violation of the rules.

These requirements are widely ignored and almost never enforced. According to some commentators, the infrequency with which attorneys report fellow professionals is inevitable and in some measure justifiable. For example, Gerald Lynch, a former law professor and now federal judge, has argued that the same values underpinning society's unwillingness to impose reporting requirements on citizens generally also apply in lawyer disciplinary contexts. In his view, the "impulse to protect one's friends and associates from harm, even from deserved punishment, is a moral and socially useful impulse precisely because it reaches beyond individual self-interest; it assimilates another's well-being to that of oneself."[8] According to Lynch, if disciplinary agencies are inadequate, "the bar should certainly act to strengthen them" rather

---

8. Gerald E. Lynch, "The Lawyer as Informer," 1986 Duke L.J. 491, 531 (1986).

than attempt to impose reporting requirements that professionals will routinely evade in practice.[9]

By contrast, other commentators, including the ABA's Commission on Professionalism, believe that reports of serious collegial misconduct are essential to protect clients and the public from abuses that would otherwise be impossible to detect or deter.[10] Even disclosure obligations that are not consistently observed can provide essential support for those who would like to come forward but fear collegial hostility or retaliation. In effect, reporting requirements make lawyers feel "less like a snitch."[11] In any event, there is an inherent contradiction in the rationale for self-regulation and the refusal to enforce reporting obligations that are necessary for its effectiveness. In justifying a disciplinary process controlled by the profession, bar leaders have emphasized the importance of insuring that individuals who "pass judgment on attorney conduct be knowledgeable regarding the practice of law."[12] If so, it makes no sense to have a disciplinary complaint process that proceeds on precisely the opposite basis, and that relies almost exclusively on clients as a source of information about ethical violations.

Yet Illinois is the only jurisdiction that has made serious (if sporadic) attempts to enforce reporting requirements. In re Himmel, 533 N.E.2d 790 (Ill. 1988), is the first published decision imposing discipline solely for a lawyer's failure to report collegial misconduct. The lawyer, James Himmel, was retained on a contingent fee basis by a woman whose former lawyer had withheld her share of a personal injury settlement. Himmel's initial strategy was to negotiate an agreement for payment under which his client would not initiate criminal, civil, or disciplinary charges. When the lawyer failed to honor that agreement, Himmel brought a successful legal claim for the amount due. However, he was also suspended for a year for not reporting the lawyer's misconduct to the bar's disciplinary authority. That decision has been highly controversial. Some commentators note with approval that Illinois lawyers' reports of misconduct have increased substantially after the court's judgment in *Himmel*.[13] Other commentators see that as a precedent

---

9. Id. at 537–38.

10. ABA Commission, supra note 5.

11. Arthur F. Greenbaum, "The Attorney's Duty to Report Professional Misconduct: A Roadmap for Reform," 16 Geo. J. Legal Ethics 259, 271 (2003).

12. Commission on the Future of the Legal Profession and the State Bar of California, The Future of the California Bar 103 (1995).

13. See Lisa Lerman, "A Double Standard for Lawyer Dishonesty: Billing Fraud vs. Misappropriation," 34 Hofstra L. Rev. 847, 891 (2006) (noting that Illinois disciplinary authorities now receive between 600 and 900 reports from lawyers annually); Laura Gatland, "The Himmel Effect," ABA J., April 1997, at 24–28.

to be avoided, particularly in light of the risks of retaliation that whistleblowing may trigger. However, there appears to be some support by courts for strengthening reporting requirements in serious cases. For example, in In re Riehlmann, 891 So.2d 1239 (La. 2005), the court imposed a public reprimand on a former prosecutor who learned that a former colleague had suppressed exculpatory evidence in a capital case. Only after the colleague had died and the defendant was scheduled for execution did Riehlmann report the misconduct.

Whistleblowing Protections

The professional risks of reporting are compounded by the absence of adequate protections for whistleblowers. In a widely publicized example, Bohatch v. Butler & Binion, 977 S.W.2d 543 (Tex.1998), the Texas Supreme Court reversed a jury award to a lawyer whose partnership was terminated after she reported a colleague's suspected overbilling to firm management. In the court's view, "[o]nce such charges are made, partners may find it impossible to continue to work together to their mutual benefit and the benefit of their clients.... The threat of tort liability for expulsion would tend to force partners to remain in untenable circumstance—suspicious of and angry with each other—to their own detriment and that of their clients...." However, the court also made clear that its "refusal to create an exception to the at-will nature of partnerships in no way obviates the ethical duties of lawyers" to report misconduct. Id. at 547.

Most ethics experts have found such reasoning highly problematic. Lawyers already face substantial disincentives to report a colleague. Why should they run the risks of retaliation when any benefit is likely to redound not to them personally but to the profession as a whole? The failure to provide wrongful discharge remedies for attorneys compounds these risks. For that reason, a growing number of courts and commentators support increased whistleblower protection, either through statutes or implied contractual provisions.[14] As they recognize, such protections are necessary to alter lawyers' incentive structures. A passage from The Adventures of Huckleberry Finn, quoted by the dissent in Bohatch,

---

14. Wieder v. Skala, 80 N.Y.2d 628 (N.Y.1992). For a case history of the Bohatch case and a critical review of its analysis, see Leslie C. Griffin, "Bohatch v. Butler & Binion: The Ethics of Partners," in Legal Ethics: Law Stories 55 (Deborah L. Rhode & David Luban, eds., 2006). For the need for stronger whistleblower protections for all professional and managerial employees, see Lynne Bernabei & Jason Zuckerman, "Protect the Whistleblower," Nat'l Law Journal, June 19, 2006, at 26. For the suggestion that safeguards must come through the legislature, not the courts, see Snow v. Ruden, McClosky, Smith, Schuster & Russell, 896 So.2d 787 (Fla. App. 2005).

makes the point directly: "[W]hat's the use you learning to do right when it's troublesome to do right and ain't no trouble to do wrong, and the wages is just the same?" Id. at 558.

Structural Problems and Reforms

Other, more fundamental, changes are also essential to make the disciplinary system more responsive to client needs. Studies by bar associations and legal ethics experts generally find three structural problems in current processes: the low percentage of consumer grievances that ever reach regulatory agencies; the failure of agencies to address minor misconduct such as negligence or fee disputes for which civil remedies are available in theory but seldom in practice; and the low percentage of reported complaints that result in significant sanctions.

Not only do few lawyers and judges report misconduct, relatively few clients are willing or able to initiate disciplinary proceedings. Sophisticated clients generally have no need to do so. Many organizational and business clients are in a sufficiently powerful bargaining position to prevent or remedy misconduct by their counsel. Lawyers' concerns about reputation and repeat business supply incentives for satisfactory performance. Where problems arise, these clients generally can afford to change counsel or bring a malpractice claim, or can at least negotiate for a reduction in fees.[15] Unsophisticated individual clients have more need for protection but often have little way of knowing whether they are victims of incompetence, overcharging, or other disciplinary violations. Moreover, many clients who have reason to doubt their lawyers' performance often lack confidence that an effective response will be forthcoming from bar agencies, or are discouraged by the complexity of complaint structures and the lack of financial remedies for their own injuries. Experts in professional responsibility often advise against pursuing a disciplinary grievance (as not being worth the trouble), particularly if there is realistic potential in a claim for malpractice against the offending lawyer. Misconduct from which a client may have benefited, such as discovery abuse or misrepresentation in negotiations, is even less likely to trigger reports to disciplinary agencies.

The disciplinary system also fails adequately to address many grievances that are in fact reported. Over ninety percent of complaints are dismissed without investigation; only about four percent

---

15. State Bar of California, Investigation and Prosecution of Disciplinary Complaints Against Attorneys in Solo Practice, Small Size Law Firms, and Large Size Law Firms 105 (2001); Geof- frey C. Hazard, Jr., and Theodore J. Schneyer, "Regulatory Controls on Large Law Firms: A Comparative Perspective," 44 Ariz. L. Rev. 593, 599 (2002).

result in public discipline and one percent in disbarment.[16] Part of the reason for the high dismissal rate is that many complaints are inherently implausible or reflect dissatisfaction with outcomes rather than professional misconduct. However, inadequate enforcement resources and jurisdictional limitations are responsible as well. The problems that consumers are most likely to experience, such as overcharging or garden variety neglect, are least likely to fall within disciplinary agency jurisdiction. Only in cases of repeated or egregious abuses are agencies likely to intervene. The theory is that clients have alternative contractual or malpractice remedies, but litigation is too expensive for most of these matters and many states have no alternative dispute resolution (ADR) systems. The ADR programs that are available often are voluntary. Clients most in need of assistance seldom find their attorneys willing to cooperate.[17] Funding constraints also prevent agencies from undertaking proactive, independent investigations, and limit their capacity to pursue expensive proceedings against well-financed large firm lawyers or to assist clients who need help in filing grievances.

So too, procedural delays and the requirement of clear and convincing proof result in dismissals of a significant number of complaints. Many jurisdictions have no time limits for resolving cases, and will "abate" disciplinary proceedings during the pendency of civil actions. Yet individuals are often reluctant to pursue bar complaints after the termination of a civil suit that was itself bitter and protracted. Extended delays also can result in the loss of crucial evidence and expose more clients to misconduct. Except in a few states, bar disciplinary agencies will not disclose the existence of a complaint unless they have found a disciplinary violation or probable cause to believe that a violation has occurred. Lawyers with multiple complaints under investigation have received a clean bill of health when a consumer has asked for information about their records.[18] Potential clients also lack a ready way of discovering sanctions even after the process is completed. Not all states publish

---

16. See sources cited in Deborah L. Rhode and David Luban, Legal Ethics 952 (4th ed. 2004). Geoffrey C. Hazard, Jr., Susan P. Koniak, Roger C. Cramton, & George P. Cohen, The Law and Ethics of Lawyering 1142–43 (4th ed. 2004).

17. "ABA Committee Proposes Rules for Lawyer Client Mediation," 13 ABA/BNA Lawyers' Manual on Professional Conduct 398 (Dec. 1997); ABA Commission, supra note 5, at 129; Ken Armstrong & Maurice Possley, "The Verdict: Dishonor," Chi. Trib., Jan. 10, 1999, at A1.

18. Rhode & Luban, supra note 16, at 953. For delays, see Michael S. Frisch, "No Stone Left Unturned: The Failure of Attorney Self–Regulation in the District of Columbia," 18 Geo. J. Legal Ethics 325, 342, 360 (2005). For a general critique, see Leslie C. Levin, "The Emperor's Clothes And Other Tales About the Standards for Imposing Lawyer Disciplinary Sanctions," 48 Am. U. L. Rev. 1, 20 (1998)

information concerning disciplinary actions, and none do so in publications designed to reach the general public.

These limitations in the current disciplinary process are not unique; similar deficiencies exist in many other legal systems.[19] The problems in this nation have prompted reform proposals along several lines. First, experts advocate providing more resources and making the process more proactive. Rather than relying almost exclusively on complaints and felony prosecutions, regulatory officials should initiate investigations based on malpractice filings, judicial sanctions, and random audits of trust funds. More steps should be taken to publicize the complaint process, to assist individuals in filing complaints, and to develop low-cost alternative dispute proceedings, including mandatory fee arbitration. Jurisdictions that have implemented such systems generally report modest success. For example, some states have client assistance programs that screen all inquiries and resolve or refer minor grievances.[20] Other nations with comparable legal systems, such as Great Britain and Australia, have similarly implemented consumer-oriented remedies.[21] However, not all the client assistance programs in this country have high satisfaction rates, so independent evaluation and replication of the most successful models should be a key priority.[22] Of equal importance is greater support of preventive policies, such as those aimed at poor office management, unrealistic caseloads, inadequate backup, and substance abuse and mental health difficulties.[23]

19. See Geoffrey Hazard and Angelo Dondi, Legal Ethics: A Comparative Study, ch. 7 (2004).

20. Massachusetts has an Attorney and Consumer Assistance Program (ACAP) that informally resolves about three-quarters of the complaints made to disciplinary authorities. Ann Kaufman, "Five Years of ACAP," reprinted in Materials for the ABA Conference on Professional Responsibility 779 (2006). The Oregon bar's Client Assistance Office also informally resolves about three quarters of its complaints within two weeks. Oregon State Bar, "Annual Report of the Oregon State Bar Client Assistance Office," (2005), reprinted in Conference Materials, supra, at 797, 804. For discussion of New York's mediation program for minor grievances, see Vivian Berger, "Mediation: An Alternative Means of Processing Attorney Disciplinary Complaints," 16 Professional Lawyer 21 (2005).

21. Rhode & Luban, supra note 16, at 953–54.

22. For example, a majority of clients were not satisfied with Oregon's Client Assistance Office, but it is unclear how much of that dissatisfaction related to unrealistic expectations. See Oregon State Bar, Client Assistance Office Survey (2004), reprinted in Conference Materials, supra note 20, at 807, 817. In other bar-sponsored fee arbitration programs, thirty to forty percent of clients who participated were not satisfied with the experience. See Deborah L. Rhode, In the Interests of Justice: Reforming the Legal Profession 181 (2000).

23. Leslie C. Levin, "The Ethical World of Solo and Small Law Firm Practitioners," 41 Houston L. Rev. 309, 385–88 (2004); sources cited in Fred Zacharias, "A Word of Caution for Lawyer Assistance Programming," 18 Geo. J.Legal Ethics 237 (2004).

A second set of proposals should focus on increasing the public's knowledge about the ethical records of attorneys. Some commentators advocate data banks and toll-free hotlines that would provide information about judicial sanctions, disciplinary actions, and malpractice judgments. Disciplinary processes should be open to public scrutiny from the time that complaints are filed. Although many lawyers oppose such open processes on the ground that disclosure of unfounded complaints would unjustly prejudice their reputations, Oregon's extended experience with public proceedings does not disclose such problems. Because consumer surveys have found deep suspicion about closed-door systems, the ABA Commission on Evaluation of Disciplinary Enforcement recommended public disclosure of complaints.[24]

A third cluster of proposals involves increasing the independence and accountability of disciplinary agencies. Although all states place such agencies under the authority of the state supreme court, only about half make them independent of the organized bar. The ABA Commission recommended such autonomy as a means of avoiding the fact and appearance of conflict of interest.[25] Some commentators have proposed further strategies to insure that disciplinary bodies are not unduly hostage to professional concerns. One possibility would be to require that the officials responsible for the disciplinary process be appointed by a diverse group, such as the chief judge of the state supreme court, the governor, and the speaker of the state legislature. Criteria for selection would be expertise in consumer protection and professional regulation.[26] Such an approach could secure greater public accountability than the current system in most states, which is to limit nonlawyer involvement in the disciplinary process to a few members chosen by lawyers.

C. Disciplinary Sanctions

Reforms are equally necessary concerning disciplinary sanctions. The sanctions currently available include:

- disbarment—a permanent or indefinite withdrawal of the license to practice law;

- suspension—a temporary prohibition on practice either for a specified period (usually ranging from several months to

---

24. ABA Commission, supra note 5; Mary Devlin, "The Development of Lawyer Disciplinary Procedures in the United States," 7 Geo. J. Legal Ethics 911, 931–32 (1994).

25. "Supreme Court Team to Study ABA Finding," Cal. St. B. J., Oct. 2001, at 5.

26. For such a proposal, see Rhode, supra note 22, at 162.

several years) or until compliance with certain specified conditions and an order of the court;

- public or private censures, reprimands, admonitions, warnings, and cautions—expressions of disapproval that establish a record of misconduct admissible in subsequent cases;

- rehabilitative sanctions—probation, mandatory education, and requirements of participation in substance abuse programs designed to correct specific conduct.

Some jurisdictions permit lawyers under investigation to resign, but treat such resignations as an admission of guilt. Attorneys who later seek reinstatement following resignation must make the same showing of rehabilitation as disbarred attorneys who seek reinstatement.

At an abstract level, there is general agreement about the factors most relevant in imposing disciplinary sanctions. Those factors include: (1) the extent to which the lawyer's conduct injured others; (2) the "blameworthiness" of that conduct; (3) the lawyer's general character, demeanor, and prior disciplinary history; (4) the need for incapacitation; and (5) general or specific deterrence.[27] But in particular cases, there is often no comparable consensus about the degree of blameworthiness and the appropriate remedy.

The Severity of Sanctions

One longstanding dispute involves the stringency of sanctions. Courts and disciplinary agencies are generally reluctant to withdraw a lawyer's means of earning a living, either through disbarment or suspension. By contrast, commentators and the public repeatedly criticize the leniency of discipline, particularly in cases involving powerful government officials, attorneys from leading firms, or repeated instances of neglect, misrepresentation, or incompetence. For example, prosecutors have positions in which unprofessional conduct can have dire consequences, but they are rarely subject to disciplinary proceedings. One study of several hundred cases of serious prosecutorial misconduct found that none resulted in public disciplinary action.[28] Other commonly cited examples of leniency include Wall Street partners who have been only suspended, not disbarred, for offenses such as lying under oath about the destruction of documents, or falsifying billing records.[29]

27. Charles W. Wolfram, Modern Legal Ethics, 110–11 (1986); see also ABA Joint Commission on Professional Sanctions, Standards for Imposing Lawyer Sanctions (1986).

28. Armstrong & Possley, supra note 15, at A1. See Fred C. Zacharias, "The Professional Discipline of Prosecutors," 79 N.C.L. Rev. 721, 755 (2001).

29. In re Cooper, 586 N.Y.S.2d 250 (App. Div. 1992); Leslie Levin, "The

Similar criticisms have focused on the light sanctions for government officials such as Bill Clinton, who made what a federal trial court found to be "false and evasive" statements in a sexual harassment lawsuit during his term as President.[30] Clinton received a five-year suspension and a $25,000 fine, which represented well under one evenings' speakers' honorarium.

A related issue involves permanent disbarment. In thirty three states and the District of Columbia, disbarred attorneys may apply for reinstatement after a prescribed period, generally between three and six years. About half of those who apply are readmitted. In the remaining states, eight allow permanent disbarment at the court's discretion; seven make disbarment permanent.[31] Critics of the reinstatement process believe that it compromises the deterrent value of sanctions, undermines public respect, and permits unacceptable levels of recidivism. In one study, a quarter of lawyers who were disciplined but not disbarred for financial violations were subsequently found guilty of further financial misconduct.[32] In other surveys, some attorneys have been disbarred multiple times for serious abuses.[33]

Other commentators, however, believe that reinstatement should remain an option. Law Professor Ronald Rotunda, for example argues:

> Because the purpose of discipline is to protect the public, if the court finds that the reason to impose the discipline has changed, and no longer exists, or that the risk to the public of future harm no longer exists, then the court should also reevaluate the need for continued discipline. Wisdom never comes to some people; we should not reject it in others merely because it comes a little late.... The possibility of reinstatement is a good policy because it serves the laudable purpose of giving the lawyer an incentive to mend his or her old ways. To take away this possibility is to take away an incentive to reform.... Proponents of permanent disbarment often claim

Emperor's Clothes and Other Tales About the Standards for Imposing Lawyer Disciplinary Sanctions," 48 Am U. 20, 83, n. 57 (1998); Lerman, supra note 13; Julie O'Sullivan, "Professional Discipline for Law Firms: A Response to Professor Schneyer," 16 Geo. J. Legal Ethics 3, 55 (2003). For other examples of undue leniency see Frisch, supra note 18, at 346–50.

30. Jones v. Clinton, 36 F.Supp.2d 1118 (E.D. Ark. 1999).

31. Nancy McCarthy, "Board of Governors Committee Seeks Input on Permanent Disbarment," Cal. Bar J., Dec. 2005, at A1, A7.

32. David E. Johnson, Jr., "Permanent Disbarment: The Case For ...," The Professional Lawyer, Feb. 1994, at 22.

33. Id. at 27.

that we should agree with their proposal because it will improve the public image of lawyers. We should resist that temptation: the organized bar should propose legal reforms because they are right, not because they might improve our public image.[34]

Generally accepted moral principles similarly suggest that strict justice should be moderated by mercy. As leaders in most states have concluded, it should not be considered impossible that lawyers could rehabilitate themselves.

Mitigating Circumstances

Further controversy centers on the role of mitigating circumstances. The ABA Standards for Imposing Lawyer Sanctions list relevant factors including: remorse, cooperation with the disciplinary process, the absence of a prior record, timely efforts to make restitution, participation in a rehabilitation program, personal or emotional problems, mental health impairments, and the imposition of other penalties. How to weigh these factors in particular cases provokes considerable dispute. Some courts and commentators are sympathetic toward offenses that appear attributable to personal problems and disabilities.[35] Other courts and commentators, primarily concerned with client protection, have been reluctant to view such difficulties as adequate mitigation. The significance of lawyers' feelings of remorse and willingness to provide client compensation is equally controversial. According to Americans for Legal Reform, it is the job of disciplinary agencies to make sure that the risk of clients is "eliminated or minimized, not excused. The kind of leniency [granted to lawyers] is not accorded elsewhere—one can hardly imagine a bank forgiving a teller's theft of thousands of dollars and keeping them on the job based on excuses such as alcoholism, mental disability, or willingness to pay it back."[36] By contrast, other commentators can readily imagine such compassion, and can cite countless celebrated examples of individuals who turned their lives around after being given a second chance.

Similar controversies involve questions about whether the attorney has "suffered enough." Some courts and commentators maintain that disbarment is gratuitous for a prominent lawyer who has undergone the humiliation of public disciplinary proceedings,

---

34. Ronald D. Rotunda, "Permanent Disbarment: The Case Against," The Professional Lawyer, Feb. 1994, at 23–24.

35. See Wolfram, supra note 27, at 96–97 (discussing cases involving, e.g.,

emotional disorders, burnout, family illness, compulsive gambling, and traumatic love affairs); Levin, supra note 29, at 49–50.

36. HALT (Americans for Legal Reform), Attorney Discipline 16 (1988).

particularly those accompanied by criminal investigations or involuntary resignation from employment. Such considerations influenced the decisions concerning Clinton and the Wall Street partners noted above. Other courts and commentators are disturbed by the class bias underlying such decisions.[37] In their view, lawyers who have attained positions of wealth and status should be held to a higher standard of conduct, particularly since their cases are likely to attract more attention than the usual proceedings and they have fewer extenuating financial circumstances. To the extent that the profession is concerned with general deterrence and the appearance of even-handedness, no special allowance should be made for the "mighty who are fallen."

Financial Sanctions

Another contested issue involves the appropriateness of financial sanctions. Unlike the disciplinary systems in other countries, American proceedings generally do not allow monetary fines.[38] The stated rationale is that such sanctions constitute punishment, and the purpose of disciplinary procedures is protection. A related concern has been that fines would make disciplinary procedures resemble those of the criminal justice system, and might accordingly require comparable due process safeguards such as proof beyond a reasonable doubt. Some commentators, however, argue that fines are an appropriate mechanism of deterrence and one commonly employed in civil as well as criminal cases. As these commentators note, the American justice system is premised on the assumption that individuals contemplating misconduct are influenced by the severity of sanctions and the probability of their imposition. Adding the possibility of significant financial sanctions might alter some attorneys' cost-benefit calculations, particularly since courts may be less reluctant to impose fines than suspension or disbarment, which involve the loss of an individual's livelihood.[39] So too, if financial penalties were used to compensate injured parties, more of those victims might report misconduct and feel fairly treated by the disciplinary process.

37. Many solo practitioners and small firm lawyers perceive such bias, which undermines the legitimacy of the system and suggests the need for more transparency in bar enforcement processes. See Levin, supra note 29, at 382–84. For the California bar's response to such concerns see State Bar of California, supra note 15.

38. Only a few states, such as California and Nevada, explicitly permit fines and less than a dozen fines per year are reported to the ABA's National Lawyer Regulatory Data Bank. By contrast, fines have long been available in British and Canadian proceedings.

39. See generally, Steven G. Bené, "Why Not Fine Attorneys? An Economic Approach to Lawyer Disciplinary Sanctions," 43 Stan. L. Rev. 907 (1991).

Discipline for Law Firms

A related issue is whether disciplinary sanctions should be directed at law firms as well as individuals. Lawyers have been among the leaders of campaigns for organizational liability in other contexts (such as those involving securities, antitrust, and environmental regulation). Many commentators believe that the reasons for institutional accountability are just as relevant for legal workplaces. In some cases, it is impossible or inequitable to single out particular individuals for sanctions. Collective liability could encourage development of appropriate mechanisms for preventing or responding to misconduct, and could avoid the need to scapegoat particular lawyers in circumstances of diffuse or shared responsibility.[40]

Two states, New York and New Jersey, have pioneered rules permitting discipline of law firms, and other jurisdictions are considering the approach. The impact of such rules is difficult to gauge, partly because they have seldom been enforced.[41] According to one New York bar disciplinary counsel, sanctioning firms may be counterproductive because it enables regulators to take the "easy way out" and avoid identifying the lawyers immediately responsible for misconduct.[42] Because organizations can't be disbarred or suspended, penalties like admonitions or modest fines may be inadequate to insure compliance.

Such considerations led the ABA's Ethics 2000 Commission to drop recommendations of discipline for law firms. Many lawyers who testified before the Commission maintained that such sanctions would "undermine the principle of individual responsibility that runs through the Model Rules."[43] Supporters of organizational liability have responded that fines and admonitions can be supplemented by requirements that firms establish review bodies to oversee compliance with ethical standards. In their view, such an approach could strengthen principles of individual responsibility by putting teeth into the Model Rules concerning obligations of super-

---

40. The Committee on Professional Responsibility, "Discipline of Law Firms," 48 The Record of the Association of the Bar of the City of New York 628 (1993); Tanina Rostain, "Partners and Power: The Role of Law Firm Organizational Factors in Attorney Misconduct," 19 Geo. J. Legal Ethics 281 (2006); Ted Schneyer, "Professional Discipline for Law Firms?," 77 Cornell L. Rev. 1 (1991).

41. Elizabeth Chambliss & David B. Wilkins, "A New Framework for Law Firm Discipline," 16 Geo. J. Legal Ethics 335, 340 (2002).

42. "Law Firm Discipline: Easy Way Out or Getting More Bang for the Buck," 15 ABA/BNA Lawyer Manual on Professional Conduct 401 (1999) (quoting Robert J. Saltzman).

43. "Ethics 2000 Commission Unveils Late Changes to Recommendations," 69 U.S.L.W. 2780 (2001).

vising attorneys. Model Rule 5.1 requires that lawyers with management authority make "reasonable efforts to ensure that the firm has in effect measures giving reasonable assurance that all lawyers in the firm conform to the Rules of Professional Conduct." The disciplinary process would obviously be strengthened by enforcement of this Rule in contexts such as discovery abuse, overbilling, or failure to implement adequate policies governing conflicts of interest and client funds.[44]

Conduct Outside Professional Relationships

Cases involving discipline for conduct occurring outside a lawyer's professional relationships raise a somewhat different set of concerns. As Chapter XI's discussion of admissions notes, the bar has been much more active in policing moral character among applicants than among admitted attorneys. From a public policy standpoint, this double standard is hard to justify. It is, of course, true that practicing lawyers have a greater vested interest in their professional licenses than applicants to the bar. But acts committed after admission are more probative of future threats to the public than acts committed before becoming an officer of the court. The difficulty, however, is that there is considerable disagreement within and across jurisdictions about how probative certain nonprofessional offenses in fact are. Particular dispute has centered on offenses such as those involving driving while intoxicated, tax evasion, minor drug offenses, and sexual activity.[45]

A number of proposals have been made to foster greater consistency in responses to nonprofessional misconduct. One approach would be for states to set forth presumptive sanctions for specific acts, and to require justifications for any departure.[46] Another approach would be to require some "nexus between misconduct and job function."[47] So, for example, acts involving dishonesty would stand on different footing than those involving sexual misconduct or personal drug use.

---

44. See Rostain, supra note 40, at 285–87. For case histories of the kind of deficient supervisory mechanisms that could be subject to sanctions, see Milton C. Regan, Jr., Eat What You Kill: The Fall of a Wall Street Lawyer (2004); James L. Kelly, Lawyers Crossing Lines: Nine Stories 183 (2001).

45. Barrie Althoff, "Ethics and the Law: Lawyer Disciplinary Sanctions," Wa. St. B. News, Jan. 2002, at 1; Carrie Menkel–Meadow, "Private Lives and Professional Responsibilities? The Rela-tionship of Personal Morality to Lawyering and Professional Ethics," 21 Pace L. Rev. 365 (2001); Deborah L. Rhode, "Moral Character as a Professional Credential," 94 Yale L.J. 491, 551–54 (1985).

46. See Levin, supra note 18, at 61–68 (advocating such an approach for all misconduct, modeled on the ABA's Sentencing Guidelines for criminal conduct).

47. Menkel–Meadow, supra note 45, at 388.

Mental Health and Substance Abuse

When mental health or substance abuse affect professional performance, the disciplinary process must obviously respond. An estimated one-third of lawyers suffer from depression or from alcohol or drug addiction. Attorneys have about three times the rate of depression and almost twice the rate of substance abuse as other Americans.[48] These problems figure in a large percentage of disciplinary and malpractice cases.[49] Given the frequency of the issue, it is striking to find little consensus concerning the effect that addiction and other psychological difficulties should have in disciplinary cases.

One area of disagreement involves the extent to which disciplinary processes should be concerned not only with fitness to practice, but also with culpability and deterrence. Some courts and bar agencies have viewed addiction primarily as a mitigating factor; others see it as an indication of unfitness. Related disagreements involve causation. Some decisions assume a relationship between addiction and misconduct; others have demanded a showing that but for the addictive behavior, the misconduct would not have occurred.[50] A further controversy involves confidentiality. Protecting information about impaired attorneys who obtain help through the bar's lawyer assistance programs encourages participation and rehabilitation, but it raises questions about how to protect clients who are at risk because of dysfunctional representation.[51]

Underlying these disputes are more fundamental issues. Law Professor David Luban observes:

> Though alcoholism is a disease, it is unlike most diseases in that it does not just happen to the victim. He brings it on himself by drinking alcohol, behavior which ... is voluntary.... Even a purely medical judgment of whether the lawyer is recovered to the point of being fit to practice is therefore partly a judgment of will power, and thus of charac-

---

48. Blane Workie, "Chemical Dependency and the Legal Profession: Should Addiction to Drugs and Alcohol Ward Off Heavy Discipline?," 9 Geo. J. Legal Ethics 1357 (1996).

49. Zacharias, supra note 23, at 241, n. 15; John Mixon & Robert P. Schuwerk, "The Personal Dimension of Professional Responsibility," 58 Law and Contemp. Probs. 87, 96 (1995).

50. Workie, supra note 48; Compare In re Kersey, 520 A.2d 321, 326 (D.C. 1987) (holding alcoholism to be a mitigating factor) with In the Matter of Crowley, 519 A.2d 361, 363 (N.J.1987) (refusing to hold alcoholism a mitigating factor); see ABA Commission, supra note 21, at Standard 9.3(h) (allowing "physical or mental disability or impairment" as a mitigating factor in the degree of discipline imposed, but noting in the commentary that this factor has been treated inconsistently by state courts and does not excuse the misconduct).

51. Zacharias, supra note 23, at 243–46.

ter. Medical [experts] try as best they can to base their prognoses on external factors—the quality of the lawyer's support group (such as Alcoholics Anonymous), his responses to counseling, the changes he has made in his environment to protect himself from stresses to which he has in the past responded by drinking, the stability and happiness of his life, etc. But in the end ... although alcoholism is a disease, not a defect of character, recovery from it will be a perpetual test of character....[52]

Although many courts and disciplinary bodies agree, they divide on how best to respond. Some are willing to give lawyers an opportunity for probation if their substance abuse was the primary cause of misconduct and they are in a structured rehabilitation program. By contrast, other tribunals impose suspension or disbarment, with the option of reinstatement after a suitable period of recovery.

Similar variations occur in cases involving lawyers with mental health impairments. A widely noted example involves Joel Greenberg, disbarred in New Jersey in July 1998, and admitted in Pennsylvania in July 1999. Greenberg lost his New Jersey license after stealing almost $35,000 from his law firm. Neither the state's disciplinary review board nor its supreme court accepted Greenberg's claim that his misconduct was a self-destructive act fueled by depression, not greed, and that his subsequent psychiatric treatment left him fit for legal practice. According to the New Jersey Supreme Court, failure to impose disbarment would impair public confidence and exonerate other attorneys who misappropriated funds in response to personal hardship. In the court's view, attorneys suffering from mental health or substance abuse should seek help before they engaged in activities that would irreparably damage their own reputation and seriously compromise the profession's public standing. By contrast, Pennsylvania bar examiners obviously accepted Greenberg's claims of rehabilitation, but refused to make any public comment about their decision due to confidentiality concerns.[53]

However such cases are resolved, virtually all experts in the field advocate greater reliance on treatment programs. Referral to such programs is particularly helpful at early stages before social stigma, physiological problems, and professional impairment become pronounced. Recovery rates among professionals who obtain

---

52. David J. Luban, "Commentary: A Professional Tragedy," Nat. Rep. Legal Ethics and Prof. Resp. (1988).

53. In re Greenberg, 714 A.2d 243 (N.J.1998); Wendy Davis, "Advice for the Disbarred, Go West," 157 N.J. L. J. 217 (1999).

adequate treatment are encouragingly high.[54] Some type of substance abuse program is available in every state, and many jurisdictions have implemented diversion systems for cases not involving serious misconduct.[55] Under these programs, disciplinary action will be stayed pending successful completion of a rehabilitation program. Encouraging greater participation in these programs should be a key priority for the profession.

Increased emphasis should also be given to prevention of disciplinary problems and accountability for bar agency performance. To make the remedial process more consistent and responsive to public concerns is likely to require structural reforms along the lines noted earlier.

D. Competence

Competence in legal practice is something everyone wants more of, but no one has a very clear sense of which efforts to promote it will be worth the cost. The contemporary campaign for increased competence began in the early 1970s, when Chief Justice Burger asserted that between one-third and one-half of lawyers appearing in serious cases were "not really qualified to render fully adequate representation."[56] Although the empirical basis for that assertion remained unclear, other commentators began offering similar assessments. Over the next quarter century, various bar organizations considered appropriate responses.

Defining the Problem

A threshold challenge in responding to professional incompetence lies in identifying the problem to be addressed. Definitions of competence in bar ethical rules and reported decisions are formulated at high levels of abstraction. The Model Rules of Professional Conduct require "reasonable diligence and promptness" and "the legal knowledge, skill, thoroughness, and preparation reasonably necessary for the representation." Rule 1.1 and Rule 1.3. The ABA's Code of Professional Responsibility prohibits "neglect" and mandates "preparation adequate in the circumstances" DR 6–101(A). Both the Model Rules and the Code also provide that lawyers who lack sufficient expertise in the field may accept employment if they associate an experienced lawyer or expect to become qualified through necessary study. Rule 1.1, Comment; DR

---

54. See sources cited in notes 48 and 49, supra; Michael J. Sweeney, "A Return to Counselor," 18 GP Solo 57 (2001).

55. Commission on Lawyer Assistance Programs, American Bar Association, 2002 Survey of Lawyer Assistance Programs (2002).

56. "Chief Justice Burger Proposes First Steps Toward Certification of Trial Advocacy Specialists," 60 ABA J. 171, 173–74 (1974).

6–101; EC 6–3. The Code's Ethical Considerations add the qualification, missing in the Disciplinary Rules and Model Rules, that the additional preparation should not result in "unreasonable delay or expense to the client." EC 6–3.

How often lawyers' performance falls beneath these standards is a matter of frequent speculation but no hard data. The fragmentary research available reveals that most qualities rated highly relevant by practitioners and employing organizations are not learned in law school or tested on bar examinations: for example, investigation, effective oral expression, maintaining client and collegial relations, document drafting, diligence, judgment, and supervisory capability.[57] According to the report of the ABA Task Force on Law Schools and the Profession, Narrowing the Gap, lawyers are not adequately prepared for their first jobs in practice; their deficiencies are also increasing as law becomes more complex and the range of necessary skills becomes more diverse.[58]

To address these problems, bar leaders generally propose: more focus on skills in bar exams, law school courses, and continuing legal education; additional "bridging the gap" training and mentoring programs for new attorneys; special assistance for solo and small firm practitioners; and improved in-house education by employers. Almost no effort has been made to assess the effectiveness of such initiatives. Moreover, the most clearly identifiable incompetence is attributable less to inadequate knowledge and skills than to other personal problems and financial considerations. To the extent that poor representation results from greed or insufficient concern for client welfare, or from inadequate stakes and client resources, the conventional proposals are not much of a solution.

Continuing Legal Education

Continuing legal education (CLE) for practicing lawyers began a half century ago, to help armed forces veterans get up to speed in the law practices to which they were returning. Attention resurfaced in the 1970s in the aftermath of the Watergate scandals, in which a substantial number of prominent lawyers were involved. About four-fifths of all states now require practicing lawyers to participate in CLE programs, generally ranging from ten to twelve hours. In most jurisdictions, part of the coursework must focus on

57. See Joanne Martin & Bryant G. Garth, "Clinical Education as a Bridge Between Law School and Practice: Mitigating the Misery," 1 Clinical L. Rev. 443 (1994); see also discussion in Chapter XI supra.

58. ABA, Section on Legal Education and Admission to the Bar, Legal Education and Professional Development: An Educational Continuum: Report of the Task Force on Law Schools and the Profession—Narrowing the Gap (MacCrate Report) (1992).

ethics. Some states demand coverage of other topics such as bias in the profession and substance abuse.

These requirements have been relatively uncontroversial. It is hard to object to having lawyers make minimal efforts to stay current in their fields and knowledgeable about ethical rules. But an analysis of CLE as currently implemented raises several concerns. Few jurisdictions impose stringent quality control, and none have compiled evidence of the effectiveness of CLE programs. In order to gain acceptance from the bar, most educational requirements are modest and some are user-friendly. For example, courses on substance abuse and emotional distress have focused on stress reduction and relaxation methods, while courses on sports law have occurred at sporting events, complete with complementary hot dogs and peanuts.[59] The problem is not simply that some classes stretch the concept of "legal education"; the more fundamental difficulty, as a District of Columbia task force noted, "is that there have been no reliable, scientific demonstrations of the efficacy of continuing legal education." Research in other professions such as medicine and engineering has found no relationship between performance and participation in continuing education.[60] Neither is it self evident that passive attendance at ungraded courses will significantly increase competence in legal practice.

That is not to suggest that all CLE is unproductive. But as one expert notes, the "major benefit appears to be skill enhancement of already motivated and relatively competent practitioners."[61] To make CLE more useful to those who need it most, commentators have proposed a range of reforms. One possibility might be to demand fewer hours but impose greater quality controls. Bar officials could require passage of an exam and deny credit for courses that bear little demonstrated relationship to performance in practice. Providers could themselves be held to educational requirements that insured some basic level of effectiveness. Alternatively, states could combine required and voluntary approaches. CLE could be mandatory for new lawyers and for other practitioners who have violated ethical rules. Attorneys who are subject to disciplinary, judicial, or malpractice sanctions could be required to take appropriate courses. Other attorneys who voluntarily complete CLE classes and pass a basic test could receive certification of their

59. Rhode, supra note 22, at 156.

60. Task Force on Mandatory Continuing Legal Education, Report to the Board of Governors of the District of Columbia Bar 26–28 (1995); Rhode, supra note 22, at 156.

61. Susan R. Martyn, "Lawyer Competence and Lawyer Discipline: Beyond the Bar?," 69 Geo. L. J. 705, 725–32 (1981).

coursework. An increasing number of lawyers are now willing to complete demanding educational requirements in order to become certified as specialists in particular fields of practice. States could encourage this trend by expanding specialization programs, publicizing their value to consumers, and improving their educational quality.[62]

E. Malpractice

Three decades ago, legal malpractice claims were so rare and practitioners were so unconcerned about liability that insurance coverage was generally not available on the domestic market. Today that situation had dramatically changed, and claims, particularly large claims, are on the rise.[63] Definitive data is impossible to come by, because insurance companies do not disclose payouts and many settlements remain confidential. However, it has been estimated that ten to twenty percent of attorneys face malpractice exposure in any given year and that insurance payouts total between four and six billion dollars annually.[64] The number of attorneys with insurance coverage varies widely by state and practice specialty, with estimates ranging from 50 to 90 percent.[65]

What accounts for the recent increase is subject to dispute. Some commentators believe that incompetent practice is growing. As competition within the profession intensifies, profit margins decrease, and billable hour expectations escalate, lawyers are under more pressure to handle matters beyond their expertise. Other commentators believe that the increase in malpractice claims has less to do with increases in the amount of malpractice than with increases in consumer expectations and in other lawyers' willingness to bring such claims. As these observers note, the bar's experience is by no means unique; other professionals have also been subject to rising numbers of malpractice complaints.[66]

The growth in claims against lawyers reflects broader changes in the structure and climate of legal practice. The increasing size and stratification within the legal community have made colleagues less hesitant to challenge each others' conduct in malpractice suits.

---

62. Rhode, supra note 22, at 156–58.

63. "Law Firms Face Sharp Rise in Malpractice Suits," Legal Times, May 10, 2005.

64. Hazard, Koniak, Cramton, & Cohen, supra note 16, at 854; "Figuratively Speaking," ABA J., Oct. 1996, at 12; Manuel R. Ramos, "Legal Malpractice: No Lawyer or Client Is Safe," 47 Fla. L. Rev. 1, 5 (1995).

65. James M. Fischer, "External Controls Over the American Bar," 19 Geo. J. Legal Ethics 59, 63 (2006).

66. Richard Pérez–Peña, "When Lawyers Go After Their Peers: The Boom in Malpractice Cases," N.Y. Times, Aug. 5, 1994, at A1; Jonathan Gaw, "Lawyers Shed Reluctance to Sue Their Own," L.A. Times, Dec. 14, 1992, at B1; Ramos, supra note 64.

Financial scandals have also prompted more civil liability claims. Individuals who have lost money in risky ventures look for deep pockets to sue and have targeted lawyers who brokered the transactions and written opinion letters on which investors relied.

Yet despite the escalation of malpractice claims, the barriers to successful actions have remained considerable. Many individuals with grievances against a lawyer are unwilling to incur the costs in time, money, and acrimony involved in filing charges. Unless liability looks clear, damages are substantial, and the defendant has sufficient insurance or legally accessible assets to make a judgment collectible, attorneys who specialize in malpractice litigation will generally decline the case.

The burden of proof necessary to establish liability is also a substantial obstacle. In general, plaintiffs must demonstrate:

- A duty of care arising from an attorney-client relationship or some other relationship giving rise to fiduciary responsibilities;

- A breach of that duty arising from failure to exercise the care that reasonably competent lawyers exercise under similar circumstances; and

- Legally cognizable damages caused by the breach, usually limited to economic injury.

Although the data on malpractice success rates are incomplete and conflicting, the best available evidence suggests that half of all claims cannot meet these requirements and result in no recovery; another quarter result in minimal judgments. Most successful claims involve fairly obvious errors, such as missing deadlines, neglecting to file documents, or failing to consult clients and follow their instructions.[67] In cases presenting less objective proof of error, clients often have difficulty establishing what exactly the attorney did or did not do, and how that conduct fell below average performance standards within the relevant legal community.

Current debates over malpractice liability center on several main issues: how to set performance standards; what proof of causation should be necessary; what should be the role of professional conduct codes; what remedies should be available; who should be entitled to sue; and what prevention strategies are most promising.

---

67. Ramos, supra note 64; ABA Committee on Lawyers' Professional Liability, Legal Malpractice Claims in the 1990s (1996). These success rates are not, however, significantly lower than malpractice claims against other professionals.

Performance Standards

Courts and commentators have divided over whether "average community" standards are the appropriate benchmark of liability and, if so, how the legal community should be defined. Should the relevant community be the locality, the state, practitioners in the field, or the legal profession more generally? A leading Vermont decision held that the state, not the locality, should provide the frame of reference. In the court's view, the "minimum knowledge required should not vary with geography.... The fact that a lower degree of care or less able practice may be prevalent in a particular local community should not dictate the standard of care."[68] That reasoning, however, raises the question of why state boundaries should be controlling. Some commentators have also objected to making liability depend on prevailing practices in the community, however defined. In their view, it gives the profession the power to dictate its own standard of conduct, a prerogative said to be unavailable to other occupations even in areas involving technical expertise. To these critics, a preferable standard would be reasonable performance under the totality of the circumstances, including clients' legitimate expectations.

As a practical matter, however, cases that are attractive enough to justify prosecution under a contingent fee arrangement (strong liability, large damages, and a financially responsible defendant) usually involve conduct that is (or is alleged to be) clearly abusive. Such misconduct would violate current as well as proposed standards of professional conduct. The difficult problem for most malpractice complainants is not the alleged leniency of the prevailing standard, but factual disputes between client and lawyer, and the traditional reluctance of courts to extend lawyer liability to victims beyond immediate clients.

Causation

A further burden for malpractice plaintiffs involves causation. In effect, they must demonstrate not only that the lawyer was negligent or guilty of other misconduct, but also that this breach of professional standards resulted in quantifiable damages. For claims involving malpractice in litigation (which comprise about half of all reported complaints), that burden often requires a trial within a trial; plaintiffs must establish that, but for the lawyer's negligence, they would have prevailed in the original proceeding. This requirement has been subject to considerable criticism. Some commentators advocate an alternative standard modeled on the test applicable in England and France, and in American medical malpractice

68. Russo v. Griffin, 510 A.2d 436, 438 (Vt. 1986).

cases. Under this test, plaintiffs who demonstrate that the defendant's substandard performance deprived them of a substantial possibility of recovery would be entitled to damages adjusted to reflect the likelihood of success.[69] Many commentators also propose a version of that test for malpractice cases involving criminal defense lawyers. The prevailing standard requires complainants to establish that they were actually innocent, and that their attorneys' substandard performance was responsible for their convictions.[70] That test is almost always impossible to meet even though, as Chapter IX indicated, the performance in many criminal cases falls below acceptable standards.

Professional Conduct Codes

A related issue involves the significance of the bar's ethical codes in establishing attorney malpractice. The Preliminary Statement of the ABA Code disclaims any effort to define standards for civil liability of lawyers for professional conduct. The Scope Note to the Model Rules states that:

> [v]iolation of a rule should not itself give rise to a cause of action against a lawyer nor should it create any presumption in such a case that a legal duty has been breached. . . . The Rules are designed to provide guidance to lawyers and to provide a structure for regulating conduct through disciplinary agencies. They are not designed to be a basis for civil liability. Furthermore, the purpose of the Rules can be subverted when they are invoked by opposing parties as procedural weapons. Nevertheless, since the Rules do establish standards of conduct by lawyers, a lawyer's violation of a Rule may be evidence of a breach of the applicable standard of conduct.

In some jurisdictions, violations of ethical rules can serve as evidence of negligence *per se,* or as evidence of failure to meet the proper standard of care. By contrast, other courts permit only indirect use (as when an expert refers to them in testifying about the standard of care).[71] This restrictive approach is hard to square with the stated purpose of ethical codes: protecting the public. It is not self-evident why this purpose would be subverted by supple-

---

69. John Leubsdorf, "Legal Malpractice and Professional Responsibility," 48 Rutgers L. Rev. 101, 111–19 (1995). For the conventional standard, see Charles W. Wolfram, "A Cautionary Tale: Fiduciary Breach as Legal Malpractice," 34 Hofstra L. Rev. 689, 716–19 (2006).

70. Ang v. Martin, 114 P.3d 637 (Wash. 2005); Wiley v. County of San Diego, 966 P.2d 983 (Cal. 1998); Wolfram, supra note 27, at 218–27.

71. Gary A. Munneke & Anthony E. Davis, "The Standard of Care in Legal Malpractice: Do the Model Rules of Professional Conduct Define It?" 22 J. Legal Prof., 33, 69 (1998).

menting the limited resources of bar disciplinary agencies with civil remedies. In any event, even in jurisdictions that are least receptive to admission of bar ethical standards, expert testimony will often incorporate these standards indirectly. For most malpractice cases, such testimony either is a legal requirement or a practical necessity to get to the jury. A competent expert is essential to establish that the lawyer's conduct failed to conform to "recognized professional standards." These standards implicitly, and sometimes explicitly, are reflected in the applicable ethical code. In effect, because the codified concept of "competence" generally mirrors prevailing standards of practice, rules restricting the admissibility of codes have limited practical effects.

Remedies

A further issue involves the adequacy of malpractice remedies. One chronic problem concerns the high transaction costs of establishing liability. Unsurprisingly, lawyer defendants are, on the whole, a litigious group when it comes to defending their own conduct. Because many cases are highly contested, less than half of insurance payouts go to injured victims.[72] A further problem is the high percentage of lawyers who carry no insurance—a number typically ranging between thirty and forty percent, depending on the state.[73] To compensate parties who cannot recover from their attorneys, virtually all state bars provide some assistance from client security funds, which are subsidized by mandatory lawyer contributions. However, most of these funds are too limited to cover more than a small fraction of client claims. Payouts are available only for intentional misconduct, and are capped at inadequate levels.

To insure more effective remedies, several reform strategies are possible. One option is to expand client security funds, either by increasing bar dues or by imposing fines in disciplinary proceedings. Another possibility noted earlier is to establish low-cost alternative dispute resolution procedures for fee disputes and malpractice claims.

A further strategy, pioneered in Oregon and debated in a growing number of jurisdictions, is to require all attorneys to carry adequate malpractice insurance. Proposals to this effect have attracted strong opposition, particularly among members of the bar who do not practice full-time or who, for other reasons, would find

---

72. Manual R. Ramos, "Legal Malpractice: Reforming Lawyers and Law Professors," 70 Tul. L. Rev. 2583, 2600 (1996).

73. Id. at 2610; Rhode, supra note 22, at 167.

liability premiums to be a substantial hardship. Critics also worry that mandatory coverage would encourage frivolous claims and would fail to distinguish among attorneys with widely varying levels of liability exposure.

Supporters of mandatory insurance respond that no increase in claims has occurred in Oregon and that premiums there are quite affordable, at rates below those of comparable jurisdictions. Part of the reason is that Oregon operates a mandatory nonprofit Professional Liability Fund that insures all the state's attorneys, eliminates expensive marketing and brokers' fees, and incorporates effective prevention initiatives. Over four-fifths of the state's attorneys support its malpractice system.[74] Many other nations also require malpractice insurance, and their successful experience suggests that mandatory coverage should be a priority for reform here. An alternative that a growing number of jurisdictions have imposed or are considering, is a requirement that attorneys disclose to clients whether they maintain a minimum level of malpractice insurance. In at least one surveyed state, after adoption of such a requirement, the vast majority of lawyers have obtained coverage.[75] An even larger number of jurisdictions require disclosure of insurance information to the state bar, which typically makes such information available to the public on a website or on request. However, as a California Task Force has noted, it is unlikely that many clients would check with the bar since most assume that their lawyer has coverage.[76]

Third Party Obligations

A final area of controversy involves the extent to which nonclients should be able to sue for an attorney's violations of professional rules. Under the traditional doctrine of privity, a lawyer could be held civilly liable only to a client, with whom the lawyer has a contractual relationship, and not to third persons, who are considered "too remote." The privity concept originally blocked actions against anyone except clients, but courts gradually have recognized exceptions to that rule. Some jurisdictions now hold that lawyers who undertake responsibilities that foreseeably affect a

---

74. ABA Commission, supra note 5, at 81–82; Rhode, supra note 22, at 163; Harry H. Scheider, Jr., "At Issue: Mandatory Malpractice Insurance: Has the Time Come to Require Coverage?—No: An Invitation to Frivolous Suits," ABA J., Nov., 1993, at 45.

75. Hazard, Koniak, Cramton, & Cohen, supra note 16, at 871; "Massachusetts Adopts Insurance Disclosure;

California Bar Task Force Releases Proposal," 22 ABA/BNA Law. Man. Prof. Conduct 62 (2006) (noting that five states have rules requiring disclosure of insurance coverage to clients).

76. See "Massachusetts Adopts Insurance Disclosure," supra note 75 (noting that a dozen states require disclosure to the bar).

third party owe a duty of care to that individual. For example, attorneys may be liable to intended beneficiaries of an estate if errors in drafting the will prevent them from receiving the bequest. Courts are also increasingly holding lawyers responsible for negligent investigations in connection with fraudulent transactions or negligent misrepresentations in opinions on which third parties can be expected to rely.[77] Such holdings are based on fiduciary/agency principles, third party beneficiary theories, or a balancing test that considers factors such as the predictability and certainty of harm and the defendant's moral culpability.[78] Underlying this line of cases is a desire to place responsibility on the individual best able to prevent losses and maintain adequate insurance.

Some courts are, however, understandably wary about overly broad extensions of lawyers' third party liability. Concerns about such malpractice exposure could compromise attorneys' loyalty to their clients and discourage attorneys from asking questions that might reveal compromising information.[79] Expansive liability may also impose disproportionate penalties on lawyers whose clients become insolvent, and the result may ultimately be escalating insurance costs that are passed on to other consumers of legal services.

Prevention

However these issues concerning the standard and scope of liability are resolved, attorneys have a strong interest in preventing disputes that might trigger malpractice claims. This interest is also shared by insurance companies, who often audit their large policyholders for risky practices and require malpractice prevention systems as a condition of liability coverage. Crucial preventive strategies include systems for identifying conflicts of interest and for reminding lawyers of important deadlines. These systems generally are most effective if they allocate responsibility for monitoring

---

77. Joan C. Rogers, "Speakers Spot Trends, Assess Changes in Malpractice Claims and Insurance Market," 22 ABA/BNA Law. Man. Prof. Conduct, 115 (2006). See John M. Freeman & Nathan M. Crystal, "Scienter in Professional Liability Cases," 42 S.C. L. Rev. 783 (1991); Stephen Gillers, "Cleaning Up the S & L Mess," ABA J., Feb. 1993, at 93.

78. Restatement (Third) of the Law Governing Lawyers, § 30; Leubsdorf, supra note 69, at 111, 130–35; Geoffrey C. Hazard, Jr., "The Privity Requirement Reconsidered," 37 S. Tex. L. Rev. 967 (1996); Forest J. Bowman, "Lawyer Lia-

bility to Non–Clients," 97 Dick. L. Rev. 267, 276 (1993).

79. Schatz v. Weinberg & Green, 943 F.2d 485 (4th Cir.1991) (denying liability to buyers who relied on closing documents that included material misrepresentations about client seller's net worth); Talton v. Arnall Golden Gregory LLP, 622 S.E.2d 589 (Ga. App. 2005) (denying liability to purchasers injured as a result of inadequate warning labels). See Fred C. Zacharias, "Coercing Clients: Can Lawyer Gatekeeper Rules Work?", 47 Boston College L. Rev. 455, 472–73, 494–95 (2006) (discussing costs and benefits of third party liability).

compliance to someone other than the person responsible for performance. An equally important strategy involves communication with clients. Attorneys should provide realistic assessments of costs, fees, delays, and outcomes. Disputes can also be preempted by detailed written retainer agreements and by ongoing reports concerning the status of the case, such as copies of major filings, notices of significant developments, and so forth. An increasing number of law firms have also made progress by establishing a specialized in-house general counsel position, with responsibilities for compliance with ethical standards and malpractice risk management.[80]

Contrary to conventional wisdom, it is not young, inexperienced attorneys who experience the most malpractice claims. Lawyers practicing over ten years account for a disproportionate share of suits. The same financial and psychological factors that lead to disciplinary charges also contribute to malpractice: unrealistic caseloads, drug and alcohol abuse, and personal stresses such as divorce and burnout. The best protection for both lawyers and their clients is a clear and consistently reiterated organizational norm of professional integrity, together with comprehensive malpractice insurance, and professional help when personal problems arise.

80. Elizabeth Chambliss, "The Professionalization of Law Firm In-House Counsel Positions," 84 N. Car. L. Rev. 1515 (2006).

EPILOGUE

Professional regulation in the twenty-first century confronts unprecedented challenges. Competition and commercialism are increasing; collegiality and civility are headed in the opposite direction. As the bar grows in size and specialization, its sense of common purpose and its reliance on informal reputational sanctions become harder to sustain. While these changes have intensified the need for formal regulation, other trends in legal markets have made effective enforcement difficult to achieve. As more of lawyers' work crosses jurisdictional boundaries, traditional state-based oversight structures face new constraints. As competition within and across professions grows more intense, the pressure to compromise competing values escalates as well. Further challenges involve the distribution of legal services. The forces of business and professional competition yield a "survival of the fittest" for lawyers who serve clients of means or who adapt practice forms to produce sufficient fee revenues. But low-income individuals often remain faced with second-class justice, or no justice at all.

These trends in legal practice generate widespread concerns but little consensus on solutions. In a bar that is increasingly diverse in background and practice setting, issues of professional responsibility are increasingly divisive. One result has been a rise of multiple, sometimes inconsistent, forms of regulation. Some states have departed from the ABA's model ethical codes; legislatures and agencies have become more willing to step in where other oversight structures fall short. This lack of uniformity poses further challenges for a profession whose work frequently crosses jurisdictional borders.

Yet the American bar has always adapted to meet the nation's pressing needs, and its own regulatory problems should be no exception. In earlier eras, issues of professional responsibility may have attracted little systematic attention, but contemporary lawyers are acutely conscious of problems in the distribution of legal services and the conditions of legal practice. Today's lawyers are also aware that if they do not actively seek solutions, others may do so for them. If the bar is to justify its regulatory independence, it must address the issues that this book has explored.

Lawyers are surely equal to that task. Leaders of the legal profession have been at the forefront of every major social reform movement in the nation's history. The challenge now is to channel that leadership inward and to make legal ethics a priority, both in principle and in practice.

*

287

TABLE OF CASES

References are to Pages.

*

INDEX

References are to pages.

†